REIMAGINING JAPAN

REIMAGINING JAPAN

The Quest for a Future That Works

Edited by McKINSEY & COMPANY
Executive editors: Clay Chandler, Heang Chhor, and Brian Salsberg

VIZ Media, LLC
a member of Shogakukan Inc. group
San Francisco
2011

Published by VIZ Media, LLC, a member of Shogakukan group
San Francisco, CA, the United States of America
Published simultaneously in Canada
Printed in Canada
First Edition, July 1st 2011

For information about permission to reprint any portion of this volume, write to:
Permission—Shogakukan, VIZ Media, LLC, P.O. Box 77010
San Francisco, CA 94107

Library of Congress Cataloging-in-Publication Data
Reimagining Japan: The Quest for a Future That Works / Executive editors,
Clay Chandler, Heang Chhor, and Brian Salsberg.
p. cm.
ISBN 978-1-4215-4086-3 (hardback)
1. Japan—Economic conditions—1989– 2. Japan—Economic policy—1989–
3. Japan—Social conditions—1989– I. Chandler, Clay II. Chhor, Heang.
III. Salsberg, Brian. IV. Title: Reimagining Japan.
HC462.95.R45 2011
330.952—dc22
2011008946

ISBN 13: 978-1-4215-4086-3
ISBN 10: 1-4215-4086-X

Executive editors, McKinsey & Company:
Clay Chandler, Heang Chhor, and Brian Salsberg
Production by Therese Khoury and Val Titov, McKinsey & Company

Book design by Robert Newman and Linda Rubes

VIZ Media, LLC, a member of Shogakukan group
295 Bay Street, San Francisco, CA 94133

To the people of Japan

Contributing Authors

Bernard ARNAULT, chairman, LVMH

Gerard J. ARPEY, CEO, American Airlines

Govinda AVASARALA, Brookings Institution

Dominic BARTON, global managing director,
McKinsey & Company

Hannah BEECH, Bejing bureau chief, *Time*

Paul BLUSTEIN, fellow, Brookings Institution

Tyler BRÛLÉ, editor-in-chief, *Monocle*

Ian BURUMA, author

John CHAMBERS, CEO, Cisco

Heang CHHOR, Japan managing director,
McKinsey & Company

Mark CLIFFORD, executive director, Asia
Business Council

Stephen R. COVEY, author, management expert

Gerald L. CURTIS, political scientist, Columbia
University

John W. DOWER, historian, Massachusetts
Institute of Technology

Nicholas EBERSTADT, demographer, American
Enterprise Institute

Charles K. EBINGER, senior fellow, Brookings
Institution

Mohamed A. EL-ERIAN, CEO, PIMCO

Bill EMMOTT, author

Kazuhiro FUJIWARA, education expert

Glen S. FUKUSHIMA, chairman, Airbus Japan

Yoichi FUNABASHI, former editor in chief, *Asahi
Shimbun*

Victor K. FUNG, chairman, Li & Fung Group

Yuji GENDA, economist, University of Tokyo

Carlos GHOSN, CEO, Renault-Nissan Alliance

Brad GLOSSERMAN, executive director,
Pacific Forum, CSIS

Senapathy GOPALAKRISHNAN, CEO, Infosys

Christopher GRAVES, CEO, Ogilvy Public
Relations

Michael J. GREEN, political scientist, Georgetown
University

Yasuchika HASEGAWA, CEO, Takeda
Pharmaceutical

Fumiko HAYASHI, mayor of Yokohama

David HENDERSON, consultant, McKinsey & Company

Kenshi HIROKANE, *manga* creator

Keiji INAFUNE, CEO, Comcept

Paul J. INGRASSIA, author

Natsumi IWASAKI, author

Naoyuki IWATANI, partner, McKinsey & Company

Pico IYER, author

Ludwig KANZLER, partner, McKinsey & Company

Richard KATZ, editor, *The Oriental Economist*

Peter KENEVAN, partner, McKinsey & Company

Alex KERR, author

Jesper KOLL, managing director, JP Morgan Securities Japan

Yoshie KOMURO, CEO, Work-Life Balance

Kenneth LIEBERTHAL, senior fellow, Brookings Institution

Peter LÖSCHER, CEO, Siemens AG

Shinzo MAEDA, chairman, Shiseido

Kumiko MAKIHARA, writer

Kevin MASSY, Brookings Institution

Bob MCDONALD, CEO, Procter & Gamble

Allen MINER, founder/CEO SunBridge

Minoru MORI, chairman, Mori Building

Ulrich NAEHER, senior partner, McKinsey & Company

Tomoko NAMBA, CEO, DeNA

Motoya OKADA, president, AEON

Takeshi OKADA, former coach, Japanese national soccer team

Gordon ORR, Asia chairman, McKinsey & Company

Edzard J. C. OVERBEEK, president, Cisco Asia-Pacific and Japan

Adam S. POSEN, senior fellow, Peterson Institute for International Economics

Philipp RADTKE, senior partner, McKinsey & Company

T.R. REID, author; former Tokyo bureau chief, *The Washington Post*

Stephen S. ROACH, non-executive chairman, Morgan Stanley Asia

Gwen ROBINSON, journalist, *Financial Times*

William H. SAITO, entrepreneur

Masahiro SAKANE, chairman, Komatsu

Brian SALSBERG, partner, McKinsey & Company

David E. SANGER, chief Washington correspondent, *The New York Times*

Kaori SASAKI, president, UNICUL International

Howard SCHULTZ, CEO, Starbucks

Klaus SCHWAB, founder, World Economic Forum

Waichi SEKIGUCHI, editorial writer, *Nihon Keizai Shimbun*

Martha SHERRILL, author

Takumi SHIBATA, COO, Nomura Holdings

Masayoshi SON, founder/CEO, SoftBank

Devin STEWART, senior director, Japan Society

Akira SUGAHARA, senior partner, McKinsey & Company

Edward SUZUKI, architect

Sakae SUZUKI, consultant, McKinsey & Company

Masaru TAMAMOTO, senior fellow, World Policy Institute

Hitoshi TANAKA, chairman, Institute for International Strategy, JRI

Peter TASKER, founding partner, Arcus Investments

Henry TRICKS, Tokyo bureau chief, *The Economist*

Bobby VALENTINE, former manager, Chiba Lotte Marines

Steve VAN ANDEL, chairman, Amway

Ezra F. VOGEL, sociologist, Harvard University

Ingo Beyer VON MORGENSTERN, senior partner, McKinsey & Company

Robert WHITING, author

Masahiro YAMADA, sociologist, Chuo University

Shlomo YANAI, CEO, Teva Pharmaceutical Industries

Tadashi YANAI, CEO, Fast Retailing

CONTENTS

CONTENTS

CONTENTS

INTRODUCTION

WHY JAPAN MUST BE REIMAGINED

DOMINIC BARTON

EARTHQUAKES ARE A TERRIFYING reminder of human frailty. They strike without warning. They kill indiscriminately. They flatten cities. The Great Eastern Japan Earthquake of March 2011 brought all that, plus a devastating tsunami and a nuclear emergency the equivalent of Chernobyl.

And yet, as the people of Japan have shown, such tragedies can also illuminate the best of human nature. Within weeks of the crisis, it was clear that, although the chain of destruction had resulted in the deaths of tens of thousands and unalterably changed the lives of hundreds of thousands more, Japan would recover. Survivors were bearing their hardships with extraordinary dignity and courage. The nation had begun mobilizing to rebuild. Though battered by one of the most powerful seismic jolts in recorded history, Japan was unbowed.

This book was on its way to the publisher when the earthquake hit. We immediately commissioned new material; many authors recast their work. The ideas and insights assembled in this volume, therefore, explore the idea of restoring Japan in a much broader sense than mending the damage done by the disasters.

In fact, Japan faces two separate emergencies. The first is the urgent need to rebuild the Tohoku region. Kobe's eventual recovery following the earthquake that flattened much of that city in 1995 offers reason for optimism about Japan's capacity to recover from geological shocks.

The second emergency is less obvious because it is ubiquitous; it has to do with Japan's long-term social and economic trends. Well before March 2011, Japan's once-formidable economy had been sputtering. Growth was lackluster. Deflation persisted. Japan's workforce was shrinking at an alarming rate, and the nation's

Dominic Barton is the global managing director of McKinsey & Company.

1

population, already the world's oldest, was also the fastest aging. The debt-to-GDP ratio was more than 200 percent, the highest in the developed world.

The country continued to excel at manufacturing; even so, many of its largest and best-known companies had lost market share to rivals from South Korea and China. Meanwhile, its service industries were global laggards. And despite a highly educated, technically savvy workforce, Japan had failed to create the sort of entrepreneurial culture that could compete with Silicon Valley. In sum, the economic model associated with Japan's rise, including such features as close collaboration between the public and private sectors and lifetime employment, had faltered. No robust new model had emerged to take its place.

When the earth moves, nothing can stop it; when a tsunami forms, it must crash to the shore. But Japan is not helpless when it comes to the social and economic factors that play a large part in determining long-run prosperity. Change is never easy, of course. As Takeda Pharmaceuticals CEO Yasuchika Hasegawa notes in his essay in this volume, "Despite our long record of withstanding sudden external shocks, we are less successful in combating gradual, long-term challenges, especially when the origins of those problems are homegrown." The important point, however, is that the future is not fated. Japan can shape its own destiny. The key variables are all within the control of the Japanese people themselves.

As McKinsey considered Japan's difficulties in addressing these long-term challenges, we decided to reach out to a distinguished group of business leaders, experts, and thinkers. We conceived *Reimagining Japan* as an effort to consider Japan's strengths and weaknesses along many dimensions, social and cultural as well as economic and political. To that end, we invited debate from an extraordinarily diverse mix of contributors; together, they bring a wealth of expertise without parallel in a single volume. These are independent voices. McKinsey did not tell them what to say or challenge their conclusions; we wanted their views to help Japan think through these difficulties.

Many of our contributors offer detailed (and sometimes contradictory) prescriptions. The head of McKinsey Japan, Heang Chhor, the driving force behind this project, suggests his own road map. But *Reimagining Japan* is meant as neither a "white paper" nor a precise policy plan. Rather, our hope is to provoke discussion and to contribute to debate about how Japan can define its future.

Naturally, this volume includes economists, academics, and CEOs (from Asia, Europe, and the United States). But it also includes contributions from a video-game designer and a *manga* artist. Baseball's Hideo Nomo and the man who saved the Akita dog breed are the subjects of other essays.

Despite the differences in the authors' backgrounds and perspectives, several themes surface repeatedly:

Openness: Again and again, authors noted that younger people seem increasingly unwilling to venture outside the safe cocoon of Japan, a symptom of a worrying insularity at a time of rapid global integration. Glen S. Fukushima of Airbus Japan notes that the number of students going overseas to study has dropped dramatically. He is not the only author to compare the country's attitude today to the Tokugawa shogunate's policy of *sakoku* (or "closed country"), where no foreigners were permitted to enter Japan, and no Japanese were allowed to leave. And Takumi Shibata, deputy president and COO of Nomura Holdings, is not the only person to call for a new Meiji, the era that followed the shogunate's demise, in which Japan embraced the world: "We must try to rekindle that positive energy."

Openness matters because in an ever-more competitive world, the only way to compete is to test yourself against the best. That is the lesson that Takeshi Okada, the former coach of Japan's national soccer team, takes from his own difficult sojourn in Germany and the experience of other athletes who have played in Europe.

As a market, Japan is big enough to stand on its own. But that size can become a trap. Venture capitalist Allen Miner demonstrates that Japan does not lack entrepreneurial verve; what is missing is the ability, or perhaps the desire, to take great ideas global. *Nihon Keizai Shimbun* technology writer Waichi Sekiguchi dissects the "Galapagos Syndrome," a term that describes the tendency of Japanese companies to make wondrous products that can work only in Japan. This is no way to become a global leader.

Diversity: Japanese society, like the best varieties of Japanese rice, has a marvelous "stickiness." Japan's people feel bound to each other. They rally together in times of difficulty, and have developed elaborate social norms and codes of personal conduct to preserve harmony. That sense of mutual obligation governed the extraordinarily civilized manner in which Japan's citizens endured the terrible days and weeks after the Tohoku disasters.

Japan's cohesiveness is often ascribed to its ethnic and cultural homogeneity. But as David Sanger of *The New York Times* notes, homogeneity also can be a disadvantage. In a global economy where rewards increasingly accrue to creative "knowledge workers," it helps to have a feel for multiple perspectives.

One dimension of this problem is English, the language of global business. The standard of spoken English in Japan is comparatively poor; as a result, not only are Japanese often uncomfortable in international settings, but the country itself can be intimidating for foreigners to navigate. Japan's largest companies might consider following the example of some global competitors in adopting English as their corporate language. Even if they do not, they must do better in recruiting and retaining Japanese with international experience, as well as foreigners who understand how to operate in Japan.

A second way to diversify is to bring in more people. Cities like London and New York get much of their energy from their global orientation; almost four in ten New Yorkers were born overseas. Could Japan, or at least Tokyo, be like that? As Japan's own workforce contracts, and as its companies push into such high-growth emerging markets as China and India, Japanese employers must learn to compete for global talent. And yet the country retains an unusually strong aversion to outsiders and immigration, an attitude reflected in the fact that it has a lower percentage of foreign-born residents than any other nation in the Organisation for Economic Co-operation and Development (OECD).

Even if Japan does not accept a large influx of immigrants in the near future, it could still bring in more points of view by taking advantage of its position as the region's most developed country. Author and former editor of *The Economist* Bill Emmott believes Japan should seek to become "Asia's hub for ideas, technology, culture." Infosys CEO Senapathy Gopalakrishnan suggests Japan create an independent global university specializing in technology and drawing in students from all over the world.

A final source of diversity could come from within: Japan's women. As a result of demographics, it is a mathematical certainty that Japan needs to expand its workforce. If the country will not accept immigrants, more Japanese need to get to work. And the largest untapped resource is women, whose attachment to the workforce is limited, with most quitting after giving birth and few building long-term careers.

Japanese businesses should diversify their boards by including more foreigners and more women. Instead, these corporations have taken the opposite approach to an extreme; the typical board member is Japanese and male, and has been working at the company his entire professional life. Boards thus composed are a closed circle that can keep out fresh ideas and new thinking. Shiseido's chairman Shinzo Maeda made it a priority to diversify the cosmetic company's board when he was CEO; among other advantages, he writes, meetings are more interesting than they used to be.

Innovation: The Japanese are rightly proud of their manufacturing expertise. And of course there is a place, and always will be, for high-value, high-quality manufacturing in Japan, just as there is in Germany and the United States. But with China (and other countries) climbing up the value ladder, mass manufacturing in Japan is the wave of the past. "No labor-intensive industry can revive Japan," SoftBank founder and CEO Masayoshi Son argues. "Knowledge-intensive industries are the only way forward." Tomoko Namba, the founder of DeNA, Japan's most successful mobile games operator, identifies a number of factors that prevent Japan from hatching successful start-ups, and hinder the ability of Japanese ventures to compete with rivals in Silicon Valley.

Japan is known for its service ethos. And yet the nation is a global laggard when it comes to such important service industries as aviation, financial services, accounting, insurance, law, and tourism. Gopalakrishnan describes Japan's service sector as "an island unto itself." In 2009, according to the OECD, Japan created only 67 percent as much economic value per hour as the United States— much of that gap came from its underperforming service industries. This is not a trivial issue, considering that services accounts for more than three-quarters of Japan's GDP. Such inefficiency saps competitiveness, economist Adam S. Posen concludes.

One problem is that Japan's education system, which served the country so well for so long in the postwar era, is not delivering as many of the flexible, creative thinkers as Japan needs for what best-selling management author Stephen R. Covey calls the "Knowledge Age." Rather than turning out clever crammers, Covey argues, Japan's educators must cultivate among students a sense of their own "primary greatness"—that is, future leaders who are self-sufficient, internally motivated, and accustomed to thinking for themselves. Keiji Inafune, a noted game creator and entrepreneur, notes that a salaryman ethos prevails in the sector, unlike the more decentralized, performance-driven US model—and Japan has gone from dominant to also-ran.

Leadership: Is Japan capable of fundamental change? Many authors—including celebrated Japan specialists Ezra F. Vogel and Gerald L. Curtis—note the shortcomings of Japan's political system, and the reluctance of the nation's political elites to abandon the entrenched factionalism and parochialism of the past. Tadashi Yanai, CEO of Fast Retailing, one of Japan's notable recent success stories, perceives a similar flat-footedness among Japan's business leaders. He worries that "other countries are growing, while we in Japan stick to our old ways."

Historians Ian Buruma and John W. Dower, however, take issue with the oft-heard assertion that Japan cannot change. Of course it can, they argue; the nation has done so many times before. Carlos Ghosn, the man who led the turnaround at Nissan, notes that "Japan doesn't always move fast, but it always catches up." And Henry Tricks, Tokyo bureau chief for *The Economist*, discerns the possible emergence of a new generation of bolder and more far-sighted Japanese leaders in both the political and corporate spheres.

Perhaps the single message that shines through most clearly in these pages is that Japan has a huge community of global friends and supporters. The world has an enormous stake in Japan's success.

To realize that hope, Japan must change. The country does not have to reject its traditional values; these can serve Japan well, as the world saw after the tsunami. But Japan must adapt those values to a changed world.

Japan balanced tradition and transformation successfully in the Meiji era, led by men of courage and vision like Ryoma Sakamoto. After World War II, a generation of entrepreneurs led by such iconic names as Honda and Matsushita helped reshape Japan's struggling postwar economy into an economic powerhouse. The Japan that emerged from those transitions was stronger, richer, and more confident.

Few of the issues the contributors to *Reimagining Japan* identify will be unfamiliar to the Japanese. Indeed, some of the essays could have been written five or even 15 years ago. The problem is that weak governments and Japan's very success has attenuated the sense of urgency.

For 20 years, Japan has drifted. To reimagine a brighter future, that must change.

—May 2011

CHAPTER ONE: RENEWAL

Photograph © The Daily Yomiuri

MARCH 11— JAPAN'S ZERO HOUR

YOICHI FUNABASHI

THE EARTHQUAKE OF MARCH 11, 2011 changed the geography of Japan—literally. Digital maps and GPS devices are likely to deviate by more than 5 meters as a result. The country has undergone a cataclysmic realignment.

Beyond this geological shift, aftershocks from the earthquake are reverberating across many dimensions of Japanese life, creating upheaval in our politics, economy, social institutions, and foreign relations. In ways many Japanese never before experienced, our national spirit has been shaken.

Throughout Japanese history, seismic disasters have often seemed to mark the dramatic end of an era. Closely following Commodore Matthew Perry's conclusion of a trade treaty in 1854 came the Ansei Great Earthquakes of 1854 and 1855; the Great Kanto Earthquake of 1923 struck shortly after the annulment of the Anglo-Japanese Alliance in 1922; the advent of Japan's lost era coincided with the Great Hanshin Earthquake in 1995. The momentous question now is what sort of change the Great Eastern Japan Earthquake will delineate.

Japan can no longer afford the delusions of "graceful decline" or "small is beautiful"—notions that appealed to many prior to March 11. Our choice is rebirth or ruin.

Unfathomable losses are the most immediate consequence of the earthquake and tsunami. Some are at least measurable, or will be in the foreseeable future—in particular, the toll in lost lives, vanished communities and destroyed property. At the time of this writing, estimates of the number of dead and missing people exceed 30,000, and calculations of the cost of rebuilding the Tohoku region are in the $300 billion range. Because Tohoku's economy was not as vibrant as that

Yoichi Funabashi is former editor in chief of the Asahi Shimbun.

of the Hanshin region, the national government will bear a higher proportion of the reconstruction costs for the March 2011 disaster than was the case after the Kobe earthquake of 1995.

But the losses are intangible as well. The compound crisis of earthquake, tsunami, and nuclear emergency has shattered Japan's image as a land of safety and security.

Japan has long been proud of the wholesomeness of its food and the reliability of its infrastructure, notably its power and transportation systems. Consider electric power: before March 2011, Japan boasted the lowest level of power outages in the world, with outstanding stability provided at low cost. As a result of the direct hit inflicted on our thermal and nuclear-based power system, that reputation is in tatters.

THROUGHOUT JAPANESE HISTORY, SEISMIC DISASTERS HAVE OFTEN SEEMED TO MARK THE DRAMATIC END OF AN ERA.

Instead of viewing Japan as a haven of immunity from danger and inconvenience, many around the world now perceive the country as fraught with peril and discomfort. This perception is certain to have an effect on foreign investment, participation in Japan's student exchange programs, and the nation's appeal as a destination for foreign tourists.

Another consequence of the disaster—clearly adverse, though difficult to quantify—is a crisis of trust. The government has performed inadequately in sharing information with the Japanese public as well as the rest of the world. Unfortunately, Japan's ineptness in communication and global literacy is a longstanding problem. According to International SOS, a company that provides organizations with emergency health care and security assistance, the inability to obtain reliable and timely information is cited by as many as two-thirds of their customers as their greatest problem when working in Japan.

More fundamental in this regard is the exposure of the too-cozy relationship between an elite cadre of "nuclear village" proponents at Tokyo Electric Power Company (TEPCO) and officials at the Ministry of Economy, Trade and Industry (METI). The lack of transparency and accountability has undermined faith in Japan's ability to manage risks properly and effectively.

Well before March 11, Japan's vulnerabilities included its fault-ridden land, a heavy reliance on oil and nuclear power, a rapidly aging population, isolated local communities, and bloated national debt. But these vulnerabilities have become more pronounced since the last comparable event, the 1995 earthquake in Kobe.

In the intervening years, Japan's nominal GDP has fallen to 479 trillion yen, from 489 trillion yen, while the central government's reliance on public debt has soared. As a result, the debt of national and regional governments has risen to more than 200 percent, from 75 percent, of GDP. Within this same time frame, the number of people aged 65 and over has increased to 29 million, or 22.7 percent, of the population, from 18.3 million, or 14.5 percent.

The events of March 11 could make Japan more fragile—and cast it into a devastating downward spiral from which recovery would be difficult. The three hardest-hit prefectures—Iwate, Miyagi, and Fukushima—have a combined area about the size of the Netherlands. These prefectures are struggling with the destruction of entire municipalities, the departure of tens of thousands of people, the abandonment of agriculture by many elderly farmers, and the uninhabitability of vast expanses of land because of radiation fears. Companies—including global firms—will move their factories to other regions, perhaps overseas, because of power shortages and damaged infrastructure.

The region has served as a power source, manufacturing supplier, breadbasket, and labor force for Tokyo, functioning essentially as an outsourcer supporting Tokyo's prosperity. The hollowing-out of this vital region will tear a hole in the economic foundation of Tokyo and Japan as a whole.

At the same time, the March 11 disaster highlighted the national strengths that provide the most promising grounds for hope. The Japanese people gained a newfound sense of unity and solidarity as they witnessed the patience, courtesy, and fortitude of those who lost homes and loved ones. The victims' ability to maintain social order even as civilization seemed to crumble about them was not only heartwarming but confidence-inspiring.

For foreigners, including Lawrence Wilkerson, the former chief of staff to US Secretary of State Colin Powell and currently a visiting professor at the College of William and Mary, the contrast with most other countries was striking. As Wilkerson observed in a column published on the website of *The Washington Note*, a popular US blog, in the aftermath of disasters in many other countries military forces are "needed for security as much as aid." But Japan's soldiers were able to concentrate almost exclusively on rescue and relief, because of the morals of the Japanese people, or, to borrow a phrase from political scientist Robert Putnam, the country's high degree of "social trust."

The epitome of this spirit is the widely reported bravery of the "Fukushima 50," who struggled to bring the stricken nuclear plants under control. The cover of the March 19 edition of *The Economist* showed workers wearing helmets and protective gear desperately trying to stop a red ball of fire—the "rising sun" from the Japanese flag—from rolling down a hill. Reminiscent of Joe Rosenthal's historic photo of US Marines raising the Stars and Stripes on Iwo Jima's Mount Suribachi, the illustration evokes the same kind of admiration among Japanese.

Japan has also reaped rewards, in the form of sympathy and support from abroad, for the role it has played as a global civilian power, including its involvement in developmental assistance, environmental protection, and disarmament. Among the many encouraging e-mails I received from friends overseas, an offer of support from Robert Zoellick, president of the World Bank, said: "It's the least we can do for a country that has been so generous to others."

Unsurprisingly, given its status as Japan's chief ally, the United States has led the way in providing such support. American troops rushed straight to the disaster area, with the aircraft carrier *USS Ronald Reagan* serving as a key command center. The United States sent 19,000 Marines and Navy sailors, 20 ships, and 140 aircraft to support the rescue effort, cementing Washington's reputation as an ally Tokyo can

A civil society: Japanese Self Defense Forces rescue survivors in Minami Sanriku two days after the tsunami.
© STR/epa/Corbis

count on. Not that the United States was alone: rescue and medical teams came from 133 countries, including Australia, China, France, Germany, Israel, Mongolia, Russia, Singapore, South Korea, and Turkey. Particularly appreciated by the Japanese public were private acts of compassion, such as the ten Pakistanis living in Chiba Prefecture who drove ten hours by truck to the decimated town of Kesennuma, where they delivered chicken curry and naan bread to 1,000 shelter residents.

The warm feelings aroused by these and many other scenes of selflessness, however, will go only so far. The task ahead will require a sustained and intense focus on recovery and rebirth—not only for the sake of the Tohoku region, but for all of Japan.

First, Japan needs to strengthen public policies aimed at protecting the lives and assets of its people from threats such as natural disasters and major technological malfunctions. Although Japan's preparedness for these kinds of events

Earthquake, tsunami and nuclear crisis have shattered Japan's image as a land of safety and security.
© Photoshot/Picture Media

is reputedly the best in the world, we now recognize the need for even greater enhancement of risk management for earthquakes, tsunamis, and nuclear power. "Human-security" policies, based on the strong authority of the central government, deserve the same priority as "national security."

Next, the switch from an energy structure that relies on oil and nuclear power to one based on renewable energy is a must. In the short and medium term, Japan has no alternative but to maintain its nuclear industry. But we should set our long-term sights on becoming a green society, with energy needs met by solar power and other renewable sources.

As this process moves forward, economic policies must guard against the possibility of a global panic originating in Japan. After guaranteeing financial liquidity and the provision of recovery capital in the near term, Japan needs to map out a credible approach to attaining fiscal stability.

THE MARCH 11 DISASTERS HIGHLIGHTED STRENGTHS THAT PROVIDE THE MOST PROMISING GROUNDS FOR HOPE IN JAPAN'S FUTURE.

The March 11 disaster came in the midst of global economic upheaval, marked by a sovereign debt crisis in industrialized countries, aging populations, inflation and neomercantilism in emerging nations, rising oil prices, and a collapse of autocracy in the Middle East. We must take care that the disruption of global supply chains caused by Japanese production cuts, as well as a sell-off in government bonds, do not trigger a global panic; markets will test the mettle of Japanese policy makers.

At the same time, Japan faces challenges in its nation-rebuilding exercise that relate to the type of country it wants to be. One consideration is the concentration of population, government, and industry in Tokyo.

The clustering of so much power, wealth, and knowledge looks more than ever like a massive risk. At the time of the Great Kanto Earthquake in 1923, the government considered, and then rejected, the idea of relocating the capital. Perhaps this time, this decision should be different. Transferring the seat of the Imperial Palace back to Kyoto as a symbolic gesture should be on the agenda for discussion. From the perspective of risk management, decentralizing governmental operations to other parts of the country would be desirable.

Fear of earthquakes and tsunamis could create even greater shifts in the mindset of the Japanese, from one that identifies Japan as a seafaring country toward one with a distaste for all things from the ocean. As concern increases about the risks of coastal living, the result could be a deepening of our tendency to look inward, causing our country to withdraw from further engagement with the rest of the world.

In other ways as well, the events of March 11 may work against Japan's integration with the global economy. The devastation of agriculture in Tohoku and the sudden increase in those 65 and over abandoning farming might appear to favor participation in trade agreements, such as the Trans-Pacific Partnership promoted by the United States, that would require agricultural reform and liberalization.

Conversely, sympathy for the plight of the farmers may strengthen the forces opposing participation.

On March 16, 2011, Emperor Akihito spoke to the nation, expressing his sympathy for the victims and gratitude to emergency responders and other relief workers. Before his statement, the Emperor declared voluntary power cuts in the Imperial Palace and residences, displaying solidarity with the disaster victims and the Japanese people.

Many people took the Emperor's message to be the most weighty of its kind since the August 15, 1945 radio broadcast by his father, Emperor Hirohito, announcing the country's surrender in World War II. Then the Japanese people heard the Emperor acknowledge that they were "enduring the unendurable and suffering the unsufferable"—and they knew that their nation was forever changed. For Japanese of a certain age, where they were and what they were doing during that broadcast has long been considered a turning point in their lives. In the same way, 2:46 PM, March 11, 2011—the moment the earth cracked in Tohoku—will mark "zero hour" for the Japanese people for years to come.

Shortly after the earthquake, several friends remarked on the phenomenon that Mount Fuji had gleamed as brilliantly as they had ever seen it in the week following that fateful March 11. Those words imbued me with a fervent desire for Japan again to rise, with all the majesty of that snow-covered summit. At the same time, a feeling of melancholy overcame me as I reflected on the pulsating spirit of noble purity that welled up among the people immediately after the earthquake and tsunami.

The images of disaster victims "enduring the unendurable" were both wrenching and uplifting. However, somewhere in those images I sensed resignation and fatalism. Does "enduring the unendurable" not resemble our resignation over the political leaders who have repeatedly betrayed us? This resignation is what I fear most.

Political leadership and a constructive contribution by the media will be critical factors. Whether these factors will be sufficient remains to be seen, but this much is certain: in the past 20 years, never have I been more sanguine about prospects for Japan's rebirth. There is an overflow of will and hope among the Japanese people as they begin rebuilding their country.

All of the above explains my cautiousness—and my optimism. I believe that Japan will be reborn.

SUMMONING THE NEXT GENERATION OF LEADERS

HENRY TRICKS

MIYAGI PREFECTURE, MARCH 17, 2011: Izumi Miura, a pharmacist in her early 20s, sits holding her knees on a blue plastic tarpaulin in the refugee center that has become her home. Her mother, who has not eaten for nearly a day, eagerly grasps four pots of yogurt proffered to her. With tears welling, she recounts how the tsunami swept away her house in the port town of Kesennuma on March 11. As Izumi's mother talks, you can sense her desperate effort to understand the calamity that nature has wrought on her life, her visions of a comfortable old age smashed into shards of matchwood.

Izumi, on the other hand, talks hopefully about rebuilding their future. I ask Izumi whether her family has any money, she shakes her head, telling me that everything they had was carried away. "It's okay," she smiles. "There's nothing to buy anyway."

We cannot know how families like the Miuras will ultimately emerge from the wreckage; or whether coastal communities such as theirs can be salvaged; or whether farming and other industries will be blighted by radiation leaks from the stricken Fukushima nuclear power plant. Nor do we know what Japan's future energy policy will be, or even whether there will be much debate about it, given the public's traditional aversion to participation in policy issues.

But we do know that Izumi—and countless others like her—have a quiet but formidable determination to rebuild the country. While the earthquake, tsunami, and resulting nuclear-plant crisis destroyed lives and livelihoods throughout the Tohoku region, people, on the whole, have looked ahead rather than back.

Some have said that only a disaster of this scale could stir Japan from two decades of unrelenting, if genteel, decline. But such claims rest on a dubious premise.

Henry Tricks is Tokyo bureau chief of The Economist.

In the wake of disaster, the world rallied to Japan; these rescue workers from South Korea were on the ground in Sendai within days of the earthquake.
© REUTERS/Jo Yong-Hak

Even before the disasters, I saw stirrings of a strong civic spirit among Japanese, ordinary people determined to address their nation's problems in the absence of bold public leadership.

In February, I visited the town of Yuda, in the northeastern prefecture of Iwate, as a guest of Yamato Holdings, a parcel delivery company known for its stylized "black cat" logo. Two years ago, one of its drivers, Mayumi Matsumoto, made a delivery to a frail, elderly woman, only to learn that the woman died shortly after Matsumoto drove away. Wracked by guilt for failing to notice the woman's grave condition, she vowed to make Yamato a lifeline for the elderly in isolated rural communities.

In the village of Munitori, near Yuda, Matsumoto discovered that the mainly elderly population subsisted on tinned food and salted salmon if the weekly delivery truck from the nearest grocer, 30 kilometers away, did not turn up. This would happen on occasion because the driver of the truck was herself elderly and could not always make the journey. With full backing from Yamato, Matsumoto organized a system to enable villagers to relay food orders each day to social workers, who would then transmit the orders to a supermarket that would package them for Yamato to deliver. The company trained its drivers to talk to residents and report on their health. Such efforts are heroic, but also highlight how easily people can slip through the social-safety net, even in prosperous Japan.

Samurai spirit

The events of March 11 revealed how fragile life can be in a country that is blighted by occasional volcanic eruptions, quakes, and tsunamis. Even before the Tohoku disaster, many elderly people in the poorer rural regions struggled to live on meager pensions. Unemployment benefits and allowances for disadvantaged groups, such as single mothers and the handicapped, often are inadequate.

As Japan picks itself up, it can draw on the renewed fighting spirit of its people to build a society better equipped to respond to such needs. The obstacles are enormous given the nation's high level of debt, aging citizenry and inward-looking orientation. But the country has faced such challenges before, specifically during the Meiji Restoration (1868–1912), which ended centuries of feudal rule, and after World War II. In both cases, decaying political systems were so discredited that a new generation of independent-minded young leaders was able to push the old guard aside. One of these was a dashing samurai, Ryoma Sakamoto, who died young in 1867—and became a star in 2010, when a television series about his life became a national craze.

EVEN BEFORE THE TSUNAMI, THERE WERE STIRRINGS OF A STRONG CIVIC SPIRIT SEEKING TO ADDRESS JAPAN'S PROBLEMS.

For now, however, it is not clear where leadership will come from. In the aftermath of the March 11 disaster, it was difficult to recall the mood of optimism among many Japanese in August 2009, when the Democratic Party of Japan (DPJ) swept into power, ending 55 years of almost unbroken rule by the Liberal Democratic Party (LDP). The DPJ has failed to live up to many of its promises, partly because of its own incompetence and partly because of obstructionism by the old guard. By early 2011, Naoto Kan, who became prime minister in mid-2010, had seen his popularity ratings slide below 20 percent.

The big question over the next few years is whether a new generation of young, energetic political leaders will emerge to help rebuild the country and shore up national morale.

Enter the realists?

Japanese society flows, like its writing system, in a rigid hierarchy from top to bottom. Every 20 years or so, change at the top becomes palpable. This is one of those times. From now until 2013, the first wave of baby boomers, born in a burst of procreative enthusiasm between 1947 and 1949, will hit 65.

Leaders of the two key political parties, the ruling DPJ and opposition LDP, typify these "boomer-snoozers," who hit the peak of their careers just as Japan's economic bubble burst in the early 1990s. Since then, they have presided over stagnation and drift. Inward-looking, risk-averse and worn down by bitter experience, they have managed to keep Japan out of a Great Depression. That is about the sum of their achievements.

A core of potential next-generation political leaders, often described as "realists" are beginning to make a mark. Two decades of national drift have stripped them of illusion. They have risen by slugging it out in urban politics, rather than by inheriting safe seats or buying their way in as did the rural political dinosaurs of old. Many members of this rising generation of politicians watched with discomfort during the 1990 Gulf War, as Japan grappled with a pacifist constitution that prevented the country from active military engagement abroad. Some of them favor changing Article 9 (which forbids acts of war by the state) and many support unpopular proposals to raise the consumption tax.

SOME INNOVATIVE COMPANIES ARE EMBRACING CHANGE IN WAYS THAT DIRECTLY CHALLENGE JAPAN'S STATIC SOCIAL HIERARCHY.

They also are acutely pragmatic. The harsh reality of urban politics and the strength of Japan's mass media have rendered them sensitive to opinion polls. That sensitivity may be an improvement over the attitude of their elders, who often ignored public opinion, but too much attentiveness to the numbers could also inhibit bold leadership.

The realists' standard-bearer in the DPJ was Seiji Maehara, an ambitious 49-year-old train enthusiast who made no secret of his belief that too much political power resided in the conservative countryside. An economic liberal, he wanted to open Japan to free-trade agreements and revive the country's industrial strength and international influence. Caught in a minor funding scandal in February 2011, he resigned as foreign minister.

Another economic liberal, Yukio Edano, appointed by Kan as the Cabinet's chief of staff, shot to prominence after the March 11 crisis. Through weeks of nationally televised media briefings, Edano came across as exactly the kind of hard-working, loyal line manager whom the public likes to trust. Others of his generation within the DPJ have been less than electric, however. Renho, a telegenic politician in her early 40s who goes by one name, made her mark by targeting excessive government spending. Named to the Kan cabinet in 2010, she sometimes comes across as more of a publicity hound than a thinker. Damningly, few of the DPJ's leaders, rising or established, traveled to the affected areas in the weeks after the disasters to visit stricken communities.

The LDP, meanwhile, is grappling with similar leadership problems. Its young-ish turks, such as Nobuteru Ishihara, the moderate 54-year-old son of Tokyo's ultra-nationalist governor, and Yoshimasa Hayashi, a former defense minister known for his clear-eyed view of Japan's problems, have failed to present sensible policy initia-tives. Both were touted as pragmatists who could work with the DPJ, and yet they seemed to lack the courage to create a coalition of common interests. As a result, other maverick LDP politicians, such as Taro Kono, who used the crisis to promote a badly needed debate on energy policy, drew new attention.

All the while, Your Party, a youthful phenomenon that gained support in the 2010 Upper House elections, has been wooing more liberal-minded urban voters. Even so, its ideology appears to be more about tinkering with the means of govern-ment—such as the bureaucracy and the Bank of Japan—than about setting out a new vision.

Business unusual

In business, the record of the boomer generation is hardly more impressive. As the world was gradually transformed by globalization, the software revolution, and the rise of new markets in Asia and elsewhere, leaders of many large Japanese companies looked inward and clung to their shrinking domestic market.

Too often, Japan's business executives speak English poorly, if at all. They seem reluctant to embrace the Western idea of restructuring. They resist changes in their corporate cultures that would allow new ideas to percolate to the top. Just as with politics, though, there is a small, postboomer clique of up-and-coming business leaders with a different outlook.

During the Tohoku crisis, companies like 7-Eleven and Lawson, the two biggest convenience-store chains, worked with the government to get their stores up and running in order to provide much-needed staples. Among such companies, there is an emerging sense—just as there is at transport company Yamato—that when the government has not created the right response, business should provide it.

Before the crisis, some innovative companies were also embracing change in ways that directly challenged Japan's static social hierarchy. Rakuten, an e-com-merce portal, has sought to make itself global, not least by requiring all employees to communicate in English even in the company's Japan headquarters. Yamada Denki, a highly successful electronics retailer, is hiring Chinese staff in Japan to train employees as executives in preparation for a big push into China. Komatsu, a heavy-machinery company, has broken traditional business taboos by pledging to use local executives to run its operations in China.

On the whole, though, Japan has stuck to a hierarchical style of business, rather than adopting the flatter, more networked approach of its global competitors. In-stead of promoting strong, entrepreneurial leadership, the country's businessmen and politicians have stuck with consensus.

All these issues challenge entrenched cultural notions, but changes in the outside world are not the only factors that make reform imperative. Japan, too, is changing, as its workforce ages and its population shrinks. Fewer workers mean the country needs to reboot productivity to maintain economic growth. The alternative is to entrench deflation and to erode living standards.

Even if Japan has no ambition to be a leading power, and would rather focus on being a leaner, high-tech economy with comfortable living standards, the country faces a huge fiscal drag as its population ages. Truly radical change is long overdue.

The first area to tackle is human resources. For too long, Japan has taken the view that the way to deal with a shrinking workforce is to supplement manpower with technological innovation, such as robotics. The country has given short shrift to the idea that in the knowledge economy, Japan needs to exploit its workers' creative abilities and not keep them chained to the factory floor.

Japan's industrial conglomerates have made a fetish of producing gadget-intensive hardware, such as televisions, mobile phones, and cars. These companies play to the strengths of their factory-based craftsmen, who are disciplined and detail-oriented. If such highly motivated workers had been freed to think laterally, Japan might not have missed one of the biggest business shifts of the last decade, away

The city of Natori, like many communities along Japan's northeastern coast, was ravaged by fire and water.
© Photoshot/Picture Media

from the machine, or "hardware," and toward the content or applications displayed on that hardware.

The imperative to loosen hierarchies is even greater in the service sector, source of 70 percent of Japan's jobs. Here women remain the nation's most under-utilized resource. Young mothers in government jobs are the only women who are routinely encouraged to return to work after maternity leave. The private sector mostly transfers these women to low-paid shifts without benefits. Childcare, meanwhile, remains expensive and difficult to arrange. All these factors not only discourage women from having children, but also rob the workforce of highly motivated talent.

Ends and means

A root cause of Japan's underperformance—afflicting both business and politics—is an inability to focus on ends rather than means.

Politicians struggle to articulate a coherent vision, and their poor communication skills result in a muddled message. Such has been the recent turnover of governments—14 in the last 20 years—that politicians plot policy initiatives in terms of months, not years. As a result, they concentrate on practical, achievable initiatives that make an instant impact—child subsidies, stimulus packages, toll road exemptions, and the like—rather than broad, strategic issues. In business, too, the priority has been to finesse the production process—that is, to make workers more efficient and preserve team spirit—rather than tackle the bigger challenge of increasing long-term profits and improving competitiveness.

The consequences of this political and industrial drift have been easy to ignore. Japan has had a hoard of savings to live on. A river of fiscal stimulus has been poured into infrastructure improvement. Cities like Tokyo remain stylish, comfortable places to live. And as the population ages, its appetite for risk seems to move in inverse proportion to its appetite for good food, a national obsession.

Despite the country's economic and political drift, Japanese have prided themselves on maintaining an enviable lifestyle. But as the burden of meeting rising health and welfare costs begins to fall on a dwindling number of wage earners, such comforts will be increasingly difficult to sustain. Corporate investment will fall as the domestic market contracts. Deflation may become endemic. The country's debt burden will keep growing. And the country needs to spend up to $300 billion to rebuild Tohoku. Power shortages in eastern Japan could last for months.

Separately, these challenges are difficult; combined, they are a force. Dealing with them will come as a huge jolt. Some will see in the country's afflictions an opportunity for reflection: on the way the nation uses energy; on the flawed relationships between the government and the power companies; on the overbuilding in coastal areas; on the patchy safety net; and on the fragility of Japan's relationship with nature.

If these reflections percolate into political debate, Japan—for all that it is suffering now—will emerge a stronger country.

REFLATING JAPAN

PETER TASKER

JAPAN'S TRIPLE DISASTERS OF MARCH 2011—the earthquake, tsunami, and nuclear contamination crisis—offered a stark depiction of the country's strengths and weaknesses. On one side of the ledger: the solidarity, courage, and extraordinary mental resilience of the many victims and rescue workers. On the other: incestuous ties between industry, bureaucrats, and politicians; blinkered strategic thinking; and a disturbing vacuum of leadership.

Coming to terms with trauma on the scale of the Great Eastern Japan Earthquake will take years, perhaps decades. But the human mind craves meaning, messages, and patterns from even the most random natural phenomena. In the immediate aftermath of the quake and tsunami, the governor of Tokyo, Shintaro Ishihara, spoke of *tenbatsu* (the punishment of heaven). He retracted the remark as the enormity of the damage became apparent. Yet many of my Japanese acquaintances, from elderly professors of history to young musicians, agreed with him. Not in the literal sense—that the victims of the disaster were in any way responsible for the tragedy that befell them—but in a metaphorical sense, that Japan had received a society-wide "wake-up call" that must be heeded.

Such an interpretation is not surprising. In both Western and Eastern mythology, natural disasters often have been viewed as portents of impending change. But change from what, and to what? The answers are not obvious. Two sentiments I heard often among Japanese as they struggled to make sense of the March 11 disasters were regret and resolve: regret for the loss of national "pride," and resolve that the drift and apathy that has characterized Japan's political scene over the last several decades cannot continue.

Peter Tasker is an author, commentator, and founding partner of Arcus Investments.

For some years now, the Japanese public has seemed resigned to the inevitability of deflation, not just in a financial sense, but in a broader sense that acknowledges a steady decline in the potential for a better life. The responses to the Tohoku earthquake suggest change may be at hand.

Clearly, ordinary Japanese are dissatisfied with the status quo. They want an end to deflation, and a return to growth; they want change in the economy, in their country's role in the world, and in relation to their own personal aspirations.

So what is the status quo, and what can be done to change it? The frequent characterization of Japan's recent past as "two lost decades" obscures a more complex reality. In the 1980s, Japan had become seriously inflated, in reputation and self-perception as much as in asset values. Books and the Japanese media often asserted Japan would **CLEARLY, ORDINARY JAPANESE ARE DISSATISFIED WITH THE STATUS QUO.** displace the United States as the world's leading economy by the turn of the century. Japanese bureaucrats and business leaders crowed that Japan had nothing left to learn from the West. In retrospect, a retreat was inevitable, and the moment of hubris was short-lived. After the implosion of the bubble economy in the early 1990s, Japan's economic performance did indeed suffer rapid decline.

As most of the world boomed through the 1990s, Japan slid into deflation and financial crisis. The response of the country's bankers and policymakers was fumbling and incoherent, albeit with some justification. Unlike the United States in 2008–09, Japan didn't have a "Japan" to learn from. As we now know from the aftermath of the global financial crisis, there are no easy fixes for the damage caused by the bursting of a large-scale bubble.

By the early years of this century, Japan's postbubble workout was largely complete and economic performance had started to improve. In 2003–08, Japan's growth in economic output was faster than America's on a per-worker basis. Corporate profits boomed, and for a while the recovery seemed to be on a secure footing. Some commentators even went so far as to claim that reforms instituted by Junichiro Koizumi, prime minister in 2001–06, had worked. Japan, they said, was back.

The euphoria was short-lived. The global financial crisis was a kind of *tenbatsu* for the entire developed world. The severity of Japan's recession revealed that, far from embarking on a self-sustaining recovery, the economy had become even more dependent on overseas demand; that there had been no recovery in wages and household income; and that nearly half the workforce was earning less than three million yen ($36,000) a year. Wage gaps widened, and indices of social well-being, such as the suicide rate, remained at worrying levels.

Japan's more recent policy failures are less defensible than its missteps in the 1990s. The Bank of Japan's justifications for inertia were convoluted and contradictory. Politicians shirked responsibility. The Democratic Party of Japan (DPJ), which won a landslide victory in the 2009 election, had one interesting idea: a substantial increase in child allowances to counter Japan's demographic shrinkage. But the proposal was watered down. Deficit hawks turned the Greek debt crisis of 2010 into a rallying cry for Japanese austerity. Officials obsessed over the possibility of a decline

Daring and cooperation can rescue the economy, too.
Photo © Kyodo News

in government bond prices, while turning a blind eye to the message delivered by the Nikkei 225 stock average, which sank to a 25-year low.

For a time, Japan's political system seemed to have shucked off the Liberal Democratic Party's post-1955 monopoly on power and graduated to the long-desired two-party system. This hope, too, did not mesh with reality. Despite winning a healthy majority in 2009, the new DPJ administration failed to make significant changes, and indeed appeared confused about what it wanted to change. Prime ministers came and went with the rapidity of new cell-phone models.

The deflation in Japan's global stature was just as severe. In foreign policy, Japan punched below its weight and, in many cases, failed even to enter the ring. As China expanded its influence, building economic bridgeheads in South East Asia, Africa, and South America, Japan grew passive. While China used its financial muscle to acquire upstream resource assets, Japan rejected the idea of establishing a sovereign wealth fund on the grounds that some investments might lose money. Instead, Japan's financial authorities kept the nation's foreign currency reserves in US Treasury bonds, mostly with short duration and low yields.

JAPAN WITHERED AS A RESULT OF DECISIONS MADE OR, MORE OFTEN, NOT MADE, BY INSTITUTIONS AND INDIVIDUALS.

Domestic interest groups, in the meantime, stymied attempts to create free-trade agreements. There was talk about turning Tokyo into a global financial center; instead, there was increasing marginalization, as intellectual and financial capital flowed instead to Hong Kong and Singapore. Japan's voice was rarely heard in forums like the G20 and the Bank for International Settlements as these entities coordinated responses to the financial crisis.

In diplomacy, a rift with China over the arrest of a fishing captain by Japanese authorities in disputed waters offered a brutal display of Asia's changing power balance. Japan's response was feeble and incoherent; China's, harsh and uncompromising. Inevitably, Japan blinked. Russia took note and immediately made the provocative move of announcing a visit by President Dimitry Medvedev to the disputed Northern Islands.

Despite great geopolitical changes, Japan's foreign ministry seemed more concerned with avoiding friction in the security alliance with the United States and putting a lid on any problems over the continuing US military presence in Okinawa. Politicians who thought otherwise were deemed irresponsible. The idea that the alliance might fall apart one day and Japan would quickly—perhaps very quickly— need the means to defend itself was considered unthinkable.

There was nothing inevitable about this story of all-encompassing deflation. Japan withered as a result of decisions made or, more often, not made, by institutions and individuals. Underlying all was a fatalistic habituation to gradual decline and complacency about the consequences.

The departure point for "reflation" should be confidence in Japan's enduring strengths. Japan is not Greece; it has the resources to fund a reconstruction program of enormous scale. Indeed, Japan is one the world's largest creditor nations, with a vast nest egg of overseas assets built up through three decades of current-account surpluses. Official opinion seems transfixed by high government deficits without considering the private-sector surpluses that have been financing them, with enough left over to finance a considerable portion of America's deficits, too.

THE MELDING OF CULTURES AND IDEAS IS THE DEFINING FEATURE OF OUR TIMES; JAPAN CANNOT STAND APART WITHOUT RISKING FURTHER DECLINE.

In the weeks after the disasters, Japanese bond yields were at the lowest levels seen in recorded history. This fact gives the Japanese government a golden opportunity to issue bonds at longer maturities, perhaps of 100 years, like the Mexican bonds floated in 2010, or better still, of no maturity at all, like those floated by Britain to finance the war against Napoleon.

There was even more leeway in monetary policy. Japan was the only major country experiencing declining prices, and market expectations were that deflation would persist for the remainder of this decade. If the Bank of Japan were to mount a Federal Reserve-scale program of quantitative easing—as opposed to the small-scale, sporadic, and badly communicated program of 2001–03—the risks of inflation rising to threatening levels are minimal. Significant purchases of government bonds by Japan's central bank would force financial institutions to put their money elsewhere, which would have the welcome effect of weakening the yen and triggering a bull market in shares and perhaps in other assets, too.

Japan's crisis of confidence has been exacerbated by its proximity to China. The rise of China and the emerging world as a whole means a loss of status not just for Japan, but for the small group of developed countries that have ruled the global roost since the Industrial Revolution. This global rebalancing of power and relative wealth is inevitable and ultimately positive, but it will generate some dangerous tensions along the way.

So the question is not whether Japan can keep pace with the fast-growing emerging economies, but how it will fare in comparison with other developed countries. In the 1990s, the answer to that question probably would have been that Japan's prospects are poor. Now the picture is less clear. Given the global financial turmoil of 2008-09, the European monetary zone's sovereign debt crisis in 2010-11, the substantial depreciation of the dollar and the pound, and the heated debate about mass immigration in the United States and Europe, Japan's structural problems, relative to those of its developed peers, suddenly seem less threatening. China is sure to face serious challenges too, not least from rising labor costs as urbanization peaks and its still-poor population rapidly ages.

Japan's proximity to high-growth emerging economies is both an opportunity and a risk. There are new markets to be cultivated, deals to be struck, and alliances to be created. Splendid isolation, or a 21st-century version of *sakoku* (the Tokugawa edict to "close the country"), are not options. The melding of cultures and ideas is the defining feature of our times; Japan cannot stand apart from those trends without risking further decline.

Still, the terms of Japan's engagement with Asia must be managed carefully. Economic growth fueled by mass immigration is the demographic equivalent of fool's gold. If immigrants integrate fully with the native population, then the different birth rates will converge and the problems of an aging society will be kicked down the road. If integration does not occur, social cohesion erodes, creating greater potential for conflict at times of economic stress. Compounding this problem is China's historic tendency to use its vast population as an instrument to project power, as seen in Inner Mongolia, Tibet, and, to some extent, in South East Asia. In Japan, immigration will increase, whether the country sanctions it or not. It is surely much better to have systems in place so that Japan can draw the people it needs on the terms it wants—and avoid the mistakes that some Western countries have made in this regard.

There are plenty of bright ideas around for the revitalization of Japan; many have been debated for a decade or more. The problem has been implementation. Nobody has cared enough; certainly not the powers-that-be, who seemed content to "manage decline," just as Britain's establishment did in the 1960s and 1970s. And not the general public, either, who have remained disengaged.

If the disasters of 2011 accomplish anything positive, it will be to break down this wall of complacency. The idea that weak leadership and unaccountable institutions have little impact on everyday life is no longer tenable. *Tenbatsu* or not, the psychological shift necessary for the reflation of Japan has started to gain momentum.

Japan's future path lies in clearing away the rubble of failed policies.
© Philippe Lopez/AFP/Getty Images

THE POWER OF *GAMAN*

T.R. REID

THE PEOPLE OF JAPAN respond well to adversity; after all, they've had a lot of practice. Japan's long history has involved a relentless series of disasters, both natural and self-inflicted. In the wake of catastrophe—be it an earthquake, a towering tsunami, or a shattering military defeat—the Japanese people tend to pick themselves up, dust themselves off, and start all over again with quiet determination, long-term planning, and a stoic commitment to hard work.

These characteristics are being tested anew after the triple tragedy that began on March 11, 2011: the largest earthquake in Japan's recorded history, the tsunami that followed, and the series of emergencies at the Fukushima nuclear plants.

For months afterward, the nation reeled from the physical, psychological, and social toll. Every evening, news programs replayed scenes of the torrents and fires that claimed tens of thousands of lives, and broadcast fresh images of the waterlogged rubble that lay strewn along hundreds of square miles. There was unending footage of grieving and increasingly restless people enduring a stressful existence in temporary shelters.

What kind of nation will emerge from this transformative event remains a matter of intense debate. Initially, at least, economists were pessimistic, in large part because the loss of the nuclear plants' power generation threatened to hobble Japan's productive capacity for months. Constant headlines about radiation triggered phobic reactions abroad regarding the safety of the country and its products.

And yet, amid the fear and sadness, there also were signs of the stalwart, resolute character traits that have brought the Japanese through so many earlier calamities. Once again, the people of Japan found ways to impose order on the chaos surround-

---

T.R. Reid is an author and former Tokyo bureau chief of The Washington Post.

Enduring adversity: At a shelter in Sendai, a boy waits for hot water to boil his noodles.
© STR/AFP/Getty Images

ing them. In the toughest circumstances, they preserved the cherished national values of discipline, harmony, and civility.

In ruined cities and makeshift relief centers, the victims displayed patience, honesty, and a refusal to panic. In one northern town, three days after the quake, a long line of customers was waiting to buy food and water at a convenience store. Then the portable generator providing the shop's power broke down. The lights went out; the cash register wouldn't open. So the customers returned their items to the shelves and waited quietly until the generator could be restarted.

That response—the reversion to national character—gave hope that Japan would manage once again to emerge intact from devastation. The damage wrought on March 11 was terrible, by any measure. Still, the Japanese have seen much worse.

Who rebuilt Kobe?

The death toll from the Great Eastern Japan Earthquake of 2011 didn't come close to that of the Great Kanto Earthquake of 1923, which left some 140,000 dead and the capital city ruined. When the earth stopped moving, the Japanese got to work and rebuilt Tokyo, bigger and more quake-resistant than before.

Amid the chaos, survivors showed discipline, determination, and compassion.
Top, left and right: © Nicolas Asfouri/AFP/Getty Images, © STR/epa/Corbis, © REUTERS/Kim Kyung-Hoon

And even that disaster was mild compared with World War II, a self-inflicted cataclysm in which 5 million Japanese died and 30 million—half of the nation—lost their homes. When the war ended, the starving, sick, shell-shocked populace, some of them dressed in makeshift smocks made from old newspapers, was left with little to eat, and few intact roads or trains. To make things worse, postwar Japan had almost no natural resources and no energy supply, having used up its coal and timber reserves in the years of battle.

But the nearly comatose country of August 1945 did have one important resource: its people. With the Japanese people's penchant for hard work, their respect for education, their habits of thrift, saving, and investment for the future, they threw themselves into the task of rebuilding a ravaged nation and a defunct economy. And of course, they succeeded: four decades after the war, the crowded island nation with few natural resources had made itself the second-biggest economy on the planet.

It's not coincidence that the Japanese tend to fight back against adversity, to work the hardest when the need is greatest. That tendency is one of the nation's most respected virtues. The Japanese have a word for it, one of their favorite words, in fact: *gaman*. This quality was emphasized in *Bushido*, the code of the samurai. It means to accept without complaint whatever life throws at you, to strap on your sandals and keep going no matter how difficult the road ahead.

I've always thought that *gaman* helps to explain the Japanese proclivity for hard work. When the odds are stacked against you, or when something horrendous happens, it's better to *gaman* than to sit around wailing in despair. Hard work becomes the medication that can ease painful memories; it gives you something to think about other than what you have lost.

The Japanese tend to believe that just being Japanese means a constant state of struggle. Even during the bubble years, when life seemed so rosy, people loved to point out the country's myriad social, demographic, and economic problems. They obsess about the obstacles in their path and the consequent need to display *gaman*.

You're never too young to learn this lesson. When my daughter was a third-grader at a public elementary school in Tokyo, she came home one night with awful news. "Dad, this is terrible!" Kate told us at the dinner table. "The teacher taught us today that Japan is a small island nation with no resources! So if we don't all work as hard as we can, this poor country can't survive."

THE JAPANESE TEND TO BELIEVE THAT JUST BEING JAPANESE MEANS A CONSTANT STATE OF STRUGGLE.

I witnessed the power of *gaman* when I covered the Great Hanshin Earthquake that was centered on Kobe in 1995. The Kobe tremor spawned no tsunami, and there was no nuclear threat; the death toll (almost 6,500) was much smaller than that of the 2011 Great Eastern Japan Earthquake. But the risk to the national economy was greater because the quake demolished the most important heavy cargo port of a nation that lived on foreign trade. It took out large sections of road and track at the heart of the national transportation infrastructure. It felled factories by the hundred and left thousands of people stranded for months in clammy, crowded, contagious temporary shelters.

The day after the Kobe earthquake, as I struggled past crumpled highways, snarled pipelines, and sundered railroad tracks, I met a middle-aged woman in a green tartan vest. She described in graphic detail the terror of the previous morning, when she watched the roof and the walls and the windows of her house crash down onto her bed. "I'm so lucky to be alive," she told me. With that, she climbed onto her bicycle and rode off through the wrecked city to bring her customers their daily delivery of the yogurt drink Yakult. That was her job—the green vest was her uniform—and the work must go on.

The job of rebuilding Kobe did go on, much faster than anyone predicted. In early April, about 12 weeks after the quake, the *shinkansen* (bullet train) line running through Kobe reopened, an important boost for the nation's transit system, as well as for its morale. By late spring, Kobe's port was repaired sufficiently to get Japan back to its normal rate of export and import. The last homeless victims left the shelters about five months after the fateful day. By mid-June, nearly all the rubbish and detritus was gone. Some six months after the Great Hanshin Earthquake, as I strolled around Kobe with my boss, he was puzzled. "When are we going to see destruction?" he asked.

Over the next year or so, I continued to visit Kobe and to marvel at the rapid pace of reconstruction. Thinking like an American, I got interested in the question of credit: Who is responsible for this? Who rebuilt Kobe?

I posed those questions to people all over the Hanshin region, and I got a characteristically Japanese answer. Nobody rebuilt Kobe, or at least, no individual did. Rather, everybody rebuilt Kobe. It was a communal effort. The work had to be done—and done fast—so people did it. The money had to be found, so the banks and the business community and the government dug deep and found it, some $160 billion in reconstruction funds at a time when Japan's economy was already in the doldrums.

Everybody rebuilt Kobe. After all, that's what you do if you're Japanese and you have just survived an epic natural disaster.

Finding the moxie

Recovery will be a steep hill to climb. The broad expanse of the damage—extending some 500 miles along the Pacific, from Aomori Prefecture in the north to Chiba Prefecture, west of Tokyo Bay—will cause major logistical problems. The uncertainty due to smoldering nuclear sites could make work dangerous, or even impossible, within a wide radius of the endangered power plants. The loss of nearly all transit infrastructure along the northeast coast will hinder reconstruction.

THE BETTER BET IS THAT JAPAN WILL DO WHAT IT HAS DONE SO OFTEN IN THE PAST: RESPOND TO BITTER ADVERSITY WITH SKILL AND FORETHOUGHT.

For all the difficulties, my bet is that Japan will do what it has done so often in the past: respond to bitter adversity with skill and forethought and a highly focused determination to get the job done. That's what *gaman* demands. True, the Japanese government is deeply in debt, but most of that is owed to its own people. It's hard to imagine that they will refuse to lend their savings to finance reconstruction.

Japan has recognized that a successful recovery along the battered northeast coast could pay double benefits. A major reconstruction program could bring new vitality to a region that has been viewed for years as a backwater, characterized by clusters of small farms and fishing villages barely connected to the bustling life of the big cities in Japan's industrial heartland. Modern seaports, state-of-the-art highways, new rail lines and airports could make Tohoku a more important part of Japan than it has ever been before.

Beyond that, an effective recovery could shore up the battered psyche of a country that has lost some of its self-confidence and drive. Since the collapse of the bubble economy two decades ago, Japan has seemed, at times, a society in despair, unsure of its stature in the world and unhappy about its prospects. A gleaming new Tohoku could be just the recipe to revive the spirits of a depressed nation.

Can this society find the moxie, the management, and the money to rebuild? The Japanese have always responded well to adversity; the nation's long history suggests that they can, and will, do so again.

KEEPING THE LIGHTS ON

CHARLES K. EBINGER, KEVIN MASSY, AND GOVINDA AVASARALA

THE ENERGY POLICY CHOICES JAPAN must make in the wake of the devastating earthquake and tsunami of March 2011 will have wide-ranging global implications. While its role as an energy power has been overshadowed in recent years by that of a rising China, Japan continues to be a major force in the global energy market. It is the fifth-largest consumer of energy in the world, the largest net importer of both coal and liquefied natural gas (LNG), the second-largest oil importer, and the third-largest producer of nuclear power.

Japan's rapid postwar growth was shaped by an industrial policy that combined increased hydrocarbon (coal, oil, gas) imports with the development of innovative energy technologies and world-class efficiency measures. Notwithstanding its vast fossil-fuel consumption, Japan has been the most energy- and emissions-efficient country in the G8 for the past 40 years, according to the International Energy Agency (IEA). Japan also has aggressive alternative-energy policies, with generous incentives and subsidies for renewables. In June 2010 the country set a target of generating 50 percent of its electricity from zero-emissions sources, including nuclear, by 2020.

Japan's postwar energy plans embraced the promise of nuclear power. Following President Dwight Eisenhower's "Atoms for Peace" speech to the United Nations in 1953, Japanese policy makers bought into the idea of nuclear power as a form of cheap, scalable power generation that would also help to minimize foreign exchange spending on oil imports and to cement ties with the United States. In 1954, the Diet passed the "atomic energy budget" despite some resistance from the scientific community.

Charles K. Ebinger is director of the Energy Security Initiative at the Brookings Institution, where Kevin Massy is the assistant director and Govinda Avasarala is a research assistant.

A child is checked for radiation in the zone around the damaged Fukushima nuclear power plants.
© REUTERS/Kim Kyung Hoon

The Iranian oil nationalization in the early 1950s and the 1956 Suez crisis demonstrated to successive Japanese governments the perils of relying on oil from the Middle East, and reinforced the idea of a link between civil nuclear power and economic and national security. To walk the line between the public's revulsion for nuclear weapons and the opportunity for greater energy security, Prime Minister Eisaku Sato set out a series of non-nuclear principles in 1967. These combined a commitment to peaceful nuclear power with a pledge never to develop, import, or own nuclear weapons.

Power authority

Japan imported its first commercial nuclear plant in 1966; by 1970, the country completed its first indigenous reactors, and the Ministry of International Trade and Industry (MITI) set a target that nuclear should account for 10 percent of power generation by 1975 and 25 percent by 1985. As with much of Japan's postwar development, MITI's projections came to pass and, by 2011, Japan had 54 nuclear plants operating. Only France relies more on nuclear power as a proportion of its power-generation capacity.

Prior to March 11, the Japanese public's acceptance of nuclear power had been on the rise: a 2009 poll by Japan's Cabinet Office showed nearly 60 percent supported nuclear power, 5 points higher than in 2005. Then came the earthquake and tsunami that hit the northeast province of Tohoku. In a poll released in early April, a majority of Japanese surveyed still backed the use of nuclear power, though support had dropped: 46 percent agreed that the current number of nuclear power stations in Japan should be retained; 10 percent said there should be more; 29 percent said there should be less, and 12 percent wanted to stop using nuclear power altogether.

BY 2011, JAPAN HAD 54 NUCLEAR PLANTS; THESE ACCOUNTED FOR 27 PERCENT OF ITS ELECTRICITY.

Following a cascade of cooling-system failures, and the subsequent explosions and radiation release at the nuclear plants in the coastal prefecture of Fukushima, the country confronted the worst nuclear accident in its history. At the time of this writing (April 2011), a mandatory evacuation zone was in place around the crippled plant, imports of some Japanese food had been banned because of fears of contamination, and the levels of radioactivity in the sea surrounding the plant were more than 1,000 times higher than the official safety limit, prompting fears that radiation could seep into groundwater supplies.

In hindsight, there is much to criticize about the stricken Fukushima Dai-ichi plant at the center of the crisis. The reactors were among the oldest in Japan, and relied on a design long supplanted by safer models. The storage of the spent fuel rods on the roof of the plant, instead of in secure pools at ground level, is a practice that has been discontinued at newer facilities. The role of Tokyo Electric Power (TEPCO), which reportedly ignored warnings about the plant's vulnerability, can legitimately be questioned. Like other nuclear utilities, TEPCO has a reputation for opacity in its disclosures regarding nuclear safety incidents.

The role played by Japan's nuclear regulatory authorities also warrants scrutiny. Even the most competent designers, corporate executives, and regulators would have had a hard time making contingency plans for the serial catastrophes that hit Tohoku. But in retrospect at least, the fact that the Ministry of Economy, Trade and Industry, MITI's successor, is responsible for both the regulation and the promotion of the industry presents difficulties. Moreover, officials often land lucrative jobs in the commercial nuclear industry after leaving government service, perhaps making them less aggressive watchdogs than they might be. At the very least, it seems plausible that newer reactor models, policed by diligent regulators and run by operators with a better record for transparency, would have weathered the crisis better.

Energy choices

Japan will pay whatever it takes to keep the lights on. The Tohoku disaster knocked out more than 12 gigawatts (GW) of nuclear power-generation capacity, responsible for around 8 percent of the country's total electricity production. Another eight GW of coal-fired generation capacity were also lost, due to damage to six coal-fired plants. The majority of this power will be restored in the next several years; Japan will also increase its imports of oil and LNG. A warning to Tokyo residents to reduce their electricity consumption by 25 percent to avoid blackouts in the summer of 2011 shows that energy planners expect the rebuilding process to be a long one.

While the economic effects of Japan's disrupted energy system are serious, the country has the money and the skills to deal with them. It is the environmental implications—specifically, the effect on the country's, and the world's, efforts to cut greenhouse-gas emissions—that will be more difficult to resolve.

Nuclear: Before Fukushima, the IEA had predicted that nuclear's share of the power supply would rise to 42 percent, from 27 percent, by 2035, requiring an increase in installed capacity to 70 GW in 2035 (the equivalent of building two dozen 1,000-megawatt nuclear power plants), from 46 GW in 2010. The country's carbon intensity—emissions per unit of economic output—was forecast to decline to less than half of 2008 levels by 2035 because of the replacement of coal plants with lower-carbon (i.e., nuclear and renewable) power generation. These projections are seriously in question.

The choice Japan makes on whether to restore its nuclear capacity will have wide-ranging implications both domestically and in the wider global energy landscape. If Japan opts not to replace its lost nuclear capacity, that decision will have serious consequences for the country's energy security and carbon-emissions profile. Renewable energy sources constitute a minimal proportion (less than 10 percent, mostly hydropower) of the country's electricity mix. Despite ambitious plans to scale up wind and solar, these sources account for less than 1 percent of the power supply, and their intermittency means they cannot replace the lost base-load of nuclear power generation. The remaining options are natural gas, oil, and coal.

Natural gas: In 2009, Japan generated 26 percent of its electricity from natural gas, almost all of it imported LNG. With a few minor exceptions, natural gas power plants escaped the devastating impacts of the earthquake and tsunami. Construction of natural gas plants is considerably cheaper and easier than those for either coal or nuclear. According to the Massachusetts Institute of Technology, the present value cost of a natural gas plant is about $850 per kilowatt, compared with $2,300/kW for a coal power plant and $4,000/kW for a nuclear power plant. Moreover, gas is much cleaner than coal, emitting only about half as much carbon per unit of economic output. Natural gas is considered a "bridge" technology, taking care of current needs as lower-carbon sources of energy are developed.

In the short term, European consumers of LNG can increase imports of pipeline gas from Russia and Algeria, freeing up extra LNG cargoes for Japan. Russian-, Qatari-, and Indonesian-based suppliers have already pledged to send Japan additional supplies. In the medium term, over the next three to five years, the global LNG market is well positioned to meet Japan's needs: LNG producers have been increasing production capacity substantially since 2007 and several new export facilities

Public support for nuclear power has been dampened in the wake of the serial emergencies at the damaged reactors.
© REUTERS/Reuters TV

are expected to come online in the next three years, including vast expansions and new developments in Australia.

In the longer term, though, a substantial increase in Japan's use of gas could constrict what may be a tightening market. Natural gas consumption is projected to increase substantially in China and India, most (in China's case) or all (in India's) expected in the form of LNG imports. China plans to build at least 13 new LNG import terminals by the end of the decade; India has two under construction and several more planned. Demand is also growing from Malaysia and Indonesia, which used to be LNG exporters, as well as Vietnam, the Philippines, Pakistan, and Bangladesh. A gas-centered recovery policy in Japan could therefore push prices up.

Oil: Japan is the world's third-largest oil consumer, behind the United States and China, consuming 4.4 million barrels per day (bpd) in 2010. Oil accounts for roughly 45 percent of Japan's total primary energy consumption, mostly to fuel cars and trucks. Since the first oil price shock of 1973–74, the proportion of oil in the electricity sector has declined steadily, to less than 10 percent, from 73 percent, because of policies to encourage the substitution of natural gas for oil in industrial processes. In the near term, oil will compensate for some of the loss of nuclear and coal installations. However, given the high cost of crude and refined fuel oil, there is unlikely to be a long-term shift back to oil-fired power.

Coal: Coal is Japan's largest source of electricity generation, accounting for 28 percent of total power production; six plants, accounting for a fifth of coal production, were damaged by the natural disasters. While the nuclear reactors damaged by the tsunami are beyond repair, the six coal plants could be back at work within a year. Coal is a contentious candidate to replace lost capacity in Japan. From the perspective of energy security, its abundance and relatively low economic cost make it an attractive option. However, in the absence of "clean-coal" technology, including carbon capture and storage, any increase in Japan's coal usage will make its emissions and environmental goals more difficult to reach.

Global implications

Japan hosted the 1997 conference in Kyoto that set the first targets to reduce greenhouse-gas emissions, and the country has remained active on the issue. It has pledged emissions reductions of 25 percent below 1990 levels by 2020 (contingent on the participation of other major economies, such as China and the United States). At Kyoto, Japan pledged to reduce emissions by 6.2 percent by 2012, compared with 1990 levels. Before Fukushima, Japan was already unlikely to meet this target; indeed, emissions had actually risen. If the disaster means less nuclear power, which is emissions-free, Japan's ability to meet its longer-term targets will be imperiled and perhaps impossible.

IF THE DISASTER MEANS LESS NUCLEAR POWER, JAPAN'S ABILITY TO MEET ITS CLIMATE-CHANGE TARGETS WILL BE IMPERILED AND PERHAPS IMPOSSIBLE.

Meeting emissions goals is a secondary consideration, though, compared with the need to rebuild the region and restore power to the economy. As the largest economy that is party to the Kyoto Protocol (China and the United States did not implement it), a decision, however justifiable, by Japan to abandon its commitments would seriously weaken the treaty.

What Japan does about nuclear power will largely decide its trajectory on carbon emissions. Before the disaster, Japan's power-sector emissions were forecast to fall 46 percent, or 200 million tons, by 2035. In the absence of nuclear power, any such abatement is unlikely to be achieved. According to the Federation of Electric Power Companies of Japan (FEPC), Japan's total carbon emissions of 1.29 billion tons in 2008–09 would have been 171 million tons higher if nuclear power were replaced by oil-fired generation—and much higher than that if replaced by coal.

The Fukushima accident has also had an immediate effect on the debate over nuclear policy around the world. Germany temporarily closed seven of its oldest plants and suspended a previous decision on life extensions for all of its 17 plants. Countries that are perceived as more favorable to nuclear power have been more measured in response. China suspended approval of new nuclear projects pending a safety review, but it is likely to continue its significant investment. Russia, South Korea, India, and France have all announced various safety revisions of their existing plants, and are also likely to continue with nuclear power as part of their energy mixes. Nevertheless, the much-heralded "nuclear renaissance," already facing financial, regulatory, and logistical challenges in much of the industrialized world, and particularly the United States, appears less likely than it was before Fukushima.

If the renaissance never happens, reducing emissions becomes much more difficult. Analysts at Société Générale estimated that a refusal by Organisation for Economic Co-operation and Development (OECD) countries to build any more nuclear power facilities, and also to allow existing plants to retire as scheduled, would add an additional 860 million tons of carbon emissions per year between 2010 and 2030. That would constitute a 6 percent increase over the projected emissions levels for the OECD during a period when their emissions were supposed to be stabilizing.

If the nuclear accident at Fukushima prompts a shutdown of existing plants or a slowdown in building new ones, other sources will have to fill the power gap; global electricity demand is expected to double between 2008 and 2035. Renewables are not going to save the day. Solar and wind, for example, are expensive and intermittent, while hydropower is increasingly unpopular. Technological advances in electricity storage, such as batteries and fuel cells, may go some way to addressing the challenge of intermittency, but they are not ready to step up. That leaves fossil fuels.

Replacement of 27 percent of zero-carbon Japanese power generation capacity with hydrocarbon-based alternatives will be costly both in economic and environmental terms. Replacement of the 14 percent of zero-carbon power generation capacity that nuclear power provides globally will be much more so.

Poor management and regulation may have contributed to the Fukushima disaster. But the larger point is this: Japan's decision to build a nuclear industry was a calculated risk, taken in the context of a range of undesirable alternatives.

With climate change politics heating up and competition for scarce resources intensifying, energy and environmental planners considering nuclear power have similar calculations to make.

CHAPTER TWO: RETHINKING JAPAN'S PAST— AND FUTURE

© Illustration by Yuta Onoda

JAPAN'S NEXT TRANSFORMATION

IAN BURUMA

NATURAL DISASTERS HAVE A WAY OF CHANGING EVERYTHING, and not just in material terms. People's expectations change. Energies are redirected. Historical time is measured in predisaster and postdisaster periods. So it will be after the Great Eastern Japan Earthquake, and the consequent nuclear crisis. Although Tokyo suffered far less damage than places further north, the city will never be quite the same city as the one I flew into from Chengdu in 2009.

Chengdu, brash, ugly, even crude in many ways, was jumping, while Tokyo felt a little laid-back, even cozy. I imagine one might have felt the same way flying from Chicago to London in the 1920s.

Cities, like countries, given a degree of freedom, are always in a state of flux, of course. London today feels more dynamic than Chicago. Tokyo is anything but stagnant. And one can only hope that some of the changes after the earthquake will not last long: the "self-restraint," in the sense of cancelled cultural events, or living in the dark because of electricity shortages, is clearly temporary. Longer-term effects are harder to gauge, but my sense is that Tokyo will bounce back.

It was not so long ago, during the booming 1980s, that young Japanese hotshots were sipping gold flakes with their tea. Up until the 1990s, the Japanese economy was still described in miraculous terms. Japanese commentators wrote best sellers describing the 21st century as "Japan's century." Tokyo was a buzzing metropolis of fashion, booms, and trends—coming and going not by the year or month, but, it seemed, almost by the hour.

As it turned out, much of this surface hype was wildly overblown. There has been a remarkable change since then, not so much in Japan, which simply slowed

---

Ian Buruma, a professor of human rights at Bard College, has written several acclaimed books about Japan.

down, but in other parts of Asia, and China in particular. In terms of economic size, China (with a GDP of $1.335 trillion) overtook Japan ($1.286 trillion) in 2010 as the world's second-largest economy.

The crowds of Chinese tourists trawling through Tokyo's luxury stores are one reflection of the change. According to official Japanese estimates, 1.5 million Chinese were expected to visit Japan in 2010 and the number is steadily rising. The notable lack of interest, according to recent polls, of young Japanese in traveling overseas might be another.

There is a hunger among young Chinese today, for money, self-advancement, adventure, that appears to be somewhat lacking in the more complacent Japanese, who are possibly hindered by social constraints, vested interests, or a general lack of new opportunities.

All that this means, perhaps, is that Japan, like Western Europe, has become a "normal," affluent, developed society. The kind of frenzy one now sees in China emerges from a sudden release of pent-up energy, which usually follows years of repression, or a great catastrophe. Like the "Japanese economic miracle" of the 1950s and 1960s, the China boom started from a very low base. The Chinese have climbed out of the wreckage of Maoism, just as the Japanese, a few decades earlier, emerged from the chaos and ruins of a calamitous war.

It would be unrealistic to expect the Japanese to repeat their rush of the mid-20th century. Even the necessary reconstruction of Japan after the earthquake won't bring back those helter-skelter days. The economy is too mature for that. It is also a good thing that most Japanese, so far, appear to be adapting with fatalistic equanimity to China's precipitous rise, despite an ugly diplomatic spat in late 2010 over territorial issues in the East China Sea. As evident in the ensuing, heated bilateral exchanges and China's suspension of key minerals exports to Japan, it wouldn't take much for mutual resentments to raise tensions between the old rivals to dangerous levels.

Tradition can be a platform for transformation.
© Jason Dewey/Stone/Getty Images

And yet, there are good reasons to hope that Japan will regain some of its old zest, if only to balance China's rising power and influence. Japan is still the richest, most potent democracy in East Asia. China remains an authoritarian state whose combination of touchiness and ruthlessness could spell future trouble—not just for Japan.

But it is China's success—perhaps more than its potential belligerence—that should make us pay attention. In a world where democracies are being seriously challenged by China's model of political dictatorship and hard-edged capitalism, we need a strong, self-confident, dynamic Japan, if only to make a better case for the advantages of political freedom.

It is easy to exaggerate Japan's present sluggishness, just as people sometimes make too much of the country's isolation during the Edo period (1603–1868). True, Japanese in the 17th and 18th centuries were not allowed to leave their country, but Asian traders and delegations, mostly from China and Korea, continued to come to Japan, and the ruling *shogun* maintained varying degrees of contact with the outside world.

Still, rather like Britain, that other island nation on the periphery of a great continent, Japan has often cultivated its remoteness, its own ways of doing things, its exclusive attitudes. Isolation tends to breed conservatism and social rigidity. Without serious challenges, domestic or external, class privileges and other forms of hierarchy solidify and block enterprise and change. It is surely not a good sign that the most recent series of Japanese prime ministers came from long political dynasties.

Japan has experienced periods of relative stagnation before and managed to renew itself with extraordinary bursts of energy, notably in the mid-19th century and after 1945. In both cases, the impetus came from abroad—and in a violent manner. The question, more acute now than ever, is whether Japan can reinvent itself again, preferably this time without the shock of outside intervention. For answers, a look at the past is always instructive.

When the Americans arrived in Japan in the 1850s, on heavily armed ships led by Commodore Matthew Perry, Japan was not exactly a poor backwater. Edo and Osaka were among the biggest cities in the world, and Japanese finance and commerce were highly developed. But political institutions, ruled by the Tokugawa *shogun* in Edo, as Tokyo was then known, had become antiquated and displayed a paralyzing ineptitude when challenged by Western might. Most politically minded Japanese knew something drastic needed to happen, but there was much disagreement about exactly what. Some wanted the samurai government to expel the "barbarians" forcibly and preserve Japan's relative isolation. Others wanted to topple the Tokugawa state and remake Japan along Western lines, that is, with a modern army, modern political institutions, and a modern empire.

The latter group consisted mostly of samurai from provincial clans who were not favored by Tokugawa patronage. One advantage of radical change (and there are many disadvantages, too) is that it breaks up hierarchies and gives hungrier, more energetic people a chance to make their mark. The toppling of the Tokugawa state and the ensuing reforms of the Meiji Restoration did just that. A new elite of businessmen, politicians, army officers, and administrators emerged from the provinces and transformed old Edo into modern Tokyo.

The "Westernizers" of Japanese society were in fact no less patriotic than the nativists who opposed changes modeled on the West. For many of these so-called liberals, learning from the West—indeed, becoming as much like a Western power as was possible—was actually a way to resist the West or at least to stop the country from being colonized. It is a strategy sometimes described as protection through mimicry. That was the purpose of "joining the West, and leaving Asia," a slogan promoted by Japanese liberals of the Meiji period. Winning a war against China, still ruled by the Qing Dynasty, in 1895, was seen as a victory for Western modernization.

The Westernization of Japan in the late-19th century was so rapid and, in elite circles, so radical that the great Meiji novelist Natsume Soseki warned his countrymen in 1914 that it would lead to a collective nervous breakdown. The ultranationalism of the 1930s and early 1940s was a symptom of this breakdown. But mimicry never really made Japan a Western, or even a cosmopolitan, nation. Even as the Japanese zealously imported foreign culture and turned it to their own ends, they preferred to keep actual foreigners at arm's length. In this respect, not so much had changed since the 17th century, when Japanese scholars were eager to learn as much as they could from Dutch books, while Dutch merchants were confined to a tiny island in the bay of Nagasaki.

Modern Tokyo, during the Meiji, Taisho, and even Showa periods, was indisputably a metropolitan city but not a truly cosmopolitan one, in the sense of welcoming people from all over the world into its fold. Foreign culture became a new form of Japanese culture. Often disdained by the West, and alienated from its Asian roots, Japan remained a fairly isolated country. The government's aim during World War II of bringing "all the world under one roof"—one imperial Japanese roof, that is—could be seen as a disastrous attempt to break out of this largely self-imposed isolation.

JAPAN HAS EXPERIENCED RELATIVE STAGNATION BEFORE AND RENEWED ITSELF WITH EXTRAORDINARY ENERGY.

Wartime defeat in 1945 did at last bring many foreigners to Japanese shores, though not in the way most Japanese might have wished. And the destruction of urban Japan, which once again broke up old hierarchies, did away with entrenched privileges and unleashed the energies of outsiders who had not been part of the cozy old system. The emergence of Sony, to mention one spectacular example, was made possible by an atmosphere of openness to fresh enterprise that no longer seems to exist today. The most effective politician of postwar Japan, Kakuei Tanaka, was a typical product of wartime chaos: a rural parvenu who bought his way into the postwar political establishment.

The enforced presence of a foreign occupation army, however, can hardly be described as a sign of cosmopolitanism. But it was certainly clear that Japanese were open to new ideas. The influence of American culture after the war was profound, in terms of popular entertainment, education, and even industry. The much-vaunted quality control system, often regarded as a typically Japanese innovation, was actually introduced in the late 1940s by an American academic named W. Edwards Deming. Well into the 1970s, even a humble English teacher from a plausible Western country would still be consulted by a surprising number of Japanese as a foreign expert on almost everything.

As was true of the Meiji years, however, the postwar remake of Japan along Western lines took place on Japanese terms, especially after the allied military occupation ended, in 1952. American-style *demokurashii*, accepted so eagerly in the immediate postwar years, quickly reverted to a very Japanese system of patronage and factional hierarchies, often based on historical family ties to particular regions.

To be sure, the system of education was sufficiently shaken up after the war to open up chances to new generations of ambitious young people. But as time went on, new and sometimes old elites, nurtured in the same high schools and universities, once again made access to top positions in politics and business harder for outsiders to penetrate. The illusion was carefully fostered that almost all Japanese were now middle class, even as the gap between the wealthy and the not-so-well-off grew apace, especially after the bursting of the 1980s "bubble economy."

Young Japanese, growing up in relative comfort in an increasingly rigid society, also became more reluctant to take risks, and even if they were keen, those risks were less likely to pay off than risks were several decades ago. This lack of risk taking, more than anything, explains why Chengdu now feels different from Tokyo, despite the greater size, wealth, and cultural sophistication of the Japanese capital.

Another wave of transformation is needed to reinvigorate Japan, to make it a genuinely cosmopolitan nation. And this time, the transformation must be a fundamental one. If Tokyo could change from a great metropolis into the cosmopolitan center of Asia by welcoming gifted, enterprising foreigners to try their luck—by opening its culture, in other words, not just to foreign influences but to foreign people, too—the city would benefit those foreigners, but even more, Japan itself.

Japan needs foreign workers not only to fill jobs that the Japanese in a rapidly aging and highly educated society are no longer willing or able to do, but the influx of fresh talent would have a big impact at higher levels, too. Academic institutions would become less hidebound and more open to new ideas, and business would be stimulated by new competition. In short, Japan would finally break out of its relative isolation.

There are many cultural and historical reasons to think of this as an unlikely proposition. Many vested interests and traditions work against opening up Japanese society to the world. And it is possible that many Japanese would much prefer to carry on comfortably in relative isolation—impervious to developments "outside." Yet, certain obvious changes that have already taken place over the last 20 years or so suggest this scenario might not be so far-fetched after all. The fact that foreigners dominate the top ranks of sumo wrestling is partly a sign that young Japanese have lost their taste for the rigors of fighting their way to the top.

But getting used to the sight of Mongolian or European champions in one of Japan's most traditional sports must surely open minds as well. The presence of foreign, mostly Chinese and Southeast Asian, staff in Japanese bars, restaurants, and other places of entertainment—such a novelty two decades ago—is now so commonplace in Japan's large cities that people barely notice it. On a higher level, who would have predicted 30 or 40 years ago that a major Japanese car manufacturer would be managed by a European chief executive—as is the case with Nissan's Carlos Ghosn? And if it can be said that anything good came from the earthquake-related disasters, one encouraging development was the help extended to Japanese victims by foreigners, including Chinese and Koreans. Not only that, but the help was gratefully received, without the bureaucratic chauvinism and prickly sense of pride that kept Japan closed to outside help in 1995, when Kobe was devastated by a quake.

The best model for Tokyo, and by extension Japan, would be London, once the imperial capital of an insular nation and now the informal capital of Europe. The rapid internationalization of London was not the result of the British suddenly deciding to open up their culture or society to foreigners. What did it was the freedom for people from other countries to follow their own interests: young French bankers, Japanese designers, Russian businessmen, German artists, and so on. It is easier to start a business, or sell art, or launch a range of enterprises in London than it is in other, more bureaucratic, more tightly regulated cities elsewhere.

The world is now facing unprecedented economic challenges. And the reaction in most countries, including Britain and even the United States, is to raise the barriers against immigrants. The instinct of Japanese bureaucrats is to do the same. But if somehow Japan could go in the opposite direction, expand its social and economic freedoms, open up more to the outside world, and encourage enterprising foreigners to compete within its borders, the transformation of an insular nation into a cosmopolitan one might just enable Japan to astonish the world once more.

The chances of this happening may not look great. But if Japanese history has shown anything, it is the capacity of Japanese, over and over again, to surprise us all—including the Japanese themselves.

A reflection on Japan's past and present.
© Andrew Pothecary

TOWARD A LASTING RECOVERY

YASUCHIKA HASEGAWA

JAPAN, AS EVERY JAPANESE SCHOOL CHILD LEARNS, is a small, crowded nation, perched atop shifting geological plates and surrounded by often violent seas. For thousands of years, people living on this volatile archipelago have coped with extraordinary natural calamities. When battered by the elements, we endure. We grieve, we join together, we rebuild—and we come back stronger than before. Indeed, our capacity to survive and even thrive in the aftermath of shocks like those we suffered this past March is part of what defines us as a nation and as a society. And so, even as I mourn the victims of the Tohoku tragedies—the tens of thousands of lives lost, the hundreds of thousands forced from their homes—I also know Japan will recover from these terrible shocks as we have recovered from shocks before.

At the same time, though, I am troubled. Despite our long record of withstanding sudden external shocks, we are less successful in combating gradual, long-term challenges, especially when the origins of those problems are homegrown. Before the earthquake struck us, our nation struggled with many such long-term challenges. As we recover from the disaster in Tohoku, we must not neglect those long-term problems. The scale of our nation's challenge is therefore huge, and the urgency for change is phenomenal. Business leaders, politicians, government officials, and citizens—all of us have to mobilize to produce the changes we need.

In the days before March 11, I felt our nation was in deadlock. If one group proposed changes, then the other parties were likely to oppose it. While the Tohoku disaster has certainly brought us closer together, we must maintain that sense of unity and purpose not only in recovering from the earthquake and the tsunami, but also in comprehensively addressing all our longer-term problems as well.

Yasuchika Hasegawa is president and CEO of Takeda Pharmaceutical Company.

The sputtering growth engine

Many of the long-term challenges that confront us are economic. The competitive position Japan has maintained over the last couple of decades is being threatened, particularly by the rising economic clout of South Korea and China. Let's look at the three elements that contribute to economic growth: the labor force, investment, and innovation.

The workforce has long stopped being a source of growth for Japan. The population is declining, and unless we begin to import foreign workers, that decline will undoubtedly continue. In terms of investment, the second element, Japan's record is poor; less than 4 percent of total investment comes from outside Japan—the lowest figure, by far, among the 20 countries in the Organisation for Economic Co-operation and Development (OECD).

The third element, innovation, should be the strongest driver of Japanese growth. But Japan has lost the innovativeness it had in the 1970s and 1980s. We continue to excel at developing and manufacturing the parts that go into machines and devices, but we miss the larger opportunities that developing new product concepts would bring. In other words, we are too focused on partial optimization and therefore miss out on radical innovation.

Consider the iPod and the iPhone. Japanese companies were already familiar with more than two-thirds of the parts used in these products, but we did not create the final product concept. Apple did this, and it was Apple that benefited most from the value created. Unless parts manufacturers have uniquely distinctive components, as Intel does, these companies are not going to do as well as those that conceive and market truly innovative products.

Mobilizing for change

Among the Japanese, tolerance for change is much lower than it is in many other populations; until this country hits bottom, our people will never get serious about change. Japanese leaders have to get their act together and show the way.

What the government should do: Japan needs to face the reality that we cannot maintain the current social welfare system with the current budgetary structure. We need to strengthen revenue stability by shifting from direct to indirect taxation. We need to consider the fact that the personal income tax and corporate income tax are too high while the consumption (or value-added) tax is too low, at 5 percent, compared with 15 to 25 percent in Europe. We should raise the consumption tax, allocate the additional revenue to social welfare, and start to reduce the public deficit.

The government should also take a stronger position in the domestic wars of attrition. For example, the top seven or eight electronic appliance manufacturers in Japan are so busy fighting each other in the stagnant domestic market that they don't have the energy to compete in the emerging markets where the real growth opportunities are. These days, the officials at the Ministry of Economy, Trade, and Industry (METI) tend to stay away from industry restructuring or reorganization. These officials must do more to avoid collective decline. If METI urged a few of these manufacturers to merge for the sake of global competitiveness, I think they would listen.

Even though Japan is a capitalist economy, direct input from influential stakeholders would be beneficial. The level of economic freedom in Japan is different from that in, say, the United States. Japan has a unique, half-socialist capitalism, so we need a more interventionist approach to sustain our industrial competitiveness. We also need to identify and mobilize around new industries that could create renewed economic growth. Many people say that environmental technologies and products could fit the bill. But today, there is no plan aggressive and coordinated enough to lift the economy.

Another government priority should be to respond to our aging and shrinking population. The population started to decline in 2008; right now Japan has 127 million people. If we could stop the decline at 110 million, then start moving up again, that would be a benefit to economic growth.

We should learn from well-designed immigration policies in countries such as Canada or Australia. For example, if you open the Canadian government home page and click on "immigration," you can immediately find the information you need and how you should proceed, in order to get permanent residence, etc. But in Japan, government officials do not want to talk about immigration. Why? Because they want to preserve the country's unique society, which they see as so homogeneous that it could not accept immigrants. At the same time, and quite inconsistently, these officials opened the floodgates to second-, third-, or fourth-generation ethnic Japanese from Brazil.

Education is another critical priority. For instance, we need to start English-language education in the first grade, as China has done in Beijing, Shanghai, and Tianjin, and in the third grade in many other cities. South Korea is also making English-language education a priority. I was stunned to learn that Samsung is implementing a hiring policy under which people need to speak English well to be considered for senior management positions. No matter how good your technical expertise and general knowledge may be, you cannot communicate and turn those assets into business opportunities without a good command of the language. Poor English skills have significantly handicapped the Japanese people and Japanese companies.

Strong leadership to guide cross-ministry initiatives is also required. For example, consider economic partnerships and free-trade agreements (EPA-FTAs). South Korea relies more heavily on agriculture than Japan does and has a farm lobby as powerful as ours. But former President Roh Moo-Hyun managed to sign EPAs with the United States and the EU. Japan has not made any progress with either region, and that puts us at a disadvantage. Our automobile manufacturers, when they export to the EU, must pay 10 percent customs. The South Korean manufacturers don't.

Although now a more challenging topic following the Fukushima incident, another example of a leadership vacuum is in the nuclear power industry. Japan gets almost 30 percent of its energy from nuclear power; we should be a leader in exporting it. But we recently lost one bid in Abu Dhabi (to South Korea) and another in Vietnam (to Russia). We did not make the kind of concerted effort needed—technical expertise from the electronics and power plant arenas, long-term financing from the banking sector, and lobbying by the government—to put a deal together.

What the private sector should do: We need bolder action and stronger leadership. For example, until Nomura acquired the former Lehman Brothers' operations in Asia and Europe, none of the Japanese megabanks had succeeded in global investment banking. This gap in our banking system is a problem because many Japanese companies have a strong desire to expand overseas, and financing and managing these deals could be a big opportunity for our financial industry. When my company, Takeda, acquired Millennium, a US company, for $9 billion two years ago, we could not use a Japanese investment banker. None had the expertise we needed.

In addition, Japanese firms lack a certain kind of assertiveness: no one wants to lead, and then no one wants to follow the leader. In my own field, for example—the pharmaceutical industry—the "drug lag" was a big deal. Many products that had been approved in the United States or Europe had not been approved in Japan. Organizations for patients and the medical community were pushing both the Ministry of Health, Labour and Welfare and the industry to get these products approved. None of the individual pharmaceutical companies, including Takeda, would raise a hand to develop unapproved products. We believed the government might make the process challenging and we could end up losing money and manpower.

In late 2008, I raised this issue to the industry association. I convinced the association to establish a nonprofit organization that would help companies get these drugs approved. The nonprofit was established in May 2009. Around the same time, the industry formed a committee to select which unapproved products should be developed first. It worked beautifully. In the United States, venture capitalists and biotech companies would have been willing to take the risk. But in Japan, people look over their shoulders to see what their peers are doing. No one takes the initiative.

How Japanese society needs to evolve. Japan must embrace the idea that, while opportunity may be equally accessible to everybody (or almost everybody), the outcomes that individuals achieve cannot and will not be the same. We cannot develop the entire nation by insisting that everyone is the same; we cannot treat people equally and disregard their individual effort and capabilities. We have to abandon this idea of rewarding everyone equally, or we will all go down the tubes.

We should also force ourselves to be much more open to the world. I have a sense that the country has become more inwardly focused; it pays insufficient attention to external issues. A case in point is that there are only about 100 Japanese students at Harvard this year, many fewer than only a decade ago. At the same time, the number of Chinese and Koreans at that university has leaped, to 463 and 314, respectively.

On the whole, there are only 29,000 Japanese studying in US colleges, compared with 75,000 South Koreans and 98,000 Chinese. To respond, we should start teaching graduate school students in English so that we can invite more foreign students. We should help to establish an East Asian Institute of Technology in Tokyo, Shanghai, and Singapore, where Japanese students and foreign students can learn together. Monte Cassim, who was born in Sri Lanka, is a former president of the Ritsumeikan Asia Pacific University in Beppu, where all the graduate programs are taught in English and where there is a 50–50 split between Japanese and foreign students. As a result, he said, the Japanese students are more serious and study much harder than they had previously, because of the influence and the stimulation they receive from the foreign students, who are "hungrier."

Re-inventing Japan: The need for leadership

We have done the analysis. We know the problems. We know what we need to do. The problem is the lack of leadership for effective implementation and execution. We need many more strong leaders to shake things up and wake people up. We need to move away rapidly from the ostrich attitude. We need to force ourselves to take more calculated risks, get better at risk assessment, and in the process shake off the paralysis caused by our usual risk aversion. My ambition for Japan is that it will maintain its high quality of life and improve its relative economic position. In terms of per capita GDP, we should be in the Top Ten. Right now, we are around No. 17, which is not good enough. I want Japan to be known as a place with a strong work ethic, cutting-edge technologies, and high standards of quality. I also want the country to be seen as a global peacekeeper.

Are these reasonable goals? Yes, but speed is key. Japan has ten years at most, and maybe as few as five, to make the drastic changes necessary. If we do not accelerate the initiatives that I have discussed here, we will fall further behind, and then it will simply be too late.

HOW TO DRIVE CHANGE

CARLOS GHOSN

JAPAN'S RESILIENCE IN THE AFTERMATH of the Tohoku earthquake has reminded the world of this nation's extraordinary capacity to face adversity and pull together. The terrifying tsunami that swept Japan's northeastern coastline engulfed towns and renewed global concerns about nuclear safety. But not even a wall of water could extinguish the courage of the Japanese people. So much was lost. And yet, as I watch Japan come to grips with this enormous tragedy, I am filled with admiration, respect, and hope. The social and cultural values demonstrated by Japan's people with such dignity, calm, and resolve amid the catastrophe reaffirm my faith in the country's ability to rally in the face of almost any challenge. My regard for those values underlies my faith that the Japanese people can not only recover from the damage inflicted by the earthquake, but also address their nation's long-term challenges.

Among the most important of these challenges is the aging and shrinking of Japan's population. This trend does not bode well for either internal demand or government finances—and the latter will have to be affected by the need to rebuild northern Honshu. But there are also reasons for hope. Japan can be extremely competitive internationally because of its cultural and social values. Japanese companies can embed these values in their global operations—in China or Thailand or wherever—and continue to grow strongly. Three particular values come to mind.

First, there is the quality of service. No other country has the same kind of reliable and predictable consumer relations, underpinned by modesty and humbleness. Second, the Japanese value simplicity. People who work in complexity often create confusion. In Japan there's not so much confusion; the Japanese know ex-

---

Carlos Ghosn is chairman and CEO, Renault-Nissan Alliance.

actly what they are doing. Finally, the Japanese excel in process; they are the masters of continuous improvement. No one executes like the Japanese; they embody focus, discipline, relentless effort, and quality combined with a respect for hierarchy. In my view, these values are relevant wherever Japanese companies want to do business. And Japan is well positioned to use these values to adapt to new realities.

The second mover advantage

If you look at emerging markets, for example, Japan doesn't always move fast, but it always catches up. Take the Chinese auto industry. At first, the Germans dominated the market, with a 70 percent share at one point. Then the Americans came. The Japanese arrived last, but little by little, they've been growing. In the Russian, Indian, and Brazilian markets, Japan wasn't the first to jump in, but once they got in, the execution was second to none. The Japanese don't give up, and they end up making a breakthrough.

The same is true for innovation. When Japanese companies innovate, it is often because there is a strong leader—a visionary founder like Akio

Ghosn's three keys for driving change: simplify, explain, connect.
© Sankei/Getty Images

Morita at Sony, for example—at the helm. The strong leader says, "We're going to do this." Everybody follows and these companies break a lot of walls and make it happen. In many other cases, however, Japanese companies move in after someone else has innovated and then surpass the original innovation. Japan has more a sense of *kaizen* than of breakthrough. They are the inventors and masters of continuous improvement.

Many people believe Japan is resistant to change, that transforming Japanese companies is impossible. That's not true. You can make any change you want in Japan, with a few conditions: you need to simplify the change, explain it, and connect the change with people. If you can do those things, you can do anything in Japan. In my experience, change is much easier here than in any other country. Japanese people take time to understand change and the reasons for it. And when they get it, they move—fast.

Consider the turnaround of Nissan, a truly remarkable accomplishment. When I became COO in 1999, Nissan was one of the most brutal, passive, reactionary companies you could imagine, with a difficult union environment. In a couple of years, the situation completely changed. The fact that the company was running out of cash when I came made all the difference in the actions I was able to pursue.

The sense of crisis helped us to do what needed to be done. This turnaround wasn't something that I did; it was a team effort by everyone at Nissan. The difference, though, was that I went to a lot of trouble to explain our situation, and why we needed to change. The employees listened and they got it. They said, "Fine, now we understand why we need to do that and why that is going to benefit us." My experience in Japan has been that if you approach change in this way, you can do anything you want.

I know Japanese companies can change, but success- **PEOPLE WHO** ful globalization, particularly in emerging markets, will **SAY THEY HAVE** put them to the test. They face difficult, sometimes painful **NO HOPE FOR** conditions. For one, there's the continuing strength of the **JAPAN DON'T** yen. In the past, Japan emphasized production at home, ex- **UNDERSTAND IT.** porting, and then building overseas capacity. With the yen **THOSE WHO KNOW** at 80 or 85 to the dollar, companies find it a struggle to **JAPAN WELL ARE** remain profitable, so resistance to building more overseas **MORE OPTIMISTIC.** factories is cracking. Motivating these decisions is not only the weak dollar, but also a weak renminbi and a weak won, which are big factors in why Japanese industries are losing market share to the Koreans in export markets such as the Middle East and South America. As a result, in the longer term, Japan will become less of a production base and more of a laboratory where the country focuses on knowledge-development efforts, such as conceiving new models, building platforms, and training people.

In addition, Japanese companies will find it increasingly difficult to compete globally without understanding and embracing diversity. In the past, the current talent pool worked because companies were present only in Europe and the United States, and had a strong base in Japan. Today, they also have to be in China, Russia, Brazil, and the Middle East, to name a few places. So all of a sudden, Japanese companies need to work with people who have very different cultures and beliefs and still find the common ground to make these workers feel motivated and part of the process. Japanese companies have a long way to go in this regard. At Nissan, 30 percent of the corporate officers are foreigners, chiefly British, French, and American. We are happy to show that diversity can work in Japan. Just because a company has more foreigners at the top doesn't mean it has lost its identity as a Japanese company.

At the most basic level, diversity in Japan means having more women in the workforce. The country needs more active people and the most obvious resource is women. I don't think Japan has a choice here. Women will have to play a much bigger role and take much more responsibility in business and society than they currently do.

There's also a broader talent issue. Companies in industries emphasizing engineering, manufacturing, and logistics have always been strong. But Japanese industries are clearly less efficient in communications and marketing, and in valuing such skills that are often necessary to be internationally competitive. When I look at Nissan's succession planning, for example, I have a lot of people suitable for jobs in manufacturing, but I have more difficulty finding the talent in such support functions as marketing and finance. The result is that when you look at sectors requiring more of this kind of talent, you tend to see average performance and un-competitive, bureaucratic, less-agile companies.

How can Japan raise the performance of these less-efficient functions? One idea is to facilitate more cross-functional collaboration and sharing of best practices. At Nissan, for example, we took industrial engineers, put them into the sales process, and told them, "Show us how we can do this better to serve the consumer." That was a very powerful exercise.

Here's another area in which Japan's corporate sector could benefit from adopt-ing international best practices: knowing the finances of the company. Many Japa-nese companies do not have a chief financial officer. There is often an accountant and a person with banking relationships, but no controllers. I remember very well that when I came to Nissan in 1999, there was no CFO. I couldn't understand the numbers. I don't think management understood where the company was making money and where it was losing money. It sometimes took us a week to determine the number of employees we had. One of the reasons some Japanese companies are struggling is they don't know if they are profitable; in fact, they don't even look for profitability. To this day, some of the companies with which we do business don't know which products they make are profitable. If you go to US corporations, you have numbers everywhere. In a certain way, these corporations are too focused on the short term because they know the numbers. Some Japanese companies don't know their numbers, so they operate more on trends. It's best to be somewhere in between.

For example, when Nissan decided to launch an electric car, everybody came to me with their models and numbers and said the project would be a financial disas-ter. But really, how do you guess the profitability of a breakthrough idea? I decided that we should collect the numbers after the project is under way, when there is market feedback. On existing businesses, however, we would continuously crunch the numbers by segment, market, and grade to make sure we know where we are.

Putting Japan on track

People who say they do not have much hope for Japan don't really understand Ja-pan. Those who know Japan well are more optimistic. As in most places, Japan operates on a spectrum from transformation to passivity, from remarkable achieve-ments to disasters.

The country clings to the status quo not because people don't want to change, but because sometimes their leaders don't have a clear sense of direction. How can people follow leaders who are lost? If there is one recommendation I would make to Japan's corporate leaders, it is to take the time to form a vision, simplify it, explain it, and make it meaningful to people. If you can do those things in Japan, the people will make change happen.

BEYOND NUTS AND BOLTS

MASAYOSHI SON

THINK OF THE NAMES associated with some of Japan's great 20th-century companies: Konosuke Matsushita, Soichiro Honda and Akio Morita. These men helped to create Japan's modern electronics and auto industries. They were men of energy, imagination and vision.

But in many cases in Japan, when founders left, the companies they built became less creative. The founders' successors didn't want to take risks or change their business models. Meanwhile, the Koreans, Chinese, Taiwanese, and Indians started to catch up with Japanese companies technologically—and competitors in those economies have big advantages in terms of their currencies and their labor costs. The result: Japan has lost its leading position in many sectors.

I believe that information technology (IT) and the pharmaceutical industry hold the keys to Japan's future. No labor-intensive industry can revive Japan; farming and fishing, for all the attention they get, are dying industries. For Japan, knowledge-intensive industries are the only way forward. And yet our government policies are not focused on such industries.

Consider the government's recent move to raise taxes on stock options, which effectively killed the use of stock options as compensation in Japan. Without stock options, it's hard to reward people for taking risks. People who don't want to take risks just stay in a company where they are comfortable.

I think Japan could change fairly quickly; one successful example could alter people's perspective and increase their confidence. Look at what happened with Apple in the US. In the early 1990s, Apple was in terrible shape, but then Steve Jobs came back, and it totally revived. Apple is now one of the most respected companies

Masayoshi Son is the founder, chairman and CEO of SoftBank.

in the world, and an inspiration to every young techie tinkering in a garage. It's important to remember, too, that Apple is no longer a manufacturing company. It designs the hardware and software, creates the business model and does very smart marketing. But the actual production gets sub-contracted to Foxconn, a Taiwanese company, and its products are mostly assembled in China.

That is the kind of model Japan should be trying to emulate. Instead, I often hear Japanese leaders or government people talk about *monozukuri*—making things. The image they seem to have in mind is of a big factory with an assembly line, workers putting stuff together with nuts and bolts. This makes no sense; nuts and bolts are Japan's past, not its future.

To follow Apple's example, Japan needs to have Apple's skills—IT, design and marketing. And it needs certain social attributes, such as passion and the desire to take risks. The government cannot, of course, create these things, but it can encourage them with smart policies, such as stock options, an active IPO market and a healthy venture-capital industry. All of these are in a relatively immature form at the moment.

The media also has an important role to play. Look at what happened to Livedoor, a very successful Internet service provider that made a number of acquisitions in Japan and the US But then the company was charged with securities fraud and delisted from the Tokyo Stock Exchange in 2006. The Livedoor story was a sensation for months, and the press was very hostile. The founder of Livedoor, Takafumi Horie, who is still fighting with prosecutors, believes he was unfairly singled out.

The Livedoor example dampened the fighting spirit of Japan's younger generation. When Livedoor's business was booming, many other Internet companies had successful IPOs. Young people with talent were inspired to work for Internet companies. Then the media went hysterical, and the politicians, too, jumped on the bandwagon. IT executives got bashed just for being young and rich. That is totally wrong.

People who work in the media are not risk takers. But they do love to go on the attack. When a big, established enterprise like Sony or Toyota makes a move, they always defend it. But when a young entrepreneur tries to do something, they look for the negative. In the US, young successful rich guys become heroes. That gives confidence and hope to the next generation. That is not the case in Japan.

My own company, SoftBank, is in a relatively good position now. We too have endured our share of bashing. But now we are now the third-most profitable company in Japan. There are other companies that are relatively young and successful—Uniqlo, Nitori, Nihon Densan. We need many more examples like these to show that Japan can create new companies able to adapt and succeed.

It's not too late for Japan to recover the fire so characteristic of great business leaders like Matsushita, Honda and Morita. If it waits another 10 years, though, to implement a clear, long-term vision of innovation and entrepreneurship, it will be.

Many people in Japan know of my admiration for Ryoma Sakamoto, the 19th century samurai who helped prompt the modernization of the country's government and economy. I try to emulate Ryoma in managing SoftBank. I want to contribute to changing Japanese society for the better. I think that's a worthy goal for all Japanese business people, whether they work for a large established company or a start-up.

DARE TO ERR

TADASHI YANAI

JAPAN'S BIGGEST PROBLEMS are conservatism and cowardice. We want stability, peace of mind and safety. But the world keeps changing. Other countries are growing, while we in Japan stick to our old ways.

One problem is that we look down on developing countries. We should be willing to learn from companies in these countries if they are better than us. But we lack the willingness to learn because we have been so successful before. That holds true for managers and employees alike.

Another problem is that Japanese business people and companies are lacking in individuality. Too many people think that everyone must be the same. That's a basic fault.

Finally, Japanese companies seem to have their eyes in the rearview mirror. They have become introspective. I think we should get back to something more like we were at the end of the war when Japan rose to prominence from a situation in which it had nothing. (It was during this period that Fast Retailing got started, in 1949.)

We've lost that spirit, maybe because we are under the illusion that we are rich and superior. But many countries are just as rich, and in Japan, income has stagnated for many people for a decade or more. Japan is still very comfortable to live in, if you are Japanese. But there's a difference between being comfortable and being viable. We are gradually losing our viability.

In short, Japan has been utterly defeated as an economy. We're losing the economic game. So why are we being so foolish? Or, more precisely, why aren't we learning from our mistakes?

Tadashi Yanai is chairman, president and CEO of Fast Retailing.

Learning from mistakes is something that Uniqlo has had to do—several times, unfortunately.

We opened our first store outside Japan in 2001, in London. And we failed spectacularly. We quickly opened 21 outlets in Britain—and shut down 16 of them by 2003. In retrospect, that was probably good, because we learned so much. Our big mistake was to try to do things the British way. We never capitalized on our strengths.

For example, we let Uniqlo's UK president create a compartmentalized management team, with area managers, store managers, assistant store managers, and then the sales staff. Store managers only spoke with other store managers. We don't have that kind of class system in Japan. Our organizations are flat.

China, the second overseas market we entered, was a failure at first, too. We faltered in China because we went too far in adapting to China. Per capita income is low—about 5 percent of Japan's—so we figured we should sell at much lower prices. That was a mistake. Uniqlo has a Japanese identity; no one wanted a Chinese Uniqlo.

Vegetables were a disaster too. We saw food distribution as a backward sector, so we went into partnership with a food group, Ryokuken, in 2002. But vegetables are not an industrial product; you don't know exactly when they will be ready or in what

Wooing the Middle Kingdom's middle class: Uniqlo's flagship store in Beijing.
© China Photos/Getty Images

volume. We eventually understood that it would be impossible to succeed unless we ran our own farms, and we did not want to be farmers. After two years, we shut operations down.

The important thing is not so much that we failed in these instances, but that we learned and eventually succeeded. In Britain, we now have more than a dozen stores, including a flagship on London's Oxford Street, and are doing well. China is our fastest-growing market, with almost 100 stores. By 2020, we hope to have more stores in China than in Japan (1,000 plus). Uniqlo's international operations are growing fast. We now have stores in 10 countries, with Thailand, Brazil and India in our sights. By 2015, most of our Japanese employees could be outside Japan.

MY ADVICE TO YOUNG PEOPLE IS SIMPLE: GET OUT OF JAPAN.

Failures are always unpleasant; from the right perspective, though, they can be useful. Our travails in Britain and China fostered resilience and led us to understand three important things. First, to create the best possible Uniqlo in other countries, we had to use the best aspects of our own organization. Second, while globalization is difficult, it is also essential. And third, to succeed outside Japan requires understanding other markets on their own terms.

In short, Uniqlo has to be both Japanese and global. The analogy to Japan as a whole is obvious.

One thing Japan has to get rid of is the idea that things are one way here and different everywhere else. The Japanese are really strong at home, and incredibly weak away from home. We need Japanese who are strong away, or who don't distinguish between home and away. We're trying to build this idea into Uniqlo's culture. For example, English is spoken at business meetings with foreigners, and we want all emails to be in English in a few years.

Most ordinary Japanese industries are bound up by government regulation, or by agreements (tacit or explicit) within the industry. The idea is to create a union or association or something and then use it to start imposing regulation and preventing competition. I hate that sort of approach. We do our best to avoid the government-industrial structures so typical of much of the Japanese economy. These are meant to be safety nets; in fact, they are shackles on global competitiveness.

My advice for young Japanese is simple: get out of Japan. One of our weaknesses as Japanese is our ineptness at communicating with other cultures. Even people who speak English well are closed off psychologically. They don't speak frankly like I do. There's this uniquely Japanese standoffishness, this hesitancy to become too involved. And it's detrimental to globalization.

All this sounds pessimistic, but I don't see this as the counsel of despair. Japan has everything—people, goods, money, technology, information. As a nation, we are honest, hard-working and serious. So why are we so weak? Why don't we use these strengths to take on the world?

If we give it everything we've got and start to move in the right direction, I'm confident that we will succeed. Even if we experience failure, we can pick ourselves up and try again. That's what Uniqlo did—and that is what Japan can do.

THE MYTH OF CHANGE-RESISTANT JAPAN

JOHN W. DOWER

ALL COUNTRIES, PEOPLES, cultures are unique, but in mainstream Western commentary no country surpasses the Japanese in being regarded as uniquely unique.

This was true in the late 19th and early 20th centuries when Japan startled the world by moving swiftly from feudal isolation to one of the "big five" powers at the Paris Peace Conference following World War I. Among the other four countries (England, France, Italy, and the United States) at the conference, Japan was the conspicuous odd fellow. During the 1930s and early 1940s, Western commentators routinely diagnosed the nation's descent into militarism and war as singular historical and psychological or sociological pathologies. The highs and lows of Japan's post-1945 experience also prompted a steady stream of *sui generis* cultural explanations. In the realm of East-is-East-and-West-is-West myth making, "the Japanese mind" holds a special, and especially tenacious, place.

Through war and peace, a few core stereotypes have dominated this myth making. The favorite characterization of the Japanese among putative Asia experts during the Asia-Pacific War, for example, was "the obedient herd." In the United States, much of the burden of explaining Japan at war fell to the urbane diplomat Joseph Grew, who was ambassador to Tokyo from 1932 until Pearl Harbor. The key, Grew explained time and again, was cognitive deficiency deriving in good part from historical backwardness. In a dispatch cabled to Washington in September 1941 (and made public during the war), he framed his view in the third person as follows:

> The Ambassador stresses the importance of understanding [that] Japanese psychology [is] fundamentally unlike that of any Western nation. Japanese reactions

---

John W. Dower is professor emeritus of history at the Massachusetts Institute of Technology, and winner of the Pulitzer Prize for general non-fiction.

to any particular set of circumstances cannot be measured, nor can Japanese actions be predicted by any Western measuring rod. This fact is hardly surprising in the case of a country so recently feudalistic.

In the six-plus decades since the war—through the whole rollercoaster ride from ruined cities to "miracles" to "bubbles" and protracted financial malaise—the obedient-herd stereotype has survived almost unchallenged. Indeed, foreign journalists and pundits seem to have an unwritten rule requiring them to cite the same Japanese aphorism: "the nail that sticks up will be hammered down." Herd behavior. Groupthink. Harmony and homogeneity. Conformity and tribalism. Them, in stark contrast to Us, with no recognition or acknowledgment of how familiar such sayings are in all societies. (Among English-language idioms, think "don't stick your neck out," "don't rock the boat," "to get along, go along.")

Beginning in the early 1990s, when the bubble burst and doldrums arrived, another cliché joined the old bromides about Japan's special character: "change-resistant." Japanese popular culture and technological innovation generally escape this sentiment, but rarely the political economy and seldom Japanese society and culture at large. Look almost anywhere in the print and online media and you will find a chorus of erstwhile Japan experts calling attention to "change-resistant bureaucrats," "a hugely change-resistant political system," "Japan's hidebound business culture and change-resistant financial system," "the change-resistant men who run Japan," "cloistered change-resistant administrations," and, more sweepingly, "the conservative, change-resistant culture of the Japanese and their change-resistant society."

Such crude cultural determinism tells us less about Japan than about our own abiding ethnocentricity. Of course history, and what Edward Gibbon called the commands of custom, matter. The history that matters most has little to do with feudalism, however, and a great deal to do with modernity as experienced by a vulnerable Asian state embedded in a fiercely competitive world defined and dominated by Western powers.

US Commodore Matthew Perry's gunboat diplomacy in 1853 and 1854 propelled secluded Japan into this global maelstrom, and the Meiji leaders' response after the feudal regime was overthrown in 1868 was the very opposite of change-resistant. This early response involved intense campaigns promoting Western-style "civilization and enlightenment" and "wealth and power"—accompanied by tutelage in the lessons of Social Darwinism—that enabled Japan to do what no other non-Western, non-white, non-Christian nation in the world succeeded in doing: join the imperialist powers instead of falling prey to them, as most of Africa and Asia did.

There were notable milestones in Japan's rapid metamorphosis into a global power, highlighted most dramatically by military victories against China in 1895 and Russia in 1905. Contrary to Joseph Grew's later postulation of incompatible Western and Japanese measuring rods, the Japanese of the Meiji era measured Western prowess and practice with exactitude. The warships they deployed in these turn-of-the-century conflicts were state-of-the-art, and the legal instruments they manipulated in the wake of their wars established them as a bona fide imperialist and colonial power: in Formosa (Taiwan) in 1895, in strategic parts of Manchuria in 1905, and in Korea in 1910.

These accomplishments stimulated both unease and approbation among the Western powers. The most striking demonstration of the latter came from England, the greatest of the imperialist powers, in the most concrete and gratifying form imaginable: bilateral military alliance. Under the Anglo–Japanese Alliance signed in 1902 and renewed in 1905 and 1911, the two nations pledged to support each other if either signatory became involved in a war with more than one power. This alliance expedited Japan's war of choice against Russia and paved the way not only for Japan's entry into World War I as an Allied power, but also the country's subsequent participation in the Paris Peace Conference, where the victors gathered to reshape the map of the world.

The termination of the Anglo-Japanese Alliance in 1923, largely at the instigation of Britain and the urging of the United States, had both near- and long-term consequences. In the near view, Japan's leaders were left without a rudder at a time when the global order was about to fall apart. Economic depression loomed. Revolutionary developments in military technology obsessed strategic planners. Competing nationalisms and ideologies undermined the fledgling League of Nations and stifled cries for peace.

This is the milieu in which militarists and so-called renovationist bureaucrats assumed power in imperial Japan, threw caution to the winds, and took the nation into war, first against China and then, in 1941, against the Allied powers that supported China and presided as colonial overlords in Southeast Asia. Japan's aggression had nothing to do with being "recently feudalistic," and everything to do with a quest for security—and ultimately autonomy or autarky—in a broken world.

The domestic triumph of the warlords was neither inevitable nor uncontested. Recent scholarship paints a picture of great tension and dynamism in 1930s Japan: cosmopolitanism and an avid embrace of "modernity" among the bourgeoisie; high levels of civilian technological innovation (as well as military technological hubris); severe disparities and antagonisms among urban and rural classes; and so on. Neither homogeneity nor harmony characterizes this era, and militarist propaganda about "a hundred million hearts beating as one" reflected an intense campaign of domestic indoctrination aimed at masking these tensions.

Post-1945 Japan is incomprehensible without an appreciation of, first, the complexity and vitality of this prewar baseline, and second, the exhaustion and deep antimilitary sentiments that accompanied defeat. Two million Japanese fighting men and as many as one million civilians perished in the Asia-Pacific War, out of a population of slightly more than 70 million. The nuclear devastation of Hiroshima and Nagasaki followed saturation firebombing of 64 large and small cities. Defeated Japan was stripped of its Asian empire, and somewhere around a quarter of the nation's wealth was destroyed. What survived was a strong bedrock of skilled human resources that had expanded greatly under the mobilization for war, and a collective devotion to starting over in a society that directed these resources to peaceful civilian pursuits.

The so-called peace constitution that US occupation authorities drafted and the Japanese Diet endorsed in 1946 has remained unchanged into the 21st century because many Japanese still remember and recite the horrors of the war and the folly of the warlords. Although the original antimilitary thrust of the constitution has been diluted through "revision by reinterpretation" and incremental rearmament, and although the charter may eventually be revised, this antimilitary legacy will never be entirely dispelled. This development is a striking about-face from the militarism that eventually triumphed in the 1930s. It is also a blessing that has become battered and warped by the peculiarly intimate and asymmetrical nature of the postwar US–Japan security relationship.

It is here in the postwar US–Japan relationship that the long-term impact, or at least resonance, of the old Anglo-Japanese Alliance, lies. Shigeru Yoshida, the conservative prime minister who negotiated Japan's transition from occupation to the restoration of sovereignty in the early 1950s, articulated this relationship clearly. A former diplomat who entered the foreign service in 1906, Yoshida regarded Japan's bilateral alliance with England in the first two decades of the 20th century as the key to the halcyon years of national glory. The ruin the militarists brought upon Japan made clear that "autonomy" was a pipe dream. At the same time, having witnessed the failure of the League of Nations-style internationalism that followed the Anglo–Japanese Alliance, Yoshida rested little hope in the new United Nations as a guarantor of peace and security. In these circumstances, he acceded to the quid pro quos the United States demanded for regaining independence under a generous, nonpunitive, multinational peace treaty: wholesale integration in Washington's Cold War policy of military and economic containment of Communism.

Railways, introduced to Japan by Commodore Perry, are among many changes Japan has embraced successfully.
© Ando or Utagawa Hiroshige/The Bridgeman Art Library/Getty Images

It is easy for outsiders to forget the conditions under which defeated Japan re-joined the so-called community of nations more than a half-century ago. It is not easy for the Japanese to forget these conditions, which continue to influence, haunt, and hamstring the nation's policy makers. Hammered out in the midst of the Korean War and just a few years after the Communist victory in China, the patchwork of intercon-nected bilateral US–Japan agreements that accompanied restoration of sovereignty was simultaneously a blessing and curse. It established the military umbrella and patron-client relationship under which Japan promoted industrial policies that led to its emergence, beginning in the late 1960s, as the world's second-largest economy. At the same time, however, nestling so firmly under the eagle's wing locked Japan into what has turned out to be a lasting and psychologically enervating status of subordi-nate, or dependent, independence.

Yoshida viewed this subordination to Washington as unfortunate but unavoid-able and by and large beneficial at the time, and envisioned Japan eventually growing out of such extreme dependency. On the latter score, he was overly sanguine. Under the quid pro quos of the bilateral security settlements, Japan agreed to rearm under the US aegis without first revising the peace constitution, with both sides wishfully assuming such revision could be carried out sooner rather than later. Additionally, the Yoshida government acquiesced in continued maintenance of US military bases throughout the archipelago, a policy that provoked vehement grassroots "antibase" movements in the 1950s and after. Okinawa was excluded from the restoration of sov-ereignty and retained as a neocolonial US military bastion, with nominal sovereignty not restored to Japan until 1972 and extensive militarized real estate remaining in American hands to the present day.

The quid pro quos for regaining nominal independence also included participat-ing in the diplomatic and economic "containment" of the People's Republic of China, which was excluded from the multinational 1951 peace conference. Even the fiercely anticommunist Yoshida thought this exclusion madness. By way of compensation, Washington promoted Japanese economic engagement in Southeast Asia; granted favorable access to US patents and licenses and general industrial and managerial know-how; and tolerated Japanese protectionism and mercantilist policies. Washing-ton also patronized the consolidation and domination of conservative political power within Japan—to the point of embracing the premiership, beginning in 1957, of the former accused war criminal Nobusuke Kishi and funneling covert funds to him in return for continued unstinting support of the Cold War agenda. The 1960 revision and renewal of the bilateral security treaty under Kishi provoked massive protests that drew participants as diverse as communists and leftists, blue- and white-collar work-ers, students, farmers, housewives, and clergy.

Japan's isolation from China continued until 1972, when the Nixon administra-tion abruptly reversed course and extended recognition to the PRC without notify-ing Tokyo of this theatrical *volte-face* until the very last moment. Japan proceeded to develop extensive economic relations with China in the decades that followed as if the two earlier lost decades were of no lasting consequence, but that is too simple a reading. Washington's cavalier treatment of Japan's leaders, loyal to a fault, survived as a symbolic marker of the inequitable nature of the relationship. Even at the peak of Japan's emergence as an "economic superpower" in the 1970s and 1980s, the nation's leaders neither did, nor could, pursue a genuinely innovative and reasonably independent external policy.

The contrast to a defeated and occupied postwar Germany is noteworthy. Although West Germany, too, fell into the US security orbit, this situation did not define the country's relations with its neighbors and the world at large. More noteworthy yet is the contrast to the independence and autonomy with which China now increasingly asserts itself on the world stage. That is an ironic development, in retrospect, when one recalls the dogmatism with which Cold War containment in Asia was promoted on the grounds that the PRC was a Soviet satellite—little more than a pawn in Moscow's grim game of monolithic Communism.

Obviously, the constraints and psychological burdens that subordinate independence has imposed on Japan's leaders since the restoration of sovereignty six decades ago have become compounded by China's emergence as the dominant state in Asia. Just as obviously, on the other hand, Japan can take pride—as China cannot—in having become a viable democracy, neither more nor less dysfunctional than the US and major nations of Europe. In this, Japan is by no means uniquely unique, and not even significantly unique, which, when all is said and done, may be what matters most.

Do these psychological constraints mean there are no powerful change-resistant forces, no hammers pounding down nails that stick up? Not at all, but we should be careful how we deploy such labels and metaphors. Where prime ministers are concerned, for example, the Japanese of recent years have been positively change-addicted. Between 1989 and 2010, no less than 14 prime ministers came and went, four of them in the less-than-four years between September 2006 and June 2010. The fourth individual in this recent accelerated parade, Yukio Hatoyama, lasted only nine months and was widely perceived as a vivid example of the hammer and nail.

Hatoyama came to power as leader of the new Democratic Party of Japan, promising to overturn the sclerotic *modus operandi* of the conservative Liberal Democratic Party, which had ruled Japan with almost no interruption since the mid-1950s. He vowed, among other things, to free Japan of excessive America-centrism by bringing about a more transparent and genuine "alliance of equals," and at the same time to promote closer diplomatic ties and deeper economic integration in East Asia. One great, immediate, concrete touchstone in Hatoyama's agenda was a pledge to close the US Marine Corps air station at Futenma in Okinawa, a long-contested site in a crowded residential area where antibase sentiments ran particularly high.

A miscellany of political factors did Hatoyama in, but the most dramatic was the Obama administration's refusal to compromise on existing agreements regarding Futenma. As so often was the case, the hand on the biggest hammer was American.

On March 11, 2011, the domestic and international challenges that Hatoyama passed on to his Democratic Party successor, Naoto Kan, were shockingly eclipsed by the earthquake and tsunami that ravaged coastal prefectures north of Tokyo and became compounded by the terrifying breakdown of reactors at the Fukushima nuclear plant. The name of the game changed unalterably, in ways that will require months and even years to evaluate.

At the same time, the international perception of Japan and the Japanese was, at least momentarily, transformed. Recognition of a shared humanity overrode all else. The dignity and discipline of the survivors, seen day after day, drew universal admiration. The Fukushima radiation crisis directed attention to risks and regulatory failures that were not unique to Japan's nuclear-energy plants. And the ripple of economic dislocations caused by the disaster became a reminder of how sophisticated and globally integrated Japan's economy is, despite the two decades of financial tribulation that have garnered so much negative attention.

Two days after the disaster hit, Prime Minister Kan declared that Japan had not faced such a crisis since the end of World War II. This comment was widely quoted, although most Japanese are too young to remember how shattered their country was when the war the militarists started came home in a rain of fire from the sky. Rapid reconstruction and recovery seemed impossible to imagine in 1945 and 1946. Yet it happened.

And it had happened before. Almost two decades earlier, the Japanese people had shown the same kind of resilience and creativity in the face of the great Kanto earthquake of 1923. A more devastating disaster than the earthquake and tsunami of 2011, the Kanto quake killed more than 100,000 people and destroyed most of greater Tokyo and Yokohama. The "reconstruction boom" that followed did more than just rebuild the metropolis; it was designed to transform the city in conspicuously modern ways that included transportation networks, parks, Western-style buildings, and commercial enterprises such as factories, department stores, theaters, and cafes. The 1945 air raids destroyed this "new Tokyo" physically, but not the spirit and human resources that made postwar reconstruction possible.

History does not repeat itself. We will not see another Japanese quest for autarky, such as occurred when the global depression that began in 1929 swamped the reconstruction boom and paved the way for the rise of the militarists. Nor will we ever again be bombarded with such hoopla as the "Japanese miracle" and "Japan as number one" that flourished in the 1970s and 1980s. That is all to the good: postwar reconstruction was no miracle and the "number-one" rhetoric was delusory. Still, it is instructive to look back to 1945 and recall what people of goodwill, standing on the cusp of the postwar world, hoped defeated Japan might become: democratic, equitably prosperous, and never again a threat to its neighbors.

Japan achieved these goals and, for all its recent travails, has not lost hold of them. Such a fusion of resilience, competence, discipline, and collective creativity in the face of daunting challenges does not appear overnight; nor does it simply vanish.

WHAT HAPPENED TO NUMBER ONE?

EZRA F. VOGEL

THIRTY YEARS AGO, *as the United States grappled with slow growth, runaway infla-*
tion, double-digit unemployment and mounting trade deficits, Harvard sociologist Ezra F.
Vogel hailed the remarkable vitality of economic, social and cultural institutions in Japan.
In Japan As Number One: Lessons for America, *first published in 1979, Vogel asserted*
that Americans had much to learn from this island nation with few natural resources—and
should discard smug assumptions of American superiority. "The more I observed Japan's
success in a variety of fields," Vogel wrote in the book's preface, "the more I became convinced
that given its limited resources, Japan has dealt more successfully with more of the basic
problems of postindustrial society than any other country. It is in this sense, I have come to
believe, that the Japanese are number one."

Japan As Number One became one of the most widely discussed books of its day, and
anticipated a wave of later titles by foreign authors debating the merits of the "Japanese
model." Vogel's book also proved a best seller in Japan. In an interview before the March
2011 earthquake and tsunami, Vogel spoke with Brian Salsberg, a partner in McKinsey's
Tokyo office, and Clay Chandler, McKinsey's Asia editor. He reflected on the impact of
Japan As Number One, and shared his assessment of Japan's performance since the
book's publication.

McKinsey: *Why did you write* Japan As Number One?
Vogel: I felt that Americans arrogantly thought everyone in other nations should learn
from the United States, and there was no need for the United States to learn from
anybody else. But I had been coming to Japan since 1958, and I saw that a lot of

---

Ezra F. Vogel is a professor emeritus of sociology at Harvard University and the author of
numerous books on Asia.

Japanese institutions were running very well. Japan had less crime than we did. The children were getting better educated. Japan's people had longer lives; their companies had loyal employees; their bureaucrats were really first-rate. At the time the economy was growing very rapidly. None of these things were very well understood outside Japan. So I wrote the book as a sort of wake-up call for Americans. That's why I picked that title, *Japan As Number One*. Of course, a lot of people didn't actually read the book, they just seized on the title. And suddenly there were all these stories in the media criticizing the book and scoffing that Japan would never be the biggest economy in the world. I never said that Japan would become the world's largest economy. What I said was that as a country, Japan does a number of things better than many other countries.

McKinsey: *The book, which was first published in 1979, became a best seller in Japan. Did that surprise you?*

Vogel: I thought it might do pretty well in Japan, but never thought it would become a best seller. I wasn't writing it to be a Japanese best seller. You know, former US Ambassador and Harvard professor Edwin Reischauer once joked that the book ought to be required reading for Americans—and banned for the Japanese.

Vogel: "I still see many strengths in Japan."
© Harvard University

One thing I think helped generate interest was that the book came out a few weeks before the first G-7 summit hosted by Japan. Then-prime minister Masayoshi Ohira mentioned it at a press conference, and said he thought it provided very good background about Japan, so a lot of the foreign leaders who were coming to the summit read the book. And of course it didn't hurt book sales in Japan when that statement appeared in the Japanese press.

But in a broader sense, I think the real reason the book took off is that many Japanese, who felt they'd been looking up to the West for so long, were just beginning to have a little more confidence in their own achievements. They were beginning to think, "By God, we've done some things pretty well," but they hadn't yet articulated that thought; now they could say, "and a Harvard professor says so."

McKinsey: *At what point did you begin to feel things were not working as well as they ought to be in Japan?*

Vogel: As a sociologist, I think about institutions. I didn't understand that financial problems could have as large an impact as they did. I was slow to understand in 1989, when the financial problems burst, how they were going to affect institutions.

Through the 1990s, and even today, I still see many strengths in Japan. That's because when countries aren't well known to Americans, Americans tend to overreact. In the 70s, they underestimated Japan; in the 80s, they overestimated it. If you really understand a country well you wouldn't have such extreme responses.

In the 90s, people said, "Japan is done for." But I said, "No, Japan is not done for." I still see many strengths—the high basic educational levels, the quality control, the ability of people to work together, the able and committed bureaucrats.

McKinsey: *Do you feel the model that worked so well before serves the country today?*
Vogel: To me the fundamental problem Japan faces now is not the aging population or anything like that; the country needs a political system with the capacity to respond effectively to problems in a long-term way. I think there was an elite community of talented people who, through the 70s, provided coherence in planning for the future. This coherence ended in the 90s, when there was a collapse of parties. Japan hasn't built the right political system to put things back together again.

McKinsey: *Are Japan's political parties developing leaders with a broader vision?*
Vogel: Taro Kono, who is director general of the Liberal Democratic Party's international bureau, is a good example of a young politician with a vision. I remember in the 70s I would ask Japanese friends who's going to be prime minister, and they would rattle off names and say, "But not Nakasone." I would ask, "Why not Nakasone?" And they would say, "Oh, no, he's too strong-willed, he doesn't follow leadership, he doesn't get along with everybody, he's too much of a loner." But when the politicians realized they had serious problems, they went to a strong leader who had a vision. [Yasuhiro Nakasone, who was prime minister from 1982 to 1987, is often described as one of Japan's most effective prime ministers.] I think Kono and Yoshimasa Hayashi are examples of politicians who could become strong leaders.

McKinsey: *During the Iwakura mission in the late 19th century, many of Japan's future leaders made a global tour of other countries in an effort to learn from them. Could something similar happen today?*
Vogel: A lot of Japanese are discouraged now. So they don't see how it would work. To me, it's awfully sad that there aren't more Japanese going to study abroad. In Silicon Valley, there are many Chinese, Indians, and Koreans, but almost no Japanese.

The same is true at the universities. Part of the problem is that the Japanese don't have good English conversation skills compared with the skills of the Chinese and Koreans. Although Japanese English is getting a little better on the average, it hasn't made a breakthrough.

McKinsey: *What are the most important things for Japan to do to begin reestablishing its place in the world?*
Vogel: One is budgeting—you can't go on with a system where such a huge amount of the national budget is in the red every year. You have to have a long-term game plan for dealing with that; to try to solve it one year before the next election is crazy. You've got to think of a sustained plan and then sell it to the people.

The second is that I think the effort by METI [Japan's Ministry of Economy, Trade and Industry] to develop new industries and new sectors is still very appropriate. Most Americans think METI decided things for industry, but that's not the way it worked. What METI did was bring together people in a sector and say, "OK, what are the collective problems we need to tackle to make this sector strong? What infrastructure do we need?" And the businesses and the stakeholders worked together with METI. You can say this approach would be going back to industrial policy, but it's not dictating to business in the way that a lot of Westerners seem to think. I still consider METI a valuable resource for the government as it thinks about the long-term.

Then there are the relationships with China and the United States. The basic goal is stability. If I had to decide, I'd probably go ahead with the move from Futenma, where American forces currently are stationed in Okinawa, to a less-populated part of the island, and then gradually draw down the number of Marines there.

With China, Japan has to publicize in more detail their recognition of World War II tragedies so the country will not be vulnerable to Chinese accusations. Then it can say, "Now, China, what are you doing to tell the truth to your people about Japan? What has China done to show how Japan has turned to peace after the war, and how much Japan helped China in the 1980s?" The Chinese aren't going to apologize, but some Chinese leaders are trying to curb their aggressive accusations.

McKinsey: *Japan's population is old and getting older. How much does this matter?*
Vogel: I'm a little skeptical about whether an aging population is as important as people say it is. I'm 80 and I'm still doing a few things!

I used to think that people should retire at 60. But when you're talking about mental labor rather than physical labor, why couldn't a higher proportion of people work until a later age? In Japan, most people work in the service sector. Why can't we extend peoples' working life five or ten years? When people tell me that Japan faces a terrible aging problem, I don't quite see it that way.

McKinsey: *Should Japan change its system to accept more immigrants?*
Vogel: The current system is cleverer than it seems. The thinking underlying the system is: "We don't give a lot of work permits, so foreigners work illegally, and if they get in trouble we can send them home very easily." So foreigners come over as students—fairly smart people come in—and they work illegally. They probably get lower pay because they are illegal; and if they do anything wrong, they get sent home. It's unfair, and it's illegal, but it's a better system than people will acknowledge openly

because they don't like to admit that they are doing things illegally. Some say Japan must admit many more immigrants. I'm not persuaded that's absolutely necessary.

McKinsey: *How would you rate Japan's education system?*
Vogel: My friends who are schoolteachers here are super. They're so dedicated! They work in the summertime, developing the curriculum for the next year; they work as a team, thinking how they can do things better. Why do Japanese students still need *juku* [privately run "cram schools" that many Japanese students attend to supplement their preparation for college entrance examinations] when the country has such dedicated teachers? It seems to me that *juku* are sending a message to kids that they really don't have to pay attention at regular school because they're going to learn the same thing at *juku* later. That's one problem. Another is that Japanese children aren't rewarded for independent thinking. I remember going to a class one time and the teacher was saying, "Okay, everyone, let's be more creative. What are the things you need to do to be creative? Write them on the blackboard."

McKinsey: *What are some of Japan's underlying strengths?*
Vogel: One is the capacity of the Japanese to listen to each other and work as a team. One of the things that impresses me most about Japan is that if you get a few Japanese together and say, "All right, here's what we're going to do," they immediately organize themselves regarding who is going to do what. They don't embarrass each other, and they don't smack each other down. There's a sensitivity and capacity to work with other people. That kind of softness in human relations is really attractive. That's one thing. Another is the incredible loyalty people show to classmates, colleagues, and business partners over a long period of time.

McKinsey: *So you remain optimistic about Japan's prospects?*
Vogel: I'm worried, frankly, because they need a system that allows politicians to think long-term, and I don't see that happening.

WHAT WENT WRONG—AND HOW JAPAN CAN GET IT RIGHT

DAVID E. SANGER

ON A DANK AND OVERCAST AFTERNOON IN TOKYO IN EARLY 1994, the founder of an old-line electronics firm told me he was convinced Japan's great postwar run was coming to an end.

"I worry that we are only good at one thing—miniaturized electronics," he said, sipping green tea in one of his company's stark reception rooms. "We haven't learned how to move on. We are an easy target."

At the time, I dismissed his comment as the musings of an aging executive with too much time on his hands and too little vision of his country's potential. After all, as a foreign correspondent based in Tokyo, I had spent the previous six years documenting Japan's remarkable rise of influence, its creation of a widely admired economic model, its construction of factories in countries that it had colonized or occupied in the first half of the 20th century, and its bold purchase of two giant Hollywood studios.

The books explaining the phenomenon of Japan to depressed Americans and Europeans carried titles that said it all: *Japan As No. 1, The Enigma of Japanese Power, and Trading Places.* Each described how Japan was on course to challenge the United States as the world's leading economic power, probably around 2010. Its rise as a political power on par with the United States and Europe, while on a slower timeline, was thought equally inevitable.

We now know that the aging electronics executive was a lot closer to the truth than the authors of those books. As it turned out, 2010 was a critical year, but not in the way predicted. It was the year China overtook Japan as the world's second-largest economy, and by the time it happened, few noticed. It had seemed so inevitable

---

David E. Sanger is chief Washington correspondent for The New York Times; *he served as the* Times's *Tokyo correspondent and bureau chief from 1988 to 1994.*

for so long that it barely merited news stories. Meanwhile, the Japanese economy remained roughly the size it was 20 years before. Japan's remarkable burst of growth, it turned out, was like cherry-blossom season: a wonder to behold, but short-lived.

Then came March 11. From a distance, those of us who knew and loved Japan could only ache as we watched a nation in misery, struck by a force of nature. Amid the carnage, and the stench of deluge, destruction, and death, Japanese wondered whether they were living through a cursed moment in their nation's history. No doubt many will remember it that way. But just as a nation destroyed by war almost seven decades ago rose again, by force of will, hard work, and an extraordinary sublimation of the needs of the individual for the society, the earthquake and tsunami that struck the nation may—just may—contain the seeds of its rebirth.

Before March 11, the most potent question about modern-day Japan seemed to be a simple one: Why did so many experts get it so wrong? How did the strengths often attributed to Japan for so many years—the high savings rates that gave the country a seemingly endless supply of capital, protected domestic markets that kept its companies afloat, comparatively low military spending, and the ethnic homogeneity that reduced internal strife—ultimately became sources of weakness?

There were many reasons. We were seduced not only by the soaring Nikkei stock market—it peaked at 38,957 on the last day of trading in 1989—but also by the illusion that the same kind of central guidance and national energy that got Japan through the first four decades of its postwar reconstruction was infinitely scalable. Certainly, Japan's bureaucrats—the men (and they were almost all men) who got the credit for figuring the system out—were convinced that the system they had invented could last forever.

In one of my first visits to the Ministry of International Trade and Industry (MITI), the supposed nerve center of the Japanese manufacturing miracle, I was ushered into the jammed office of the head of the auto division. While his scores of aides had their heads down at battered gray desks, looking busy, he showed me the giant map of the United States that covered the back wall. The map was dotted with colorful pins, one for every Japanese auto or auto-parts factory built on American soil. On closer inspection, I saw it was no ordinary map, but one that divided the country by its congressional districts. MITI was not only planning Japan's expansion, but also keeping count of how many members of Congress had a stake in Japan's continued success. There was no government office in the United States, I recall thinking, that had a similar map of American manufacturing influence across Japan, or Germany. MITI's plan certainly looked like it had legs.

What did I miss? Something simple: Japanese bureaucrats knew how to map the known world, but not the unknown territory of innovation. Because the country's savings were kept in the Postal Savings System, for example, they were not deployed into new technologies, at home or abroad, that could keep the miracle alive.

A protected domestic market assured that Fujitsu and NEC enjoyed a stable, hard-to-invade base, but it also kept the country from competing with an array of new, game-changing technologies. More importantly, the protected home market discouraged companies from taking risks. So Japan failed to anticipate the rise of the Internet, the creation of Google and other search engines, the invention of the iPhone, and the transition from big computer programs to killer apps.

Even Japan's ethnic cohesion—often cited in the 1980s as a critical source of competitive strength because it avoided the messy racial and ethnic tensions that absorbed other societies—turned out to be long-term competitive disadvantage. Without question, Japan's treasured homogeneity has its advantages, as the world saw in the country's response to the March 11 disaster. There was no looting. There were no riots. Quietly, Japanese re-created their social structure in orderly high school gymnasiums, looked for the missing, and took care of those whose lives had washed away. It was hard to imagine any other country responding to natural disaster with such quiet dignity.

AN ENTIRE GENERATION HAS BEEN RAISED TO ADULTHOOD WITHOUT FEELING THE SENSE OF OPTIMISM THAT ONCE PULSATED THROUGH THE NEON STREETS OF GINZA.

But such orderliness, we've learned, also comes at a price. For decades it kept the country from assembling the kind of diverse, international workforce needed to understand markets outside its own, and from importing the youthful, creative people who would bring in ideas not "Made in Japan." What serves a nation so well in times of crisis, it turns out, can also hold it back in global competition.

To anyone who lived in Tokyo when diners in the Ginza sprinkled gold on their sushi and Japan was the world's largest aid donor, the question loomed: How could this national self-deception go on for so long? Japan's first reaction to the slump of the early 1990s was that this was simply a cyclical downturn. Certain that healthy growth would soon return, banks remained in denial about the state of their balance sheets or the pernicious effects of deflation. Sit tight, the Japanese assured themselves, and things will all bounce back.

Meanwhile, the Liberal Democratic Party (LDP), which had ruled since the 1950s, was deeply dependent on those same banks and businesses to keep its coffers full. It froze in the headlights. The LDP's power structure was based on the status quo. When it was forced into action to spur the economy, it reverted to the same kind of pork-barrel projects that seemed to pay off in the 1960s and 1970s. But these projects did not pack the same punch. More train lines were built, but to places few wanted to go; more bridges, across lightly traveled waters. The LDP continued lavish subsidies to farmers, a key element of its constituency, without asking whether it made any economic sense for Japan to cling to the myth of itself as a rice-growing culture.

At the other great economic-policy power centers—the Ministry of Finance and the Bank of Japan—officials ran out of ideas once interest rates bottomed out near zero. The modern samurais had fired every arrow, and it was not enough. That created a national sense of powerlessness, and fearful investors grew more fearful.

Even when Japan recognized a problem and tried to take action, the results seemed to fall short. Before the downturn took hold, for example, the government recognized that there were cultural barriers to innovation, so it talked up a new culture of risk taking and promoted Japanese "Silicon Valleys." I visited many of these, including the "Science City" at Tsukba and smaller innovation centers from Hokkaido to Okinawa.

The projects were promising, the researchers delighted in their freedom from the humdrum of ordinary corporate life. Some of their ideas took hold.

But Japan was still missing some critical elements: these places were islands, rarely linked to great universities or an eager community of venture capitalists. Risk taking was carefully circumscribed. There were far more marginal improvements than conceptual breakthroughs, and too few pathways to the market.

These missteps help to explain why Japan lost its economic edge, but they fail to explain its erosion of political influence. In the 1992 book, *A Japan That Can Say No*, Akio Morita, then-chairman of Sony, and Shintaro Ishihara, a stalwart nationalist and mayor of Tokyo, wrote that "Japan can change the whole world balance of power. . ."—in part because the rest of the world needed Japan's trading surpluses, and would therefore seek its approval.

The thesis was stated so baldly that many Japanese recoiled in embarrassment even at the time. But there was a core of truth to it. If well managed, the Japanese state could have found ways to leverage its power around the world. And it tried, if half-heartedly. Starting in the mid-1980s, long before the crash, various government reports proposed schemes for Japan to "internationalize," and put its ugly World War II legacy behind it. Inside the LDP and out, some people even advocated a policy of liberal interventionism, to demonstrate that Japan knew how to use its power for good. In this spirit, Japan sent armed forces overseas on peacekeeping missions.

But each foreign mission risked a backlash at home. Japan's financial contribution to the Gulf War in 1991 (about $13 billion) was doled out so slowly that the country got little credit for it. When Japanese peacekeepers in Cambodia in 1992–93 took casualties, the national will to send the young into harm's way, even for humanitarian purposes, seemed to crumble. The country did send troops to Iraq and provided logistical support in Afghanistan, but still seemed uncertain of its purpose. Were the troops sent to further Japan's national interests, or simply to show solidarity with its biggest ally?

The domestic allergy to foreign military interventions quashed real debate about whether Japan had a need, or a moral obligation, to send its forces to protect Rwandans, or to help oust Saddam Hussein from Kuwait, or to deal with the Taliban. Countless times, Japanese friends told me that these conflicts were, in the words of an old saying, the "fire on the other side of the river." To many Japanese, this restraint was laudable, considering the disasters that befell the country when it wandered far from its shores between 1910 and 1945. But the result was a nation that assumed someone else would make the world safe for Japanese commerce.

Japan seemed to believe "internationalization" could be limited to exporting capital and foreign aid. Its international influence came to be measured in the number of factories built in Thailand and bridges constructed in Cambodia. But once Japan could no longer finance projects on that scale, its influence began to rot—first subtly, then disastrously. When the flow of aid slowed down, the rest of the world stopped paying as much attention to Tokyo.

Twenty years of slow growth and deflation have hollowed out Japan's hopes for an international role, and greatly diminished the desire for leadership. An entire generation has been born and raised to adulthood without feeling the sense of optimism and global power that once pulsated through the neon streets of the Ginza.

The evidence lies in the country's reluctance to create or join global coalitions. There are exceptions of course: the Kyoto climate-change protocols were a major Japanese project, and an important one. The country has been a leader in calling for nuclear disarmament ever since Hiroshima and Nagasaki. But when it comes to contributing to global security, Japan continues to take a back seat. Rather than focus on the broader threats that North Korea poses to the region, or to the depredations that

Ginza in the Bubble Era: Did the lights burn brighter then?
© Michael S. Yamashita/Terra/Corbis

country has imposed on its own people, Japan has fixated on the tragic cases of Japanese kidnapped long ago by North Korean infiltrators. Those episodes certainly have to be resolved, and the political pressures to understand them are tremendous. But it is hard to formulate a grand strategy against a brutal regime with such a narrow focus.

Washington became frustrated with Japan, and somewhat impatient. As a result, the Obama administration largely thwarted Japan's already limited ambitions. The current administration has not, for example, gone out of its way to campaign on Japan's behalf for a permanent seat on the United Nations Security Council. Why, the administration implicitly asks, should it go to the mat for such an insecure, self-absorbed ally? When President Obama visited India in late 2010, and called for that country to join the Security Council, he made little mention of the long-time American support for Japan to take a seat of its own. Whether an oversight or a deliberate omission, the slight was a reminder that, in the months before the earthquake, Japan's influence in Washington had ebbed.

The question for Japan, even before the earthquake and tsunami, and more urgently now, is how it can break out of this cycle of decline. A first step—albeit one that will be a tough sell politically, especially at a time of economic weakness and recovery from tragedy—seems obvious: Japan has to open its borders to more immigrants. Not just cheap labor, which often finds its way into the country anyway, but the kind of young talent who will see opportunities to help revive a country that has long been in love with technology but finds itself short of the spirit it needs to make the next leap.

The hard part is convincing the Japanese that their current immigration policies are hurting themselves. On visits to universities during my time in Japan, I often mentioned the story of Andrew Grove, the co-founder of Intel. As a young man, Grove fled Hungary, then landed in the United States and went on to develop a technology that remade computing. Had Japan's immigration policies been more open, I asked, would Japan have been the country that first commercialized the microprocessor?

The point never seemed to make an impression with my audiences. But today, after history has repeated itself at Google (one of whose founders is a Russian immigrant) and countless other successful start-ups, it might. It's impossible to count the lost revenue of a what-if. But there is no dispute that the country's political class has failed to grapple with the question of whether a shrinking Japan can sustain itself without welcoming new immigrants and the new ideas they bring.

A second critical step is to get out from under the mountain of government debt—something that will be even more difficult, given the need to rebuild Tohoku. Still, investing less in the elderly and more in the young is vital. Given the talent in the country, there is no reason Japanese universities should not be among the best in the world, attracting students from across the globe. By and large, these universities are not. Japan did not have a single business school ranked in the top 100 in the most recent *Financial Times* MBA survey. In the annual *Times* (of London) Higher Education ranking, Tokyo University (No. 26) was the only Japanese institution to make the top 50, and only two made the top 100—as many as Ireland.

Japan also needs an investment strategy that takes account of China's move into the heart of the high-technology arena that has traditionally been a Japanese strength. When I talk to Japanese politicians and bureaucrats, they often sound as if they are waiting for China's own economic bubbles to burst. That may happen. But hoping that China trips up is not a strategy.

Recovering from the disasters of March 11 could provide a framework for Japan's renaissance. The country suddenly has a new national mission—something that has been missing for two decades. Just as a previous generation of Japanese rebuilt Tokyo, Hiroshima, and Nagasaki, the current generation has an opportunity to remake an area that missed the first Japanese miracle. Best of all, this generation has the world rooting for it.

Northeastern Japan can become, with the right incentives and the right investments, the birthplace of all those things the Japanese determined were missing from their national economy. Where better to put the mix of universities, start-ups, and venture capital than in the ruins around Sendai? What better memorial to those whose lives were tragically washed away than a world-class center to build structures that can withstand the earth's worst forces; energy technologies that can make the crippled Fukushima power plants seem like a relic of a past age; and social networking technologies that spread the best in Japanese community-building? Japan has done it before. The country can do it again.

Just as Japan needs an economic strategy that confronts the realities of a rising China, it needs a security strategy that recognizes the changing contours of power in Asia. So far, Japan does not have such a strategy. Twenty years of recession have deepened Japan's isolationist tendencies. But it is clear that if Japan wants to play a significant, if diminished, role shaping the new Asia, it has to prepare its bureaucracy, and its people, for a dramatically changed environment. In short, Japan must reach a national consensus on where its strategic interests lie. It needs something approaching a grand strategy.

Developing such a strategy won't be easy. Ever since World War II, there has been fear that any public discussion of Japanese strategy would be exploited by its neighbors, who are always quick to remind Japan of its imperialist past and the atrocities that accompanied its occupation of much of Asia. But not every strategy has to contain an imperialist taint. And at a moment when China clearly has a vision of what its sphere of influence will look like a decade or two from now, the bigger risk for Japan is to enter the next decade without some guiding principles. Otherwise the country will never know when to push back, how to set limits, or even how to cooperate in facing joint threats. A country that does not understand its own national interests has a greater, not a lesser, chance of being sucked into conflict.

Take the most likely scenario for a crisis: the end-game in North Korea. If North Korea implodes, there will be a scramble for control of the Korean Peninsula; if it explodes, the results could be even worse. The South Koreans, the Americans, and the Chinese each have the rudiments of a strategy for how to handle those possibilities; their challenge is to make sure they don't trip into conflict while executing them. Japan has huge interests in managing North Korea's demise, but as one senior Obama administration official put it to me, "If there is a Japanese strategy for dealing with North Korean collapse, it's a well-kept secret." Would Japan urge South Korea to take effective control of the peninsula? Would it stand by if the Chinese try to take over?

Those are only a couple of the questions Japan needs to consider in responding to China's new assertiveness. Beijing appears to be spending less time these days talking about the country's "peaceful rise," and more about asserting exclusive control over vast waterways, including the South China Sea. The diplomatic blowup between China and Japan in the fall of 2010, triggered by a Chinese trawler captain who rammed a Japanese Coast Guard vessel near the Senkaku Islands, blindsided Tokyo. The Democratic Party-led government initially took a hard line, detaining the Chinese captain. But the government folded as soon as China threatened to cut off imports of rare-earth minerals needed by Japanese industry. The incident was ugly enough, but it also demonstrated what happens when Japan stumbles into such incidents without a clear sense of strategic purpose.

As the weeks following the earthquake demonstrated, the immediate tensions between China and Japan can be overcome. While the Chinese did not rush to Japan's aid the way Japan's allies did, they offered enough to create the promise of at least a temporary warming of relations. It is an opportunity that both countries should seize, since history does not suggest there will be many moments of common interest.

Over the longer term, the structure for developing a true national security strategy for Japan is already in place: a tight three-way alliance between Washington, Seoul, and Tokyo. But to make it work better, Japan has to stop debating the not-in-my-backyard issues, such as where to base U.S. troops on Okinawa, and start considering how it can strengthen its relationships in order to set limits on China's ability to rewrite the rules unilaterally.

Japan has traditionally shied away from this kind of issue, largely because of the overhang from its brutal World War II history. But more than two generations have passed since then, and Washington has moved from worrying about Japan's intentions to worrying that Japan assumes the United States will provide for Tokyo's security without commensurate contributions—and sacrifice. Because a series of Japanese prime ministers have ducked those issues, the US alliance with South Korea has become far stronger than the one with Japan.

Japan has much to offer, both in its character and in its hard-earned wisdom. It has an industrial base that was once the envy of the world, and could be again. Its financial managers have learned from bitter experience what happens when balance-sheet problems are left to fester. It appreciates that Japanese exceptionalism was largely a nationalistic myth—and that the country's success is linked to that of its neighbors and allies. It has learned that when political influence is built solely on money, a market downturn affects national power.

The issue is whether Japan, jarred by tragedy and unified by the need for recovery, can lift its politics from two decades of parochialism in order to restore the growth and influence it once enjoyed. Now may be the moment.

DEMOGRAPHY AND JAPAN'S FUTURE

NICHOLAS EBERSTADT

BARRING THE UNIMAGINABLE, just 30 years from now, Japan will be a far smaller and vastly more aged country than the one we know today. On the cusp of this monumental demographic transformation, Japan is gradually but relentlessly evolving into a society whose contours and workings are the stuff of science fiction. Aging and population decline will profoundly alter the realm of the possible for Japan—and will have major reverberations for the nation's social life, economic performance, and global position.

Japan's future population profile has largely been set: more than 60 percent of the people who will inhabit Japan in 2040 are living today. Between now and then, the country's population prospects will be driven by three distinctively Japanese trends:

1. Excellent general health. The Japanese are perhaps the world's longest-living people, with an overall life expectancy today of 83 (86 for women); the outlook is for further improvements. Despite salutary trends in "healthy aging," this increase in life expectancy can only mean that a growing share of the population will be increasingly frail—and that their need for pensions, medical services, and long-term care will grow.

2. An unusually strong aversion to immigration. Alone among the world's richest nations, Japan has reported net *out*-migration over the past four decades. According to the Organisation for Economic Co-operation and Development (OECD), in 2007 Japan naturalized fewer than 15,000 new citizens, far fewer than Switzerland—a country with highly restrictive naturalization laws—and just 6 percent of Japan's population. As of 2010, Japan was home to an estimated 2.2 million foreigners, less than 2 percent of the population.

Nicholas Eberstadt is a political economist and demographer and is the Henry Wendt Scholar in Political Economy at the American Enterprise Institute in Washington, DC.

3. Extremely small families. Japan recorded its first postwar instance of sub-replace-ment-level fertility (that is, fewer than 2.1 children per woman; the rate in Japan is less than 1.4) in the 1950s and has not seen a single year of above-replacement-level fertility since 1974, according to the Japan Statistics Bureau. Barely 40 percent as many Japanese babies were born in 2007 as were born in 1947, and the outlook is for fewer births still in the decades immediately ahead—as far as the demographer's eye can see.

We can get a sense of the shape of things to come by comparing the 2010 popula-tion profile for Japan with the country's projected profile for 2040, Thirty years from now there will likely be fewer Japanese people under the age of 65 than there are today, and many fewer under the age of 50—but many more over the age of 75. This Japan could have more people in their 80s and 90s than it has children under 15—and the number of centenarians would be not that much lower than the number of babies born each year. As of 2040, according to these projections, 34 percent of the Japanese population will be 65 or older, and 13 percent—every eighth person—will be over 80. Every week between now and 2040, Japan's median age is set to rise by two days; by 2040, it is on track to be 54 years, up from 44 today.[1]

But there is more. The Japanese family is being shaken by truly seismic shifts that promise to produce a society with all but unrecognizable kinship patterns. Tra-ditional "Asian family values"—universal marriage and childbearing, and lifelong marriage—are eroding. There is a headlong "flight from marriage" by younger women. Between 1970 and 2005, the proportion of never-married Japanese women in their late 30s soared to 18.4 percent, from 5.8 percent, according to recent re-search by the Asia Research Institute.

An increasing number of Japanese people are choosing to be childless. Roughly 13 percent of today's 50-year-old Japanese women have never married—and more than 20 percent of them do not have children.[2] Projections by Japanese researchers sug-gest the corresponding proportions by 2040 could be as high as 24 percent and 38 percent, respectively—meaning that nearly one in four women in this future Japan would complete their childbearing years without ever taking a husband, and nearly two out of five would never have a child.

Divorce no longer bears a stigma, and it is already more common in Japan than is realized. According to one study, a young woman's odds of eventual divorce in Japan are now about 30 percent—higher than in Norway, Finland, or France.[3] This trend means the outlook for marital breakup in the decades ahead is likely to rise signifi-cantly for the decreasing proportion of those who marry in the first place. Thus the Japan of 2040 will be not only be shrinking and elderly, but also increasingly filled

1 Miho Iwasawa and Ryuichi Kaneko, "Trends in partnership behaviours in Japan from the cohort perspective," *Eurostat Methodologies and working papers: Work session on demographic projections, Bucharest 10-12 October 2007*, pp. 65–76.
2 Ibid.
3 Ryuichi Kaneko, "Population Prospects of the lowest fertility with the longest life: The new official population projections for Japan and their life course approaches," *Eurostat Methodologies and working papers: Work session on demographic projections, Bucharest 10-12, October 2007*, pp. 169–188.

with aged isolates, divorcees, and adults whose family lines end with them. Japan's robust (if sometimes stifling) networks of family relations—a pillar of Japanese society throughout history—stand to be severely eroded.

What will these impending demographic and familial changes mean for the Japan of 2040? Here are a few of the most likely implications:

The looming era of institutionalization. This aging society will be a shrinking society. Japan's total population is projected to decline from about 127 million today to some 104 million in 2040, an 18 percent drop (Exhibit 1)[4]. The decline of the working-age population (ages 15 to 64) is likely to be even steeper: a plunge to 57 million, from 81 million, or 30 percent. Viewed another way, while the total population is projected to fall 1 percent a year until 2040, the manpower pool will shrink at almost double that rate, 1.8 percent. Fewer people, then, will be paying for more numerous older dependents.

Not the least of the problems attendant to extreme population aging may be Alzheimer's Disease (AD), which can be long-lasting, utterly incapacitating, and demanding of constant attention. At present, there are no effective preventive or curative medications for AD—and scant indications of promising treatments in the

Exhibit 1
Population by age and sex, 2010 vs. 2040 (projected)   ☐ 2040 ■ 2010

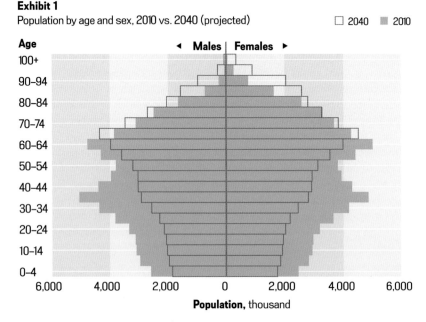

Source: US Census Bureau, International Data Base
4 In this graphic, I use projections from the US Census Bureau, but projections by the UN Population Division, or Japan's official Statistics Bureau, look very much the same.

current R&D pipeline. A study commissioned by Alzheimer's Disease International hypothesizes that by 2050, one of every 20 Japanese could suffer from AD.[5]

The caregiving implications of such an outcome are staggering, but given the erosion of the Japanese family, a steadily increasing proportion of Japan's senior citizens will have no children to turn to for support. Under such circumstances, an increase in long-term institutionalization looks all but inescapable.

Demographic simulations by Japanese researchers suggest that by 2040, nearly 10 percent of women over 65 might be living in institutional settings.[6] At any given age, Japan's seniors are likely to be healthier and fitter 30 years hence. But the country's coming gray wave will necessarily focus ever-greater salience on their obligations from—and to—the rest of society.

The brave new nature of childhood and youth. In the recent past, children in Japan were plentiful, while elders (who could expect a measure of social veneration) were scarce. By most projections, there will be three Japanese over 65 in 2040 for every child under 15—an almost exact inversion of the ratio as recently as 1975. How will Japan's children 30 years hence be treated by a society in which a large minority of adults opted not to have children, and in which the median age of an aging electorate will itself be approaching 60?

AGING AND POPULATION DECLINE WILL PROFOUNDLY ALTER THE REALM OF THE POSSIBLE FOR JAPAN.

It is easy to imagine that children will become increasingly prized, even treasured. It is also possible to envision a future in which Japanese boys and girls could regard themselves as entitled, and their obligations and duties to their elders as onerous or even optional. The hopes and expectations falling on this dwindling cadre of youth will be truly enormous—and for some fraction, unbearable.

Japan is already a witness to the phenomena of Not in Education, Employment or Training (NEET) youth. The acronym refers to those who are opting out of existing Japanese social arrangements by declining to pursue education or employment. In the more pathological extreme, known as *hikikomori*, a kind of acute social withdrawal, these individuals shut themselves off and retreat to a life of video games, the Internet, and *manga* in their own rooms within their parents' home. None of these alternative futures are mutually exclusive. Suffice it to say that childhood and young adulthood in this future Japan will certainly be different—and perhaps more difficult—than ever before.

The struggle to grow. With two "lost decades" of economic growth immediately behind it, and a serious crisis now besetting the world economy, the Japanese economy faces a future in which simply sustaining positive economic growth will be a chal-

---

5 See, for example, "Dementia in the Asia Pacific region: the epidemic is here," report by AccessEconomics PTY Ltd. for Asia Pacific Members of Alzheimer's Disease International, September 21, 2006, available electronically at http://www.alz.co.uk/research/files/apreport.pdf.

6 Tetsuo Fukawa, "Household projection 2006/07 in Japan using a micro-simulation model," *IPSS Discussion Paper Series*, Tokyo, 2007-E02, National Institute of Population and Social Security Research.

lenge. Even if the older Japanese retire at a later age, the country's workforce will almost certainly be much smaller than it is today. Extreme aging will also place pressure on the nation's savings rates—and thus, other things being equal, on investment for growth.

From a macroeconomic standpoint, Japan already has the OECD's highest ratio of gross public debt to GDP (some 200 percent). Recent projections by researchers at the Bank for International Settlements suggest that, on the country's current budgetary path, this ratio could rise to a mind-boggling 600 percent by 2030.[7] While Japan might be able to service such a mountain of public financial obligations without risk of sovereign default, the implications for economic performance are hardly auspicious.

As for real estate, this market is unlikely to be a growth area for a depopulating nation, considering that Japanese researchers anticipate the country will have roughly 20 percent fewer households in 2040 (38 million) than it does today (47 million). Country properties, however, may offer attractive opportunities to the discriminating investor: projections from the UN Population Division suggest Japan's rural population will fall by some 40 percent between 2010 and 2040, while the country's urban population will drop only slightly.

Even in the face of these economic pressures, Japan does have options. The first is to build on its generally strong school system: improving educational attainment (and implementing a lifelong approach to education and training) could increase productivity. Japan is a world leader in research, development, and "knowledge production"; strengthening these capacities for technological innovation, and applying technological advances and breakthroughs broadly throughout the national economy, could also stimulate growth. In addition, far-reaching structural reform could have beneficial spillovers for Japan's long-run growth. Seizing those as-yet-ungrasped opportunities for reform, however, will require widespread determination. Will that prove to be too much to ask from an aging, risk-averse national electorate?

A less crowded, "greener" land. With depopulation and the emptying of the Japanese countryside (Japan's rural population in 2040 may be smaller than at any point since the late 1800s), Japan will have more living space and arable land per person. Given the country's ongoing improvements in energy efficiency and green technologies, environmental quality could improve appreciably. In this sense, depopulation could coincide with improvement in natural amenities and quality of life.

A nation of immigrants—and emigrants? Japan is an increasingly cosmopolitan country, and the Japanese are enthusiastic international travelers. But they are also acutely sensitive to the "other-ness" of *gaijin*, and immigration has been strikingly limited. It is not altogether impossible that attitudes toward foreign labor could change, but it is fantastic to imagine this society accepting the millions of immigrants that would be required to prevent labor force decline. The UN Population Division once estimated that Japan would need a total net immigration of 17 million

---

7 Stephen G. Cecchetti, M. S. Mahoney, and Fabrizio Zampoli, "The future of public debt: prospects and implications," *BIS Working Papers*, Number 300, March 2010.

between 2000 and 2050 to forestall depopulation—and a net inflow of more than 30 million people aged 15 to 64 (or almost 650,000 per year) just to keep the country's working-age population from shrinking.

No less intriguing, however, is the proposition that a depopulating Japan might turn out to be a major supplier of *emigrants*. Given the cost of aging, Japan might, for example, establish "health care colonies" in places like India or the Philippines: spots where large populations of elderly Japanese could enjoy a good quality of life at a fraction of the cost at home. Younger Japanese, for their part, might find it attractive to embrace new opportunities abroad, rather than stay in a shrinking, dying Japan.

• • •

Population projections, of course, are just that: projections, based upon assumptions. A significant turnaround in Japan's demographic outlook cannot be ruled out—but we must recognize the narrow limits of the possible. It is difficult to imagine anything that could reverse, or even delay, an era of unprecedented aging.

Is it possible to boost birth rates appreciably over the long term? Probably not. The Democratic Party, elected in 2009, is trying. It is proposing more day-care services and other child-friendly policies—including much higher payments to new parents—in an effort to encourage larger families. The problem is that such policies have had limited success at best in the societies that have attempted them.

Continental Europe, for example, is home to a broad range of child-friendly programs—but none of these countries has a fertility rate above 2.1 children per woman, the level at which population remains stable. In pro-natalist Singapore, the total fertility rate was a mere 1.22 as of 2009, according to Statistics Singapore, lower even than that of Japan.

It is remotely possible that some great change in public attitudes—an ideological or religious movement or the like—could sweep Japan and revitalize the desire for larger families. But to date, these changes have never occurred in an affluent open society where fertility levels have sunk as low as Japan's are today. For better or worse, depopulation and pervasive graying look to be Japan's lot.

FADE TO GRAY

BRAD GLOSSERMAN

FOR TOKYO'S DISCERNING RESTAURANT-GOERS, Café Rottenmeier in Ikebu-kuro offered a new wrinkle on fine dining. Named after the stern *fraulein* of the hit 1970s *anime* series, "Heidi, Girl of the Alps," Rottenmeier's waitresses were gray-haired, bespectacled grannies who reminded customers to stop slouching and or-dered them to behave themselves. The café, which was conceived by artist Miwa Yanagi and open for a few weeks as part of the 2010 arts Festival/Tokyo, was created as a statement about Japan's tendency to worship young women, although it is the oldest, grayest country in the world.

Yanagi's premise was, of course, ironic. It was also a disturbingly astute vision of Japan's future. Some 23 percent of the Japanese population was aged 65 or older in April 2010; by 2055, that demographic will reach a staggering 41 percent. The country's population is shrinking, projected to fall from 127 million today to 90 million by 2055. In the countryside, the aging phenomenon is well advanced: the average age of a Japanese farmer is 66 and less than a third of the country claims residence in rural areas.

The challenge of an older population is not unique to Japan. Most developed nations face a "gray" future, and China is set, as a result of the one-child policy, to become the first country to become old before it becomes rich. But the degree and speed of Japan's transition stands out.

There are ways, theoretically, that Japan could counter population decline. It could import labor, but the sheer number of workers it would need to import—hundreds of thousands every year just to keep the labor supply steady—makes that

---

Brad Glosserman is executive director of Pacific Forum CSIS, a non-profit foreign policy research institute affiliated with the Center for Strategic and International Studies in Washington, DC.

option implausible for a country historically hostile to immigrants. Technological fixes, such as robots, can help to compensate for labor shortages. Finally, and potentially most significantly, Japan could give women real options so that they would be more inclined to have more children. But resistance to such change, I have concluded, is deeply ingrained. Japan has been alerted to the consequences of its treatment of women for decades, has felt the effects for years, and yet continues to trundle along without altering its course.

Japan as number 11

The most obvious and alarming implications of an aging society are economic. A graying population drains a nation of its economic vitality. Japan will likely still be wealthy in 2030, but it will be living off that wealth, not generating new capital. Foreign investment, already low, will be diverted to bigger, more dynamic markets (except for businesses that target older consumers). Local savings not drawn down to pay for retirement will likely flee in search of more lucrative returns.

Delaying retirement cannot solve the problem. Rising productivity demands constant change and adaptation. Entrepreneurism and innovation are more closely associated with youth; older workers are more conservative and more risk averse. By every measure, the economy will shrink, and so will the tax base, at the very time an aging society will be demanding more social services.

The IMF estimates that Japan's GDP could fall 20 percent, in real terms, over the next century compared with what it would be if population size remained constant. Household wealth will stop growing and begin an absolute decline over the next two decades. By 2024, household wealth will have returned to 1997 levels.

Equally important but less tangible, demographic change threatens to suck the vitality out of Japanese society. Tokyo is likely to be home to an ever-larger proportion of the Japanese population. There will always be pockets of youth and activity— Shibuya will continue to be the epicenter of youth culture—but city life as a whole will slow down. Urban life will become increasingly stratified by age and income level, with a relatively affluent older generation consuming its savings and a less well-off youth and middle-age cohort struggling to make ends meet as a rising share of their income is consumed by taxes. A geriatric Japan won't be a preferred destination for tourists unless they are elderly themselves, looking for a safe, secure, and comfortable vacation experience.

Younger Japanese will likely resent the burdens they must shoulder—high taxes, the care of aging parents and grandparents—and the diminishing say they have over their future. Energetic and creative individuals will move abroad in search of opportunities, leaving the quiescent, the stolid, and the unimaginative to constitute the mainstream of Japanese society. In short, every development will reinforce the country's downward slide.

More than 30 years ago, Ezra Vogel's best seller, *Japan As Number One*, focused international attention on the country's meteoric rise and reshaped expectations of its potential. Today, the IMF estimates that Japan will rank eighth among nations, in nominal GDP, by 2050; Goldman Sachs anticipates a steeper slide, estimating that Japan will be number 11.

The limits of hard power

Japan's relative economic decline will have profound implications for its international standing. Since the founding of the modern state, national wealth has been an important source of power and status, often used to underwrite strong militaries. Even postwar Japan, which has constitutional limits on military spending, developed a formidable military machine. (A defense budget limited to 1 percent of GDP still yields a chunk of change when it is 1 percent of one the world's largest economies.)

But Japanese defense expenditures have been declining in real terms since 2002 and that downward trajectory should steepen as the society ages and governments must make choices among spending priorities. An older society is more likely to put scarce tax dollars into health care and other domestic needs rather than expensive defense systems. Even more significant, however, will be Japan's reluctance to send an increasingly precious resource—the younger, most productive members of society—into harm's way. And remember, the military, which has not been a popular career in postwar Japan, will have to pay high salaries to attract personnel in a market characterized by labor shortages.

Postwar Japan has, of course, been notably reluctant to use its not-inconsiderable military to advance its national interests. That reluctance isn't a bad thing but there are ways, other than combat, that militaries can contribute to international peace and security; for example, Asia experiences natural disasters on a far-too-regular basis and militaries have proven to be the most effective first-responders. New security threats, such as piracy and terrorism, demand coordinated responses. There is growing demand for peacekeepers to create and preserve peace in fragile or failing states.

Tokyo's Café Rottenmeier: Sit up straight and mind your elders.
© Kazuhiro Nogi/AFP/Getty Images

Japan recognized this new opportunity—some would say "demand" —to demonstrate such support in the aftermath of the first Persian Gulf War, when the country passed legislation that legalized its participation in such efforts. But a changing demographic profile is likely to scale back the contributions Japan can make in this area. And to the extent that it doesn't do the difficult and dangerous work, it is going to lose its place at the international table to those that will.

Other factors will also shrink Japan's international stature. In the 1980s, Japan articulated the idea of "comprehensive security," a concept that put as much emphasis on political and economic means as military ones to secure its national interests. For Tokyo, Overseas Development Assistance (ODA) was a key part of this idea. Tokyo used ODA to foster mutual understanding and closer diplomatic ties; generosity gave Japan considerable international clout and prestige.

The government and the private sector worked hand in hand to underwrite the economic development that served as a springboard for East Asia's growth and extended Tokyo's influence. Opinion surveys in Southeast Asia confirm that Japan's readiness to provide funds, through the public and private sectors, boosted the country's popularity and image. At a minimum, ODA has mitigated some of the lingering memories of World War II.

Japan was the world's leading provider of ODA from 1991 to 2000; since 1997, though, the budget has declined about 40 percent in real terms. Japan ranked third as a provider of assistance by 2006 and fifth by 2007. Diminishing national resources that result from an aging society will make that decline sharper still.

That retrenchment will be paralleled by gradual economic disengagement. A shrinking domestic market might seem like a reason to become more international but younger Japanese people appear increasingly isolationist. Opinion surveys and anecdotes reveal that a growing number of younger people feel no need to learn English or venture beyond their shores for experience or opportunity. Part of the reason is that businesses, which funded much overseas education, have cut back. An equally important explanation is that the younger Japanese simply feel no urgency to leave the cocoon of their comfortable society. And if they are like this at 20, imagine how they will see the world when they are 50, or 80.

There is another way Japan's economic stagnation could hurt: Tokyo recycles its still-impressive trade surplus—about $30 billion in 2009—by investing in US Treasury bills. This policy has underwritten US consumption of Japanese goods and helped the United States cover its budget deficits. As of August 2010, Japan held $836 billion in T-bills (second only to China).

An aging Japan will no longer be able to recycle those surpluses. Actually, an aging Japan will not have those surpluses: its trade accounts will fall into deficit and funds that are available, along with previous holdings, will be needed at home.

This change of position will be gradual; moreover, rising powers like Brazil, South Korea, and India could take up Japan's slack. But the United States cannot simply assume a soft landing. For one thing, China and South Korea are aging, too. They will increasingly need those funds themselves, to finance domestic investment and to pay for pensions and health care. The Chinese may begin to wonder why they are financing a rival power. So it is somewhere between possible and plausible that this loss of cheap capital could drive up the cost of borrowing in the United States—and thus have profound implications for US fiscal and economic policy.

The possibilities of soft power
Soft power is the ability of a nation to rally other countries behind its leadership on the basis of shared ideals and values. (Hard power employs force or coercion.) Soft power shouldn't be confused with popularity or attractiveness; the fact that *anime* or *manga* are read the world over doesn't mean that Japan is more likely to be listened to.

The point is that while the negative implications of Japan's demographic transition are serious, some positive outcomes are also possible with the deft use of soft power.

For example, the emerging profile of a militarily weaker and substantially older country should once and for all drive a stake through the heart of the regional bogeyman that sees (or pretends to see) Japan as a country yearning to return to a nationalistic imperialism. A nation that can no longer staff or finance its military cannot be considered a threat to its neighbors. That reality should stop the need to demonize Japan, reduce tensions in northeast Asia, and eliminate one reason for military buildups.

In fairness, part of the demonization is the outgrowth of domestic politics in other countries; a foreign scapegoat is always handy. But to the extent that there are genuine concerns about Japanese intentions, relentless aging will help kill those worries.

An innovative and ambitious Japanese leadership could use demographic change to drive a fundamental shift in foreign policy. Two decades ago, there was a certain hubris associated with Japan's rise to international prominence. No more. Now there seems to be comfort in the idea of being a "middle power" that could spearhead regional diplomacy, and encourage greater cooperation among like-minded and similarly situated countries. South Korea is the most obvious partner, but Australia also fits the bill.

As a first step, Japanese leaders could recognize that the existing territorial conflicts with its neighbors are simply not worth contesting. Renouncing those claims— Japan has territorial disputes with South Korea (the Liancourt Rocks in the Sea of Japan); China (the Senkaku/Daoyutai islands); and Russia (the Northern Territories/ Kuriles)—would not only eliminate an irritant in bilateral relations but also set a powerful diplomatic example of how a nation can resolve thorny and enduring disputes.

The counter-argument is that Tokyo would look weak, making the country vulnerable to predatory diplomacy and bullying. Given the conflict with China in 2010 over the Senkakus—the only disputed islands Japan actually possesses (the others it is contesting)—it is fair to say that relinquishing them might send the wrong signal to Beijing. But in the case of South Korea and Russia, I think Japan could make a strong argument that it was practicing principled diplomacy and developing a national security strategy better suited to its needs (and this argument might eventually be true even of the Senkakus). Eliminating these sources of contention—and remember, we are talking about mostly uninhabited specks of rock—will reduce lingering suspicions of Japan and thus ease relations with its neighbors.

A country with diminished resources—as will be the case with Japan—will likely find it easier to reach out for help in dealing with shared problems. And those countries will be less hesitant about reaching back. China, Japan, and South Korea, for all their differences, have many cultural convergences. They confront the same trends and pressures, such as nationalism, aging, and reconciling Confucian societies with Western influences. Geographic proximity means that they are equally affected by problems such as sea-lane security, environmental degradation, and instability in North Korea. There is every reason for these countries to work together to solve future challenges. And working together on shared concerns is the best way to build the trust that will be the foundation of a stable and secure regional order that successfully deals with a rising China.

Japan can be a catalyst in this effort—in effect, turning its relative weakness into a diplomatic strength—by becoming an important part of something greater than itself. In the way that France has used its position in the European Union to remain a key regional power, Japan can leverage its own relatively weaker position to remain a force in Asia.

Pushing on an open door

At key moments in history, the Japanese have grappled with fundamental choices. During the Meiji Restoration, national leaders had to decide whether to open the country to the world or try to stay closed. Then, after the devastation of World War II, Japan had to give up its imperial ambitions; it rebuilt itself to become, for a time, the world's second-largest economy.

Since the end of the Cold War, Japan has chosen the path of least resistance, putting off any real debate about the future. Still, 20 years of economic stagnation have divided Japanese society. Some argue that the country must abandon the economic policies that propelled it into the upper-most ranks of nations. Others consider that course far too risky. In the absence of consensus, the country has drifted.

But the failure to make a choice is, of course, a choice in itself. Japan, in essence, has opted for slow and genteel decline rather than upend a social order that has delivered great benefits to most of its citizens. Japan has chosen the devil it thinks it knows—demographic decline—over radical changes that do not come with any guarantee of success.

As a result, Japan appears to be at the mercy of forces—demographic transformation and economic decline—that defy political manipulation. A thoughtful and assertive strategy that exploits the country's soft power could, however, help to compensate for the loss of its absolute power. Going in this direction requires leadership, vision, the readiness to make hard choices, and the ability to follow through on them.

In short, soft power demands wisdom, a virtue that often—but not always—comes with age.

CHAPTER THREE: RESTRUCTURING JAPAN INC.

Photograph © Winhorse

ASIA'S SLEEPING GIANT

STEPHEN S. ROACH

TWO DECADES AFTER THE SPECTACULAR IMPLOSION of Japan's "bubble economy," the lessons of the descent—to say nothing of the torpor that has followed—remain vital to the global debate. After all these years, there is still considerable disagreement over where Japan went wrong and what the rest of the world can do to avoid a similar fate. Indeed, the search to understand how Japan lost its way has assumed even greater significance in the aftermath of the Great Financial Crisis of 2008–09.

Curiously, that debate had become somewhat less intense inside of Japan in recent years. A long and arduous postbubble shakeout gave way to a grim sense of resignation. The demographic headwinds of an aging, and now declining population, in conjunction with the political instability following the dismantling of a long-entrenched leadership structure, dulled any sense of reawakening. Losing the distinction as the world's second-largest economy only deepened Japan's wounded sense of national pride.

But now Japan faces a new crisis. The devastation of the March 2011 Tohoku earthquake, and the tsunami and Fukushima nuclear emergency that followed, has galvanized a nation mired in two lost decades. Out of crisis often comes reawakening. Today's Japan has just such an opportunity.

But as was the case in the aftermath of the Hanshin earthquake that devastated Kobe in 1995, there are no guarantees that the inevitable rebuilding will spark a sustained economic revival. While the Japanese economy did, in fact, rebound in 1996, weakness quickly resumed in 1997. A key lesson from that earlier period:

Stephen S. Roach is a senior fellow in the Jackson Institute for Global Affairs at Yale University and non-executive chairman of Morgan Stanley Asia.

Contributing to TFP?
© Yoshikazu Tsuno/AFP/Getty Images

postdisaster rebounds do not alleviate the need for any nation to come to grips with its deep-rooted economic malaise.[1]

There is still intense debate over how Japan should do that. Many in the West cling to the view that Japan's lost decades are traceable more to policy blunders than to structural problems in the Japanese economy.[2] If only Japanese policy makers had been quicker and more forceful in their response, goes the argument, Japan would have lost just years, not decades.

Significantly, this same mind-set pervades the current debate in the West, where policy activists are adamant in insisting that aggressive stimulus is needed to ward off a Japanese-like endgame in the United States and Europe. The Federal Reserve's

1 The comparisons between these two major earthquakes in Japan may, however, be very misleading. In terms of the sheer physical shock, the current disaster dwarfs that of some 15 years ago. With a magnitude of 9.0 on the Richter scale, the Tohoku quake released about 350 times more energy than did the Hanshin quake with a magnitude of 7.3. And, of course, the earlier disaster did not have catastrophic—and potentially lasting—nuclear ramifications.

2 See Adam S. Posen, Restoring Japan's Economic Growth, Institute for International Economics, 1998.

move in 2010 to implement yet another round of quantitative easing is very much an outgrowth of the view that has long guided US monetary policy in fending off the risks of a Japanese-style deflation—the need to err on the side of a quick and massive postbubble stimulus.[3]

If only the solutions were that easy. The policy blunder excuse—namely, the relative impotence of timid responses by both monetary and fiscal authorities—stems from the standard postmortem on the Great Depression of 1930s. Just as the Keynesian prescription of policy activism is widely viewed as the cure to that catastrophic period, a similar remedy is deemed to be appropriate for Japan as well as for other major economies struggling in the years following the crisis of 2008–09.

But is it? In Japan, a postbubble slowdown in productivity growth suggests a very different diagnosis of the problem. Specifically, consider the record on total factor productivity (TFP)—the growth in a nation's output that is traceable to the improved efficiency of the economy rather than to increases in the number of workers and the amount of machinery. By this measure, Japan's once rapidly improving efficiency came to a virtual standstill in the 1990s. According to one highly credible estimate, gains in TFP averaged just 0.2 percent per year over the 1991-to-2000 postbubble period, a dramatic deceleration from the 2.4 percent average annual rate of the 1983-to-1991 prebubble interval.[4]

This estimate suggests Japan's economy was afflicted by something other than macro policy errors. The most persuasive explanation focuses on the reluctance of Japanese businesses—banks and nonfinancial corporations alike—to embrace aggressive restructuring strategies. Put another way, the real villain in Japan's postbubble malaise may well be the notorious "zombie" syndrome: the productivity-inhibiting role of life-support credit lines that many banks provided to increasingly sclerotic companies that otherwise would have failed.[5]

The walking dead can hardly be expected to spark productivity enhancement in Japan or, for that matter, in any nation. That lesson seems all but lost amid the plethora of bailouts governments around the world undertook in 2008–09. From Wall Street, to AIG, to Detroit, the United States has certainly flirted with its own generation of zombies. The same can be said of Britain and Europe. Think RBS, HBOS-Lloyds, Fortis, Hypo Real Estate, and on and on. Too big to fail, they call it

---

3 See Alan Ahearne, Joseph Gagnon, Jane Haltmaier, Steve Kamin, et al., "Preventing Deflation: Lessons from Japan's Experience in the 1990s," Federal Reserve International Finance Discussion paper No. 729, June 2002, and Ben S. Bernanke, "Deflation: Making Sure 'It' Doesn't Happen Here," speech before the National Economists Club, November 2002.

4 See Fumio Hayashi and Edward C. Prescott, "The 1990s in Japan: A Lost Decade," *Review of Economic Dynamics*, 2002. While these estimates are very much at odds with a more optimistic assessment of total factor productivity presented in Posen (op. cit.), they are broadly consistent with a fairly detailed analysis provided by Takanobu Nakajima, Koji Nomura, and Toshiyuki Matsuura, "Overview of the Japanese Economy During the Lost Decade," in *Total Factor Productivity Growth: Survey Report*, Asian Productivity Organization, 2004.

5 See Ricardo J. Caballero, Takeo Hoshi, and Anil K. Kashyap, "Zombie Lending and Depressed Restructuring in Japan," National Bureau of Economic Research Working Paper No. 12129, April 2006.

in the West. But how different is that from Japan's zombies and from the postcrisis problems that arise from the compassionate but ultimately counterproductive actions aimed at containing the damage during moments of crisis and distress? If the Japanese experience is relevant, this same defense mechanism could sow the seeds of the West's own protracted period of postbubble stagnation, in other words, a globalization of Japanese-like lost decades.

Some of Japan's woes, to be sure, stem from plain bad luck. The global recession of 2008–09 came at a time when the Japanese economy appeared to be on the mend. But the steep downturn that ensued was a grim reminder of the limits of postbubble resilience, especially for an externally dependent Japanese economy whose fortunes are tightly intertwined with the global trade cycle. When world trade plunged by a record 11.3 percent in 2009, there was no place for Japan (or, for that matter, any export-led economy) to hide. For Japan, that relapse—its fourth postbubble downturn—further soured the national mood. And now an earthquake-related recession seems like yet another unfortunate turn. The lesson for Japan, or, for that matter, any economy: anemic postbubble economies are particularly relapse-prone in the event of a shock.

Unlike earlier travails in Japan's postbubble malaise, the authorities have been quick to respond to the Tohoku earthquake. However, if the core diagnosis of the underlying problems is structural and not because of a lack of sufficient cyclical stimulus, the policy prescriptions are very different.

The limits of cyclical stimulus as a remedy for structural weakness are particularly relevant for the Japanese economy in light of the major demographic challenges of a now-shrinking population.[6] A declining population means that only limited economic growth can come from consumers, whose spending still accounts for nearly 60 percent of Japan's GDP. That, in turn, forces Japan to consider two possible offsets: a turnaround in productivity growth or a new impetus from exports and external demand.

On the productivity front, the good news is that corporate Japan has finally come to grips with tough competitive challenges. The once-sacrosanct institution of lifetime employment has been all but dismantled. And a broad cross-section of businesses have made meaningful progress on the road to restructuring. All of Japan's major banks have been reconstituted and recapitalized, and restructuring has strengthened many of the country's major nonfinancial companies such as Nissan (cars), ANA (airlines), Marubeni (trading), Kawasaki Kisen (sea transport), Kobe Steel (steel), Kajima (construction), and Obayashi-gumi (construction). As a result, the inefficiencies of "zombie congestion" have begun to recede.[7]

6 According to the United Nations World Population Prospects, Japan's population peaked at 127.449 million in 2005 and is estimated to have declined to 126.995 million in 2010. A further sharp decline to 101.659 million is projected by 2050.

7 A recent extension of the analysis of Caballero, Hoshi, and Kashyap confirms a significant reduction in the incidence of Japanese zombies since 2002; see Shin-ichi Fukuda and Jun-ichi Nakamura, "Why Did 'Zombie' Firms Recover in Japan?" Center for International Research on the Japanese Economy (CIRJE) Discussion Paper F-751, July 2010.

When it comes to additional measures that might enhance Japanese productivity, there is ample low-hanging fruit. Three areas offer particularly significant potential:

1. Japan has been a laggard in embracing corporate strategies that use information technology (IT) to boost productivity, especially in labor-intensive service industries. This reluctance is an outgrowth of the legacy effects of lifetime employment and the related unwillingness of Japanese companies to substitute advanced technologies for labor. Recent trends are more encouraging. As of 2008, IT-related investment had risen to 24 percent of total Japanese capital expenditures, more than double the 11 percent share in 1990. That brought Japan's IT expenditures up to 6.7 percent of its GDP—second among major economies to the United States, where the share was 7.4 percent of GDP, but ahead of China (5.9 percent), Germany (5.4 percent), and France (5.2 percent).

2. The privatization of Japan Post—a major objective of the Koizumi government—has stalled. As a result, the lumbering bureaucracy of a government-owned savings system has retained its distortive role in allocating capital. The privatization effort needs to be restarted, with an aim of allowing this massive pool of state-controlled savings to seek higher productivity-enhancing returns in the private sector.

3. Japan's outsize government debt load, in addition to posing concerns about long-term stability, has important implications for productivity as well. With public-sector debt now at 200 percent of GDP—and rising, especially in the aftermath of the Tohoku earthquake—Japanese savers are overinvested in low-yielding government securities. That asset allocation soaks up too much of the nation's scarce capital, thereby inhibiting corporate investment and related productivity enhancement strategies.

However, even if Japan were to act on this agenda and realize a sustained improvement in productivity, a significant portion of those gains would be offset by the effects of a declining population. That, in turn, puts the squeeze on Japan's domestic income-generating capacity and leaves the nation with little choice other than to look offshore in its search for growth.

The export sector has been Japan's strongest source of growth for quite some time. After slipping to less than 10 percent of GDP in the mid-1990s, the export share almost doubled to some 20 percent in 2007 before plunging during the recession of 2008–09. A key factor behind this development was a stunning shift in the mix of Japan's external markets. The United States had long been Japan's largest export market, accounting for 30 percent of total Japanese exports as recently as 2001. Those days are now over. Today, China is Japan's largest export market, purchasing about 20 percent of Japan's overseas shipments, well above the sharply diminished 16 percent share now going to the United States.

This change in Japan's export mix has come at a fortuitous time. Up until recently, much of China's demand for Japanese goods—sophisticated machines and components in particular—had been aimed at producing exports for shipment to the United States and Europe. But now China, in response to a confluence of internal and external pressures, is about to change its own growth model in a fashion that could be hugely beneficial to Japan. After 30 years of export- and investment-led growth, China seems likely to shift to a more consumer-focused economy. With Chinese imports consistently running between 25 and 30 percent of its GDP in recent years, this transformation should provide a major impetus to China's trading partners.

No economy stands to gain more from the coming shift in China than Japan, which now ranks as China's No. 1 foreign supplier. In 2009, Japanese sales into Chinese markets totaled $131 billion, nearly 30 percent higher than No. 2 South Korea. Consequently, Japan is not only well positioned to source a meaningful portion of China's likely increase in consumer products (ranging from motor vehicles and appliances to pharmaceuticals and cosmetics), but also has a comparative advantage in many of the special products and technologies that China needs to satisfy its increasingly urgent alternative energy and environmental objectives.

GAINS IN TOTAL FACTOR PRODUCTIVITY AVERAGED JUST 0.2 PERCENT PER YEAR FROM 1991-2000, DOWN FROM THE 2.4 PERCENT AVERAGE FROM 1983 TO 1991.

Therein lies what could well be the most promising opportunity to end Japan's corrosive string of lost decades. Although fraught with obvious risks, a China-centric impetus to Japanese exports offers great potential. Yet, as the spat over the Senkaku and Diaoyu islands in 2010 indicates, there is always the possibility that a long history of bad blood between the two countries could lead to a damaging rupture in economic ties. Notwithstanding this setback, the record in recent years actually provides grounds for optimism. Time and again, economic pragmatism has trumped political frictions in cementing increasingly tighter trade and direct-investment relations between Japan and China. As far-fetched as it may seem today, the establishment of a free-trade arrangement between these two nations could well be the icing on the cake for an export-led renewal of Japanese economic growth.

In the past 20 years, Japan's postbubble healing has been long and arduous, with far too many setbacks along the way. Understandably, the Japanese spirit is wounded. But there are now grounds for encouragement, especially on the productivity and export fronts. With a disciplined and focused policy agenda, Japan can find a way out. All that is missing now is leadership and a strong national resolve. The focus and indomitable spirit of post-earthquake Japan are especially encouraging in that regard.

Meanwhile, the jury is out on whether the Western world can escape a Japanese-style fate. There are certainly some disconcerting similarities, especially the predictable outbreak of postbubble denial that always seems to pervade the political response and the policy debate. Unfortunately, the more the rest of the world remains convinced that it can borrow from Japan's failed macro policies, such as quantitative easing and massive government borrowing, the greater the risk other countries will suffer lost decades of their own.

SEND IN THE SAMURAI

ADAM S. POSEN[1]

FOR SEVERAL DECADES, business and economic pundits have exoticized Japan's economy. The supposed lost decades since 1990 have only heightened perceptions of a country whose economic system operates in unique ways, not subject to standard economic analysis. Surprisingly, the global financial crisis of 2008–09 seemed to reinforce the sense of Japanese economic performance as being unusual and long lost, even as several major economies show distinct parallels to Japan's postbubble experience. This view of Japan as atypical and mysterious is, however, unfounded and can lead to deeply mistaken conclusions about the country's longer-term economic prospects. The tragedy of the March 2011 earthquake and tsunami will do nothing to dislodge the Japanese economy from the long-term development path common to all advanced economies.

As portrayed in the work of the legendary Japanese film director Akira Kurosawa, there are universal concerns for all humans, Japanese or foreign, and these can be conveyed by globally shared forms of storytelling. So, too, can there be a common understanding of the Japanese economy using a general analytical framework. The story to be told is not *Rashomon*, where it is anybody's guess what happened to Japan in the 1990s. Nor is the story *Ran*, where one critical event—an asset price bubble and its implosion—determined the course of the next decade. The story of Japan's economy in the 1990s is that of *Seven Samurai*, in which a terrible negative shock disrupts the normal cycles of Japanese economic life, eroding communal

---

1 The views expressed in this essay are solely those of the author.

Adam S. Posen is a senior fellow at the Peterson Institute for International Economics in Washington, DC, and an external member of the Bank of England's monetary policy committee.

prosperity until strong leadership requiring significant sacrifice is exerted to restore normality. Seen that way, the future for Japan's economy is of continued normality in the absence of new, self-destructive social or policy paths—and the ability to overcome even a horrendous natural disaster.

In more direct terms, for all of Japan's cultural distinctiveness, the country's economy is governed by the same forces and processes that govern the macroeconomic performance of other advanced capitalist economies. In fact, Japan in the 1990s shared many problems that are characteristic of the United Kingdom, the United States, and other European economies today; those episodes, in turn, have much in common with previous generations' experience in the Great Depression of the 1930s. Japan responded in the same way other economies have when confronted with a similar kind of financial shock.

What stands out about the Japan experience is the duration of its Great Recession. Yet, Japan's lasting economic underperformance in the 1990s was attributable to readily comprehensible macroeconomic and financial policy mistakes recognized by some at the time.[2] The Bank of Japan was slow to cut interest rates, and still slower to adopt additional monetary stimulus measures after the bubble collapsed. The Japanese government raised the consumption tax significantly in 1997, cutting off the first recovery from the crisis, and throughout the 1990s engaged in far less actual fiscal stimulus than advertized, let alone needed. Bad real-estate loans were allowed to fester, eating away at the capital of the entire banking system over the course of the decade, creating instability and capital misallocation. Stronger, more responsible macroeconomic policies could have prevented the initial recession of 1992–95 from deepening and dragging on until 2002. Unfortunately, the current global financial crisis reveals other countries' similarities with Japan extend to political economy to some degree, as manifested in the reversals and half-measures in macroeconomic stimulus and bank recapitalization in those countries as well. If anything, recent experience demonstrates that Japan is an even more normal economy than commonly realized.

THE STORY OF JAPAN'S ECONOMY IN THE 1990s IS THAT OF *SEVEN SAMURAI*: A TERRIBLE NEGATIVE SHOCK DISRUPTS THE NORMAL CYCLES OF JAPANESE ECONOMIC LIFE.

Perhaps because of the persistent false perception of exceptionalism, current commentary about Japan's economy often overlooks or dismisses how well its economy performed in the 2000s until the global crisis hit. In fact, once the policy mistakes of the 1990s were reversed by then-Prime Minister Junichiro Koizumi and Cabinet Minister Heizo Takenaka, the Japanese economy recovered strongly and in a sustainable manner.[3] In contrast to claims that Japan was fundamentally

2 Adam S. Posen, *Restoring Japan's Economic Growth*, PIIE, 1998.
3 Adam S. Posen, "The Realities and Relevance of Japan's Great Recession: Neither *Ran* nor *Rashomon*," STICERD Public Lecture, London School of Economics, May 24, 2010. Available at: http://www.piie.com/publications/interstitial.cfm?ResearchID=1592.

unsound and perhaps incapable of growing, real GDP growth actually returned to its long-term trend rate, consistent with the view that policy mistakes rather than structural issues had held Japan back. Furthermore, the recovery was no mere sopping up of idle labor and equipment, which would have run out when spare capacity had been used up. In fact, the recovery of 2002–08 was the longest unbroken expansion in Japan's postwar history.

The real evidence of Japan's underlying economic vigor comes from the fact that Japan's recovery was driven by ongoing progress in productivity. Japanese annual total factor productivity (TFP) growth was the highest or second-highest among the G-5 (France, Germany, Japan, the United Kingdom, and the United States) in most of the last decade's pre-crisis years. (TFP refers to the growth in national output that cannot be attributed to increases in labor or capital, that is, growth attributable to technological and process improvement.) Over the period between the start of Japanese recovery (2002: Q2) and the start of the global crisis (2008: Q3), Japan had the highest average annual GDP growth per worker, and by a large margin the highest annual TFP growth, during a period when all the major economies were doing well. Some critics have claimed falsely that it was a decline in Japan's productivity—the country's structural problems catching up with it—that caused the recession, rather than a decline in demand driven by the crash and subsequent policy. Yet, the recovery of Japanese corporate investment and productivity as soon as macroeconomic problems were resolved gives the lie to this view.[4]

Thus, Japan's prospects over the coming decades should be fine for a normal country at the global technology frontier, with ample savings, and secure property rights. The economy should grow over time at approximately the rate of productivity growth—around 2 percent annually—adjusted for changes in prices and population size. The country should have normal business cycles and be vulnerable to external or further weather shocks, but not display any unusual patterns.

Yes, the Japanese population is aging rapidly, but what matters for human welfare and for sustainable performance is *per capita* income growth, and demographics do not prevent sustained growth by that measure. The meaning of the terrible loss of life in Japan's 2011 earthquake and tsunami cannot be captured in economic metrics. But from the narrow view of longer-term economic prospects, the loss is insufficient to alter the country's current or future workforce on a national scale.

Yes, the outstanding public debt level is very high, but the national savings available to fund government borrowing remains far larger still, indebtedness to foreigners remains insignificant, and Japan has $3 trillion (around two-thirds of GDP) in foreign assets to draw down if needed. Given the absence of foreign creditors who could cease to lend money and even sell off Japanese debt, the likelihood is very low that the Japanese government would suffer the "sudden stop" of credit that has afflicted other countries. Rebuilding the devastated parts of Japan's northeast regions

---

4 Adam S. Posen, "Unchanging Innovation and Changing National Economic Performance in Japan," in Richard Nelson, Benn Steil, and David Victor, eds., *Technological Innovation and Economic Performance*, Princeton University Press, 2002, pp. 74–111. Available at: http://www.piie.com/publications/wp/01-5.pdf

would cost on the order of a few percent of GDP spread over three to five years, and thus be readily financial. Absent a flight of domestic savings from Japan, which would drive up interest rates on government debt, the long-run fiscal situation can be managed with moderate adjustments of the kind also needed in the United States and other market economies.

Most troublingly, Japan has suffered persistent deflation, with the attendant drag on the economy. But even deflation is surmountable in the years to come. Just as the long recovery of 2002–08 finally brought inflation back above zero before the crisis hit, the current recovery will bring Japan back to price stability. An inevitable depreciation of the yen against the euro, the Chinese yuan, and other currencies pegged to the yuan, will in coming years help overcome deflationary trends, as will mounting global upward pressure on energy import prices.

It is of course possible to list those areas begging for structural reform in Japan, most notably the underutilization of female and younger workers and the inefficient service sector. While intolerance is the major cause of these deficiencies, and while that intolerance is distasteful to many Japanese as well as to most Western observers (including myself), the significance of such deficiencies in purely economic terms should be kept in perspective. Throughout most of Western Europe, youth unemployment is high and service industries are protected from competition; the US labor market also has been showing recent signs of what used to be called Eurosclerosis. If anything, fixing this situation gives Japan a potential remedy for some labor

They provided leadership in the face of crisis.
© 1954 TOHO CO., LTD. © 1954 Seven Samurai TOHO CO., LTD

supply shortages that will emerge as its population ages. With Japanese birth rates
so low, there is little need for welfare state expansion on the scale required in some
other countries to increase female employment. Thus, for Japan, structural reform
is a matter of attitudes more than of money. The now-urgent need for improvements
in the Japanese energy grid and in nuclear safety is material in human terms, but
will not be major drivers of productivity trends one way or another.

More dangerous than structural limitations is the possibility of Japanese policy
makers repeating the macroeconomic mistakes of the 1990s, errors that, unfortunately, now find an echo in the United States and Western Europe. The greatest risk
is that Japanese policy makers will again underestimate the potential growth rate
of Japan and keep monetary or fiscal policy too tight out of fear the economy might
overheat or tax revenues prove insufficient. That sort of mistaken forecast by policy
makers could become a self-fulfilling prophecy, which could play out in two possible
ways. First, tight policy could lead to poor growth that would be seen to vindicate
the mistakenly low estimate of economic potential. Second, long-term underemployment of workers and equipment could lead to actual erosion of supply capacity,
that is, unemployed workers could be deemed unemploy-
able, and production lines could be scrapped without being
replaced.[5] That danger is the primary reason for stating
clearly the facts of Japan's strong recovery in the 2000s,
when mistaken policies were reversed, and for grasping
the positive implications of that recovery for the country's
growth potential.

BELIEVING IN THE ECONOMY'S ABNORMALITY LEADS TO DEEPLY MISTAKEN CONCLUSIONS ABOUT JAPAN'S LONGER-TERM ECONOMIC PROSPECTS.

To ensure further against macroeconomic mistakes, Japan can institutionalize rules to govern policy making, rather
than leave policy open to the mistakes of overly conservative
bureaucrats with too much discretionary power. One good
measure in this regard would be for the Bank of Japan to
adopt a public inflation target set well above zero, which would force the bank to take
steps to resist deflation, rather than to worry solely about risks of high inflation. Japan's system for public budgeting could be changed in ways that would offer more au-
tomatic stabilization, which would mean a higher tax burden and lower expenditures
when times were good, and a lower tax burden with higher expenditures when times
were bad, without any assessments—let alone decisions—to be taken by officials. To
do so, the government could shift to more mechanical methods of revenue collection
without loopholes, such as the value-added tax, rather than allow small businesses to
self-report their incomes and take deductions. A more transparent and rules-based
means of allocating tax revenues between central and prefectural governments would
also limit the room for official mistakes in times of recession. The exceptional monetary and fiscal response to the March 2011 earthquake and tsunami would have fewer
disruptive side effects if such a policy framework were in place.

5 Adam S. Posen, "The Central Banker's Case for Doing More," *PIIE Policy Brief* No. 10-24, November.
Available at: http://www.piie.com/publications/interstitial.cfm?ResearchID=1680

Japan need not be satisfied with being a normally growing advanced economy (though too much melancholic comparison to past economic glories would itself be unreasonable if not harmful). As noted, Japan already holds its place at the top table among the major economies in terms of productivity growth, which for an advanced and aging economy is the one source of sustainable good performance. Yet, if Japan were truly to open its labor markets to female workers, extend liberalization of its service industries beyond just the financial sector, and expose its protected industries to greater international competition, the Japanese economy could be all the more successful for years to come.

In particular, if Japanese business can further overcome the mutual distrust among Japan's Asian neighbors to enable continued investment in the region, as well as to accept inward investment on a much greater scale, Japan could become a still-greater managerial, financial, and technological hub for the developing economies of the world's fastest-growing region. Given the fundamental strengths of Japan's normal economy, and absent all-too-normal policy mistakes, there is an excellent basis for an ongoing upward trajectory. If the natural vulnerabilities shown in Japan's quake and tsunami give more impetus at the margin for Japanese companies to move physical capital and production abroad, while retaining human and intellectual capital ownership, so much the better.

In a sense, the Japanese economy is becoming British. No longer a dominant player, and unable to reclaim (exaggerated and unsustainable) past glories, Japan, like Britain, must recognize that its best hope for the future lies with sensible macroeconomic management, a stable world-class financial system, high flows of foreign direct investment in and out of the country, and the export of business services to accompany those investments. Some high-value-added manufacturing will remain onshore, and soft exports such as cultural goods and tourism will play an increasingly important role.

Most advantageously, the economy will be tied to the asynchronized business cycles of two much larger economic regions, Greater China and NAFTA America, just as the UK's trade and relationships straddle the euro area and NAFTA America. Japan's economy will remain sufficiently large and on its own cycle that, like the United Kingdom, it can benefit from keeping its own currency and thus monetary independence.

That is not a hugely exciting future, nor a terribly distinctive one. But it does imply that Japan will have a nice economic garden of its own to tend, a goal upon which both Japanese and British concepts of normal life rightly place high value. As Kurosawa shows in *Seven Samurai*, and as the world has seen in the response of the Japanese people to the earthquake and tsunami disaster of March 2011, a return to normal hard work and rewards in conditions of social peace is something for which to be grateful.

LEARNING FROM THE "LOST DECADES"

MOHAMED A. EL-ERIAN

IT IS TIME TO REASSESS the familiar narrative about Japan's decline as a global economic power. For years now, conventional wisdom has attributed Japan's disappointing economic performance over two "lost decades" to a combination of uniquely Japanese failings: economic policy errors, weak corporate governance, and a reluctance to undertake pro-market reforms. But in light of the difficulties facing policy makers in Europe and the United States to respond to shocks to their own economies in recent years, that judgment—and its implied assumption of Western superiority—now seems simplistic and unfair.

Indeed, Western policy makers' recent disappointments suggest that restoring growth in the wake of wrenching economic downturns is a far more complicated business than most economists have led us to believe—regardless of whether those downturns were brought on by the implosion of a speculative stock and property bubble (as we saw in Japan in early 1990s), or a financial panic and disorderly deleveraging triggered by the failure of a leading financial entity (the crisis that swept Europe and the United States after the fall of Lehman Brothers in 2008), or a sovereign debt crisis (such as the one that engulfed the peripheral countries of the European monetary zone in 2010–11).

Reappraising how the Japanese "miracle" came undone, and why it was so difficult to revive after the asset bubble burst, is a matter of more than academic interest. The importance of the Japan question also transcends the narrow debate about whether the various criticisms heaped on Japanese policy makers over the years were undeserved. Correctly interpreting Japan's postbubble experience has direct

Mohamed A. El-Erian is CEO and co-CIO of PIMCO, and the author of When Markets Collide: Investment Strategies for the Age of Global Economic Change *(2008)*.

relevance to the ongoing discussion of how today's policy makers should respond to the challenges now facing the global economy. More broadly, a thorough reevaluation of the Japanese experience is vital to an informed understanding of the limits of traditional economic policy measures in reviving growth after episodes of severe financial trauma.

Learning the right lessons from the Japanese experience takes on new significance as Japan embarks on a major reconstruction program following the triple calamities of March 2011—the devastating earthquake, the tsunami, and resulting nuclear crisis. In the course of these reconstruction efforts, many aspects of the Japanese economy will be reset. Japan's politicians and policy makers will be called upon to provide a unifying vision that combines recovery with a return to high medium-term economic growth.

Well before the failure of Lehman Brothers, American academics and policy makers had formed a consensus that missteps by Japanese policy makers were to blame for Japan's 20 years of lackluster economic growth. In this view, Japan might have averted a protracted slump had the nation's central bank lowered interest rates more aggressively, and had fiscal authorities given increased government spending measures more time to take effect before talking up the need to restore fiscal discipline.

After Lehman Brothers' collapse, in rallying support for bank bailouts and government stimulus packages, officials from both the Bush and Obama administrations claimed that the United States could learn valuable lessons from Japan's

Bernanke and Shirakawa: Two puzzled central bankers.
© Tomohiro Ohsumi/Bloomberg via Getty Images

mistakes. The Japanese experience, they argued, demonstrated the need for an un-ambiguous policy narrative, bold and concerted action from government and the central bank, and unyielding commitment to avoid deflation at all costs.

When US growth stuttered despite strong stimulus measures in 2009–10, Treasury Secretary Timothy Geithner invoked the Japanese experience in arguing for even greater government intervention in the US economy. Similarly, Federal Reserve Chairman Ben Bernanke cited the need to avoid Japan's "mistakes" as justification for two rounds of quantitative easing, increasing the money supply through extraordinary Federal Reserve purchases of government bonds and other securities.

But now the simple story about how Japanese policy makers got it "wrong" is being challenged by developments in the West—and particularly economies that relied heavily on financial engineering. It is increasingly evident that the dynamics of postbubble economies are highly complex. Among the complications: the per-sistence of "balance sheet issues" facing lenders, companies, and households still struggling to reduce debt well after authorities have flooded the financial system with cheap credit; and "structural rigidities," such as the inability of private firms to resume hiring in an environment where households have cut back on spending and individuals are worried about losing their jobs or homes.

After extraordinary monetary and fiscal policies in the United States failed in 2009–10 to deliver fully on policy makers' growth and employment expectations, analysts are reconsidering how much standard macroeconomic policies can achieve in postbubble industrial economies. At its core, this reconsideration is a reassess-ment of what policy makers can deliver at a time of major national and global re-alignments. Do we expect too much of governments and central banks? How and what should policy makers communicate to the public when their policy instru-ments are dulled by debt overhangs, structural imbalances, and a private sector intent on reducing leverage?

The economies of Japan and the United States differ in many respects, but there are fundamental similarities. Both experienced significant, multiyear asset price bubbles in the run-up to financial dislocation. During these bubbles, the behavior of households and companies reflected a consensus that asset price surges would con-tinue forever. In both countries, the eventual collapse of asset prices undermined private-sector confidence and severely weakened the banking system. Economic activity declined; banks scrambled to rebuild capital badly depleted by large credit losses; the flow of credit slowed and, for some borrowers, came to a complete halt; and households deleveraged, some by choice and others of necessity.

To counter this disruptive chain reaction, authorities in both countries took ex-treme measures, injecting emergency liquidity into the system and using public bal-ance sheets to absorb private losses and keep the system afloat. In both cases, crisis-management responses were successful in reducing the risk of economic collapse.

But having staved off catastrophe, governments and central bankers in both na-tions proved far less successful in restoring postcrisis growth. In the United States, as in Japan, the recovery has been weak and protracted—in absolute terms and relative to policy makers' expectations. The shock to public finances has proved more durable than expected. The rehabilitation of banks and credit mechanisms has been slower and more painful.

CONVENTIONAL WISDOM, ESPECIALLY OUTSIDE JAPAN, HAS HELD THAT JAPANESE POLICYMAKERS WERE TOO COMPLACENT IN THE POST-CRISIS PERIOD.

While policy makers in both Japan and the United States may share an inability to reignite robust postcrisis growth, it does not necessarily follow that authorities from the two nations are struggling for the same reasons. There are crucial differences in the context of each economy's postbubble challenges. First, Japan's problems were—and remain—compounded by the country's aging population and shrinking workforce. The United States, with its more liberal immigration policies and younger population, is not similarly constrained. Second, overall global growth conditions were supportive of Japan's attempts to reinvigorate its economic growth, while the United States must grapple with a global slowdown and, in 2011, a set of supply-and-demand shocks emanating from unrest in the Middle East and disasters in Japan. Finally, Japan was aided by the willingness of the rest of the world to accommodate a weaker yen, while a weakening of the dollar has provoked much more of a global outcry.

The dominant view among economists—at least those outside Japan—remains that Japanese policy makers were too complacent in the postcrisis period. The Bank of Japan was too slow to combine policies of zero-interest rates and quantitative easing, while the Ministry of Finance was too eager to restore its credentials for fiscal prudence.

By contrast, the US policy response is seen as more proactive and robust. The Federal Reserve moved almost immediately to a policy of very low interest rates and asset purchases. In November 2010, the Fed embraced a more expansive policy of quantitative easing, known as QE2, this time aimed at turbocharging asset prices and promoting growth, as opposed to the narrower objective of stabilizing and normalizing markets. Meanwhile, in a rare instance of bipartisanship, the US Congress in the last weeks of 2010 set aside concerns about the mounting national debt and approved an additional round of fiscal stimulus.

The US approach has been praised for averting a global economic meltdown, but it has drawn its share of criticism. Some warn that low interest rates and deficit spending will culminate in a burst of inflation. Others lament that the Federal Reserve has compromised its independence, becoming little more than an adjunct of US fiscal policy. Many point to the weakening of the dollar as evidence that the Fed will end up debasing the currency with disastrous repercussions.

US trade partners, meanwhile, complain that the cheaper dollar threatens the global recovery, pressures commodity prices, and risks a round of global protectionism and competitive currency devaluations. Japanese policy makers have been increasingly public about the challenges facing the United States, and the inadvisability of drawing simple conclusions from Japan's experience. At an October 2010 meeting of the IMF and World Bank in Washington, Bank of Japan Governor Masaaki Shirakawa warned: "If foreign countries mistakenly draw the most crucial lesson from Japan's experience as the necessity of short-term stimulative policy measures, they will face a risk of writing the wrong policy prescription." Easy money alone, Shirakawa argued, "cannot solve the problem. Structural reform is indispensible."

My own view is that the world is reaching a reassessment in its understanding of Japan's economic experience. It is possible that the US approach will prove successful in reviving "animal spirits" of consumer and investor confidence, and achieve a successful transition from temporary sources of growth (policy stimulus and inventory cycles) to permanent ones (sustainable private-sector demand and investment).

That is certainly my hope, as the welfare of millions, if not billions of people around the world, is at stake. A strong and sustainable US recovery, if it materializes, would effectively put an end to the debate about what the Japanese authorities should have done back in the 1990s and even the 2000s. The lesson nearly everyone would draw is that Japanese authorities should have acted more aggressively.

IN THE U.S. AND POSSIBLY ELSEWHERE, WE ARE AT A CRITICAL JUNCTURE IN TERMS OF REVISITING JAPAN'S POLICY EXPERIENCE.

But we must also consider the possibility that the US approach will fail to deliver a rapid return to high growth and job creation. In that case, the US economy could suffer adverse side effects from its leaders' aggressive, interventionist policy approach. Those side effects could include further misallocation of resources, credit-market distortions, and damaged credibility for the Federal Reserve and other policy-making institutions. There could also be global consequences in the form of currency tensions, capital controls, protectionism, higher commodity prices, and a new wave of political instability in the emerging world.

In these circumstances, the conventional wisdom regarding Japan would have to be revisited. The emphasis on "policy mistakes" would be rejected in favor of a new recognition that postbubble dynamics are complex—too complex, perhaps, to be dealt with by demand-management policies alone. The United States would sadly be added to the long list of countries to have struggled through long, slow, postbubble workouts.

My view is that this second outcome is the more likely. The consequences of such a scenario are profound. I can think of at least five:

First, there would be much greater emphasis on the need to communicate early on the implications of national and global realignments. Leaders from all nations, rich and poor, would have to be more open about the nature of the economic challenges faced by their citizens—and more humble in acknowledging limits to the ability of governments and central banks to resolve those problems quickly. In this sense, the economic narrative of advanced economies would start to sound more like that in developing countries.

Second, the presumption for policy makers would shift from the comfort of (seemingly predictable) cyclical responses to the much more difficult task of identifying, designing, and implementing structural reforms. Here again leaders would do well to "come clean" in acknowledging that economics is not an exact science, that the consequences of economic policies are not always predictable, and that governments cannot guarantee economic outcomes.

Third, multilateral institutions must recognize the need to move more rapidly and proactively in dealing with financial crises, and to develop a deeper understanding of how financial systems interact with the broader economy. An acceptance that postbubble economies take many years to recover implies a much greater focus on cross-border coordination to prevent financial shocks.

Fourth, the policy options facing large economies such as the United States could no longer be viewed in isolation. We must move beyond narrow debates about whether there should be more or less fiscal stimulus, more or less quantitative easing, and higher or lower taxes, and opt instead for a more holistic discussion involving tax reform, medium-term budgetary responsibility rules, infrastructure investment, and interstate regulation.

On top of these four challenges, there would be a fifth consequence—one of even more direct relevance to Japan. In the event of a long, slow global recovery, Japan would face a convergence of dangerous conditions: weak demand for Japanese exports, further worsening of public-debt dynamics, and an accelerating decline in domestic productive capabilities.

A long, slow recovery of the global economy would add to the tremendous pain and loss suffered by Japanese society as a result of the earthquake, tsunami, and nuclear crisis. In such a world, Japan would have to face up to the risk of substantial deterioration in its economic prospects. No longer could Japan hope to maintain living standards by drawing on its current account surplus and accumulated wealth. No longer could it afford to fall back on old excuses—such as the need to preserve the homogeneity of the Japanese population—to justify refusal to liberalize immigration policies. No longer will it be possible for Japan to rely on building factories abroad to offset the declining fortunes of the domestic economy.

This seemingly grim scenario (and it is a scenario, not a baseline) could have a positive aspect if it helps to bring about a recognition of new realities, coupled with a new willingness—in Japan, the United States, Europe, and at the multilateral level—to tackle holistically and head-on the challenges of the modern global economy. In the process, structural reforms would attract as much attention as demand-management policies. And a renewed effort would drive the reform of global governance to reflect the facts of today rather than the entitlements of yesterday. Over time, such a shift would improve the well-being of millions, if not billions, of people around the world by helping to establish a more effective global economic system that would lay the foundation for sustainable and balanced growth. In the specific case of Japan, it would ensure that the vast human suffering and physical damage of the March 2011 catastrophes are followed not only by postdisaster reconstruction but also by a period of breakout economic growth.

POISED FOR PROSPERITY

JESPER KOLL

I HAVE ONE OF THE MOST DIFFICULT JOBS IN THE WORLD. I'm a professional Japan optimist. I've been singing Japan's praises since arriving in Tokyo in
1986. Unfortunately, I have found it harder and harder to maintain credibility, what
with deflation battering the economy, nominal national income stuck at 1993 levels, industry after industry losing out to global competitors, and—for the past two
years—the government borrowing more than it collects in revenue. At times I feel
as though I'm observing the elite of Easter Island back in the 13th century: what
were they thinking as they cut down that last tree? Can it be that the combination of
demographic destiny, entrenched vested interests, and cultural stubbornness leaves
no other outcome but the relative and absolute decline of a once-great national
economy?

It doesn't have to be this way. Unlike the Easter Islanders, Japan's elites know
something is deeply wrong. But they can't agree on how to fix it. Some say taxes
should go up, others say expenditures must be slashed. Many insist the Bank of
Japan should print more money. There is no consensus on what went wrong, and
therefore no consensus on how to put things right. Common ground seems particularly elusive in the years following the pro-business, reform-minded Koizumi
administration, which—deservedly or not—is now perceived to have done as much
to stigmatize economic reform as it did to promote it.

To be a Japan optimist, it is essential to consider both the demand- and supply-
sides of the national economy and to remember that on both sides obstacles to
renewed dynamism are surmountable. On the supply-side, Japan's economy is constrained by excessive rules and regulations. On the demand-side, it suffers from

---

Jesper Koll is head of Japan equity research at JP Morgan Securities Japan.

popular anxiety about underfunded pensions and the possible bankruptcy of public services. Wise leaders can fix both problems with relative ease.

Path to prosperity, step one: Clarity of purpose
"In times of political confusion, and under an arbitrary government, many will prefer to keep their capital inactive, concealed and unproductive, either of profit or gratification, rather than run the risk of its display. This latter evil is never felt under good government."

These words from the French entrepreneur and economist Jean Baptiste Say are the best description of the vital feedback between public policy and private "animal spirits." They offer an apt summary of conditions in Japan over the past two decades. As public policy keeps flip-flopping, the government sends mixed messages on national goals. Privatization of the postal savings system? Yes! Then....no. Fiscal consolidation? Yes, then no, then maybe. The Bank of Japan's antideflation drive? Yes, but, well, maybe not. Such unpredictability has had a predictable result: Japan's bewildered firms have slowly but surely curtailed investment at home. What's killing the Japanese economy is not the strong yen or high tax rates. It is the lack of clear focus in public policy.

CAN IT BE THAT THE COMBINATION OF DEMOGRAPHIC DESTINY, ENTRENCHED VESTED INTERESTS, AND CULTURAL STUBBORNNESS LEAVES NO OTHER OUTCOME BUT THE RELATIVE AND ABSOLUTE DECLINE OF A ONCE GREAT NATIONAL ECONOMY?

What should that focus be? First and foremost, Japanese economic policy must come to the rescue of the nation's producers and entrepreneurs. Business investment and private risk-taking are what create jobs and incomes. Examples abound of highly successful new entrepreneurs in Japan. Most of them built their empires in the domestic economy. According to *Forbes* magazine, Japan's richest man is Fast Retailing's CEO Tadashi Yanai, whose wealth burgeoned over the past decade as he aggressively expanded his chain of Uniqlo stores. Asia's youngest self-made billionaire is neither Chinese nor Indian, but 33-year-old Japanese entrepreneur Yoshikazu Tanaka, founder of the social networking site Gree. Meanwhile, the founders of Mixi, DeNA, and Rakuten are also climbing the wealth-creation ladder in Silicon Valley style.

So entrepreneurship and the creation of wealth and jobs are possible in Japan. The problem is that the successes have been restricted to retail, a sector that was the focus of aggressive deregulation during the 1990s, and "new economy" sectors involving the Internet and digital media that, because of their relative novelty, escaped entanglement in the regulatory dragnet.

Path to prosperity, step two: Supply-side power
Deregulation and market-oriented policies could unlock private risk capital and entrepreneurship in Japan. In key sectors of the Japanese economy—financial services, construction, telecommunications, healthcare—regulations strangle growth. During the post-Koizumi era, each of these areas has swung back toward tighter rules.

Japan is a long way from Easter Island.

Specifically, policy should promote producers in sectors where Japan has natural strengths. Such policy is hardly a novel concept for Japan, where in the first few decades after World War II bureaucrats famously selected industries to benefit from subsidized loans, protection from foreign competition, and supportive regulation and other forms of government backing. But now it's time for different policies to achieve similar goals—with a primary emphasis on deregulation and the opening of markets to foreigners, rather than the heavy-handed interventions of the past.

First, Japanese policy should avoid the "me-too" approach of copying the strategies of other economies. An example is the pro forma efforts launched every couple of years or so to turn Tokyo into a dynamic financial center like Hong Kong, Shanghai, or Singapore. By now it is clear Japan does not really want to create the conditions for such a center—and in any case its aging population will generate lower and lower savings, which means that finance is a sunset, not a sunrise, industry. Japan would be better off reinforcing and supporting its own domestic megatrends and natural growth opportunities. I see at least four areas in which Japan has the potential to leverage inherent social and cultural attributes to realize substantial economic returns:

- Rojin *power*. No country is better suited to create a network of healthcare facilities, retirement communities, hospices, and the like that would set new global standards for how societies provide for their *rojin*, or seniors.
- *Soft power*. Given the global admiration for Japanese fashion, design, new media, and architecture, the country can become a magnet for firms in those fields from all over the world.
- *Agri-power*. With a shift in focus to eco-food, safe food, and innovative food, even Japan's famously inefficient farmers could become world-beaters.

- *Destination power*: Since neighboring countries are generating millions of newly prosperous citizens who want to tour the world, Japan should make itself much more inviting to these travelers.

None of these activities involves significant manufacturing. Each is labor intensive, offering reasonable pay for jobs requiring relatively high levels of education and creativity. (Although developing labor-intensive industries might not seem suitable for a nation facing a long-term decline in population, unemployment among Japanese youth is running close to 12 percent—five times the historic average, a disgraceful and deleterious problem. Let's not wring our hands about Japan's shrinking labor force until the youth unemployment rate has dropped back below 5 percent.) And each of these sectors could benefit substantially from an overhaul of rules and regulations that would foster competition and entrepreneurship.

UNLIKE THE EASTER ISLANDERS, JAPAN'S ELITES KNOW SOMETHING IS DEEPLY WRONG. BUT THEY CAN'T AGREE ON HOW TO FIX IT.

One of the promising sectors mentioned above—tourism—already offers a positive case study. The decisive move by then-transport minister Seiji Maehara to deregulate and liberalize Haneda Airport is a classic example of how political leadership can overcome old-style vested interests, stir animal spirits, induce investment, and deliver job growth. Indeed, deregulation has done so much sooner than skeptics had believed possible. The defeat of the powerful forces protecting Narita Airport's international flight monopoly has brought Tokyo airport access much closer to that of Singapore and Hong Kong—a huge boon to the potential wave of tourism from Asia's burgeoning middle class.

More of that kind of market-oriented creativity could boost prospects further for destination-power Japan. How about the other sectors?

Consider the idea of becoming an "elder-care power." This sector is bound to grow, with the natural aging of society generating rising demand for healthcare services, ranging from nursing to home care to staff positions at old-folks' homes. Yet the sector suffers from a terrible shortage of nurses, estimated at around 30,000 to 50,000 over the next decade. In a country with such high youth unemployment, this mismatch should not be tolerated and leaves much hope for simple reform to boost employment and incomes.

Why don't more young Japanese become nurses? The intense training requires four years of study, followed by a demanding test; yet three or four years into a nursing job, the income is usually less than what people can earn working part-time at a Starbucks or the post office. And, unlike the highly regulated workdays that nurses must endure, those part-time jobs offer much greater flexibility and freedom. The doctors' association bears part of the responsibility for this mismatch, because its lobbying power helps keep a lid on the pay of nurses in public hospitals (the motive being to limit the wages that private doctors must pay their nursing staff).

Raising nurses' pay, as well as reviewing and deregulating nursing qualification standards and job rules, could go a long way toward eliminating the nursing shortage and cutting down youth unemployment. The government can afford to relax these rules; jobs created bring in tax revenues, and reduced unemployment cuts down social spending. Remember: the starting point is a recognized shortage of nurses—excess demand relative to effective supply. Closing that gap in labor markets is a powerful example of how supply-side economics should work.

There are similar opportunities in agriculture. Currently, the government subsidizes farmers mainly by providing a combination of price supports and protection from imports. Shifting to a system in which farmers received guaranteed minimum income would free up supply potential, without excessively reducing farmers' living standards.

The end of price supports would entice farmers to drop the wasteful production of foodstuff such as low-grade rice currently grown only to gain artificially high prices guaranteed by the government. Farmers could then devote land to raising production for potentially lucrative foreign markets. If this shift were coupled with agricultural land reform—allowing existing parcels to be merged for larger-scale production—Japan could conceivably become a substantial food exporter in the foreseeable future. Demand for safe, eco-friendly, and tasty food products is rising fast in Asia, China in particular. There is also increasing demand for the highest-grade rice, fresh fruit, specialty vegetables, and even dairy products and meat. Asia's increasingly luxury-seeking middle class has already proven to be an attractive market for Japan's famous *koshi hikari* rice, and in the wake of problems regarding products such as milk powder in China, the brand value of made-in-Japan food is surging in the region. The farm lobby, which prefers the current system, will fight hard to resist, but Japanese agri-power can rise and leave its reputation for poor competitiveness behind if the government implements the right kind of reforms—another illustration of the possible supply-side revolution.

Japan's potential soft-power in areas such as media, design, and fashion is well recognized. As science fiction writer William Gibson wrote in *Wired* magazine: "When I want to see the future, I go and spend a week in Tokyo." Public policy should promote more aggressively the education of designers, architects, and artists as part of a national effort to attract Asia's emerging creative class. Just as Toyota decided two decades ago to build a car-design center in France, companies based in Asia and elsewhere should be encouraged to set up their cutting-edge design centers in Japan. Special tax benefits for design centers could yield big economic dividends, as would more public sponsorship of film festivals and art fairs.

Ultimately, though, these supply-side policies can't succeed unless they are matched by demand-side measures designed to get Japan's consumers spending.

Path to prosperity, step three: Tax reform
Poll after poll finds that Japan's citizens are anxious about the future. Among their biggest fears: uncertainty about whether the state's promises to cover graceful retirement can be honored. This uncertainty is what drives workers to save so much of their paychecks, depresses demand, and worsens the vicious deflationary cycle

in which consumers defer making purchases, since they expect they will be able to buy later at cheaper prices.

Magic bullets are exceedingly rare in public policy, but in this case, one is available: Japan should pass a law that automatically raises the consumption tax from its current 5-percent level by an additional one percentage point every year on April 1. And this law must leave unspecified how many consecutive years this step-up is supposed to happen. The government should declare that, *toriaezu*—for the time being—the consumption tax will be going up with the start of the new fiscal year.

A *toriaezu* tax hike makes sense economically and politically. The economics aims directly at both deflation and fears of a bankrupt pension, social welfare, and heath care system. Japan's demographics make the case for a consumption tax particularly compelling; as the nation's workforce shrinks, fewer people earn income that can be taxed, so the best way for the government to collect the revenue it needs is to tax at the point of consumption. The problem is that at 5 percent, the revenue generated is woefully insufficient.

With government debt almost twice the size of Japan's gross domestic product, the risks are considerable that financial markets may at some point lose confidence in the country's ability to pay its obligations. Most economists calculate the consumption tax would need to be raised to some 20 percent to ensure that markets maintain faith in Japan's long-term fiscal soundness. Such estimates are excessively precise; it is simply impossible to calculate what exact rate for the consumption tax would be optimal for Japan. Hence, my proposal to—*toriaezu*—hike the tax by 1 percentage point every year. This steady increase will enable policy makers and the public to see the impact on total tax revenues as the rate gradually increases.

Accompanying the tax hike should be clear legal requirements that the added revenues can be used only to fund pension, healthcare, and social security. The "bullet" must be directed at what worries the Japanese people, not local construction firms. Once consumers feel confident their pension and health benefits are secure, they are bound to loosen their purse strings.

Agri-power: Is *koshi hikari* a source of future strength?

Fear not: a 1 percentage-point-per-year consumption-tax boost is not big enough to cause serious damage to the economy. On the contrary, the effect is bound to be positive, because public awareness of the pending steady rise in sales taxes will help pull Japan out of its deflationary mindset. When consumers know that the tax on the items they are considering is headed inexorably upward, they lose their incentive to wait for prices to fall. To be sure, not all of the tax hike will be passed on to consumers; some of it will be absorbed by companies. But wage bargaining in Japan will start to change, with unions and workers bound to demand a minimum one percentage-point increase in their pay. This increase matters a lot; the deflation mindset stops when real wage bargaining begins.

And what of politics? Any tax increase will be unpopular. But the gradual increase I'm proposing would be less objectionable than many alternatives—and it would prompt a crucial shift in the national mindset. In decades past, the game has been to postpone the inevitable and then postpone it again. In fact, politicians have won elections based on their promises to refrain from raising the consumption tax. Every delay has exacerbated the fiscal deficit problem and raised the likelihood of drastic action in the future; for every year that the consumption tax has not been hiked by 1 percentage point over the past decade, it will have to be raised by almost 2 percentage points in every future year to compensate. Surely it is easier to endure a 1 percentage-point increase each year for some period of time rather than undergo the shock of a 5- or 6-percentage-point boost all at once. As is so often true in economics, the sooner you act, the better.

Once a 1 percentage point annual hike is agreed to, the fiscal policy debate can begin to "normalize." The worry mongering about the necessity of prompt action to prevent a fiscal crisis will stop, and neither the opposition nor the ruling party will be forced into embarrassing contortions in which they acknowledge the need for action but insist that it needn't happen on their watch. This normalization would be possible because concrete steps toward lower deficits and better public finances would be actually underway.

Eventually, when Japan's fiscal health is clear to all—whether restoring that health takes a consumption tax rate of 8 percent or 10 percent or even 14 percent—politicians can turn to the happy subject of halting further increases. Of course, some politicians may want to start repealing the law right away, but I am prepared to trust that Japanese voters will recognize such a step as disastrous. Indeed, both the ruling Democrats and the opposition LDP seem lately to have recognized the need to raise the consumption tax. It's not too far-fetched to imagine that this "magic bullet" could provide the basis for bipartisan agreement on economic policy.

Not all optimists are starry-eyed; my confidence in Japan's prospects is rooted in reality. Empowering people and entrepreneurs, and enacting sensible tax increases, can put Japan back on a track toward prosperity. This two-pronged approach would mark a fundamental break with the enterprise-stifling policies of the past, reverse the damage done by politicians unwilling address voters' concerns about their future, and lead Japan from its lost decades into a era of newfound purpose and hope.

IS JAPAN PAST ITS COMPETITIVE PRIME?

KLAUS SCHWAB

WHEN JAPAN HOSTED THE OLYMPIC GAMES IN 1964, the event was a coming-out party—Japan was back. From 1960 to 1990, Japan's GDP grew at an average annual rate of 6.2 percent as the country established itself as a global manufacturing, financial, and innovation powerhouse and a peaceful, prosperous, and largely content society. But a massive real estate and asset bubble built up in the 1980s: this bubble burst in 1991, and the after-effects are still being felt. Growth has averaged just 1 percent a year since then, according to the World Bank.

Despite this difficult economic situation, Japan remains one of the world's most productive and affluent countries. While China has overtaken Japan as the world's second-largest economy, Japan's per capita income is still many times higher than the PRC's.

For more than 30 years, the World Economic Forum has examined the factors that enable national economies to achieve sustained economic growth. We define competitiveness as the set of institutions, policies, and factors that determine the productive level of an economy. That level of productivity, in turn, sets the level of prosperity that can be earned.

The Forum's Global Competitiveness Index (GCI) measures 12 factors that are critical to productivity (Exhibit 1). Japan has ranked in the top ten of the most competitive economies since the first GCI in 2005; in the most recent year, the country was sixth out of 139. In most areas, Japan compares well with the United States and consistently outperforms the Organisation for Economic Co-operation and Development (OECD) average and China.

Klaus Schwab is founder and executive director of the World Economic Forum.

Japan's competitive strengths

Japan excels in the more sophisticated areas that drive competitiveness. It is the world leader in the business sophistication category and ranks fourth in innovation. It also performs well in infrastructure (11th), and in the quality of health and primary education (9th). The size of its domestic market generates significant economies of scale and related efficiency gains. In its macroeconomic performance, however, Japan falls far short—ranking 105th.

Japan boasts an exceptional capacity to innovate, thanks to high investment in research and development. Total spending on R&D has been rising steadily over the past decade, to 3.8 percent of GDP (the fifth-highest ratio in the world), up from 2.8 percent in 1997. In this dimension, according to the World Bank, Japan outperforms the United States (2.7 percent), Germany (2.6 percent), and the OECD average (2.5 percent) by a sizable margin. Japan also possesses excellent academic and research institutions, which produce a large pool of highly qualified scientists and engineers. Furthermore, research collaboration between the universities and the private sector is intense, ensuring that innovations get to market rapidly.

As a result, Japan has been a prolific innovator. Twenty-one percent of the 167,349 patents for inventions granted in the United States in 2009 were from Japan (Exhibit 2). That percentage is equivalent to the shares of Germany, South

Exhibit 1
Japan's performance in the Global Competitiveness Index
Scores are on a 1–7 scale (7 = best)

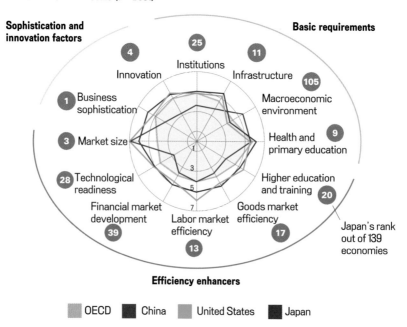

Korea, Taiwan, Canada, the United Kingdom, France, and China combined. Japan earned 50 percent more patents than the countries of the European Union, which has a population three times that of Japan. Only the United States (49 percent) earned more patents.

Statistics from the World Intellectual Property Organization tell an even more compelling story. Over the past decade, Japan's share of patent applications rose to 20 percent, from 10 percent, while those from the United States declined significantly (Exhibit 3). While patent filings are not an infallible proxy for innovation, they are a broadly useful metric—and there certainly cannot be innovation without invention.

Buttressing Japan's innovation capacity is the high degree of sophistication of its business sector, where the country ranks second to none. Japanese businesses are generally present at the top end of the value chain. Their comparative advantage resides in the unique processes and products they design; they are trendsetters. Japanese firms use sophisticated market tools and strategies, and, sourcing from a broad base of suppliers, exert control over the entire distribution chain. Furthermore, strong and deep clusters encourage innovation by fostering competition and concentrating talent and capital. Japanese consumers are also extremely demanding, encouraging businesses to maintain high levels of quality.

Exhibit 2
U.S. patents granted to residents of Japan

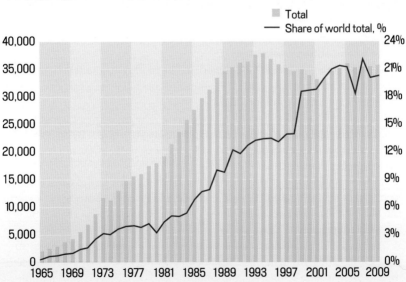

Source: United States Patents and Trademarks Office, 2010

Exhibit 3
Patent applications by country of origin (%)

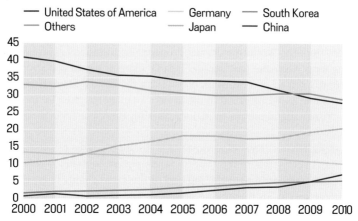

¹ Provisional and incomplete data.
Source: World Intellectual Property Organization, 2010

It is no surprise, then, that Japanese companies have excelled in automobiles, electronics, cameras, and game software. They manufacture machinery and a wide range of instruments requiring high precision and quality. It's true that Japan has lost ground in a number of industries, but the country remains a world leader in the automotive and IT industries, as well as in robotics, environmental services, and solar energy. Japan was a pioneer in mobile phone technology.

Japan's competitive weaknesses
While these strengths are real and important, the country also suffers from a number of weaknesses that have eroded its competitiveness. If these weaknesses are not addressed, Japan risks continued decline.

For a start, Japan's fiscal position is alarming. The government budget deficit, made worse by the recent financial crisis, reached 11 percent of GDP in 2009. Government debt represents a staggering 218 percent of GDP, by far the largest debt burden among the advanced economies. Most of the debt is domestically held, which lessens the currency risk; Japan is not about to go the way of Greece. But the high level of debt still raises the cost of capital; and given the country's low growth and low inflation, this level of debt does raise troubling questions about long-term fiscal sustainability.

The origins of these cavernous deficits and mounting debt are deep and structural. Japan's society is aging, as a result of higher life expectancy and lower fertility, and there is little immigration to compensate. Foreigners account for only 1.6 percent of the population (the OECD average is 10 percent). Moreover, Japanese women are not highly active in the work force, as reflected in the country's low female-to-male participation ratio (Japan ranks 83rd).

This combination of factors has caused the dependency ratio—the number of individuals, chiefly children and the elderly, compared with the number of those available to provide such support—to worsen rapidly since the early 1990s. The ratio currently stands at 53 percent—that is, 53 dependents for every 100 actives—the highest ratio in the world. And it is going to get much worse: by 2050, the OECD estimates that figure will exceed 100 (compared with an average of 89 for the other members of the OECD). This trend raises important questions about the ability of the government to meet its future commitments to healthcare, long-term care, and pensions. The current government has promised to cut the public deficit in half by 2015. This promise will be extremely difficult to keep, but must be kept to set the public finances on a more sustainable path.

Another concern is taxation. The corporate tax rate, at 56 percent of profits, is already among the highest in the OECD. (Only Spain, Belgium, France, and Italy apply higher rates.) Indeed, business executives in Japan who responded to the Forum's annual Executive Opinion Survey named taxation as the second-most problematic factor for doing business, just after policy instability (Exhibit 4). Well aware

Exhibit 4
The difficulties of doing business in Japan

% of responses

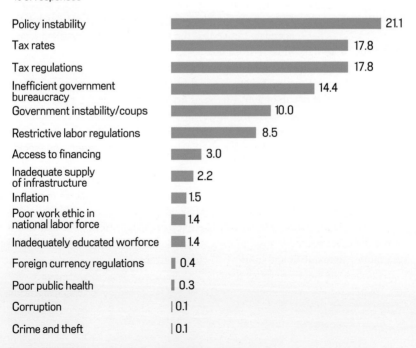

Policy instability	21.1
Tax rates	17.8
Tax regulations	17.8
Inefficient government bureaucracy	14.4
Government instability/coups	10.0
Restrictive labor regulations	8.5
Access to financing	3.0
Inadequate supply of infrastructure	2.2
Inflation	1.5
Poor work ethic in national labor force	1.4
Inadequately educated worforce	1.4
Foreign currency regulations	0.4
Poor public health	0.3
Corruption	0.1
Crime and theft	0.1

Source: World Economic Forum, Executive Opinion Survey 2010

of this burden, the government is considering lowering corporate taxes. The difficulty will be to do so while not worsening the deficit.

The macroeconomic environment is challenging enough; the larger problem, though, is that Japanese politics is in disarray. There have been six prime ministers since 2006. This kind of churning makes much-needed reforms difficult to implement. Businesses lack visibility because of shifting agendas. Indeed, respondents to the survey in Japan cite political instability as the single most problematic factor for business, so it's not surprising that business doesn't trust the country's politicians (Japan ranked 58th) or their ability to spend money wisely (91st). In other words, the business community thinks that taxes are not only too high, but also that it gets too little in return.

TWENTY-ONE PERCENT OF PATENTS GRANTED IN THE U.S. IN 2009 WERE FROM JAPAN —EQUIVALENT TO THE SHARES OF GERMANY, SOUTH KOREA, TAIWAN, CANADA, UNITED KINGDOM, FRANCE AND CHINA COMBINED.

Finally, the data show that a number of policy rigidities hamper business and employment creation. For instance, the World Bank estimates that it takes on average 23 days— 10 more than the OECD average—and eight procedures to set up a business in Japan. In addition, the job market is characterized by a number of rigidities that discourage job creation and hinder creativity in the workplace.

Looking ahead: A strategy for renewal

The role of the World Economic Forum is to bring together decision makers to have productive and honest conversations about the shape of global, regional, and industrial agendas. I hope that the Global Agenda Council on Japan, a gathering of leading thinkers from business, government, and civil society convened by the Forum, can help Japan's leaders come to concrete solutions to these pressing problems. Because if there is one thing everyone can—and must—agree on, it is that delay is not an option; a sense of urgency is a necessary start.

Japan's alarming macroeconomic and political difficulties require profound fiscal and government reforms. Based on recent conversations with numerous senior Japanese leaders, it is clear to me that the unstable political situation and gloomy economic indicators are taking a toll.

Even so, the country should avoid becoming too inward-looking and losing its self-confidence. Japan has successfully addressed major issues such as energy efficiency, healthcare, pollution, and social-safety nets. The country can build on this track record. Having observed Japan closely for decades, I have faith that it can harness its considerable strengths—in education, social stability, technology, and innovation—to maintain and improve its competitiveness.

"CREATIVE DESTRUCTION" IN JAPANESE POLITICS

GERALD L. CURTIS

THE MAJOR FEATURES OF Japan's political system—features that contributed greatly to the nation's postwar success—have been weakened or destroyed by the very success they helped produce.

Institutions that once promoted Japan's economic recovery, growth, and social stability have proved ill-suited to managing a mature economy. The intimate relationship between business and government; the alliance between bureaucrats and ruling-party politicians; lifetime employment; seniority-based compensation schemes; the "main bank" system for funneling capital to manufacturers; the Finance Ministry's convoy system for keeping banks afloat—these and many other features of the postwar political economy no longer dominate the Japanese political landscape.

Moreover, Japanese society has changed in ways that make it impossible to resurrect these institutions. The public is no longer willing to tolerate old-style machine politics and its backroom wheeling and dealing. In a more pluralistic and diverse Japan, formerly tight-knit communities have become less so, as have political parties and business, professional, and labor organizations that buttressed the old-style institutional arrangements.

The consequence is a kind of groping for a new way of conducting politics—one that must achieve better results before long, lest Japan be destined for inexorable decline. Evolving new institutions and procedures is inevitably a complex and contentious process, but Japan's political leaders must act quickly and decisively.

Gerald L. Curtis is a professor of political science at Columbia University and a visiting professor at Waseda University.

Continued paralysis of the Japanese political system can only erode and eventually destroy the dynamism and potential that exist in Japanese society.

Recent events underscore the urgency of political change. The March 11, 2011 earthquake and tsunami, which brought so much death and destruction and left hundreds of thousands homeless, followed by the radiation leaks at the Fukushima nuclear reactors, have made the need for far-reaching political change all the more apparent. Prime Minister Kan rightly characterized the situation as the worst crisis that Japan has faced since the Second World War. The need for political leaders who can articulate a persuasive vision for Japan's future—not only for the devastated areas of the northeast but for the nation as a whole—has never been greater. Whether Japan's political leaders can rise to the challenges created by the crisis, however, remains to be seen.

A kind of political ceasefire ensued in the weeks immediately following the earthquake. Speculation about Kan being forced from office or calling a snap election disappeared. Stunned by the enormity of the tragedy in the northeast, the public clung to the hope that the Kan government would manage the crisis competently. Opposition party politicians, for their part, quickly recognized that playing politics with the disaster would provoke a national backlash; even Kan's sharpest detractors emphasized their readiness to cooperate with the government. But that was the immediate response. When politics reasserts itself, as it inevitably must, the key question is whether Japan reverts to the patterns of political debate and competition that prevailed before March 11 or whether this unprecedented tragedy helps produce much needed and fundamental political change.

Well before the crisis, it was clear that Japanese voters had lost patience with old-style politics. In September 2009, with the victory of the Democratic Party of Japan (DPJ), Japan's political history appeared to be starting a bright new chapter. After decades of rule by the Liberal Democratic Party (LDP), public hopes ran high that the formation of a DPJ government, led by Yukio Hatoyama as prime minister, would mark a change in politics for the better. Voters relished the prospect that the end of LDP control would end two decades of economic stagnation and transform a political system that catered more to special interests than to the needs of ordinary Japanese.

Those hopes were dashed by the self-destruction of the Hatoyama government. The triggering event for the Hatoyama cabinet's demise was a dispute with the United States about military bases in Okinawa, but the fundamental cause was the public's loss of confidence in Hatoyama's very ability to govern. Public enthusiasm for the DPJ gave way to a deep-seated pessimism that no one in the Japanese political class could provide the leadership the country so sorely needs.

Whether Hatoyama's successor, Naoto Kan, will fare much better remains to be seen. He got off to a lackluster start. The DPJ suffered a major defeat in an Upper House election held shortly after Kan came to power in June 2010. The prime minister himself helped bring about that loss by proposing—then hastily withdrawing—an increase in the national consumption tax. A few months later he came under withering criticism for capitulating to Chinese pressure amid a flare-up of territorial tensions. So far, the public reaction to his promise to craft a new economic growth strategy has run from indifference and skepticism to outright hostility.

The public's disappointment with the DPJ is matched by a lack of enthusiasm for the LDP or for any of the several small parties that have recently been created by defectors from the LDP. Japanese politics, like the economy itself, has fallen into a deep funk with no clear way out.

What makes this situation especially worrisome is that Japan's political problem cannot be chalked up solely to the absence of dynamic leaders and the failure of any of the political parties to come up with policy ideas that might arouse public enthusiasm. Those features of the current Japanese political scene are more the consequence than the cause of the nation's political malaise.

The daunting reality is that Japan's political system is in the midst of a period of "creative destruction"—in which the accent has been more on the destructive than the creative side of the process. To replace institutional arrangements that have sunk into obsolescence, some new ones have emerged, along with a number of reforms and policy innovations. But like so much else about economic, social, and political change in Japan, while the direction has generally been right, the pace has been all too slow.

During the long reign of the LDP, it responded pragmatically and flexibly to changed circumstances in order to secure its overriding objective of holding onto power. For half a century, its formula kept producing electoral success, but the party finally ran out of steam. The public's tolerance for political corruption decreased and its criticism of LDP ties with special interests grew. The election system was changed from a multi- to a single-member district system, thereby transforming intra-LDP competition into interparty competition. Factions weakened over time. Powerful party leaders left the scene. Changes in political funding rules made it more difficult to raise money. After hoping against hope for some two decades that the LDP might get its economic policies right, the public finally had enough and voted it out of power.

The DPJ has not replaced the LDP as the dominant party. Its hold on power is tenuous. Stability in voting behavior has given way to wild swings. Most Japanese voters identify with no party and shift their vote, when they vote, from one party to another, depending on their level of dissatisfaction with the incumbent government and the popularity of party leaders. A stable two-party system may evolve, but considerable time must pass before the features of a post-LDP-dominant system come into full view.

The collapse of LDP rule has been accompanied by the dramatic decline in the prestige, power, and morale of Japan's famed mandarin class. The popular notion that bureaucrats rather than politicians have been the policy makers in the Japanese government is only a half-truth. The true half is that Japan's elite bureaucracy has been a key player in government policy making. But it was so in alliance with senior politicians in the LDP, not in place of them.

That alliance has crumbled. The LDP found it convenient to blame bureaucrats for the nation's woes rather than acknowledge its own culpability. And the DPJ made bureaucrat bashing and a promise to have politicians rather than bureaucrats make decisions a key plank in its platform.

The problem is that in a country without think tanks like those that can be found in Washington, London, or Paris—or in Seoul or Beijing, for that matter—and with few policy intellectuals, the bureaucracy is the source of most policy expertise. Many in the DPJ and in the cabinet seem to believe that their commitment to exercise political control *(seiji shudo)* means that politicians should abjure the advice of bureaucrats, make policy decisions, and order the bureaucracy to implement them.

The result is a decision-making system in considerable disarray. It was to be expected that creating a new relationship between politicians and bureaucrats to replace the LDP–bureaucrat alliance would take some time. But more than a year after coming to power, the DPJ has yet to make significant headway in constructing a coherent decision-making and crisis-management system. In the meantime, governance suffers from an amateurish, flying-by-the-seat-of-your-pants quality.

Moreover, neither the DPJ nor the LDP has been able to articulate a vision for the country and a strategy for realizing it that the public finds compelling or even comprehensible. This lack of vision stands in stark contrast to the situation that prevailed in the postwar period up to the 1980s, when there was a deep and broad consensus in Japanese society, and among its political elite, that the priority was for the nation to secure its place among the most economically advanced countries.

Deep fissures divided postwar Japanese society. Conservatives and liberals fought over whether to revise the American-drafted Constitution, whether to opt for alliance with the United States or unarmed neutrality, and whether to return to an idealized past. But amid all this *Sturm und Drang*, the Japanese were united in their desire to catch up with the West and to do so by peaceful means.

In the aftermath of the Pacific war, Japan devised one of the most successful economic-development models in history. This model combined rapid economic growth with an equitable distribution of income and political democracy. Bitter differences on other issues had the effect of reinforcing the consensus to prioritize growth. Institutions were designed to foster close government–business cooperation and to provide economic security to the great mass of people during a time of enormous social change. Japan evolved intricate and elaborate informal networks of elite coordination to keep the nation on track as it pursued its catch-up goal.

This system worked remarkably well until the goal it was designed to accomplish was realized. Since the mid-1980s, the catch-up project having been mostly accomplished, Japan has been seeking a post-catch-up consensus on goals and institutional reforms that would substitute for the no-longer-effective informal elite coordination institutions of the past.

All the while, the strength of formerly powerful institutions has ebbed. Large integrative interest groups—such as the medical association, the Japan Agriculture (JA) network of farm cooperatives, the business community's Keidanren, and the major labor union federation—have lost much of their ability to aggregate political demands and to mobilize support for political parties. These institutions, in a Japanese variant on a trend observable in all advanced democracies, have suffered from fragmentation and a proliferation of special interests seeking to influence government policy. Peak associations like Keidanren used to be key elements in the LDP and the opposition party's electoral machines. They do not fulfill that function any longer, thus weakening formerly stable voting blocs, exacerbating the tendency for voters to swing their support from one party to another, and making it all the more difficult for political leaders to rally broad public support.

Also enfeebled is the close and cooperative relationship between the state and business that for so long characterized the Japanese political economy. The Japanese never bought into Adam Smith's notion of an invisible hand; their assumption was that the very visible hand of the state should hold on tight to the hand of business so that together they could find the optimum way to achieve the nation's catch-up goal.

That close government–business relationship no longer exists. Japanese corporations competing in a dynamic, fast-changing global market are not waiting for or willing to accept the kind of administrative guidance that the Ministry of Industrial Trade and Industry (MITI) used to exercise or the informal guidance that the Ministry of Finance (MOF) once exercised over the banking system. In the financial realm, regulatory reform has also substantially altered the old ties between the state and the private sector, as supervisory powers over banks no longer reside with the MOF but rather in a separate Financial Services Agency.

Japan carved out its own singular approach to managing the relationship between business and the state, following neither an American capitalist model nor a socialist one. But it is not clear what economic philosophy drives the current government. Prime Minister Kan has made "jobs, jobs, jobs" his key slogan, but his approach emphasizes the role that government can play in creating jobs by pouring more public money into healthcare and other social services and gives scant attention to what the government should do to create incentives for business to generate employment. Former Prime Minister Koizumi had it right when he argued that deregulation was key to restoring Japan's economic vitality, but this is not a view shared by the current DPJ government.

Given the enormity of the challenges that confront the Japanese political system, it is no easy task for Japan's political leaders to muster the political will to make the kinds of bold policy changes that are needed and get the support of a risk-averse public for them. But it would be a mistake to write Japan off as a nation whose future has passed.

The economist Joseph Schumpeter employed the term "creative destruction" to describe the interplay of chaos and innovation in markets. A similar process has been at work in Japanese politics over the past two decades—and has brought important changes. The new arrangements emerging include both formal institutions and informal ones. Traditional institutions of the labor market are giving way to more flexible arrangements. There are ongoing programs to bring about education reform, immigration reform, changes in the system used for the training of lawyers, and a rebalancing of power between the central government and localities, as well as policies to encourage women to seek professional careers, to mention just a few. None of these programs has advanced far enough, but the destruction of long-established institutions and the process of creating new ones in their place continue unabated.

How quickly and successfully changes occur will depend to a considerable extent on the quality of political leadership. Prime Minister Kan may be the last of the generation of politicians currently over 60 years of age to head the government.

The last lower election that brought the DPJ to power saw the largest turnover from incumbent to new candidates since the American occupation purge of Japan's political leaders, in the late 1940s. That purge opened the way for younger politicians with new ideas to come to power. The 2009 Lower House election may prove to have much the same consequence.

The question is whether the younger, emerging generation of politicians will be able to make politics catch up to the society that Japan has become. This new generation of politicians needs to articulate a set of national goals that captures the nation's imagination; they need to figure out how to mobilize the bureaucracy rather than demoralize it and also how to tap into expertise in the private sector and academia and nurture a new generation of policy intellectuals; they need to develop the communication skills to marshal public support for the policies they advocate.

Is the emerging generation of Japanese leaders up to this task? No one can say for sure, but in many respects these new political leaders are quite different from those who preceded them. Most of them come from backgrounds other than the bureaucracy or local politics, the traditional recruiting grounds for national politics. As a group, leaders from this emerging generation are more diverse than their predecessors. These younger leaders have not been socialized into the traditional Japanese way of politics and for the most part embrace values that are not compatible with old-style factional politics. The nation's future depends not only on whether they can think about policy and politics in innovative and imaginative ways, but also whether they have the persuasive powers to secure the necessary backing from the public.

Given enough time, new and more effective political institutions will emerge in Japan; eventually the creative aspects of the process will trump the destructive aspects. And there's the rub. The process of creative destruction is a race against time. For Japan, the question is whether the creative aspects of its political system can prevail in time to avert a future of drift and decline.

People around the world have marveled at the bravery and civility of Japan's people in the face of earthquake, tsunami, and nuclear hazard. But perhaps those most impressed by the generosity and resilience of the Japanese people have been the Japanese themselves. There is a sense of rediscovered pride in the strong social bonds that have enabled the nation to pull together in this time of extraordinary difficulty and dislocation. Many Japanese have found satisfaction in the durability of traditional values they thought had disappeared; they are expressing a quiet faith the country's ability to prevail rarely voiced over the past two decades of economic stagnation.

Can Japan's political leaders tap into that new energy and enthusiasm for change? Can they put to good use the renewed sense of self-confidence the crisis has generated? If they can, Japan faces a much brighter future than almost anyone thought was possible before disaster struck. But if they do not, the public will be alienated from the political system in a much more profound way than at anytime since the Second World War and Japan's decline will be inexorable. That is the choice that Japan now faces.

WHAT WOULD DRUCKER DO?

NATSUMI IWASAKI

IN 2006, NATSUMI IWASAKI, *a television and comedy event producer with a passion for online games, was struggling to mobilize an effective Final Fantasy team. He discovered the blog of a fellow gamer hailing the ideas of American management expert Peter Drucker. Iwasaki began studying Drucker's ideas and was immediately captivated by their relevance, not just for online games, but also for many forms of competition—and indeed many aspects of daily life in contemporary Japanese society. Iwasaki was particularly struck by Drucker's use of the word "management." In Drucker's writing, the term implied something very different from what was commonly understood in Japan. For example, in baseball—a sport with which Iwasaki, a former high school pitcher, had firsthand experience—the manager of a US major league team was a leader and a coach. In Japan, however, the role of "manager" (manejaa) was a humble one that typically involved cleaning up and keeping track of equipment. The more Iwasaki reflected on this difference, the more profound it seemed to him. He began writing about Drucker's ideas on his own blog. And in December 2009, he published a novel, What If a Female Manager of a High School Baseball Team Read Drucker's 'Management'?*

Iwasaki's novel became a runaway best seller. By the end of 2010, What If... (or, as the book's title is commonly abbreviated in Japanese, Moshi Dora) had sold more than 2 million copies and become Japan's No. 1 best-selling book. Moshi Dora also spawned a manga and popular television anime series, and is being adapted as a live-action movie.

The story's heroine is Minami Kawashima, a Tokyo high school student who is unexpectedly asked to become a manager for the school's baseball team. Searching for guidance in how to perform her duties, Minami stumbles across Drucker's 1973 clas-

---

Natsumi Iwasaki is author of What If the Female Assistant of a High-School Baseball Team Read Drucker's "*Management*"?

sic, Management: Tasks, Responsibilities, Practices. *She decides to use Drucker's principles—especially his emphasis on the importance of setting clear goals, identifying "customers," and thinking rigorously about how to satisfy them—to rally the school's demoralized team. True to Drucker's vision, she resolves to help the team qualify for the national high school baseball championship at Koshien Stadium. In striving to attain that lofty objective, she and members of the team realize that their customers are their parents, classmates, and supporters in the local community. Inspired, they pull together and begin to excel.*

McKinsey asked Iwasaki to explain how he hit a home run with Moshi Dora*—and how the wisdom of Drucker might help Japan cope with its many challenges.*

"How would Japan change if the prime minister read Drucker?"

I have received many such questions since my novel became a best seller. As the title suggests, the story focuses on Drucker's *Management: Tasks, Responsibilities, Practices.*

Peter F. Drucker was born in Vienna in 1909. He published his first book in 1939, and continued to be active as one of the world's most respected authors for the next 60 years. When he died in 2005, he was regarded as a giant of business management, and his reputation continues to grow. Drucker has carved a place for himself not just in the history of the 20th century, but in the history of humanity.

THERE IS A REASON WHY ORDINARY JAPANESE CITIZENS, NOT POLITICAL AND CORPORATE LEADERS, HAVE TURNED TO DRUCKER FOR ANSWERS.

In my book, the main character, Minami, is in secondary school. Circumstances conspire for her to become a manager of the baseball team, and she begins to work toward the unbelievably far-fetched goal of reaching the national tournament, even though the team has never before made it beyond the preliminaries. More than 100 schools compete for the spot from the West Tokyo District. It is an incredible undertaking to make the top of that heap.

Minami's first step is to get a copy of Drucker's *Management.* She then uses Drucker's theories as a reference point for thinking about the baseball team, asking herself: Who are the baseball team's customers? What do those customers want? What is innovation?

Such questions have relevance beyond business (or baseball). Many people have read my book—not just managers, but also retirees, workers, housewives, business students, and even high school and elementary students. Their reading often leads them to reading *Management,* too. Since the publication of *Moshi Dora,* sales in Japan of Drucker's own books have soared.

So it is not surprising that many people have asked me how Drucker's ideas might apply to politics and other issues. Each time, my answer is the same. Drucker says that society is moving from centralized authority to decentralized authority. The time will come when each individual will act as a manager at the level of the family, community, or enterprise.

That is why the question—"How would Japan change if the prime minister read Drucker?"—is meaningless.

Moving beyond politics

In the past, the political sphere exerted a great deal of power in Japan, but it is now on the wane. The diminished influence of politics became clear in 2009 with the historic change in government from the Liberal Democratic Party to the Democratic Party of Japan. That handover marked an extraordinary shift away from the political machine that had been in power ever since the end of the war. But there was almost no change in society itself. What the 2009 election did was to make us aware that we, the Japanese people, have to take responsibility for reform ourselves; we cannot simply rely on the politicians. We have begun to see ourselves as managers of our own lives.

That is why *Management* is relevant for ordinary Japanese—not just for business or political leaders, but for everyone else. I believe Drucker's ideas can help us all to find a new way of life.

We need not belabor the fact that Japan's economy and society are exhausted. After 45 years of almost uninterrupted growth, we have been in a consistent defla-

Smile, Mr. Drucker, the world is still listening to you.
© George Rose/Getty Images

Natsumi Iwasaki's book helped launch a "Drucker boom."
© Itsuo Inouye/AP

tionary trend for 20 years. The end of economic expansion brought a cooling of our enthusiasm and ardor. The collapse of Lehman Brothers and the ensuing financial shock in 2008 sent Japan into recession. Unemployment emerged as a significant issue. Falling results gave many companies an excuse to lay off large numbers of employees on fixed-term contracts. These people spilled over into the streets with no prospects for reemployment, which only exacerbated the country's sense of stagnation. Sentiment became even darker and more anxious.

The experience of high economic growth brought education to all corners of the Japanese population and increased people's sense of participation in their society. The experience of the bubble economy taught us the emptiness that lurks on the other side of affluence and made possible a more skeptical take on the idea of unlimited growth. The experience of stagnation and deflation taught us to understand other people's pain. The experience of falling birthrates and aging demographics gave us a renewed awareness of the importance of children and communities.

And then in 2010 there was the "Drucker boom." People began turning to *Management* for hints on how to live and be happy while confronting the issues of economic stagnation, deflation, and a fast-aging population—a combination of circumstances Japan has never experienced before. In this context of questioning and social change, many people were receptive to Drucker's message. He wrote about the power of individuals to set specific goals, define values, and find creative ways to overcome challenges that benefit not only themselves but also the larger society.

In my book, Minami incorporates many different ideas in her management of the underdog high school baseball team. She eventually succeeds, and the team goes to the national high school championship tournament at Koshien Stadium, one of Japan's most important sporting events. A single, ordinary citizen is successful in energizing her community. I would like to see the same thing happen in many other aspects of Japanese society.

Circles, big and small

In the past, our society was structured like a giant triangle. People, goods, and money all converged on the triangle's apex in Kasumigaseki and Nagatacho (the government districts of Tokyo) before being showered back on the outlying districts.

But politicians and bureaucrats are playing ever-diminishing roles. We are entering the decentralized era that Drucker wrote about. Think of Japan as a society that is formed by the overlap of small circles into one very large circle.

The managers of these circles are individual citizens who discover and polish their own strengths. Their efforts require, as Drucker wrote, thinking about the customer and defining a coherent set of values. It is also important to make use of the expertise and experience of older people.

Considering Japan this way, growth becomes about more than just bringing together circles to make them bigger; it is about individuals finding the right circle, regardless of size. Drucker argues that size defines strategy and strategy defines size. Rather than a society that seeks numerical growth, as Japan did in the past, I think we need to create a society that seeks optimal quality.

What Japan is going through will not be unique. Its historic experience—high economic growth, bubble economy, and subsequent economic stagnation, deflation, and falling birthrates—will inevitably be replicated by countries around the world.

Already, some countries are experiencing high economic growth, and others are going through the rupture of a bubble. Some have begun to worry about economic stagnation, deflation, and falling birthrates. These countries and others can learn from what Japan has begun to do—accept economic stagnation, deflation, and falling birthrates, and try to discover how people can live happily in those circumstances.

Japan was at one point the world's second-largest economy. (Now we are third.) Having become aware of the fallacy of unlimited growth, we must adjust to our role as a lifestyle leader. It is up to us, both as individuals and as a country, to find a way to live happily even in economic decline.

Japan's today is the world's tomorrow. In Drucker's sense, our customer is the world, and Japan can best serve it by creating new values and new ways of living.

SMALLER COULD BE BEAUTIFUL

MARK CLIFFORD

ALMOST BY ACCIDENT, Japan is conducting a great experiment. No other significant country has ever seen its population plummet so fast without disease or war.

A Japanese baby today is born into a country of nearly 127 million people. If she
lives out a typical Japanese lifespan (86 years now for women, and continuing to
lengthen), when she dies near the end of the century Japan is likely to have only
about half as many people as it had on the day of her birth.

A Japanese child born today, over the course of her life, will watch her country
complete a fascinating two-and-a-half-century arc. The journey so far has taken
Japan from a small, isolated island nation to an industrialized phenom that peaked
for a time as the world's second-largest economy. Now, as China passes Japan in
the GDP league tables, Japan is charting a path that will see it once again become a
small island nation on the periphery of a teeming, dynamic continent.

Therein lies Japan's greatest challenge in coming decades: to ensure that its impending smallness is beautiful. With the right leadership and the right policies, the
country can succeed. Counterintuitive though it may seem, Japan's relative decline
could be a positive development for its people. In the happy version of Japan's future, productivity improvements and technological advances combine to put Japan
in the top rank of the world's most livable and environmentally friendly nations.
Japan would use its stock of physical and intellectual capital, along with its engineering and manufacturing prowess, to build cities that were no longer as crowded
but featured today's amenities and much more.

A less-populous Japan, with most of its people clustered into a handful of big
cities, would allow for a greater expansion of natural parks. Large swathes of the

---

Mark Clifford is executive director of the Asia Business Council.

archipelago could revert to wilderness, and these renewed natural spaces would sustain the development of a profitable ecotourism industry. Agriculture would remain important as a way of life for a significant minority—and as a major source of food for consumers who prefer the *terroir* of home-grown Japanese products. High-end manufacturing would lead the world and engineering and science would remain national passions; so, too, would the task of preserving Japan's traditional arts and crafts. In an increasingly globalized and homogenized world, Japan would stand out as a rich country that, more than any other, had preserved many of its defining characteristics, from its appreciation of fine food and elegant design to an affinity for craftsmanship, precise organization, and social harmony.

GET A LIFE, FOREIGN PUNDITS SNEERED IN THE '70S AND '80S. WELL, MANY JAPANESE ARE DOING JUST THAT.

The outcome of this grand experiment could be a healthy, prosperous, and contented society whose members enjoy the best of city and country life. Growth would be modest, but the standard of living would be high. Part of the economy would be well integrated into the global economy, through a handful of large corporations. But for many of the people, the small island economy would provide ample opportunity, with the wealth generated by the export sector paying for the imported goods that the Japanese need but cannot produce.

These blissful conditions won't materialize automatically. A perfectly plausible alternative is a dystopian spiral into poverty driven by higher government debt, sluggish productivity growth, and the burden imposed on ever-fewer workers of caring for a relentlessly increasing number of elderly.

To avoid that outcome, Japan must start now with a hardheaded look at how to cope with its extraordinary situation. There can be no more denial, no more pretending that the demographic ship will somehow dramatically alter course. Wise government policies must ensue, starting with measures to enhance output in some of the economy's least-productive sectors, notably services, so that the falloff in the workforce does not deprive the nation of the resources its living standards require. Accompanying those policies must be a commitment from virtually all segments of society to change social and business relations in ways that make the most of the population's graying. None of this will be painless, but if Japan seizes the opportunities presented by its human "hollowing out," it could emerge as a pacesetter for other countries facing population shrinkage.

Plotting an escape from Japan's demographic predicament requires a clearer understanding of how the nation got into that predicament in the first place. In his comedy *Lysistrata*, the Greek playwright Aristophanes had the women of Athens go on a no-sex strike until their men stopped the Peloponnesian War. But what Japanese women are doing is no laughing matter. They have gone on a serious baby strike—and for understandable reasons.

Japanese women have decided not to have many babies in a society where kids too often mean the end of a career, the end of independence, and the start of a race to get little Hirotaro into the best kindergarten. Small wonder that "office ladies" are ubiquitous in Paris and Hong Kong, where they frequent the boutiques of Chanel and Louis Vuitton. These women might be living with their parents, but they are saving their salaries for *haute cuisine* and designer handbags. Is that really an irrational choice given what motherhood means in Japan?

At some point a desperate Japan might possibly implement policies that would encourage more childbearing. Women would need greater opportunities in the workplace and the sort of pro-family policies adopted in countries such as Sweden (where working parents get 16 months of paid leave after having a child). Perhaps even more unlikely, Japan could welcome immigrants, who have contributed to economic prosperity in places as different as Hong Kong and the United States, Canada and Singapore. But significantly altering Japan's demographic destiny would take a shock of almost unimaginable consequences.

The *bonsai* model: small and beautiful.

As the Japanese embark on their experiment, they have already created an enviable lifestyle that is well worth preserving. Back in the 1970s and 1980s the West derided the Japanese for being nose-to-the-grindstone workaholics. Get a life, foreign pundits sneered. Well, many Japanese are doing just that. Tokyo's 160,000 restaurants boast more Michelin stars among them than all the eateries in Paris and New York combined, and whether these establishments serve elaborate *kaiseki* cuisine or humbler meals, their customers revel in savoring locally sourced ingredients. While developing Asia is in a fevered art boom, with *nouveaux-riche* collectors vying for attention, Japan's exquisite museums rank among the world's finest. Abandoned islands and rural areas host sculpture parks and art festivals. And of course, Japan's public spaces are safe, thanks to one of the world's lowest violent crime rates.

The problem is that the Japanese won't be able to enjoy their good food, fine art, and well-maintained trains—much less designer handbags—if they don't have the money to pay for them. Caring for the burgeoning number of elderly will place enormous demands on future resources. So will raising the tax revenue needed to ensure that the government's debt burden does not reach financial crisis–inducing levels. Generating those resources will not be easy at a time when the size of the labor force is plummeting.

Ultimately, the success of Japan's experiment in demographic downsizing will turn on whether productivity—output per worker—can improve fast enough to offset the decline in people. The good news is that Japan's factory workers are among the world's most skilled and its citizens among the world's most educated. The big worry, from a productivity standpoint, is that Japan has rejected the rough-and-tumble of Anglo Saxon–style market capitalism. If the price of having fewer losers is fewer winners, that is a price Japan has so far been willing to pay. But if the happy version of Japan's future is to prevail, policymakers will have to accept more competition.

Just as important as enhancing productivity is the test that Japan's social cohesion will undergo. Leadership will be needed—not just from politicians, but also from the media, nongovernmental organizations, artists, and other opinion shapers. Society will need to build a new generational consensus if the elderly aren't to be seen simply as a burden. A key element is to keep the older Japanese population economically active as long as possible. Retirement ages should increase dramatically. That change implies re-thinking the hierarchical nature of work. Can Japanese companies keep workers in place for an extra 10 or 20 years but demote them in the organizational hierarchy? That would be sufficiently tough in Silicon Valley, let alone Japan. But it is an issue that Japan—and many other countries—must confront.

The elderly will need to be more involved with children and younger adults, whether formally in the educational system or outside it. This involvement could take many forms; perhaps the most promising is the transmission of Japanese craft, design, and culture. There must be a conscious policy of generational bridge building to prevent age apartheid, with continued support for social services for both the young and the old—whether that support involves spending money on improving schools or building hospices. The alternative could be older voters who want to cut educational spending because of falling student rolls and younger voters who refuse to support healthcare for the aged.

If Japan succeeds in utilizing the advantages of declining numbers, one area in which it will undoubtedly shine is environmental sustainability. The filthy air and mercury poisoning scandal of the post-World War II growth years gave way four decades ago to a remarkable energy conservation effort. Japan, always reminding itself that it's a vulnerable island nation with no oil, is now the most energy-efficient large economy. And it's set to get better. From aggressive carbon-cutting targets to the rooftop gardens literally sprouting across Tokyo, there's a nationwide effort to live efficiently.

Low carbon needn't mean dreary. Tokyo is virtually the only Asian capital where bicycling is part of normal middle-class life rather than something endured only by the poor. Public transport in Japanese cities is cheap and reliable.

Japan's environmental thrift complements the global leadership of its companies in areas such as solar power, energy-efficient cars, and a host of other ecofriendly technologies. The value of that expertise will grow as the world moves toward a low-carbon future. But for Japan to sustain its edge, it must continue investments in R&D and science and engineering education, as well as foster a more entrepreneurial, risk-oriented culture that will promote the commercialization of the ideas generated in university and corporate labs.

For a wealthy population essentially to turn its back on growth is a radical rejection of everything that modern market economies stand for. Such a shift is all the more poignant in the case of Japan, given what has happened in the 150 years since the Japanese decided to imbibe the spirit of scientific and technical progress from the West while preserving the best of their traditional society. Japan was a pioneer at the time of the Meiji Restoration, showing in the decades that followed that an Asian nation could play catch-up with the Western powers. Tragic and misguided as the country's military aggression during the 1930s and 1940s was, Japan's initial wartime success in 1940–41 inspired a generation of independence fighters to take up arms against colonial powers.

More positively, Japan's post-1945 economic success was an inspiration to its East Asian neighbors. Its best decades of postwar growth led the way for the wave of countries that followed in its wake—from Taiwan and South Korea in the 1970s and 1980s to China today. All the while, Japan has been unmatched in retaining its national character. Although traditionalists are forever bemoaning the loss of Japan, it has a unique identity. Indeed, Japan has balanced tradition and modernity with exceptional finesse.

So if any country can provide a model for a way to decline gracefully, it is Japan. Its sobering and remarkable experiment has just begun—and the world must hope, for its own sake as well as Japan's, that the ending is beautiful.

REFORMING JAPAN, NORDIC STYLE

RICHARD KATZ

NOWHERE IS THE KEYNESIAN notion that ideas matter, for good or ill, truer than in Japan, where false choices are the biggest obstacles to economic and institutional reform.

Take, for example, the reformers who, in the tradition of former Prime Minister Junichiro Koizumi (2001–06), can envision change only in the harsh magic-of-the-marketplace version popularized by Ronald Reagan and Margaret Thatcher. To gain efficiency and GDP growth, Japan's Thatcherites seem to say, the country must accept falling real wages and the second-highest poverty rate among the rich countries (after the United States). Already, one-third of Japan's workforce is relegated to part-time or temporary employment, under which they must submit to lower wages and less job stability. That is one reason why household income, hence consumer demand, is so low and why Japan seeks the Sisyphus-like remedy of an ever-rising trade surplus to drive demand for its output.

In a country with egalitarian values, that kind of economic development has produced a backlash. Many within the fractious Democratic Party of Japan (DPJ), which came to power in 2009, argue that Japan must shore up income equality and job security by returning to the practices that led to the "lost decades"—wasteful public works, protection of inefficient economic sectors, and zombie firms. Prime Minister Naoto Kan sometimes criticizes deregulation as a job-destroyer.

If the debate remains locked in this mode, Japanese voters will reject change. And without the right reforms, aging and inefficiency will doom Japan to stagnant or declining living standards. Fortunately, the fundamental premise of the debate is

---

Richard Katz is the editor of The Oriental Economist Report.

misguided. Equality *and* growth; efficiency *and* security; full employment *and* rising wages—these can be allies, not alternatives.

Growth and efficiency can provide the means to finance rising wages and a social safety net. In return, a properly woven safety net can encourage the public to accept the creative destruction that underpins growth by aiding the re-employment of those who suffer in the process. In Japan, unfortunately, the safety net has taken the form of protecting weak industries and firms via regulations and anticompetitive business practices. Such practices have merely proven that those who sacrifice growth for the sake of security risk ending up with neither.

There is a different, better way. The Nordic countries— Denmark, Finland, Norway, and Sweden—have a safety net that not only buffers the jobless from catastrophe but also fosters growth. According to the Organisation for Economic Co-operation and Development (OECD) data, Danish workers in 2008 enjoyed the highest real wages in Europe, the second-lowest unemployment rate in the OECD, and the greatest income equality. Swedes enjoyed one of the highest rates of real wage growth over the past decade, and ranked second in income equality. Finland and Norway were sixth and seventh.

IN JAPAN, A WORKER'S PRIMARY SOCIAL SAFETY NET IS HIS JOB. THAT CREATES TREMENDOUS POLITICAL PRESSURE TO KEEP MORIBUND AND MEDIOCRE FIRMS GOING.

Like Japan, the Nordic countries are homogeneous, highly educated, former one-party democracies. Norway even hunts whales. These countries, like Japan, enjoyed stellar postwar growth, then went into deep crisis. In Sweden, according to the International Monetary Fund (IMF) and World Bank, GDP declined 6 percent from 1991 to 1993; unemployment rose from 2 percent in 1988 to 9.4 percent by 1994; and the budget deficit peaked at 13 percent of GDP. Denmark's "lost decade" began with a recession in the early 1980s. In 1982, the ruling Social Democratic government threw up its arms in despair and turned the government over to the opposition without an election. The economy grew just 0.6 percent from 1987 through 1993; in 1993, according to the IMF, unemployment peaked at 12.4 percent.

Unlike Japan, however, the Nordics recognized their problems. Breaking with one-party democracy, they engaged in an ultimately fruitful trial-and-error process of institutional and structural reform. Their equivalent of Japan's quasi-Thatcherite "Koizumians" became less neoliberal, while the Social Democrats adapted their egalitarian and redistributionist desires to the needs of market-led growth. The Nordics recovered, and they are now among the most competitive, prosperous, and contented countries in the world.

Between 1995 and the onset of the global slump in 2008, according to the World Bank, Finland and Sweden achieved the fourth- and fifth-highest rates of per capita GDP growth among a group of 19 rich countries, at 3.5 percent and 2.7 percent respectively (the United States came in tenth, at 2.2 percent). Sweden and Finland came in third and fourth in productivity growth. In Denmark, the rate of private-sector productivity growth more than doubled, to 2.5 percent, from 1.1 percent. Danish unemployment had fallen to 3.3 percent just before the recent global recession; Swedish unemployment was more stubborn, at 6.2 percent.

Can Japan say "flexicurity"?

The key to the Nordic turnaround is "flexicurity," an unwieldy term coined by Danish Prime Minister Poul Nyrup Rasmussen in the 1990s to describe policies that fuse the ideals of flexibility and security. In the United States, there is lots of market flexibility, but workers have limited security and income inequality is high. In Japan and continental Europe, there is lots of security for those with a full-time regular job, but much less security for the rest and less flexibility in the economy as a whole. Companies that cannot easily let go of workers during slack times are reluctant to hire even during good times—one of the reasons that youth unemployment in Japan has hit 10 percent, and is more than twice that in France and Spain.

By contrast, the Nordic model combines the growth-enhancing flexibility of the market with a high degree of income security and equality. Flexicurity means that rather than trying to protect a particular job at a particular firm, the system instead seeks to provide employment security—generous unemployment compensation, assistance in finding work, plus pension and healthcare plans not tied to any particular position. Jobs come and go. Companies come and go. But workers find new jobs, the economy gets more efficient, and real wages keep rising.

It is cheaper and easier to lay off workers or even close down a plant in the Nordic countries than it is in Germany or France. More than 30 percent of Danes change jobs every year, the highest figure in the OECD; 11 percent lose their jobs and another 20 percent quit to find better ones. Generous unemployment insurance in Sweden and Denmark replaces some 75–90 percent of a low-income worker's wage, while effective labor-market programs help workers retrain or get a new job quickly. Flexicurity is a kind of *kaizen*—the Japanese term for continuous improvement—for both people and the production process.

Workers unafraid to lose their jobs make no political demands to keep zombie firms or industries alive. Nor do they fear that competition, globalization, or new technologies will ruin their lives. On the contrary, in Sweden, 80 percent say that increased trade is a good thing.

The difference with Japan could not be starker. In Japan, a worker's primary social safety net is his job (women, by and large, are outside this system, as they are much more likely to be temporary or part-time workers). If his firm

At one of IKEA's Japan stores, learning to work the Swedish way.
© Yoshikazu Tsuno/AFP/Getty Images

downsizes or goes under, the worker is in big trouble, because he will find it difficult to get an equivalent position at another firm. That form of employment uncertainty creates tremendous political pressure to keep moribund and mediocre firms going.

Moreover, the seniority wage system rewards workers who stay at their job and penalizes those whose jobs disappear. The pension and unemployment systems penalize workers who move from firm to firm. Finally, a series of court decisions have made layoffs difficult. No wonder that in Japan (and continental Europe), nearly half of all workers have stayed at the same firm for more than ten years, compared with 26 percent in the United States and 31 percent in Denmark.

REFORM HAS NOT BEEN WIDE ENOUGH, OR DEEP ENOUGH, TO CREATE A BROAD-BASED PRODUCTIVITY REVOLUTION.

With Japan's working-age population shrinking, increased output per worker is the only source of GDP growth—but productivity is rising at a limp 1.5 percent a year. The country currently is so far behind in so much of its economy that it could gain a huge boost just by bringing productivity in laggard industries closer to global standards. Despite stellar performance in a few sectors like autos and electronics, Japanese manufacturing as a whole is 30 percent less efficient than manufacturing in the United States. For example, the food processing industry has productivity only 40 percent of US levels—and is falling. Farming, construction, and much of the service sector are even worse off. Post-1995, two-thirds of the acceleration in productivity growth in the United States came from old-economy industries like retail and rust-belt manufacturing that used new technologies or simply reorganized themselves under the pressure of competition. In short, it is not exotica like nanotechnology, but improvements in every sector of the economy, old and new, that will revitalize Japan.

Improvement in efficiency is where flexicurity comes in. Within the OECD, efficiency improvements *within* each firm account for less than half of the growth in Total Factor Productivity (TFP), a figure that measures the use of both capital and labor. Some 40 percent of the improvement results from newer firms displacing older ones; 13 percent from more efficient firms taking away market share.

Japan misses much of this potential because it has the lowest rate of firm turnover in the OECD. New firms bring in new technology, new attitudes, and fresh blood. But the death of old, inefficient firms is equally critical. Moribund firms trap capital and labor. In Japan, regular workers' flexibility at leading firms is largely limited to moving from one subsidiary to another within a conglomerate. Years ago, when steel sales declined and labor rigidities prevented steelworkers from moving to new firms, Nippon Steel set up money-losing flower shops just to provide work.

The birth and death of firms is a form of Darwinian natural selection. Most new firms do not succeed—but those that do change the economic ecology around them.

What happens if the destruction is too destructive? What if lives shattered by the destruction are unable to recover because of barriers to entry, rigid labor markets, and the like? In that case, people will resist change—and that describes Japan.

There is an additional problem. While there is lots of competition in Japan's efficient export-oriented industries, many of Japan's domestically oriented sectors might
as well have signed mutual nonaggression pacts. For proof, look at how market share
in some industries, such as flat glass or polyethylene film, did not change for decades.
Studies have shown that the best predictor of firm performance is the fierceness of
the competition it faces. And yet, the latest "growth strategy" document of the DPJ
and the Ministry of Economy, Trade and Industry (METI) claims the key to increased
competitiveness is to reduce competition even more by mergers. This is simply wrong.

Japan has instituted significant changes in the last decade, in the areas of finance, retail and wholesale trade, energy, telecommunications, corporate merger
policy, and the role of state enterprises. But reform has not been wide enough, or
deep enough, to create a broad-based productivity revolution. Moreover, some of
the changes advertised as reform are actually retrograde steps, such as mergers that
reduce competition, or labor "reforms" that were advertised as increasing flexibility
but actually allowed firms to shift to lower-paid irregular workers. Except for a very
encouraging improvement in distribution—the subject of major reform—most of
the change has been in the same few sectors that have always worked hard at up-
grading their productivity, such as autos, machinery, and electronics. Japan is getting
the most reform where it needs it least and the least reform where it needs it most.

An Iwakura Mission for the 21st century

Japan and the Nordics share a communitarian, egalitarian ethic, where people
do not fear government involvement in the economy. One important difference,
though, is that in Japan, people doubt whether, in return for their high taxes, the
government will spend the money in ways that benefit society as a whole. Based on
experience, they believe that money will be wasted on special interests, such as the
notorious bridges to nowhere.

In the wake of the catastrophic earthquake-tsunami of March 2011, there will
clearly be a need for a huge rebuilding program. But observers will also want to see
whether any of the infrastructure—from bridges to the nuclear power plants—were
more vulnerable to damage because of lax enforcement of safety and quality standards regarding public works and the politically connected utilities.

Since the Iwakura Mission of 1871, when Meiji Japan sent diplomats and students around the world, Japan has proved adept at seeking out and adapting lessons
from the rest of the world. Japan cannot adopt the Nordic model wholesale, nor
should it want to. Herring and sushi may look alike, after all, but they taste different; economic change, too, has to take account of local preferences.

But flexicurity is a system that is working, something that cannot be said of the
Japanese economic model at the moment. There are many individuals in Japan's
political parties, ministries, business, press, and academia who recognize the need
to surmount the false choice of growth versus security. However, they have not co-
alesced into a force. As Japan seeks solutions to its problems, the country would be
wise to pick and choose among the world's best practices—including, of course, its
own. In doing so, it should look at itself in a Nordic mirror.

CHAPTER FOUR: RE-ENGAGING WITH THE WORLD

© Illustration by Phil Couzens

JAPAN'S GLOBALIZATION IMPERATIVE

GORDON ORR, BRIAN SALSBERG, AND NAOYUKI IWATANI

FOR ALL THE INTERNATIONAL SUCCESS of Japan's big, well-known companies, many still lag behind their global rivals in the most important markets. Why are General Motors and Volkswagen more successful in China than Honda and Toyota? Why are LG and Samsung bigger in India than Panasonic and Sony? Why is IBM larger in Japan than Fujitsu is in the United States?

These questions are more than academic. Survival for many Japanese companies may depend on their ability to greatly increase overseas revenues and profits, given demographic and economic trends that suggest slower or stagnant growth in the home market. Even Japanese companies with established global businesses face stronger competition and must rejuvenate their overseas business models.

Building a globalized company will require many Japanese executives to think in new and unfamiliar ways about organization, marketing, and strategy. The approaches that proved successful in the past—for example, replicating practices from the Japanese market in foreign operations—have outlived their usefulness.

The good news is that the sleeping giant that is Japan Inc. has begun to awaken. There's an uptick in international mergers and acquisitions, a new sense of urgency in boardroom discussions, and a few bold moves by Japan's more progressive companies to use English as a global corporate language and to recruit talented non-Japanese executives. Still, as with most such awakenings, the pace is slow and the approach often opportunistic and confused rather than strategic.

Gordon Orr is a senior partner in McKinsey's Shanghai office and the chairman of McKinsey Asia. Brian Salsberg and Naoyuki Iwatani are partners in McKinsey's Tokyo office.

A matter of survival

Japan's biggest companies have been losing relative market share over the past ten years: their proportion of the Fortune Global 500's total revenues decreased to 13 percent, from 35 percent, between 1995 and 2009. One of Japan's longtime strengths is electronics, for example, but its share of the world's export value of electronic goods has fallen from 30 percent in 1990 to less than 15 percent today, according to the Japanese Ministry of Economy, Trade, and Industry. Many Japanese companies have no alternative to globalization if they hope to continue growing.

A shrinking consumer base and lagging productivity

For the past 40 years, Japanese companies achieved global leadership by dominating their home market, but no longer. Japan's population is expected to fall from 127 million today to less than 100 million between 2040 and 2050. A declining population will almost certainly reduce the absolute level of private consumption, along with tax revenues and, potentially, overall GDP. Private consumption in Japan, at the end of 2008, stood at 220 trillion yen ($2.7 trillion), 59 percent of GDP. It is (optimistically) forecast to reach 293 trillion yen in 2040, with an underlying assumption of an absolute increase in GDP per capita of more than 50 percent—something that is difficult to fathom in the current deflationary environment.

THE GOOD NEWS IS THAT THE SLEEPING GIANT THAT IS JAPAN INC. HAS BEGUN TO AWAKEN.

Another economic issue is lagging productivity at home. Despite a handful of world-leading industries and companies, Japan has among the lowest labor productivity rates of any major developed country. Japanese companies are therefore generally less competitive and more vulnerable to foreign attackers at home. Japanese workers tend to be among the world's most diligent, but they are both collectively and individually inefficient—particularly those who do not toil in factories. Our conversations with senior executives suggest that Japanese managers are acutely aware that their headquarters are overstaffed, that employees focus more on work effort than on impact or outcomes, and that Japanese companies have hobbled efficiency by limiting outsourcing and offshoring to a handful of IT-related functions.

Foreign inroads

Meanwhile, foreign competitors have penetrated Japan's once-insular market, taking advantage of the Japanese consumer's enthusiasm for digital commerce and new openness to foreign products. In many ways, these consumers, long touted as unique, behave increasingly like their counterparts in Europe and the United States: what they want is value. In a Japanese context, value means products that look attractive or stylish but are nonetheless significantly less expensive than traditional offerings.

With a few exceptions, Japanese companies have been slow to offer such value, giving foreign competitors a chance to muscle in, especially those that have significant control of product distribution. Businesses have attracted consumers around the world by offering some combination of value and an exciting shopping experience (Costco, H&M, IKEA, Zara) or a simple, intuitive user experience (Amazon, Apple). Other companies, such as Wal-Mart, use their global footprint to bypass Japan's multilayered distribution system and thus to introduce products at prices significantly lower than the Japanese competition's. While the overall share of foreign competitors remains small, their growth rates often far exceed those of most larger Japanese rivals.

A tired innovation model

Japanese companies once were leaders in providing innovative products appealing to consumers in developed markets. But consumers in fast-growing emerging markets have different needs. Japan has found that trying to identify them in R&D labs at home—the typical approach—is a challenge. That issue is not relevant only to emerging markets; Japanese companies must get closer to their customers everywhere. The current, made-in-Japan model is insufficient.

In fact, the emerging corporate-innovation model is globally collaborative, with product ideas, customer insights, money, and talent coming from all over. Procter & Gamble, for instance, reports that more than 50 percent of its innovation initiatives involve collaboration with outsiders. Shiseido executives say they can't assume that all of the company's innovations, both in beauty care products and in channels, will come from Japan; hence the 2010 acquisition of US-based Bare Escentuals, for $1.7 billion. What makes traditional Japanese lab-based R&D less effective today? In short, increased competition from China, South Korea, and Taiwan; the wide availability of component parts; and an increasingly fast speed to market.

Investment in research and development is often seen as a proxy for innovation, and it is true that Japan is a leader in R&D, spending 3.8 percent of GDP on it. But this view misses a crucial point: innovation across many categories once dominated by Japan now comes from outside the country. A 2010 report by the US-based National Association of Manufacturers listed Singapore and South Korea as the world's top two countries for innovation—far ahead of Japan and even ahead of the eighth-ranked United States.

Getting to global

Many Japanese companies should be global leaders, given their manufacturing and technological prowess and overall size and scale. But they are not. We analyzed the ten largest Japanese companies in each of 16 industries to better understand their global profiles. On average, Japan's ten largest companies in 15 of these industries—automotive is a notable exception—are less global than their overseas peers, as measured by the percentage of revenues, assets, and stock ownership outside Japan. By those measures, Japanese companies made no progress toward globalization from 2006 to 2009 (exhibit).

Averages don't tell the whole story, and some Japanese companies are quite global even by these standards. For most, however, globalization is a work in progress. McKinsey's experience in Japan suggests five steps—across organization, marketing, and strategy—that its companies should take to globalize successfully.

Exhibit

The Globalization Box Score measures a company's level of globalization
based on the share of its revenues, assets, and stock ownership,
as well as on the number of its leadership positions that are external to
its home country.

For the top 10 public companies by revenues across 16 selected industries,[1]
n = 160

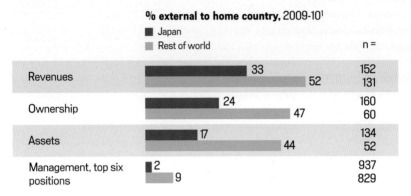

% external to home country, 2009-10[1]

■ Japan
▨ Rest of world   n =

		n =
Revenues	33	152
	52	131
Ownership	24	160
	47	60
Assets	17	134
	44	52
Management, top six positions	2	937
	9	829

To ensure a representative analysis, we categorized Japan's public companies
into the following 16 industries.

Automobiles and parts	Food and beverages	Personal goods
Basic materials	Health care	Retail
Construction and materials	Industrial goods and services	Technology
Consumer electronics and leisure goods	Media and telecommunications	Travel and leisure
Durable house products	Oil and gas	Utilities
Financial services		

[1]Specifically, for Japan, the top 10 Japanese companies in each industry; for all others,
the 10 largest non-Japanese companies by revenues.

Source: Bloomberg; McKinsey & Company analysis

Making the case for globalization

Many Japanese companies understand the benefits of globalization. But their executives may lack a compelling "globalization story" for employees—global goals,
aspirations, and value propositions. Are these widely understood and properly communicated in a way that excites and energizes the organization while addressing
the anxiety that comes with big changes in direction? Spending time and effort
developing such messages may seem trivial, but a globalization effort won't get far
unless employees are on board.

Shiseido illustrates some attributes of a successful case. The company's senior
executives must, for example, explain the globalization story in a way that makes

it meaningful to other employees. When Shiseido's Shinzo Maeda (now the company's chairman) became chief executive officer, in 2005, he made globalization a top priority. Maeda constantly reminds employees of the company's vision: to "become a global player representing Asia with its origins in Japan." This positioning clarifies the company's overall strategy—reinforced by a major acquisition and the establishment of a global rotation program—without diminishing the home market's importance.

Senior executives should understand a company's distinctive strengths and capabilities clearly and ensure that they form part of its global strategy. For Shiseido, this means training and technology. The company extensively trains thousands of beauty consultants each year and has implemented the same approach in China, Russia, and the United States. While many Shiseido products don't bear the corporate brand name abroad, most are sold as the fruits of Japanese research and technology.

JAPAN ACCOUNTED FOR 35 PERCENT OF THE FORTUNE GLOBAL 500'S REVENUES IN 1995—AND ONLY 13 PERCENT IN 2009.

Strong—and sometimes not so popular—acts by senior executives can back up the talk. Upon assuming the top job, Maeda jettisoned some smaller, long-established brands, while doubling down on global megabrands better positioned to become category leaders at home and abroad, though he left room for local brands. He also hired an experienced foreigner, Carsten Fischer, to run Shiseido's international business, which currently accounts for more than 40 percent of the company's revenues. Fischer demonstrated his desire to be part of the Japanese team by shunning a corporate office, opting for an open cubicle among the rest of the staff.

Adopting English as the company language

Making English the main company language may be controversial and difficult to execute. But its importance in a globalization effort cannot be overstated, especially for monocultural Japanese companies. Our experience suggests that the decision to conduct most of the company's business and internal interactions in English was an important success factor for the globalization efforts of multinational companies such as France's Danone and Israel's Teva Pharmaceutical Industries.

The move to English is critical because it opens up a world of talent. Everything else in the globalization journey follows from gaining access to a higher-quality employee pool. It's hard to get a rich exchange of talented people across units and geographies without a *lingua franca*. As irritating as it may be to cultures that speak other languages, the trend toward English is unstoppable—nearly one billion people use it as their first or second language. Talented Asians with global aspirations tend to learn English, not Japanese or Russian.

How will Japanese companies adopt English? That's a big question. In 2009 Japan had the lowest score of any of the International Monetary Fund's advanced economies on the Test of English as a Foreign Language, administered to foreign students who .want to study in the United States. It had the second-lowest score among Asian nations, outperforming only Laos.[1] Still, companies like Rakuten and Uniqlo have announced that they will make English their corporate language by 2012, and Nissan and Takeda conduct many meetings in English. Should prestigious schools such as Tokyo University or a few of the leading Japanese companies make high English scores a prerequisite for acceptance, we would imagine a rapid increase in overall English ability.

Designing an aggressive talent-management strategy

Typical Japanese executives have never held an international assignment or worked outside their companies or business units. Nearly all senior executives are Japanese. Such professionals may be quite capable of managing domestic businesses but are increasingly ill-prepared to run global enterprises in fast-changing, competitive markets. Japanese companies are painfully aware of this handicap. A 2010 government survey of 263 senior executives found that the single biggest hurdle for globalization was the "securing and training of human resources in Japan."

In general, the Japanese corporate human-resources model lends itself well to domestic business but not to international. The defining characteristics of Japanese talent management are well known: tenure-based advancement, egalitarian compensation, and lifetime employment. The HR function focuses almost entirely on recruiting at the university level and on greasing the wheels of the lockstep, tenure-based promotion system. International experience not only isn't essential to advancement but also is often seen as a negative. Japanese organizations tend to be monocultural and monolingual, making it difficult for foreigners to succeed. Also, women have trouble advancing: Japan placed 94th of 134 countries in the World Economic Forum's Gender Gap Index 2010. Among high-income countries, only South Korea had a lower score.

Most Japanese companies need to rethink HR's role and to adopt an employment strategy incorporating new approaches to career paths, compensation, and performance evaluation. Some, like Komatsu and Shiseido, are moving ahead, but elsewhere progress is slow. Best-practice talent-management programs apply meritocracy at all levels and emphasize diversity. They manage talent strategically to attract the best people and find places for them, not just to fill open positions. These are the basic steps Japanese companies can take to upgrade their talent management:

- *Embrace diversity and set aspirational targets for women, foreigners, and Japanese managers from other companies and industries.* We are not recommending a quota system, but without targets there is no way to guide the HR organization or track progress.
- *Create a global rotation program open to the top 100 to 200 executives, enabling them to work abroad in other parts of the company.* The program should guarantee their original positions and tie promotions to participation. Globalization and similar strategic projects can help improve this group's capabilities and experience.

---

1 Daisuke Wakabayashi, "English gets the last word in Japan," wsj.com, August 4, 2010.

The right recipe for globalization: Combine multinational talent and foreign language capability. Season with overseas training. Mix vigorously.

© Illustration by Dan Page

- *Hold HR more accountable for talent strategy and development rather than just internal placement and recruiting.* This responsibility includes establishing a broad leadership-development program and giving support to coaching for managers.

Komatsu, for example, has its own in-house management-training program. Local executives manage most of the company's major country operations, and employees know that overseas experience offers a path to rapid advancement. In fact, more than two-thirds of Komatsu's executives in Japan have had meaningful work stints abroad. Shiseido, joining the ranks of Nissan and Sony, hired a foreigner as its top executive managing the international business and installed one of Japan's first up-or-out employment policies: if managers fail to be promoted within a certain time, they will be asked to leave.

Building a global marketing function

In recent years, Japanese consumer product companies have had trouble turning their technical and manufacturing prowess into brand equity and products tailored for foreign consumers. Indeed, they have spent too little time trying to understand consumers and are often disconnected from the markets where they want to build share. Many executives of Japan's largest consumer companies privately acknowledge that they have fallen behind the likes of Apple, P&G, Samsung, and Unilever in their efforts to ensure shopper-focused rather than R&D lab–centric product development.

Some of the best-known Japanese companies lack proper marketing functions, believing that a product-development group, a sales team, and a contract with a leading Japanese advertising firm will suffice. But this approach has had its day. The ever-faster pace of product development—homogenizing products, prices, and channels—makes marketing and branding more important than ever. Samsung, for example, introduced the Galaxy Tab in November 2010, just six months after Apple launched its iPad.

World-class marketing organizations have several points in common: a meaningful role for global marketing in the innovation and product-development process, the presentation of a consistent customer experience, the ability to absorb insights from other industries or markets, and the use of cutting-edge techniques to better understand consumer needs. A few Japanese companies, such as Toyota and Nintendo, have both strong global brands and well-developed marketing capabilities, but these are exceptions.

Brands are immensely beneficial to their owners when they have unique value propositions effectively communicated to strategically selected customer segments. But the concept of brand management is alien to most Japanese consumer companies. Each business unit and geography tends to control the brand on its own turf, and that sometimes leads to an inconsistent brand identity or experience. In 2010, only five Japanese companies made the WPP BrandZ Top 100, an annual ranking of brands based on inputs from over one million consumers globally. They accounted for less than 5 percent of the total brand equity value created by enterprises on the list.

In the majority of global companies that have built substantial brand equity, the most important marketing decisions are made by the chief executive officer, the equivalent head of an autonomous business unit, or someone, such as the chief marketing officer (CMO), who reports directly to the organization's most senior decision-making position. In these companies, it's the CMO who makes the final call on the balance between global and local marketing, on trade-offs among go-to-market channels, and on how much to invest in new advertising media. However, fewer than 1 percent of Japanese companies with revenue above $1 billion have a CMO, compared with more than 10 percent in US companies of equivalent size. Of the top 12 Japanese beverage manufacturers, for example, we could find only one with a separate marketing organization reporting to the CEO.

How can a Japanese company with global aspirations become truly brand-oriented?

- *Decide which powers accrue to the CMO position and where it should be in the organizational structure.* At least until global brand-equity thinking becomes second nature in a company, the CMO must have disproportionate air time at all key decision-making forums.
- *Recruit marketing talent worthy of the brand-value goals.* The key positions must be filled with people who are as fluent in global marketing insights as they are in Japanese culture. To bring in alternative ways of thinking, it will be necessary to recruit marketing talent from other industries or geographies.
- *Reallocate power to global business units and brand "owners."* Matrix structures—characteristic of organizations in which both country managers and global brand and business unit owners share power—do have their challenges. Yet delegating all decision making to a specific geography is unlikely to create successful global businesses. Marketers increasingly tend to identify "tribes" of consumer archetypes that cross borders. Each archetype involves similar products and brands. Meanwhile, the Internet's increasing power has forced companies to coordinate marketing messages globally. For Japanese companies, shifting to a model that looks more like the approach of the world's leading global consumer companies is worth the short-term pain that adopting it would entail, and will probably raise their global brand equity.

Getting more from strategic corporate development

Any serious globalization attempt will inevitably lead to more M&A, joint ventures, and alliances, as well as greater use of other expansion models. It's clear that Japanese companies will have to move aggressively in this arena, since in many markets organic growth—important as it is—will not provide the scale needed for competitiveness.

Japanese companies are not shy about doing overseas deals. In fact, M&A has increased recently, in part because of a stronger yen and the increasing recognition that the domestic market is shrinking. Over the years, some individual deals have proved successful. But only a few Japanese companies have tried and perfected a serial-acquisition strategy, such as those of Cisco Systems and P&G, considered models in this area. One company that's trying is Rakuten, Japan's leading online shopping site, which completed deals in China, France, Indonesia, and the United States, all within a 12-month period.

Besides M&A, many companies have tried partnerships with trading concerns, minority joint ventures, and alliances. Generally speaking, these approaches have disappointed, in part because they neither build capabilities nor help companies share best practices; at best, they provide an international revenue stream or rudimentary access to new markets. Indeed, many Japanese multinationals act more as holding companies for international subsidiaries than as truly global organizations. When they buy companies, they do minimal integration, except to consolidate revenue—ignoring opportunities for cost-cutting, engaging talented employees of the acquired enterprise, and identifying its best products and taking them global. In some cases, Japanese acquirers have even found themselves acquiring minority interests in companies that have competing interests, leaving the target companies paralyzed on how to grow.

Senior Japanese executives express frustration to us about this kind of ineffective postmerger management, which often stems from language and other cultural barriers. More than one Japanese company we know of has made an overseas purchase and then sent a team to the acquired company's headquarters, only to return with little to show for the effort because of communication challenges and a lack of clarity about how to share best practices.

We have observed some companies trying to globalize by experimenting with business models that are pointedly unlike those at their core. In one approach, the Japanese company creates a "second home," which offers freedom from the constraints of headquarters—meaning more room for across-the-board experimentation and for decision making free of home market bias. Existing businesses run from the Japanese headquarters remain undisturbed, while managers can share with headquarters the lessons learned in the second home. Executives can create one by reorganizing the company to eliminate the distinction between domestic and foreign markets, acquiring a foreign business and using it for pilots and experimentation, and moving a business unit to a foreign country.

Panasonic is moving in this direction. In late 2010, its president, Fumio Ohtsubo, announced that the company would eliminate the distinction between domestic and global markets in its consumer products marketing operations. This decision comes two years after the company retired the Japan-only National brand and refocused its efforts on developing affordable products for emerging markets. Komatsu, the world's second-largest maker of construction equipment (after Caterpillar), conducts annual reviews of its business units' operating plans not at the Tokyo headquarters but in each of the company's eight major markets, to signal their importance.

Another way for Japanese companies to grow internationally involves joint ventures with domestic competitors. In many cases, these companies can't compete for overseas projects, because of high costs, a lack of scale, or inexperience navigating in foreign markets, so they could consider collaborating. We find more and more examples of this approach, including an agreement between Hitachi and Mitsubishi Heavy Industries to cooperate on railway systems in overseas markets.

• • •

Globalization is a means to an end. The end is to create and sustain a self-reinforcing cycle of profit growth and value creation, access to a richer asset and talent pool, and a more compelling value proposition for employees and investors. Getting there will be difficult. Many Japanese companies must make big changes, but most will start the journey with considerable advantages: scale, relative strength in the home market, formidable quality standards and service, and experience working with an aging and digitally sophisticated population. At the time of this writing, Japanese companies also have a strong currency for doing international deals.

Nevertheless, the path forward will seem difficult for most senior Japanese executives, figuratively standing on the shore and looking across the ocean to a world whose language many of them don't speak and whose habits and successful behavior seem radically different from their own. Even if they have concluded that some things in their companies must change, it may be difficult to imagine how to move the organization in a new direction. The most expedient path, we would argue, is "getting the boat pushed out into the current" by ensuring that faster globalization becomes a leading priority over the next few years.

HOW SHISEIDO WENT GLOBAL

SHINZO MAEDA

GLOBALIZATION HAS COME TO SHISEIDO—and in a big way. Overseas sales now account for more than 40 percent of our revenue, compared with 10 percent a decade ago. As our financial profile changed, we realized our company, too, must change. In a sense, Japan is in a similar position. As a nation, we are not big enough to go it alone, and our population is getting smaller; our future has to be in connecting more often with more of the world.

If Japan's companies are to globalize, the people who work at those companies must globalize, too. That is not easy. Japanese people don't have much experience with different cultures; historically, we haven't been good at handling diversity, and we are not that eager to try.

Consider the makeup of the boards of Japanese companies. There are few non-Japanese directors—even as foreign share ownership of Japanese companies has risen sharply—and few women. At the end of 2009, 19 of the Japanese companies in the Fortune 200 had no women directors, the most of any country represented on the list. Among those companies were many that have global scale. Overall, fewer than 2 percent of Japan's corporate board members are female. In part, the homogeneity of Japan's large companies reflects the fact that their boards tend to be drawn from the ranks of experienced senior managers, and there are few women or foreigners in these positions. Regardless of the cause, the effect is that Japanese boards lack diversity.

The commitment to change that pattern has to start at the top. Since 2006, Shiseido has made a conscious effort to diversify our board. Out of 13 board members (including two external directors, a position added in 2006), seven are not the old-style members, that is, Japanese men who had worked for Shiseido their whole

---

Shinzo Maeda is chairman of Shiseido, and was president and CEO from 2005 to early 2011.

lives. We have three board members who are women, and one who is not Japanese. Together, these individuals bring a new level of objectivity and a broader perspective because they have different backgrounds and areas of expertise.

OVERSEAS SALES NOW ACCOUNT FOR ALMOST 40 PERCENT OF OUR REVENUE, COMPARED TO 10 PERCENT A DECADE AGO.

As a result, discussions at our board meetings have become much livelier. In the past, our meetings proceeded much like those at other large Japanese companies. We spent about 40 minutes reviewing written documents diligently prepared for us by the staff, and about 10 minutes commenting on those documents. We didn't often dispute or even question staff recommendations. But now our meetings are very different. We insist that written materials are distributed well in advance. Board members are expected to have read the documents carefully before the meeting. We spend about 10 minutes discussing the prepared materials, and devote the remaining 40 minutes to group discussion. This procedure might seem like a small change, but it has strengthened the position of primary decision makers, and thereby transformed the whole dynamic of our approach to management.

Cascades and M&A

There's a Japanese saying that change starts at the top and then cascades to lower levels. That's been true for us. Once we made the commitment to embrace diversity at the top, everything else began to cascade in the right direction. Now we are pushing for diversity at every level. We have established a global rotation program to ensure that our Japanese employees get overseas experience, and are sending more of our young employees to work in our foreign subsidiaries. We have established a global grading system to evaluate the depth and breadth of our employees' understanding of overseas markets, and are pushing our Japanese employees to learn foreign languages, especially Mandarin. We are working hard to encourage global mobility and to create a more inclusive culture, with common values and principles around the world. There is a need to have a strong group feeling among all Shiseido people, whether they are Japanese or not.

At the same time, we're working to create new opportunities for women and non-Japanese employees in Shiseido's operations around the world. Already more than half our overseas managers are women. Globally, more than half of our sales representatives are non-Japanese. In China alone, we now have more than 10,000 employees. And we are working to create new training and career development programs for our non-Japanese colleagues. In 2008, for example, we opened the Shiseido Training Center in Shanghai, to train our ever-growing number of Chinese employees as well as the employees of our business partners.

We're also trying harder to understand our overseas customers and business partners. In 2006 we opened research centers in Europe and Southeast Asia. These centers conduct research into the regulatory frameworks relating to cosmetics in individual countries and are being integrated into a planned global Technology Management System.

As we grow and diversify, we are making greater use of foreign languages, especially English, in our internal communications. We haven't formally declared English our official corporate language; that's a big step that will take time and preparation to implement. But already in our international division we communicate in English, and we all recognize the need to engage with customers, partners, and co-workers beyond Japan in a common language.

Not just cosmetic: Shiseido is betting big on the Chinese consumer.
© Everett Kennedy Brown/epa/Corbis

Another dimension of our globalization policy is time. Shiseido used to plan in three-year increments. Now we are creating ten-year scenarios as a way to think about where to find growth and how to build global capabilities. That was part of the reason for the $1.7 billion purchase of Bare Escentuals in March 2010. This was one of the biggest deals ever made by a Japanese cosmetics company, and a major deal for Shiseido, which historically has done few acquisitions. Bare Escentuals has a substantial presence in the United States, and we have kept its top management, a decision that reflects our belief that Japanese companies should leverage more non-Japanese talent, particularly in local markets. We have many joint ventures outside Japan. Bare Escentuals will be another global brand for Shiseido, and it connects us to a different corporate culture.

The timing of the acquisition—in the midst of the global financial crisis—was also notable. As a country with few natural resources, Japan tends to be prudent. Although an excellent quality, prudence too often translates into an aversion to risk. But because Shiseido had begun to work in a more integrated way and developed a better grip on its overseas operations, we had the confidence, the analytical skills, and the people to seize the opportunity. If we had had only Japanese board members, I am convinced we wouldn't have been able to move with such speed. We'd still be negotiating.

Japan, Asia and the world

The level of cultural understanding needed to operate successfully in cosmetics is much higher than in, say, a technology company, where there are global metrics and standards. Beauty isn't like that; you need to understand local sensibilities in a nuanced way. Japanese companies have often found this nuance difficult to appreciate, which is why few fast-moving Japanese consumer goods companies have expanded globally.

Shiseido was born and grew up in Japan, but in a sense we have always been global. Our founder, Arinobu Fukuhara, a Navy pharmacist, founded the company in 1872 on the Ginza as Japan's first Western-style pharmacy. After a trip to the United States, in 1902, Fukuhara brought the first soda fountain to Japan. The name "Shiseido" itself is derived from a passage in the classical Chinese cosmological text, the *I Ching*.

But more than anywhere else, Shiseido is part of Asia and we should see ourselves as representing Asia, the way L'Oreal is associated with Europe or P&G with the United States. Those are global companies, but with distinct roots. Shiseido is seeking a similar balance: to be true to our Japanese origins and our global responsibilities while also being seen as part of Asia.

This is the right place for us. In terms of skin color, skin texture, hair colors, and other characteristics, the Japanese are more similar to other Asians than they are to Europeans or North Americans, so there is a natural affinity between the region, its people, and our products. Moreover, the Asian market is growing fast. According to the Asian Development Bank, there were about 1.9 billion Asian people in 2008 who could be characterized as middle class, 30 percent more than in 1990. We are not far away from having a billion middle-class Asians, and many of them will have enough money to enhance their beauty.

Just look at China. Beginning in 1983, Shiseido shared technology with a state-owned cosmetics company as a way to build relationships and learn about the market. We opened a research center in Beijing in April 2002, so that we could fuse Chinese social norms with Japanese research expertise. The center helped us develop Aupres Eternal Total Recharge cream for the China market, as well as Sinoadore, which incorporates elements of traditional Chinese medicine.

This effort is paying off. Revenues in China are approaching $1 billion, and we anticipate 15 to 20 percent sales growth for the foreseeable future. And it could be much higher than that. Right now, about 60 million people in China use cosmetics; we expect that number to rise to at least 200 million by 2015. Moreover, Chinese are heavy users of skin-care products, a cosmetic category that is a strength of ours. *Ad-Age* recently ranked Shiseido as the leading skin-care brand in China, in part because Chinese consumers place a high value on Japanese technology. You can see this preference every day in the Ginza, where tour buses spill out Chinese shoppers in front of department stores; for many, the Shiseido counters are their first stop. In China itself, we are adding hundreds of stores every year, and already have more than 5,000.

China has been a long haul for us, and there is still much more to do. Our next challenge in the China market will be to develop a new sales model that is not just a replica of the model we use in Japan but a completely new approach tailored to the unique conditions of the Chinese market. But I believe Shiseido has succeeded so far because we got a number of basic things right. First, we created products exclusively for the China market. Second, we learned to reach different customers by selling our products across a variety of different channels, including department stores, drug stores, and specialty outlets. And finally, we made an effort to identify and promote local talent, an effort that is part of our larger globalization effort.

We are still Japanese, and are proud of our heritage. Now, however, we have shown that we can also be citizens of the world. I am confident that Japan can do the same.

UNLOCKING
SAKOKU

GLEN S. FUKUSHIMA

SAKOKU **(LITERALLY, "LOCKED COUNTRY")**—the policy under which no foreigner could enter or any Japanese person, under penalty of death, leave the country —defined Japan's foreign policy for more than two centuries. The Tokugawa shogunate enacted this policy through a series of edicts issued between 1633 and 1639; the edicts remained in effect until 1853, the year US Commodore Matthew C. Perry forced the reopening of Japan. Until the Meiji Restoration of 1868, no Japanese person could legally leave the country.

This period of self-imposed seclusion has had a profound effect on the course of modern Japanese history. Even during the era of miraculous economic growth from the 1950s to the 1980s, Japan's idea of internationalization was to export people, manufactured products, and capital, rather than to import any of these commodities into Japan. One consequence is that Japan still has, by far, the lowest level of inward foreign direct investment (as a percentage of GDP) of any of the 34 Organisation for Economic Co-operation and Development (OECD) countries. Since the bursting of the economic bubble in the early 1990s, Japan has shown a marked tendency to turn complacently inward, while the rest of the world—especially Japan's neighbors in Asia—has engaged with outsiders more actively than ever.

Over the past decade, Japan's presence on the world scene has declined precipitously. At international conferences, the number of Japanese participants has declined sharply. Those Japanese people who attend rarely engage in the active give-and-take that people from other countries do routinely. The Three S's for which Japanese participants attending international forums became famous in the 1980s— sleep, silence, and smile—persist even today. The test of successful moderators at

---

Glen S. Fukushima is chairman of Airbus Japan and former president of the American Chamber of Commerce in Japan.

international conferences, the joke goes, is that they are able to get the Indians to stop talking, and the Japanese to start.

Similarly, the number of Japan's young people studying abroad, particularly in the United States, has plummeted, as the number of Chinese and South Koreans has surged. Of the top ten countries sending students to Harvard University, nine now send more students there than they did ten years ago. The one exception is Japan. Between 1999 and 2009, the number of Chinese students at Harvard increased to 463, from 227, and the number of South Korean students increased to 315, from 183. By contrast, the number of Japanese students at Harvard dropped to 101, from 151. Last year there were only five Japanese undergraduates enrolled at Harvard and only one in the freshman class.

JAPAN HAS THE LOWEST LEVEL OF INWARD FOREIGN DIRECT INVESTMENT IN THE OECD— BY FAR.

At the end of 2010, the Ministry of Education released statistics confirming this trend. According to the ministry, the number of students studying overseas peaked, at 82,945, in 2004, and then declined for four straight years. In 2008 (the latest year for which statistics were made available), only 66,833 Japanese were studying overseas. Of these, 29,264 students were in the United States (down 13.9 percent from 2007), 16,733 in China (down 10.2 percent), and 4,465 in Britain (down 21.7 percent).

There are many reasons for these trends. For one thing, many young Japanese are simply not interested in going abroad. Japan has become so safe, secure, and comfortable that there is little incentive to live abroad, where one has to speak foreign languages, deal with peoples of other cultures, engage in difficult negotiations, or deal with unfamiliar and competitive situations. The water may be murky; the natives unfriendly. Tokyo has more Michelin-starred restaurants than any city in the world, the people are polite and civil, the streets are clean and safe, and the trains run precisely on time. Why go anywhere else?

According to a poll of Japanese in their 20s conducted by the Japan Travel Bureau in 2009, the second-most frequent reason cited for not going abroad (27 percent) was a lack of interest in foreign things. The fourth reason (24 percent) was the responders' fear of going to dangerous places and catching contagious diseases. Even those Japanese who have recently joined trading companies or the Ministry of Foreign Affairs are less eager to study or work overseas than were their peers of 20 or 30 years ago.

Then there is the job market, which is both short of jobs and tightly controlled. College students feel compelled to start looking for employment from the first day of their junior year, leaving them little time to study abroad. For these students (and their parents), studying abroad is a luxury they can ill afford, especially since few Japanese companies and organizations give credit to their new recruits for overseas experience. At the same time, Japanese organizations are less likely to send their employees overseas for extended study. Some of these entities can no longer afford to; others don't want to pay for MBAs and then see these graduates lured away by foreign companies that often have a greater appreciation for this kind of education. There is also a widespread belief, particularly among the Internet-addicted young, that they can learn what they need online. These young people see little point in attending international conferences or conducting research abroad.

Fundamentally, young Japanese do not want to go abroad because Japan generally does not reward them for doing so. In many cases, studying abroad can actually be a detriment rather than an asset for this group. Stories abound of Japanese students who earned an MBA at a leading business school abroad but, upon returning to headquarters, were assigned the task of language interpreter rather than a line position where they could put their foreign education to substantive use.

The dearth of incentives to venture abroad has created a kind of vicious cycle in which fewer Japanese students apply to foreign universities, and those who do apply are less competitive than their classmates. Applicants from China, India, South Korea, and other countries often go through an intensively competitive process in their home country to gain eligibility to study in the top American universities. They have strong English skills and are highly motivated and competent in their areas of specialty. Once enrolled in American universities, they work hard and strive to achieve, since how well they do academically in the United States can affect their future career prospects.

Consider South Korea, where ambitious young students often relocate to English-speaking countries (including Singapore and Malaysia) to study English in order to apply to universities in Australia, Britain, Canada, and the United States. *The New York Times* recently reported that several private preparatory schools in South Korea provide intensive education in English in order to prepare their graduates for attendance at selective American colleges.[1] One of these schools requires mastery of two foreign languages besides English in order to graduate. Harvard had 37 South Korean undergraduates last year, more than from any foreign country except Britain and Canada.

The reluctance of Japan's youth to venture abroad would be less a cause for concern if Japanese universities were world-class, and Japanese society accepted talent from around the world. The reality, however, is that few Japanese universities are highly rated by international standards, and Japan still remains relatively closed to outsiders, even to highly trained professionals. This reality means that Japanese students who do not spend time abroad will miss the opportunity to experience the new insights, fresh perspectives, and sense of discovery that can result from exposure to the stimulation, diversity, and competition found outside of Japan.

In addition to limiting Japanese youths' perspective, the lack of overseas experience will make it harder for these students to gain fluency in foreign languages. The abysmal level of English-language instruction in Japan has resulted in the country's annual ranking near the bottom among Asian countries on the Test of English as a Foreign Language (TOEFL). In recent years, Japan has ranked above Afghanistan and Mongolia on the test, but below North Korea.

1 "Elite Korean Schools, Forging Ivy League Skills," April 27, 2008

DESIMA ISLAND.

For hundreds of years, Japan restricted contact with outsiders to Nagasaki's Dejima Island.
© Mary Evans/AAP

Such results are embarrassing; the larger problem, however, is that the lack of overseas experience reduces the opportunities for young Japanese people to establish the friendships and human networks that are becoming increasingly important in this shrinking world. Whether in politics, government, business, law, journalism, or academia, important global connections are formed through direct and frequent human contact, and sustained and strengthened through air travel and information technology, including the Internet. By turning inward and not venturing abroad, Japanese professionals will find themselves increasingly bypassed and marginalized. Such marginalization is a loss for both Japan and the global community, which have much to learn from, and share with, each other and no shortage of issues on which to work together.

What can be done to reverse this insular trend?

1. The Japanese political leadership should explicitly encourage Japanese students to study abroad. Ex-Prime Minister Yukio Hatoyama (Stanford), Secretary-General Katsuya Okada (Harvard), National Strategy Office Secretary-General Motohisa Furukawa (Columbia), and ex-Chairman of the House of Councilors Satsuki Eda (Oxford) are among the Democratic Party of Japan leaders who have benefited from their study abroad, as have members of the Liberal Democratic Party, including ex-Defense Minister Yoshimasa Hayashi (Harvard), ex-Chief Cabinet Secretary Yoshihisa Shiozaki (Harvard), and ex-Deputy Minister of Justice Taro Kono (Georgetown). A nonpartisan commit-

tee of Japanese political leaders who have studied abroad should be created to encourage Japanese students to follow in their footsteps.

2. Just as Japan has set targets to increase the number of foreign students who study in the country (300,000 students by 2020), the country should set targets to increase the number of Japanese students who study abroad. The Japanese cabinet recently moved in this direction when it announced in June 2010 an economic growth strategy that includes "dispatching 300,000 Japanese youth abroad" by 2020. However, the plan does not include any specific steps, programs, or funding.

3. Additional funding—from foundations, companies, and the government—should be provided to support promising Japanese high school and college students to study abroad.

4. Schools and companies in Japan should create incentives to stimulate young Japanese, both students and office workers, to study abroad. Finally, if the Democratic Party of Japan adheres to its pledge during the Lower House election of 2009 to establish a National Strategy Council, one of the council's first tasks should be to forge a comprehensive national security strategy that includes reversing the current Japanese trend of isolation, insularity, and seclusion. Reversing that trend is particularly important given the triple disasters of the earthquake, tsunami and threat of nuclear radiation that hit Japan on March 11, 2011.

The collapse of the Berlin Wall in November 1989 ushered in the end of the Cold War. In the 20-plus years since that event, globalization—of politics, economics, finance, business, technology, culture, and education—has been the single most important force affecting the lives of ordinary citizens around the world. It is ironic that, just as other countries are engaging more actively than ever to create networks of individuals, organizations, and nations and enhance their well-being and prospects for the future, Japan is turning inward and fading from the world stage. Reversing this trend should be a high priority if the Japanese government wishes Japan to play the positive and constructive global role it has the potential to do.

NO PLACE
TO BELONG

YUJI GENDA

IN OCTOBER 2010, I participated in an international conference on labor economics held on Cheju Island, South Korea. The session was an acute reminder of how globally minded South Koreans are—and how starkly their external orientation differs from the prevailing mindset in Japan. Profiles of the speakers, projected on an overhead screen, included brief summaries of their educational backgrounds. Of the South Korean academics my age and younger, every one held a PhD from a US university.

One of the best-known examples of South Koreans' global mindedness is Kim Yu-na, the female figure skater who earned a gold medal at the Vancouver Olympics. Yu-na's father, recognizing his daughter's talent when she was just seven years old, prepared to send her overseas for training as a skater. When Yu-na became a teenager, her mother accompanied her to Canada while her father remained in South Korea to earn money. Yu-na's parents gave their full support to her overseas training. This willingness to send children abroad and involve the entire family in helping children improve their performance in an international arena is typical not only of the Kims, but also of the entire South Korean elite.

South Korea's companies, too, invest heavily in helping their people gain overseas experience. Samsung Electronics, for example, each year selects 200 to 300 employees who have been with the company for more than three years and sends them abroad as part of its "regional specialist" system. The goal of the program, which costs Samsung an estimated 10 million yen (or about $120,000) per participant, is to help employees understand the cultures as well as the economies of its foreign markets.

Yuji Genda is a professor of labor economics at the University of Tokyo Institute of Social Science.

South Korea's population is half that of Japan's, and its birthrate is falling faster than Japan's. South Koreans are keenly aware that engaging with the outside world is their only hope for survival.

Inward-looking Japan

While South Koreans have adopted a positive outward-looking mindset, we Japanese are inward-looking. Consider the statistics for foreign travel. More than 16 million Japanese venture abroad each year, according to Japan's justice ministry, but growth in outbound travel comes mainly from the increasing number of seniors, who are using their generous pensions to venture abroad. By contrast, the number of travelers in their 20s has fallen since 1996.

People travel abroad for many reasons—business, honeymoons, sightseeing and the like. So the most important indicator of young people's exposure to other cultures might be the number of Japanese students venturing overseas for higher education. According to a 2010 report by Japan's Ministry of Education, Culture, Sports, Science & Technology, the number of Japanese students enrolled in foreign universities has been declining since 2004.

THE NUMBER OF JAPANESE STUDENTS ENROLLED IN FOREIGN UNIVERSITIES HAS BEEN DECLINING SINCE 2004.

Perhaps it is unfair to label the youth of Japan as "inward-looking" simply because fewer of them are traveling overseas. It may be that many young Japanese are eager to venture abroad but unable to do so because of financial constraints; if so, we may see more young people venture out as the yen continues to appreciate and the number of international flights from Haneda Airport increases.

But when I say that Japan's youth are "inward-looking," I also am thinking of the large and growing number of young people who are hidden in their own shell and cannot be drawn out for any reason. In a sense, Japanese society is full of inward-looking young people, regardless of how easy it is to live in Japan.

Withdrawing from society

Most symbolic of these inward-looking young people are the *hikikomori*, or recluses, who have withdrawn from society entirely. In official statistics, people are classified as *hikikomori* if they have not left their room or house for six months or more. In 2010, the Cabinet Office, with the advice and cooperation of specialists who support young people, conducted its first survey on the *hikikomori* phenomenon. It found that Japan had at least 700,000 recluses. The survey also found that 1.55 million people felt that they had a tendency toward reclusiveness.

At a seminar, I spoke to a man in his 30s who had experienced *hikikomori*. I asked, "What did you do while you were at home?" He said, "I kept thinking about the meaning of it all." As he thought incessantly about meaning—of life, work, and himself—he didn't know whether he was coming or going. He was in over his head, and became frightened to go out into the world. That is the essence of *hikikomori*. It's not a matter of laziness; it is about being overly serious and cautious.

Young people staying put

I was born in 1964 and, when I graduated from high school, Japan had already gone through the period of high growth. However, in our generation, most people thought they had to go to the city to accomplish something. If you did not go to school or get a job in Tokyo or Osaka, you did not know whether you had a future.

But now my classmates who stayed in the relaxing countryside and have families with at least two kids seem to be living happier lives. These days, young people who live in rural areas have far less interest in moving to the city than did their parents at a similar age. While there will still be many youths who strike out for the big cities in search of opportunity, a growing number of Japanese young people would rather just "stay local," whether for school or work. Perhaps this "stay local" mindset reflects an increased affection for one's hometown. But it is also true that the development of the Internet and spread of cable TV have eased the feeling among people in the countryside that they are somehow deprived or missing out. High school girls in rural areas who check the latest information on Shibuya fashion on their cell phones can know as much as their urban counterparts about what is hip.

Country dwellers can use Amazon to buy books and order what they want online, when they want, wherever they are. Some might say there is nowhere to have fun in rural areas, but with the development of traffic networks, such as expressways, it is increasingly common for those in their 20s to go into the city on weekends. So why bother living in such a crowded and draining place?

Other factors sap young people's will to venture from home. As the population ages and the birth rate continues to fall, many parents feel an increasing need to keep their eldest children close, so that these children can look after them in their old age. Traditionally in Japanese families, the eldest son or, in some cases, the eldest daughter inherits the family home, obliging younger siblings to seek their fortune in the big cities. But in today's era of subreplacement fertility rates, the majority of Japanese children are firstborns. Parents fear that their children will go to the city and never come back. And so, with ample pensions, parents lavish their children with money and real estate. Children, mindful of their parents' concerns, hesitate to move to the city.

Some families want their children to go to an urban school, but cannot afford to support them. Young people from rural areas who have found jobs in the city do not necessarily earn large incomes. Often they struggle to find permanent jobs, or can find permanent positions only at a low wage. Many young people discover that they cannot make ends meet in the city without support from their family in rural areas. Whether in the city or countryside, nonpermanent work is the only option for many and life is hard for the young, no matter where they are. Many young people conclude it is better to live at home, where at least food and shelter are guaranteed.

"No place to belong"

In the 1990s, after the Bubble Economy collapsed, many young Japanese began to complain that "I can't find the work I want," or "I can't live in a way that lets me be true to myself." Over the past decade, as working hours have grown longer and cases of depression have multiplied, young people worn down from the stress of work or personal and professional relationships have begun to say, "Enough! I can't deal with it anymore!" In the aftermath of the "Lehman shock," many young people, unable to find solace in their work or their family life, lament bitterly that there is "no place to belong" *(ibasho ga nai)*.

Of course there is nothing wrong with remaining rooted to the same spot. In a sense, people who have the latitude to gaze inward forever can be considered comparatively happy. But it is the fear that sooner or later these Japanese youths will have nowhere to belong that drives many of them to cling so tenaciously to what they have now. Such inward-looking young people have no hopes or desires, and no zeal for life.

When foreign pressure eventually shatters the shell that protects them, how will Japan's inward-looking youth react? That question worries me. People who have never engaged with the outside world have weak resistance, with no immunities to withstand an external shock. Lacking defenses, they are quick to give up, choose a self-destructive path, or lose touch with reality.

Talent development strategy

To avoid such outcomes, we need to help young people turn their gaze outward. As we did during the Meiji Restoration, we should select young people with leadership potential who can be entrusted with the nation's future. We must, of course, seek out youths with strong basic academic skills, but beyond that, we must choose those persons with flexible minds open to communication with other cultures as well as youths who have a deep understanding of their own society. The nation should not only invest heavily in opportunities for these youths to travel and build skills, but also sponsor their studies overseas.

In Japan, where criticism of bureaucracy abounds, there is still powerful resistance to the notion of elite education. And yet, given the current instability of global affairs, it is clear that people with overseas experience and perspective are indispensable to the nation's future well-being. Public opinion must be given due heed. But what is needed now is a political initiative to develop outward-looking future leaders.

Whether the state is capable of fairly and efficiently selecting competent young people is a valid concern. If the state is to acquire that capability, it must first break free of the insular, ad hoc, and bureaucratic mentality that predominates today. Next, we should create a "Ministry of Children and Youth" with a mandate to provide young people with a more international, long-range perspective. Should that sort of dramatic transformation prove impossible, the next best alternative is to work with our universities. Professors with trust-based global relationships should shoulder the responsibility of sending Japanese students abroad and, on occasion, welcome students from other nations to Japan. Becoming a new "haven of knowledge" for the 21st century is a way for universities to survive in the face of the falling birth rates and declining enrollment. If we are to develop leaders capable of supporting the nation's future, we must put greater effort than we have previously into establishing such havens of knowledge.

Japan's youth: feeling squeezed.

We should not be so narrow-minded as to fret that some of the young talent in whom we invest may not return to Japan and thus turn out to be a waste of money. In every field of endeavor, youths from Japan must become more active internationally; if we succeed in that goal alone, Japan would realize tremendous value.

To transform Japan's reclusive, inward-looking youths into outward-looking leaders, we must develop the proper educational resources. I once had the opportunity to propose employment measures for young people to the Minister of Health, Labour and Welfare. My advice: "It's important for the government to support young people. But it is also important to *support young people who support young people.*" In addition to the 700,000 *hikikomori* cases, the government estimates that at least 600,000 Japanese youths can be classified as "NEETs"—so-called because they are "Not in Education, Employment or Training." But rather than trying to provide direct government support for 100 recluses or NEETs, we would achieve better results by developing ten young people capable of working with those 100 people.

Into an unknown world

As a nation, we must give careful consideration to the type of institutions and infrastructure necessary to encourage our young people to look outward and engage with the rest of the world. But young people themselves must also take the initiative. If, for whatever reason, they are unable to venture abroad, they should make an effort to plunge into an unknown world closer to home. That world could include participation in sports, art, a community festival, or a nonprofit organization. Young people will find many unknown worlds waiting to be explored right in their own neighborhoods.

When the day comes that once again Japan's young people strive to participate in unknown worlds—as they also seek a stable place to belong—new hope will emerge for Japanese society.

THE YOUNG AND THE HOPELESS

MASAHIRO YAMADA

OVER THE PAST DECADE, Japan's youth have developed a new yearning for stability. Rather than tackling challenges and taking risks, they seek out the most stable life course available, holding fast to the assumption that the economic conditions of tomorrow will be much the same as those that prevail today. This attitude can fairly be characterized as "conservatism" in that it seeks no change in existing social systems.

Young Japanese have come to cherish security over adventure. Fewer young people are venturing abroad. The number studying abroad is in decline, as is the number visiting foreign countries as tourists. Japan's youths have grown especially wary of volatility in the workplace.

Each year, the Japan Productivity Center conducts a survey of the attitudes of the nation's newly hired workers. The survey has found a steady increase over the past decade in the number of respondents who say they want to "keep working for this company until retirement"; in 2010 the percentage of respondents agreeing with that statement reached a record 57 percent, up from 20 percent in 2000. Conversely, the number of new employees indicating a desire to switch jobs or start their own businesses is in decline. A separate survey by the Japan Management Association (JMA) has found an increase in the number of new hires favoring the seniority-based waged system over a system in which pay is based on skill or merit. The JMA survey also showed an increase in the number of respondents expressing an aversion to a foreign posting.

The new strain of conservatism is also evident in surveys measuring the attitudes of women. A number of surveys since 2000 show a growing preference

Masahiro Yamada is a sociologist at Chuo University.

among young women for becoming housewives. The percentage who agree with the statement "the man works, the woman takes care of the house" rises notably as women move into their 20s and 30s. Increasingly, women say they would rather marry a man with a stable job and acceptable income than have a career of their own.

The values reflected in such surveys hark back to social patterns prevailing from the end the war, through Japan's high-growth era and on into the 1980s. In those years, it was taken for granted that after graduation men would join a company and be employed until retirement, while women would become housewives and raise children. Today's youth long for that kind of stability.

Lifetime employees and "liquid" laborers

What is the source of this conservatism, this satisfaction with the life courses of the past? I think it is the fact that, over the last 20 years, the work environment for young people has changed, while the employment practices of Japanese companies have not.

Since the implosion of the "bubble," Japan's economy has changed significantly. We have not merely struggled through a cyclical downturn; rather, the economy has undergone a fundamental secular shift. Japan, like much of the rest of the world, has experienced the sort of transformation described by former US secretary of labor Robert Reich in his book, *The Future of Success.* Our economy is **EIGHTY PERCENT OF UNMARRIED JAPANESE BETWEEN 18 AND 35 LIVE WITH THEIR PARENTS.** more global than ever. There is a new premium on the services sector. Automation and information technology play a more important role than ever. These changes have revolutionized the nature of work.

During the industrial age, the common pattern was "Fordism": men worked as skilled laborers and held the same job for life. In Japan such workers were called *"kaisha-in"* (literally, a company member); once hired, they had every reason to expect stable jobs until retirement. Women married *kaisha-in*, became housewives, and also had stable lives.

In the modern economy, companies require two different groups of workers: those with high levels of expertise and professionalism regardless of their gender, and less-skilled "liquid" laborers, who work only when the company needs them. This pattern is common in all developed countries.

In the postbubble era, Japan shied away from restructuring its economy, protecting many traditional industries that were no longer competitive. In the 1990s, new service industries like convenience stores and fast food emerged alongside these traditional industries. New ventures in information technology also flourished. Many of these new sectors required large numbers of nontraditional (nonfull-time) employees. When the Asian financial crisis struck in 1997, labor laws were loosened to allow the manufacturing sector to cut costs by using nontraditional employees. These laws began the transition to an economy that requires large numbers of "liquid" workers not only in services and manufacturing, but even in government and public services. At the same time, however, the economy still retains more traditional full-time employees than it needs.

One shot at stability

Large companies and the public sector in particular have retained the practices of mass hiring of new graduates, employment for life, seniority wages and different treatment for full-time and nonfull-time employees. Becoming a full-time employee of a large company or government agency is almost a guarantee of employment for life. You have one shot at securing such a position: the moment of graduation. It's true that the number of midcareer hires is rising. But in the private sector, the people in demand for those positions are experienced full-time employees at other companies—workers already awarded lifetime jobs. Meanwhile, the public sector has age restrictions.

Over the course of a lifetime, the difference between full-time employees and "liquid" employees is vast. The disparity goes beyond wages. As a full-time employee of a large company, it is almost impossible to get fired. The probability that your employer will go bankrupt is minuscule. A nontraditional employee has no guarantees. He or she is excluded from training and education opportunities and,

Liquid laborers have many sorrows to drown.
© Composed by Kenneth Y Huang/Flickr/Getty Images

in a variety of forms, denied the benefits of unemployment insurance and pensions. The opportunities to restart are few. The prospect of ever becoming a full-time employee is remote.

As demand grows for liquid laborers, Japan's youth are paying the price. Because it is so difficult to shed full-time employees, companies with too many workers cope by hiring fewer new graduates. The result is a large and growing pool of young workers unable to find full-time jobs when they graduate. Since the late 1990s, young graduates who failed to win full-time positions found employment as liquid laborers. Previously, such jobs had been offered to housewives and students looking for part-time work; today they are filled by young graduates, both male and female. Thus, while Japan's overall unemployment rate is not as high as that of Europe or North America, employment conditions are much worse for young Japanese workers who fail to secure full-time positions at graduation than for those who do.

Because changes in Japan's labor environment have not been matched by changes in employment practices of Japanese companies, the nation's young people confront a world in which life is stable and good for those who manage to find a position inside the traditional system. Those on the outside feel all but abandoned.

Parasites in fantasyland

Young Japanese with a chance of winning a position within the traditional system go to extraordinary lengths to get one. Once inside the system, they cling fiercely to their entitlements. For today's graduates, the most popular jobs are with stable companies and local governments. As they approach graduation, Japanese students expend a great deal of energy on the search for a stable job or a spouse with a stable job. Once hired, young Japanese tend to be risk-averse, shunning job changes, eschewing entrepreneurial opportunities, and avoiding foreign postings. The prevailing perception is that change is dangerous; that any attempt to find work outside the embrace of a large, established company is doomed to failure; and that efforts to change society as a whole are futile.

Young Japanese who find themselves shut out of traditional employment are hardly more adventurous. For the most part, their earnings are meager. They toil at jobs with few benefits and little hope of advancement or even continued employment. Some are exhorted to "try again" for full-time positions. But in Japan's closed labor system, chances of success are slim.

It's worth noting that nearly 80 percent of unmarried Japanese between the ages of 18 and 35 live with their parents; among unmarried nontraditional workers, the rate is even higher. By remaining with their parents, young employees with low incomes can enjoy a decent life, provided they never marry or seek financial independence. I have called this group "parasite singles"; I believe the parasite-singles phenomenon to be one of the primary reasons for Japan's declining birthrate.

A defining characteristic of parasite singles is that they cling to unrealistic dreams. Men imagine they will become rock stars or famous photographers. Women dream of marrying a man with a high income and a stable job. These fantasies,

179

however improbable, are parasite singles' best hope for making any kind of life on their own.

As their dreams die, parasite singles often seek other forms of escape. Men turn to *pachinko* or online games, places where effort is rewarded and friends abound. Having never been fawned over in the workplace, some men find solace in visits to "maid cafés" where they pay for the privilege of being flattered. Women tend to obsess over celebrities, chasing the latest stars in dream worlds of their own.

It is an irony that Japan's *anime* character and game industries, so popular overseas, have developed largely to fulfill the fantasies of disaffected workers at home. They are a kind of "dream industry." Parasite singles try not to think about what will happen after their parents die.

Over the years, youths willing to take risks and try new jobs or lifestyles have become a smaller minority in Japan. And this minority is fleeing. In particular, young women who aspire to more meaningful careers and lifestyles are increasingly seeking refuge overseas.

In the face of so many roadblocks, is there any future for Japan itself? If nothing changes, full-time employees will have no energy for innovation. Nontraditional employees will grow old in their escapist fantasylands, only to confront serious problems in maintaining their living standards when their parents die. Ambitious youths will seek opportunities abroad.

The end of lifetime employment

Economic conditions no longer permit everyone to become a full-time employee. The implications of that change are clear: the time has come to do away with a system that apportions total stability to a shrinking elite of full-time employees while granting none to anyone else. The mass hiring of new graduates must stop. The institutions of lifetime employment and seniority-base wages must be reconsidered. We must also mend the yawning gaps in social safety nets that, in the current system, treat people differently depending on whether they are full-time employees, nonfull-time employees, or self-employed.

The practice of mass hiring at graduation is not essential to the function of Japan's economy; it is not the norm in Europe or North America. The Netherlands, for example, has largely eliminated the gaps in benefits for full-time employees and nontraditional employees. In many of these countries, young people still face many challenges in the job market. But at least they are not divided, as they are in Japan, into "winners" and "losers" the moment they graduate. In other countries, young people are granted the space to think about their futures and to experiment with different options.

Japan, too, must provide this space for growth. We must create an economy that affords stability even for those who do not become full-time employees with big firms, as well as those who choose to leave such jobs to strike out on their own. In so doing, we could provide our children with the opportunity and confidence to take on new challenges, and the motivation to make the most of their own skills and talents.

IS JAPAN A VAMPIRE FINCH?

DEVIN STEWART

FOR YEARS, telecoms executive Takeshi Natsuno wondered why NTT DoCoMo's advanced cell phones weren't selling overseas, until in 2007, it struck him: the phones were so advanced and so different that they had little connection to the rest of the world. They were the technical equivalents of the vampire finch, a species of bird found on the Galapagos Islands that has evolved a unique long, pointed beak precisely adapted to its environment—and found nowhere else.

Natsuno, who is widely considered the mastermind behind the i-mode mobile platform that looked likely to be a world-beater in the early 2000s, came to call this phenomenon the "Galapagos Syndrome." Around the same time Natsuno began using the term, so did former Nomura Research Institute consultant Naohiro Yoshikawa, who recently published a book on the subject, *Galapagos Ka Suru Nihon* (*"The Galapagos-ization of Japan,"* 2010). It's impossible to know exactly who used the term first, but Nastuno and Yoshikawa are widely credited with bringing the phrase into wider currency.

Indeed, "Galapagos" has assumed the status of a Zen interjection; the term crops up constantly. Many conversations about Japanese characteristics—the poor standard of English, say, or the veneration of manufacturing—are punctuated by the word "Galapagos," followed by silence and nodding heads.

As a phrase, "Galapagos Syndrome" is an elegant synthesis of many concepts. It refracts other common expressions, such as "island-nation thinking" (*shimaguni kanjo*) and the belief in Japanese uniqueness (*nihonjinron*). Like many terms that capture a moment in time, the meaning of Galapagos has broadened beyond its

---

Devin Stewart is senior director of corporate, policy, and lecture programs at the New York City-based Japan Society.

original business context. Instead, it is often used as a shorthand for other trends that hint at Japan's growing insularity.

Consider, for example, the phenomena of *hikikomori*—hundreds of thousands of Japanese shut-ins who refuse to leave their homes and have given up on social life. *Hikikomori* has nothing to do with business, but it is still considered a symptom of the Galapagos Syndrome. Or look at Japanese newspapers, which are notoriously Google-unfriendly, lacking permalinks; the *Nihon Keizai Shimbun*, one of the world's largest newspapers, requires a written application to approve links to its homepage. That's considered a form of Galapagos, too. Why has Japanese undergraduate enrollment in US universities dropped 52 percent in the last decade? Galapagos.

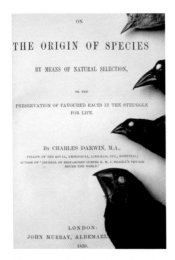

The vampire finch could be Japan's national bird.

© Frans Lanting/Terra/Corbis

The concept resonates because it taps deep into Japanese norms: Reserve is a valued trait in Japan, and shyness is almost considered a virtue. But the last thing Japan needs is to curl up inside its shell. An isolated Japan would lose both international influence and economic competitiveness.

To think about it another way: Name a global Japanese corporate powerhouse that is not a manufacturer. Except for Nintendo, Japanese brands are best known for their manufacturing prowess. That's partly because Japan is great at manufacturing—and partly because excelling in services requires a more global mindset. "Isolation hurts Japan's economy, especially in services," Robert Dujarric of Temple University Japan wrote in the *Japan Times*. "It puts them at a severe disadvantage when competing with foreign rivals run by multinational and multicultural staffs."

Another economic side effect attributed to the Galapagos Syndrome is that the products of Japanese research are increasingly evolved, yet nonetheless separate from global society. According to Hajime Ito, a former government official now in the private sector, and Jun Kurihara, a senior fellow at Harvard, Japan leads in number of patents in solid waste management and is number two after the United States in air pollution control, water pollution control, medical technology, pharmaceuticals, and biotechnology. But it doesn't even make the top 10 in cited research or core articles in the same fields.

Why? Ito and Kurihara blame Japan's penchant for keeping knowledge to itself, combined with the declining number of Japanese students at overseas universities. To be sure, the number of college-age students has been falling for decades, and 20 years of economic uncertainty have weakened the ability of families to finance overseas university tuition. But there is more to it than that. "An international degree is not as valued" in Japan as it used to be, Harvard president Drew Gilpin Faust told the *Washington Post* in 2010.

Questions and answers

There are three overlapping schools of thought about the Galapagos Syndrome. One is resigned acceptance: Leave us alone so that we can get on with our lives. A form of nationalism is associated with people in this camp; they believe that the country should rely on its uniqueness, whether it be organic farming, raising the world's most expensive beef, or forging super high-tech steel. Proud of Japan, they don't see Galapagos as much of a problem. Norihiro Kato, a professor at Waseda University, has come to embody this thinking. He published a much-discussed essay in *The New York Times,* arguing it was a relief when China surpassed the Japanese economy to become the second-largest in the world: Japan, he wrote, could now focus on quality of life instead of worrying about growth.

THE PRODUCTS OF JAPANESE RESEARCH ARE INCREASINGLY EVOLVED YET NONETHELESS SEPARATE FROM GLOBAL SOCIETY.

Then there are the wishful thinkers. These people believe that the Democratic Party of Japan's victory in 2009 constituted a genuine shift of power away from the bureaucrats toward the people, and that it is only a matter of time before a more competitive two-party political system helps to revive society and its marketplace of ideas. This group also includes two other categories: foreigners (often those new to Japan) awed by Japanese technology and efficiency, and observers who discern the beginnings of a quiet revolution in Japan's lively youth culture. The wishful thinkers acknowledge that Galapagos Syndrome is a problem for Japan, but profess confidence that eventually it will run its course, or that Japan will heal itself with its inherent social anti-bodies.

Finally, there are the disillusioned internationalists. Typically, these are elite policymakers, conservative intellectuals, and businesspeople such as Ito, Kurihara, or Hiroshi Mikitani, the founder and CEO of Rakuten, who is making English his company's official language. These observers not only acknowledge that Galapagos Syndrome is a problem, but warn that it is getting stronger, and that Japan is worse off because of it. After witnessing decades of political inertia, they think it may take a genuine shock—say, a debt crisis—to create the conditions for change. The pessimists are patriots, too. But they see the country's greatness tied to a cosmopolitan future in which it is fully engaged and globally competitive.

Coping with Galapagos

It's common for outsiders to diagnose Galapagos and then prescribe immigration (to bring in fresh ideas and a broader tax base) and higher education reform (to open people's minds). But such remedies are easier prescribed than administered. Take immigration. John Haffner, author of *Japan's Open Future* (2009), estimates Japan would need to boost its intake of foreigners to as many as 650,000 people per year in order to stabilize the nation's declining population. Japanese notions of identity and economic realities render such a move undesirable; it is not going to happen.

As for education, the trends are in the wrong direction. In the respected 2010 *Times Higher Education* survey, only five Japanese universities cracked the top 200 (down from 11). Not a single Japanese business school made the *Financial Times'* top 100. It is no stretch to link the relative decline of Japan's universities with the country's overall fall in power and competitiveness. And it surely does not help that young people who do study abroad can be stigmatized when they return, missing out on the hiring season and often not as highly regarded as those who stayed home to study at Japan's elite universities.

It's possible, perhaps even probable, that Japan will make some moves to globalize education and to increase immigration. It is certain, however, that these steps will be limited, and gradual. So maybe it makes sense to look to business, where the term "Galapagos Syndrome" originated, for clues about how to deal with it.

Consider Sharp, a tech company that has exhibited classic Galapagos symptoms. Sharp had a PC business whose products were technically sound but incompatible with global standards. In 2010, recognizing that it could not compete, Sharp bowed out of the PC game. Instead, it introduced an Android-powered e-book tablet—and named it "Galapagos."

The idea, the company said, was to give the term a positive connotation, symbolizing the steady and constant evolution of services and experiences; for example, periodic software updates that ensure that the device keeps improving. At an event explaining the new product, company executives displayed a slide that read: "Galapagos is NOT Galapagos," with the first instance of the word written in English and the last in Japanese *katagana* script. Ironically, that is a distinction that could only make sense in Japan—and it's worth noting that the Galapagos tablet will be available only domestically at first. But at least Sharp is trying. "Instead of Japan getting down on itself," one executive told *The Wall Street Journal*. "We need to find a way to maximize what we've got."

That's surely the right idea—not just for Sharp, but also for Japan: To recognize its weaknesses, and then to build on its strengths. It is, as a matter of fact, what DoCoMo failed to do. Though it was far ahead of the mobile game in the early 2000s, it was never able to break into overseas markets in any significant way; almost all i-mode customers are in Japan. As for the Galapagos tablet, the jury is still out.

Japan is not helpless. There are things the country can do, such as offering incentives for students to study overseas; opening its economy to competition; and engaging in higher-profile economic diplomacy. All of this could help to connect Japan more closely with the world outside the archipelago.

If, that is, it so chooses. Because the fundamental question is this: As a society, is Japan satisfied with gentle decline? Are they perfectly okay with being vampire finches—leading a safe and pleasant life in an isolated island outpost? If that is the case, then Galapagos is not really a syndrome, but an affirmation of Japan itself.

THE NOMO EFFECT

ROBERT WHITING

HIDEO NOMO WAS A GOOD, if not great, pitcher, as well-known for his audacious leap in the mid-1990s from the rigid world of Japanese baseball to America's big leagues as he was for his famously unhittable forkballs.

Yet, he is arguably the most significant sporting figure to emerge in contemporary Japan.

By becoming the first player to break out of the confines of Japanese baseball and succeed in America, the most competitive arena in his sport, Nomo inspired a whole generation of Japanese athletes to test themselves abroad.

On a broader level, what is called the "Nomo effect" reached into fields as diverse as business, science, and the arts, and influenced bold individuals willing to forsake Japan's cozy traditional order to compete or engage with the rest of the world. In Japanese sporting circles, a wave of Japanese baseballers went to the United States to play after Nomo blazed the trail in 1995.

Some became overnight sensations. Nearly all drew admiration at home as well as abroad. But back when Nomo, at age 26, stunned fans at the end of Japan's 1994 baseball season by announcing his retirement and his intention to play in America's big leagues, his defection enraged much of Japan.

The media labeled him an ingrate and a traitor, while critics condemned him to the modern-day equivalent of *mura hachibu* (village ostracism) before he even left the country. For a time, his own father stopped speaking to him.

At that stage, Japan was suffering what one commentator described as a severe case of "sports anonymity." Aside from the odd international marathon win-

Robert Whiting is an author and journalist who has written several acclaimed books on contemporary Japanese culture.

ner, judo champion, or occasional women's volleyball victory, the country's finest athletes were all but unknown outside Japan. In the 1988 Summer Olympics, for example, the country won only 14 medals, fewer than Romania and less than half as many as South Korea.

Beyond sport, a larger sense of obscurity afflicted the nation. From the Sony Walkman to Toyota cars and *anime* characters, Japan had produced many products that were famous the world over. But there were very few world-famous Japanese people.

Nomo's influence helped change Japan's image, both domestically and internationally, not least in emboldening other Japanese athletes to follow his example. More significantly, his success in America helped Japan's battered self-esteem and, in the process, probably did more than any politician had done to improve cross-cultural relations.

Nomo played in the United States for 12 seasons, and while he could not keep up the high standard of his first few years, his influence endured. Today, it is no longer surprising to see Japanese athletes compete and win in the global arena. In the 2004 Olympics, they won 37 medals, and the country has qualified for every soccer World Cup since its first one in 1998.

Among the new breed of sports champions to emerge were gold medalist hammer thrower Koji Murofushi; two-time world figure skating champion Mao Asada; and star footballer Hidetoshi Nakata, a self-proclaimed Nomo fan who moved to Italy in 1998 to join Perugia and became the first Japanese to play for a European club. In a Nomo-style ascent, Nakata, then a star player of Japan's fledgling J-League, disproved critics who said he was too small, too weak, or simply not good enough for world-class soccer by becoming one of Italy's top players.

The impact was profound. By the end of the 1990s, millions of Japanese were spending their weekends watching satellite broadcasts of European soccer and their weekday mornings watching Major League Baseball, while tens of thousands embarked on overseas tours to see the games firsthand.

While the Nomo effect went way beyond sport, it was in baseball, appropriately, where the phenomenon was most apparent. Hideki Matsui, the once-prized slugger for the dominant Japanese team, the Yomiuri Giants, was named the Most Valuable Player in Major League Baseball (MLB)'s 2009 World Series, while Ichiro Suzuki, having broken numerous long-standing American batting records, now seems destined to become the first Japanese player to be enshrined in the US National Baseball Hall of Fame.

When Ichiro, as he became widely known, broke the 82-year-old record, in 2004, for most hits in a single season, the *Asahi Shimbun* declared that Japan's citizens, "once seen in the US as a faceless people obsessed with exporting cars and consumer electronics," were now cast in an entirely new light thanks to "the excellent play of the Japanese players and their positive personalities."

Ichiro was as flashy as Nomo was low-key. Known for his Oakley sunglasses, goatee, and unusual batting form, Ichiro became a US cultural icon. In the process, he helped make Japan and being Japanese "cool" in the eyes of many Americans.

All together, 41 of Japan's finest baseball players have followed in Nomo's foot-steps. Virtually none suffered the criticism he endured. Indeed, by 2001, when Ichiro went, going to the United States was the thing to do. The Japanese play-ing professional baseball in the United States were national heroes; *kimono*-clad grandmothers and grade-school children alike could reel off the starting lineups of the Mariners, the Yankees, and other teams that had bought prominent Japanese players.

"None of us would be here had it not been for Nomo," Hiroki Kuroda told *The Los Angeles Times* in 2007, after he left the Hiroshima Carp to sign with the Dodgers. The Seibu Lions, meanwhile, became one of the biggest financial beneficiaries of the Nomo effect, when the Boston Red Sox paid the team $52 million just for the right to negotiate with its star pitcher, Daisuke Matsuzaka, in 2006.

America's "discovery" of Japanese baseball prowess, just like Japan's emergence from international sporting obscurity, might seem late in coming. But it is worth remembering that before the Meiji era (1868–1912), when Japan had undergone centuries of self-imposed isolation, the country had little knowledge of the Western concept of sport, that is, athletics for fun. There was *sumo*, born from ancient Shinto rites; the martial art of *kendo*; horseback riding; and swimming—the last three cul-tivated primarily for purposes of military training.

But when Japan eventually opened its doors to the world, baseball—taught by imported American experts—became the rage. The Japanese found the one-on-one battle between pitcher and batter similar in psychology to that of a mar-tial arts encounter, and liked the group aspect of baseball's nine-man teams as well. They grafted the old samurai philosophy of endless training, self-sacrifice, and development of spirit onto the game, and renamed it *yakyuu*, or field ball, to distinguish it from its American cousin. *Yakyuu* went on to become Japan's national sport. One early sign of the seriousness with which Japan embraced it came in 1896, when the First Higher School of Tokyo, a tightly disciplined squad whose practice motto was "Bloody Urine," swept a se-ries of games against a team of amateur Americans. In bold headlines, the newspapers hailed the victories as tri-umphs for the nation. Winning these games helped Japan believe it could compete with the West. As one historian remarked, "Foreigners could not hope to understand the emotional impact of the 1896 victories but they helped Japan, struggling towards modernization after centuries of isolation, begin to deal with a tremendous infe-riority complex it felt toward the more industrially advanced West."

NOMO'S SUCCESS IN AMERICA HELPED JAPAN'S BATTERED SELF-ESTEEM AND PROBABLY DID MORE THAN ANY POLITICIAN TO IMPROVE CROSS-CULTURAL RELATIONS.

Over the next few decades, baseball continued to thrive, and after the hugely popular 1934 tour of Japan by Babe Ruth and other stars, the Nippon Professional Baseball (NPB) league opened for business in 1935, led by the Tokyo Giants, a team that went on to become a national institution.

After World War II, as Japan rebuilt itself from the ashes of defeat and set about becoming a manufacturing powerhouse, Japanese athletes—fed on more nutritious diets—became bigger, stronger, and better, and baseball continued to thrive.

American scouts eagerly attempted to recruit players like Sadaharu Oh, who would go on to hit a world-record 868 home runs. But Oh stayed put, bound to Japan by protectionist sentiment and the demands of a circumscribed loyalty. "I wanted to try my hand in the US, but I couldn't leave," said Oh. "Even if the rules had allowed it, the fans never would have forgiven me."

Then Hideo Nomo changed everything. The son of a fisherman in Japan's Inland Sea region, Nomo was 6' 2" tall, and weighed 200 pounds. He could throw a baseball more than 95 miles an hour, and his famous "forkball" dipped 12 inches as it zipped past baffled batters. Nomo was one of the best young pitchers in Japan. Yet he had been stuck for five years since signing on in 1990 with the relatively obscure Kintetsu Buffaloes. He wanted above all to test his skills against the best in the world—and knew that meant playing in the United States.

Nomo understood the vast differences between the baseball worlds of the two countries. In Japan, teams were poorly funded advertising vehicles for corporations. Players toiled in cramped ballparks, traveled by train, and stayed in business hotels. In America, baseball was big business. MLB players performed in deluxe stadiums, traveled by chartered jet, and stayed in five-star hotels. They did not carry their own bags. Nor did they have to practice year-round; the slogan "Bloody Urine" had no place in their ethos. And thanks to their powerful union, they made several times as much as their counterparts in Japan.

With a far more independent spirit than his confreres, Nomo bridled under a demanding, disciplinarian manager whose motto was "pitch until you die" and whose cure for a sore arm was to order a hapless pitcher to throw harder. Although player agents were banned at the time by feudalistic Japanese team owners, Nomo joined forces with Don Nomura, a Los Angeles-based agent who had found a little-known loophole in the Japanese Uniform Player Contract.

The contract stated that a player who retired must return to his former club—if he stayed in Japan. Going to a foreign country to play, however, was not mentioned. So at the end of the 1994 season, Nomo announced his retirement from the Buffaloes—much to the disbelief of Kintetsu executives—and then announced he had signed with the Los Angeles Dodgers.

The bitter criticisms of Nomo's "treachery," however, began fading rapidly when he started winning—and a country that had long measured itself against the United States suddenly began taking pride in his achievements. His games were telecast live to Japan and watched by enthralled early-morning commuters on huge outdoor screens called "Jumbotrons."

When Nomo was named the starting pitcher in the 1995 All-Star game, Japan's then-prime minister, Tomiichi Murayama, called him a "national treasure." The *Asahi Shimbun* deemed Nomo's success a "catharsis" for the Japanese fed up with constant US carping about Tokyo's trade policies.

Ironically, Nomo received far more attention in Japan as a successful US major leaguer than he ever had as a member of the lowly Buffaloes. American fans embraced him, too, intrigued by the talented young player who had joined the Dodgers speaking not a word of English. Attendance soared when he pitched; *Sports Illustrated* put him on the cover.

Over 12 seasons in the United States, Nomo attracted huge publicity and made millions of dollars in endorsements. His influence went far beyond his performance statistics—not least in the way he inspired many of his fellow countrymen.

Many believe that had it not been for Nomo, baseball superstars such as Ichiro and Matsui would not have had the nerve to make the leap across the Pacific. Others argue that internationalization would have come to Japanese baseball anyway, considering the 1990s globalization of the sports business—from American basketball to English Premier league soccer.

Indeed, as Itaru Kobayashi, an official with the Softbank Hawks baseball team and a former player, remarked, "Those Japanese stars might have gone overseas anyway, eventually, but probably not so soon, not without the Nomo precedent and the toughness and courage he showed."

Even Japan's baseball team owners got into the international spirit when they took, in the early 2000s, the unheard-of step of hiring a total of four American managers. One of them, Bobby Valentine, experimented with a softer, more progressive management style, and seemed vindicated when his team, the Chiba Lotte Marines, won the Japan Championship in 2005. Japanese companies, wrote the president of Nippon Metal, should learn to treat

Nomo changed the game.
© Jed Jacobsohn/Getty Images

employees "the way Bobby does." Trey Hillman, another American manager, led Sapporo's Nippon Ham Fighters to the Japan Championship in 2006.

The Nomo effect is also a likely factor in other changes that took place in Japanese society. Hallmarks of Western-style individualism, from job-hopping to litigation and even bleached-blond hair, all taboo in the pre-Nomo era, gradually became an accepted part of the culture. Even Japan's stay-at-home ballplayers caught the spirit: inspired in part by Nomo's confrontational stance, they launched, in 2004, Japan's first players' strike, when the owners threatened to reduce the number of teams.

In the corporate world, perhaps the most notable example is the case of Shuji Nakamura, who invented the blue LED in the early 1990s while working for Nichia. The company made a fortune from his invention; all Nakamura received was the company's thanks and a 20,000-yen bonus ($250). Initially, press reports in both Japan and abroad cited this humble reward as an example of the superiority of the team-oriented Japanese business model.

Some years later, however, in 1999, Nakamura left Nichia to become a professor at the University of California, Santa Barbara, and sued his former company over the miniscule bonus. He eventually was awarded 840 million yen (more than $10 million), the largest settlement ever paid by a Japanese company for an invention.

ASSERTING A PHILOSOPHY OF SELF-RELIANCE AND INDIVIDUAL ACHIEVEMENT, JAPANESE ATHLETES, BEGINNING WITH NOMO, OPENED THE DOOR WIDE TO A CONFIDENT EMBRACE OF INTER-NATIONALIZATION.

The rough parallel to the spirit of Nomo's behavior—leaving a Japanese institution to claim his rights—was widely noted at the time. A string of similar lawsuits followed, including one in 2006, when electronics giant Hitachi was ordered to pay more than $1 million to an employee who developed crucial DVD technology, and another the same year, when Ajinomoto was ordered to pay $1 million to an employee who invented an artificial sweetener.

Clearly, what succeeds in Japan is no longer defined just by the Japanese. The respect goes to those with the courage to test themselves against the world's best—and to succeed. Just like Nomo.

Asserting a philosophy of self-reliance and individual achievement, Japanese athletes, beginning with Nomo, opened the door wide to a confident embrace of internationalization that companies like Uniqlo are walking through. But there has also been a reaction against this internationalization, as Nomo could attest.

When he returned to Japan, Nomo joined his old team as a coach. Two years later, he was fired: the manager did not care for his Western ways of thinking, an opinion widely shared by other managers, even though Nomo was later hired as a spring training coach by the Hiroshima Carp. And when even Bobby Valentine eventually wore out his welcome, his successor was a tough, old-school Japanese manager, who promptly won a championship. By 2010, all four American managers were gone. Yutaka Enatsu, a well known columnist and former star player, was not sorry to see the Yankees go home: "There's no need for *gaijin kantoku* (foreign managers)—not in Japanese baseball."

Hillman, who left Japan in 2007, would not have been surprised by the comment. In talks to business groups in Sapporo, he had criticized the tendency of many Japanese baseball managers to browbeat, intimidate, even physically abuse their players. "To say they were not interested in my style of leadership would be a gross understatement," Hillman later said. "The people in the audience told me that I should be more like that or I would lose control.... The old ways may have softened, but is Japan really changing? The answer is not very much."

The reality is that despite some fundamental changes ushered in by Nomo and other pioneers, the Japanese still prefer many of the old ways, even when those methods are no longer effective. This is demonstrably the case with Japan's professional baseball world, now grappling with falling spectator numbers, dwindling budgets, and powerful competition from MLB's slick marketing machine.

To better compete with American baseball, NPB would have to restructure, or to merge with America's MLB. League revenues in Japan have stagnated at about $1 billion since the mid-1990s, while MLB's have quadrupled, to almost $7 billion. Even so, Japan's baseball *shogun* have said they will not consider either option.

Most Japanese teams remain (unprofitable) public relations vehicles for their corporate owners. The Nippon Ham Fighters, for example, are owned by a pork producer. So every time the team is mentioned in the media, it is free publicity, which is much cheaper for the company than buying advertisements.

The result is that there is comparatively little investment in developing the game. In short, with a protected, and rather cozy, domestic market on which to rely, Japan's baseball management is reasonably content with what it has. It values its unique traditions and style more than the opportunities that could beckon with a more daring approach, even as television ratings slide and attendance wanes. The parallel to Japan's sputtering economy is irresistible.

Of course, Nomo, Nakata, and the rest were part of an era in which the outside world, in the form of the Internet and satellite television, permeated Japan's daily life in a new way. Still, it is no stretch to argue that these athletes did much to improve their country's global image and inspired others to reject the unwritten but binding rules that both unite and constrict Japan.

These athletes' example taught Japan that you don't have to do everything in a group or join a big company in order to succeed. The athletes showed the merits of an alternative model, based on grit and self-reliance. They were not afraid to stand up to an insular, quasi-feudal system that restricted their talents and tempered their spirit.

The Nomo effect is real. Tradition dies hard in Japan, where centuries-old habits are not easily disrupted. And tradition is often a good thing—such continuity is one of the society's charms. But there are consequences, too, when the claims of tradition calcify a decaying reality.

So Japanese baseball continues to be characterized by a militaristic mind-set and a plodding, predictable style of play. Japanese soccer's choreographed "reset and resume" pattern still rules the pitch. And many Japanese companies continue to manage from the top-down as they jealously guard their domestic niche.

Change in Japan sometimes comes in increments, sometimes in fits and starts—and sometimes when a young pitcher boards a plane to Los Angeles.

MANAGEMENT LESSONS FROM THE DUGOUT

BOBBY VALENTINE

After an injury-marred ten-year major-league career, Bobby Valentine turned to coaching, then spent eight seasons as manager of the Texas Rangers, leaving in 1992. He joined the Chiba Lotte Marines in the Japanese Pacific League in 1995 and returned to Japan in 2004, after managing the Texas Rangers and the New York Mets. Valentine took a distinctly unorthodox approach to his job as Chiba's manager, and appeared vindicated when the team won its first championship in more than 30 years. The first non-Japanese manager to win the Japan Series, he became something of a gaijin icon; at the Chiba ballpark, even the sake and bubblegum were branded with Valentine's image. His success led to the hiring of other foreign managers; at one point, Westerners ran four of the 12 professional Japanese teams.

A happy Valentine.
© Toshifumi Kitamura/AFP/Getty Images

But when Valentine's team faltered, he lost the support of owner Akio Shigemitsu, who decided not to renew his contract after the 2009 season. A protest campaign gathered more than 100,000 signatures in his support. Nonetheless, Valentine left Chiba—and was replaced by a Japanese manager. Valentine is now a baseball analyst with ESPN. In an interview with McKinsey, Valentine reflected on his experiences in Japan.

Bobby Valentine has managed in the major leagues in both Japan and the United States.

DID I BRING SOMETHING UNIQUE and different to Japanese baseball? Perhaps, but some people thought I was unique and different in the United States, too.

I do not think of my time in Japan as a series of cultural battles won or lost. Instead, I consider the experience a fascinating journey that gave me a unique perspective on the world of baseball—and by extension, on both the United States and Japan, my first and second homes, respectively.

On the basis of my first experience in Japan, in the mid-1990s, I believed I understood some of the needs of the players and fans. When I came back, in 2004, I tried to fulfill those needs, and found the task extremely challenging, but also very rewarding. I wanted to make a difference, and I think I did. I had enough autonomy to experiment. I could fail and not have to hang my head in disgrace. My status as an outsider certainly helped. I was not invested in the status quo. Japanese managers have made it to the top: why should they challenge the system that got them there? I didn't have those concerns.

I fell short on many of the things I was hoping to accomplish—not because of lack of effort, but because of lack of time. In Japan, change takes longer. But I think I helped to get the conversation going.

IN JAPAN, IT IS NOT UNUSUAL FOR PLAYERS TO PRACTICE NINE HOURS A DAY IN PRE-SEASON, TO PRACTICE ON DAYS 'OFF' DURING SEASON, AND TO HAVE POST-SEASON PRACTICE IN AUTUMN. I CUT BACK.

Practices and principles

One thing I wanted to do was to connect with the fans more and to create ways for them to connect with the team. When I left Japan, I called Chiba's "the greatest fans in baseball"—and I meant it. Japanese fans as a whole are great, one of the things I love about the game. But they were literally and figuratively fenced off from the team and the players.

I think the reason for this separation is historical. Professional baseball began in Japan after the barnstorming tours in the 1930s, particularly the one in 1934, when Hall of Famers Babe Ruth, Lou Gehrig, Jimmy Foxx, and Charlie Gehringer played and Connie Mack managed. The games were a huge success, attracting about half a million fans and selling out Japan's biggest stadiums. When Ruth, Gehrig, and the rest were in Japan, there was the perception that these megastars were bigger than life.

The executives at *Yomiuri Shimbun*, one of Japan's national newspapers, had done a lot to promote the tour and sensed that Japan was ready for a professional league run as a business. It did not escape their notice that sports could help sell newspapers, too. Their interest was the origin of Japan's first pro team, the Yomiuri Giants. So when Japan began its own league, in the 1930s, it replicated the only image of pro baseball players that the country knew—a kind of hero worship. Babe Ruth (*Beibu Ruusu*) was mobbed in Japan, and had to be fenced off from the crowds so people did not get too close. That concern for safety started the practice of separating the players and the fans, and it lasted. And lasted.

Beibu Ruusu was a hit in Japan.
© Mark Rucker/Transcendental Graphics,
Getty Images

I thought this separation was unfortunate. Japanese fans come before the first pitch and leave after the last. Regardless of score or performance, they support their team. They give their money, their loyalty, and their passion, and what do they get? Not enough.

I came to Japan with the idea that the fan base deserved a more personal association with the team. So we had days where fans and players were together on the field; we had fan appreciation events; we let kids run the bases after games; and we cut down the fence near the dugout so that fans could get autographs. The team became invested in the community, sponsoring, for example, blood pressure stations where people could get tested during games. I went out of my way to meet fans wherever we played; sometimes I even gave dance lessons before games. These kinds of things are common in the United States (except, perhaps, for the dance lessons!), but they were innovative in Japan. Chiba became known as the most fan-friendly team in Japan. I'm pleased I was part of that.

Players deserved attention, too. They needed more than a uniform and a paycheck; they needed to have their personalities become known. They needed to be valued as individuals as well as members of the team. So, in an attempt to change a workplace environment where everything else in life was second or third to the job of baseball, I let them grow their hair if they wished and ensured that they had free time with family and friends. I wanted to remove the "us-against-them" mentality between management and players. Coaches in Japan are known to slap their players; there was traditionally a kind of militaristic mind-set where the general (manager) is the end-all and the soldiers (players) exist to give everything for him.

In Japan, it is not unusual for players to practice nine hours a day before the season, to practice off-days during it, and to have autumn practice afterward. I cut back on practice time. At Chiba, we practiced a lot, but we also rested enough, so that the strength of body and mind was still there at the end of the long season.

During the seven years I was in Japan, I saw other organizations begin to adopt some of these principles. For example, some ballparks began to tear down the barriers that separated fans from the players. I also began to see managers smiling and hugging players rather than hitting them. I cannot take credit for these changes; but I do think I was part of a larger process.

One thing that hasn't changed, and I wished it would, is the economic structure of the game. I was in Japan in 1995, the year Hideo Nomo left for the Los Angeles Dodgers; he was the first high-profile player to go to the United States. I wasn't opposed to him leaving, but he opened the door to many others who think of the United States as a place where the grass is greener. It's a problem for Japan that so many of its stars are now playing outside the country. Rather than have these players leave for New York or Seattle, I believe Japan needs to be fertilizing and watering its own grass.

My dream is for Japanese baseball to be able to compete, both on and off the field, with the best teams in the world. When Chiba won the Japan Series in 2005, I challenged that year's American champs, the Chicago White Sox, to a true World Series. For Japan to maintain this level of playing, and to prevent Western baseball from making more inroads into the Japanese talent pool, the structure of Japan's game has to change.

Changing baseball in Japan comes down to finances and talent development. There are 12 teams in the Japanese major leagues, but sometimes it feels as if only one or two teams matter and the rest exist simply to provide competitors on the field. In Japan, the big boys don't like to play with others; they don't share and don't care if their weaker siblings are ever good enough to compete.

This financial area is where I think I encountered the most resistance from other teams. While I recognize there is dissatisfaction about economic disparities among the US major-league teams, there is more cooperation and more revenue sharing than in Japan. As for the issue of talent development, Japan needs to give more amateur players the chance to go professional. Only about 100 men per year are selected into the pro game. If Japan expanded the minor leagues, the country would create a talent base that could replace some of those who seek the greener American grass.

Game analysis

Japanese baseball culture differs from that in the West. Players are more disciplined. They appreciate practice (major-leaguers in the United States seem to resent it) and they execute the finer points of baseball at a higher level than many US major-league players. I think Western players could learn much from Japan about discipline and respect for the game.

In turn, Japanese players could learn more about technique—the actual mechanics of throwing or swinging or playing defense. I'd also like to see their natural abilities flow a little more. There is less testing and challenging of the conventional wisdom in Japanese baseball; things are done a certain way because that is how things have always been done.

As for Japan as a country and a culture: I loved it and I miss it. I enjoyed the orderliness, cleanliness, and friendliness of Japanese society—from the appearance of the people to the streets to the food. Of course, I missed American food, friends, and family, too. And sometimes I found that the sameness of Japanese society could be tiring. But there are many, many things about Japan—hot springs and bullet trains for a start—I wish I could import.

Japan and the United States are obviously very different societies, but I treasure them both, and feel truly lucky to have been, for a time, a man of two countries.

I loved Japan.
© Toshifumi Kitamura/AFP/
Getty Images

SUMO WRESTLES WITH GLOBALIZATION

HANNAH BEECH

IN THE BEGINNING, before there was a nation called Japan, there was sumo. As an exhibit at the sport's museum in Tokyo explains: "According to Japanese legend the very origin of the Japanese race depended on the outcome of a sumo match." The supremacy of the Japanese people on the islands of Japan was established, as the legend goes, when the god, Takemikazuchi, won a sumo bout against the chief of a rival tribe.

No wonder, then, that sumo, more than any other athletic endeavor, is thought to embody the soul of the Japanese nation. For 1,500 years, religiously inspired ritual has guided every lumbering step taken by sumo wrestlers. Clad only in loincloths, their hair swept into topknots that were the peak of fashion 150 years ago, the men of sumo are supposed to serve as oversized poster boys for the ultimate Japanese virtues: dignity, honor, discipline, and strength.

But the guardians of this most Japanese of sports can no longer claim this responsibility as their birthright. For here is the blond topknot of an Estonian ex-bouncer called Baruto (real name: Kaido Höövelson) and the hairy chest of Bulgaria's Kotooshu (born Kaloyan Stefanov Mahlyanov). There is the telltale cellulite of a trio of Georgian wrestlers, whose bodies accumulate fat quite differently from the way the Japanese physique does. And everywhere, it seems, are the wide cheekbones of Mongolian athletes.

Since 2003, only two men have been promoted to the exalted status of *yokozuna*, or grand champion, the sport's highest rank to which a mere 69 wrestlers have clambered since 1789. Both are from the land of Genghis Khan: Asashoryu (né Dolgorsuren Dagvadorj) and Hakuho (formerly known as Monkhbatyn Davaajargal).

Hannah Beech is Beijing bureau chief of Time *magazine.*

Well beyond the Mongolians, in just over a decade, foreigners have so dominated sumo that more than half of all high-ranked wrestlers are now *gaijin*, the colloquial term for "foreigners." At the 2010 autumn tournament in Tokyo, only one Japanese man competed in the top two echelons, and he was a 37-year-old journeyman past his prime.

The reason for the foreign invasion is simple. The number of Japanese sumo recruits dwindles each year. What average Japanese kid today wants to grow up— and out—to become a sumo wrestler? Ask any high school or middle school sumo coach what's happened to recruit numbers, and he'll tell you they've gone way down. The training is too rigorous, the bottoms too bared. And in a country where being rotund is no longer a sign of prosperity but a marker of overindulgence, all that fat is considered unsightly, even if it is wrapped around a lithe and limber fighting machine.

"You look at the Mongolians who come today, and they have the hungry, strong bodies of kids who grew up doing hard labor on the farms," says Michinori Yamada, longtime coach of the top-ranked Saitama Sakae high school sumo team. "Japanese families used to send their boys to sumo stables to ensure they got enough food. Now, Japanese kids eat what they want, they go to college, and they don't want to work so hard."

Here, sumo, once again, is a few thunderous steps ahead of Japanese society. Even though change was forced on the sport, the stampede of foreigners into sumo signals a rare instance in which Japan is tackling one of its biggest problems: a growing labor shortage. Indeed, sumo's *gaijin* experiment carries resonance far beyond the *dohyo*, as the sumo ring is known. After all, if this quintessentially Japanese sport can accept—and even celebrate—foreigners, perhaps the rest of the nation can do the same in other fields.

Of course, international wrestlers still face persistent discrimination, the thousand small indignities that can wear down even a 200-kilogram behemoth. Still, it is now virtually impossible to imagine sumo without athletes whose names are spelled in *katakana*, the Japanese alphabet reserved for foreign words. Imagine: the last time a Japanese-born wrestler won an official tournament was back in 2006. International athletes don't just dominate sumo. They *are* sumo.

Naturally, foreigners can't just turn up in a sandpit and start grappling away. They must learn passable Japanese, especially to match the local athlete's ability to mumble mind-numbingly dull postmatch platitudes. They must train their stomachs to crave not just a Japanese diet, but also a voluminous sumo diet of traditional stews and other foods. They must accept the isolation of a system in which each sumo training stable is allowed to house only one foreign-born athlete.

Foreign wrestlers, like their Japanese counterparts, must also hew to a hierarchy that would make even Confucius wince. Here's a typical day in a sumo stable, where all the athletes must live and train for the duration of their careers: reveille is at 5:30 AM, then comes a full morning of hard practice. Lunch is eaten in order of rank, followed by a session with a topknot hairstylist and a couple of hours of naptime.

Then the wrestlers-in-training go on to bathroom-cleaning and other chores, a session at the gym, and dinner preparations.

From 7:30 PM to 10:30 PM, the athletes are given free time. After that, lights go out. Wrestlers all sleep in the same room. The rest of the day, junior stablemates must act as glorified servants to their elders. Pride is brutally checked: low-ranked wrestlers are banned from giving out autographs and don't merit a salary at all, merely a living stipend. Even *yokozuna* are paid just $300,000 a year, a sliver of what a baseball star or top footballer earns.

Within this rigid arrangement, foreign wrestlers, no matter their athletic prowess, are held to a higher standard than their Japanese counterparts. When a pair of Russian wrestlers was caught smoking marijuana in 2008, their transgressions were taken as proof of foreigners' innate unruliness. Then there's the case of Mongolian former grand champion Asashoryu, who despite unquestionable dominance in the ring, was deemed by the local press as lacking *hin*, or dignity.

THE STAMPEDE OF FOREIGNERS INTO SUMO SIGNALS A RARE INSTANCE IN WHICH JAPAN IS TACKLING ONE OF ITS BIGGEST PROBLEMS: A GROWING LABOR SHORTAGE.

Practically everything Asashoryu did reeked of a lack of *hin*: failing to defer to a sumo elder in a bathhouse hallway, tugging on an opponent's topknot, pumping his fist before a fight. Early in 2010, the Mongolian got caught up in a drunken scuffle outside a Tokyo nightclub. Though Asashoryu flagellated himself, apologizing in a suitably abject Japanese fashion, he was forced into early retirement. "If Asashoryu had been Japanese, there would have been some criticism but it would not have been as severe," says Takanobu Nakajima, a university economist who is also vice chair of an advisory committee formed to rejuvenate the sport.

Hawaiian-born Konishiki (who started out life as Saleva'a Atisano'e) arguably received even worse treatment in the 1990s, when the 287-kilogram wrestler was denied an expected promotion to *yokozuna* by the Japan Sumo Agency (JSA), the sport's governing body, presumably because he was a little too individualistic, or perhaps a little too, ahem, American.

Nevertheless, foreign-born wrestlers can thrive in Japan and have done so. Hakuho, Asashoryu's Mongolian successor as *yokozuna*, is as bland and deferential as Asashoryu was controversial and cocky. Naturally, he is beloved by his Japanese fans. So, too, is Estonia's Baruto, who has been dubbed sumo's Leonardo DiCaprio by the local media. (OK, maybe there's a passing resemblance between the two, but, really, not all blond, blue-eyed foreigners look alike.) At one tournament, elderly ladies with powdered faces and dowdy cardigans waved Baruto-emblazoned fans while screaming *"Kawaii!"* ("cute!"). Quite an honor for the son of former Soviet cattle farmers.

International talent has undoubtedly enhanced the action inside the *dohyo*. Nevertheless, all is not well in the house of sumo. Attendance is down, and hard-core fans are dwindling. It might be easy to blame the sport's waning popularity on the *gaijin*. But most of sumo's woes are home grown. In 2007, the sport was rocked by the hazing death of a 17-year-old Japanese recruit at the hands of his stablemates, who were armed with bottles and a baseball bat.

More damaging has been a 2010 scandal in which 65 wrestlers admitted to participating in illegal betting rings formed through underworld contacts. Mind you, the athletes weren't punting on sumo. Instead, they were wagering on baseball, card games, and—gasp!—golf. But most betting is illegal in Japan and its presence in sumo stables highlighted the sport's longstanding relationship with another Japanese institution: the *yakuza*.

Although organized crime bosses' patronage of sumo wrestlers has been an open secret for decades—a well-worn career trajectory for retired sumo wrestlers

Sumo doesn't push foreigners out.
© Kyodo News

has been as Mafioso-style bodyguards or even enforcers—the betting scandal forced fans to face up to the extent of *yakuza* involvement in a sport whose athletes are expected to act as moral paragons of society. More than a dozen wrestlers were suspended from the sport for their illegal wagering. But the scandal has radiated out from sumo. In November 2010, through a crackdown kick-started by the sumo investigation, police arrested a person thought to be the No. 2 man in the *Yamaguchigumi*, the nation's biggest crime syndicate.

Disgust with the *yakuza* connection ran so high that some of sumo's top corporate sponsors pulled out of the 2010 summer highlight, the Nagoya *basho*, or tournament. (At the Nagoya stadium itself, signs outside warned: "Gangsters keep out.") NHK, the country's national broadcaster, which has for decades devoted weeks of airtime to sumo's six annual *basho*, halted live coverage of the 15-day competition. It was the first time since 1953 that a live sumo feed had been cut, a shocker akin to a TV blackout of the soccer World Cup.

Presumably, NHK was also still smarting from an incident in 2009 in which, Japanese police contend, gangster bosses bought front-row seats at a sumo tournament so their jailed blood brothers could see them on TV and feel a surge of *yakuza* pride. "This is the kind of crisis you may only see once in 100 years," said NHK's president Shigeo Fukuchi, explaining the network's sumo embargo. The subtext was even more alarming. Would sumo, that klieg-lit display, beloved as much as a cultural touchstone as a display of physical prowess, actually exist in a century's time?

The answer, at the start of 2011, was not heartening. Far from reforming itself, the house of sumo imploded further, as if acting out a slow, ritualized form of suicide. For years, the specter of match-fixing has dogged the sport. But confirmation appeared to come when more than a dozen wrestlers and coaches were implicated in fixing matches and using cell phones to coordinate the collusion. The evidence, police say, was collected from mobile phone messages as a by-product of investigations into the 2010 gambling scandal. So grave were the allegations that the JSA canceled the 2011 spring *basho* in Tokyo. It was the first time a tournament had been canceled since the end of World War II, when a bombed-out stadium prevented matches from being held.

To some critics, the match-fixing scandal has delivered precisely the kind of killer blow they hope will finally knock some sense into sumo's elder statesmen. Following the allegations, everyone from Japan's prime minister to ordinary housewives had an opinion on what the sport needed to do to reform itself. Many urged the JSA to inject fresh blood by appointing outsiders to the notoriously closed body. Others argued that sumo should lose its cushy, tax-exempt status and be forced to compete in a leaner, meaner environment. Whatever the solution, one thing is clear: Japanese society is demanding big changes from its sport of giants.

At the same time, it's worth noting that not a single foreign wrestler was banned from the ring because of the match-fixing and gambling imbroglios. Indeed, in the end, what may save sumo is the unlikely combination of foreign wrestlers and national traditions that verge on the sacred. For decades after the war, Japan maintained a sort of embarrassed silence over its national faith, which combines elements of both Shinto and Buddhism in nature worship and a pantheon of indigenous deities.

Nevertheless, sumo is still deeply rooted in Japanese religious traditions. Suspended over the *dohyo* is a Shinto shrine roof. Before matches, wrestlers sip holy water and purify the ring by sprinkling salt. Once in the sacred space, they clap their hands together to summon the gods. Even the referees wear peaked black hats similar to those of Shinto priests.

Do most wrestlers, even those who are Japanese, truly understand the significance of all this religious regalia? Probably not. Ask the young recruits at Saitama Sakae High School, which boasts one of the nation's best sumo teams, about the sport's hallowed nature, and they will stare blankly. What they like is a good "wrassle"—in extraordinary surroundings.

For more than a divine spirit, what Shinto confers upon sumo is a sense of high theater. An average sumo match lasts but a few seconds. The surrounding pageantry—the *yokozuna's* ritualized *dohyo* dance, the priestly keen of the referee, the spray of white salt against brown sand—is what separates sumo from the slapstick hype of the World Wrestling Federation. It is the same indefinable quality that makes one intuitively understand when a product or design is Made in Japan. Does it really matter if the victor in a sumo bout is a Georgian who moonlights selling yogurt on Japanese TV?

Perhaps an individual spectator pining for the days of two of the last great Japanese wrestlers, brothers Takanohana and Wakanohana, may become irritated. But traditions in Japan are so deep that they can subsume even seemingly unyielding concepts like ethnicity. Yes, Japan is a largely homogenous and sometimes xenophobic island-nation. Even in the face of a mounting labor shortfall, many Japanese people are unwilling to accept the need for, say, Indonesian nurses or Chinese convenience-store clerks.

Still, Japan's ability to elide matters of race is not limited to the sumo ring.

Sadaharu Oh, the Japanese baseball hero, was born to a Chinese father and faced schoolyard discrimination because of his ancestry. Yet his long-standing home-run record is still hailed as the ultimate display of Japanese fortitude. Masayoshi Son, the founder of SoftBank, is ethnically Korean; yet his business success is praised as one of the last great examples of Japan Inc.'s bravura.

Maybe Japan is uniquely Japanese and national comparisons cannot be drawn. But it's still worth thinking of how other sports have adapted and flourished because of an infusion of foreign talent. The apotheosis of America's national pastime, Major League Baseball, is no less American because of the stream of foreign players from places like the Dominican Republic and, yes, Japan. The same can be said for the National Basketball Association, whose popularity in the United States hasn't waned at all even as the league's rosters have become more international.

Can sumo, as the physical repository of all things Japanese, survive and thrive in the same way? In fact, reforms have already begun. The JSA is a tradition-obsessed bulge of bureaucracy lacking the flexibility of its charges. But the governing body, if only through sheer necessity, has accepted foreigners into the sport, albeit with reluctance and continuing constraints, including the rule introduced in 2010 to limit each of the 50-plus sumo stables in Tokyo to just one foreign-born wrestler. The new rule is a parochial—even protectionist—policy the sport hardly deserves. But so far the restriction has failed to stop the rise of talented foreign wrestlers.

At the same time, the JSA has moved to tackle its gangster problem with more than the usual quick bow of contrition followed by years of inaction. Committees have been formed, the JSA's management shaken up, and wrestlers put on notice that the wink-and-nod attitude toward the *yakuza* will no longer be tolerated. (Given Japanese baseball's success with striking out *yakuza* influence, sumo should be able to succeed with a similar purge.)

The biggest challenge, though, will be to change the salaryman attitude that pervades sumo, an exchange of individual freedoms for lifetime employment that in this day and age no longer feels like such a good—or even realistic—deal. Stablemasters may argue that it's only through the severity of sumo life—the hazing, the curfews, and the constant toilet-scrubbing—that discipline is instilled and loyalty is retained. But if the monastic rigor of sumo stables deters so many potential wrestlers, surely the rules can be relaxed. In the 21st century, does it really make sense for the JSA to demand, for instance, that its athletes abstain from driving cars during tournament weeks?

And as sumo changes, Japan must do the same. The salaryman culture, with all its inefficiencies and inequalities, should not hold sway in the 21st century. Young Japanese have already abandoned its peculiar ethic. In today's competitive economic environment, the country's companies can no longer just expect to lead the world, or live in isolation from it. Sumo proves that foreign blood can invigorate without destroying the ineffable Japanese-ness of the sport. In the same way, unless the Japanese start suddenly procreating more or drastically shortening their life span, immigration will be the best solution for energizing a shrinking, aging society. Says economist Nakajima: "We live in a global economy now—Japan must change, and sumo must change."

In the meantime, sumo's sacred heart will carry the sport through to the next century. "When we visit retirement homes, old people like to touch us and sometimes are brought to tears," says retired wrestler Yoshinori Tashiro. "There's something spiritual about sumo."

Certainly, when the sport's *colossi* parade into the ring to open and close each tournament, even the stale stadium air feels consecrated. Slick with perspiration, trembling with determination, the wrestlers circle the ring, bring their hands together, and bow their heads to the gods. It is an act of divination that is quintessentially Japanese. No blond head or Mongolian cheekbone can change this singular moment of worship.

BEND IT LIKE NAKATA

TAKESHI OKADA

JAPANESE PEOPLE OFTEN have a kind of inferiority complex. After the rain, we look down at the puddles instead of looking up at the rainbow. That's too bad, because soccer, as it is played in Japan, has many virtues. For instance, Japanese players are much better than Brazilian players at carrying out instructions from their coach.

And yet that same willingness to follow instructions to the letter can be a liability unless combined with the recognition that, in the end, you have to use your own judgment. So when I coached the Japanese team, the first thing we did was work on forming a positive mental attitude, or at least we tried to eliminate this inferiority complex.

Competing in Europe helped a lot of Japanese players overcome this attitude. When Hidetoshi Nakata came back after spending seven years in Europe, for example, I noticed that he never said he was hurt. Even when he was fouled, he stood up right away. Other Japanese players then followed his example; he had a huge impact on the team.

Just living overseas can help you toughen up and build your character. When I was younger, I went to Germany for a year. I didn't speak much German. I had to find a place to live by myself, buy and register a car, and do everything on my own. I didn't even know where to dispose of my garbage. It was a rough experience, but it gave me self-confidence.

But young Japanese today have no interest in going overseas. They are different in this regard from youth in my day, when we all wanted to go abroad and see the world. Why is that? Because life in Japan has become so comfort-

---

Takeshi Okada is a former coach of Japan's national soccer team.

Heading off that inferiority complex.

© Paul Gilham/FIFA via Getty Images

able. People feel that life here is not perfect, but it's good enough. Everyone is satisfied, and I think that attitude is really dangerous. We're all wallowing in affluence, so there's no reason for any of us to push or challenge ourselves anymore.

WHEN I WAS YOUNGER, I WENT TO GERMANY FOR A YEAR. I DIDN'T EVEN KNOW WHERE TO DISPOSE OF MY GARBAGE. IT WAS A ROUGH EXPERIENCE, BUT IT GAVE ME SELF-CONFIDENCE.

When I coached the team, we made "challenge" our rallying cry. The idea was: "Don't just stay where you are: push yourself harder, further." Soccer players don't improve in a steady, linear way. They have good days and bad days. The problem with Japanese players is that they psych themselves out: they have a bad day, and then they compare that experience to their good days and get depressed thinking they are in a slump or declining, instead of realizing they are experiencing a little hiccup, a temporary setback on the way to even greater heights.

I admire people like Shunsuke Nakamura, who did well in Scotland, but struggled when he joined Reggina in Italy in 2002. Even so, he didn't give up; he took the risk. Now he is back playing in Japan, and is a better player for his experiences.

Before the last World Cup, I told the team that when our opponents tried a long shot we should be aggressive and get right up in front of them, the way players do in Europe. The European style is different from that in Japan. Our players who had experience in Europe understood immediately, and responded. The other players didn't know what to do. We played Cote d'Ivoire and England. After those games, the whole team finally got it. We all saw that we needed to be more forceful in going on the attack.

In the Information Age, you can obtain a lot of knowledge about the tactics of other teams just from reading or surfing the Internet. But that is no substitute for real-world experience.

I've been asked how I built Japan's team and I'm happy to explain. But I also tell people that there are many variables; no single formula applies. Especially in soccer, there's always an unpredictable "X factor" that's hard to control for. Even if you gather eleven excellent players, does that mean they will become a good team? Not necessarily. So when someone asks me how I built such a good team and I tell them, that person will sometimes respond, "Aha, now I get it! I'll do it that way!" Well, no, that's not how it works. You have to see the whole picture.

The first thing, of course, is to open your mind. And it's helpful to read books and analyze examples of others who have succeeded. But every team is different. At the end of the day, leaders have to make their own decisions about what will work. They have to listen to individual players, understand how these particular players work together, and then exercise their own best judgment.

That's why I think young people—our future leaders—should take the leap and venture abroad. They need to broaden their horizons and discover new sources of growth.

CHAPTER FIVE: REDEFINING JAPAN'S FOREIGN RELATIONS

Photograph © Michael Hitoshi/Stone/Getty Images

A TALE OF TWO FUTURES

BILL EMMOTT

THERE WAS NOTHING SURPRISING: long before it happened, in 2010, Japan knew China would overtake it as the world's second-largest economy and that Japan would no longer stand out as Asia's economic powerhouse. But the reality was still unnerving—and deeply challenging. And this was even before the most challenging event of all, the devastation and nuclear shock delivered to Japan on March 11th, 2011.

How will Japan react to an Asia with three great regional powers (China, India, and Japan) rather than one? With several technological leaders rather than one? With financial, military, diplomatic, and environmental complexity rather than simplicity? How might that reaction be altered by the events of March 11th? The answers to those questions will shape Japan's destiny.

On the face of it, there is more opportunity than threat in these new geopolitical circumstances. Situated in the world's fastest-growing and most dynamic region—with industrialization and urbanization proceeding rapidly in both India and China, and with regional trade booming—Japan has a great geographical privilege. Already, China is Japan's largest trading partner (and South Korea's, too). India is still too poor and always too far away to loom as large, but trade with it is growing, as is Japanese investment there.

Still, being rich, modern, and Asian does carry risks. Throughout history, whenever new powers have risen to challenge the existing hegemons, conflict has occurred. Moreover, in Asia there is not just the obvious risk of conflict between, say, China and the long-standing power of America and its ally, Japan. There is also a risk of conflict between the two rising giants themselves—China and India—and of recurrent tensions with their neighbors over territorial claims and other disputes.

Bill Emmott, who has written several books on Japan, is the former editor of The Economist.

The last Sino-Indian war occurred less than half a century ago, in 1962. The last war between China and its neighbors occurred in 1979, when China invaded Vietnam and absorbed a shocking defeat. The battle between India and Pakistan for Kashmir is still going on. The last relic of World War II stands in Japan's backyard, with the continued division between North and South Korea, with all its associated tensions. Four of the world's eight declared nuclear-weapons states are in Asia, three of them having made their full declarations only in the past 15 years (India, Pakistan, and North Korea). So, although Asia has been more peaceful during the past 30 years than in the century before, the guns will not necessarily remain silent.

That is a great worry for Japan, whose post-1945 constitution limits its military options; the country remains dependent on its security alliance with the United States. The way in which tensions can be created by a seemingly small incident was shown in September 2010, when a Chinese fishing boat rammed Japanese coast guard vessels near the Senkaku Islands, and caused the worst friction between Japan and China since 2006, with the end of the five-year prime ministership of Junichiro Koizumi, whose insistence on visiting the controversial Yasukuni war shrine caused an annual freeze in relations.

A QUIET LIFE AMID GENTEEL DECLINE COULD LOOK TEMPTING TO MANY JAPANESE.

There is also a further, distinctly Japanese risk: that the country will react to these dangers and to the pressure of commercial and cultural competition by turning inward and becoming isolationist. This inward turn had already been happening in recent years, at least in a mild way, a trend exemplified by the decline in the number and proportion of young Japanese choosing to study and work abroad. And one risk arising from March 11th is that this trend might now be reinforced, with Japan inevitably preoccupied with the reconstruction effort, but also conceivably more cautious, defensive, and inward-looking.

That option is a serious temptation for several reasons. History is one; the Tokugawa shogunate closed the country for more than two centuries after 1635. Second, a country with a population of 127 million, even a slowly shrinking one, can offer its people a wide range of life choices and a strong culture. Third, with a weak economy and an aging population, there is little stomach for a fight with China, even if the battle is metaphorical rather than martial. A quiet life amid genteel decline could look tempting to many Japanese. There are plenty of straws in the wind that suggest that choosing this option is far from theoretical: the decline in the number of Japanese studying abroad, for example, or the continued resistance of major corporations to internationalize their management.

For Japan to isolate itself, however, would be a tragedy and a delusion. It would be a tragedy because the country has a genuine opportunity to prosper and even to increase its influence in the region. To reject that possibility is to condemn future generations to an unnecessary decline in living standards and life chances. It would be a delusion because the outside world, and especially Asia, is always going to penetrate Japan's society, economy, and politics. Turning inward would likely mean only that this penetration will be more damaging and disturbing than it needs to be. And turning inward would surely make the rebuilding of Japan following March 11th harder, not easier, by restricting the mental and physical resources that would be available.

There is, in contrast, a powerful and positive future for Japan to choose. That future can usefully be divided into three main parts.

1. To become the region's most productive and innovative services economy. In the service sector, Japan is currently either a laggard or is losing its lead. In aviation, shipping, financial services, design, media, entertainment, retailing, advertising, marketing, accounting, the law, tourism, hospitality, health care, education, and many other industries concerned with knowledge and with human interaction, productivity is poor, internationalization is weak, and vested interests predominate. Liberalization, to the extent that it has happened at all, has been hesitant and inconsistent.

2. To be Asia's hub for ideas, technology, culture—indeed everything to do with knowledge. Japan, despite its head start in prosperity, has failed to become Asia's hub for ideas or culture, and the country's lead in technology is narrowing. Japanese universities have few international faculty members, and there are not enough foreign students to make the country an ideas hub. Culturally, the country is important in

Here's to a truly Asian future.
© Barbara Walton-Pool/epa/Corbis

popular music, design, architecture, animation, and *manga* cartoons, but it cannot be accurately described as a truly Asian cultural center. South Korea has been a strong rival for more than a decade now, and there will soon be new competition from India and from China.

3. To be part of the creation and leadership of a pan-Asian community analogous to the European Union. For all the talk about community building, existing regional institutions and relationships remain shallow. Japanese diplomacy has long been directed at deepening those relationships and, in recent years, bringing India into these discussions, chiefly through the strangely named East Asia Summit. Prime Minister Yukio Hatoyama, during his brief period in office (September 2009 to June 2010), described the construction of Asian community institutions as among his top priorities. Little has actually happened. There is a rich alphabet soup of organizations, but none involves real obligations, such as the pooling of sovereignty and exchange of binding commitments that has built the European Union. Even the free-trade arrangements are shallow by comparison with the EU or the North American Free Trade Agreement.

The thing to imagine—to reimagine—is what Japan's position could be like in 20 or 30 years' time if the country went in the direction of openness and deeper engagement by remedying today's shortcomings and really gripping the future with both hands. And then compare that vision with one in which the status quo continues.

Start with services and knowledge, for they are the heart of a modern economy—and Japan is still Asia's richest, most sophisticated, and most modern economy. Imagine if in the next two or three decades, the country to which Japan's Asian neighbors look first for high-quality design, art, financial services, and health care—was Japan. The price that can be charged for these services is high, and so are the profits. At a time when manufacturing exports may well have declined as competition from elsewhere intensifies, these and other services could by then be Japan's most important source of foreign exchange.

These services would also provide ample employment suitable for an aging population. If Japan can build on its current status as the region's most digital nation, with the fastest and most innovative communications system, it could also be the region's most entrepreneurial nation by then, with a huge variety of service companies, all over the archipelago, enabled by that technology.

To achieve this influence will, however, require a radical program of liberalization. For a start, this effort would require the fundamental reform of the antitrust agency, the Japan Fair Trade Commission, to enforce competition throughout the economy. Then Japan needs to tear down specific barriers to entry in industries such as the law, telecom, wholesale and retail distribution, and transportation (including access for low-cost airlines). The vitality and innovative force that such a program would release could prove a huge asset in stimulating the rebuilding and reshaping of post-tsunami Japan.

Imagine, too, that Japan's universities—Tokyo, Kyoto, Doshisha, Waseda, Keio, Kyushu, and many others—become by 2030 the region's go-to campuses for brilliant researchers and star students, either in Japan itself or on cloned campuses dotted around the world. These institutions could become go-to campuses for several reasons: the freedom of thought and expression in Japan compared with China; the superior quality of Japanese life; and the flowering of private funding. For this scenario to happen, though, most teaching would have to be in English and performance measurement (and pay) for faculty would have to spread.

Achieving these objectives would be genuinely difficult, but not impossible. Tokyo, Keio, and Waseda have already inched in that direction. Unless they and other universities turn inching into striding, however, they are going to face decline as public funding shrinks and as Japanese student numbers relentlessly fall. To maintain a position as intellectual centers, Japan's universities need to globalize, recruiting more foreign students and faculty. Only if they do so will they become true centers of innovation and forces for change.

Under pressure of competition, openness, and far more productive services, Japanese companies would surely be stimulated to invest more in R&D and technology. That effort, though, would be stronger if links between private companies and universities were to become closer, which will occur only when universities become more open to collaboration. In culture, too, freer competition would break up the old, slow-moving oligopoly of mass-communication companies that have throttled the creativity of Japanese artists. The era of great movie directors such as Akira Kurosawa seems a distant memory. It doesn't need to be that way.

Finally, let's turn to the third element—the creation of an effective pan-Asian alliance. Japan's position in Asia is analogous to that of France in the European Union (even if its historic distancing from Asia is more reminiscent of Britain's attitude to Europe). In the EU, France has sought two main things: to use EU institutions and the need for compromise as a way to prevent its bigger neighbor, Germany, from dominating the continent; and to use the EU as a fulcrum to leverage greater influence for itself on the world stage.

For Germany, read China, with of course big differences, especially in political systems. But Japan's interests—like France's in the EU—depend crucially on ensuring that China's growth occurs within a cooperative framework of regional rules and institutions that help to channel China's behavior and restrain it from dangerous excesses or unilateralist moves.

Japan's influence is likely to decline as the country's economy slips down the rankings, as public resources for overseas aid decline, and as a move into current-account deficit promises to reduce capital exports. So imagine if by 2030 Japan could be the country that had built a strong pan-Asian community, with some elements of pooled sovereignty and a strong habit of cooperation. As the region's richest and freest democracy, Japan would hold a strong moral position within such a community.

Officially, such an alliance has been the policy of the Ministry of Foreign Affairs for most of the past decade and was embraced by Prime Minister Hatoyama in 2009. But action was been conspicuously absent. Japan needs to initiate a series of projects, probably best begun in economics and the environment, in which countries in the region learn to exchange obligations and take on commitments—as the

European Coal and Steel Community began the process of European integration more than half a century ago. By showing a willingness to cede some sovereignty, Japan would encourage others to follow its example. Over several decades, broader institutions could be built. The difficulty lies in persuading giants such as China and India to cede any sovereignty; the only way to achieve that would be by leading, bringing enough other Asian countries along in order to make the giants feel the advantages of being a member of the club, rather than an entity on the outside looking in.

Japan could seek to be a critical player in alliance building within this institution, as it could be friendly with India, Indonesia, Singapore, and perhaps even a unified Korea. Japanese diplomats, like the French (and British) in the EU, could be admired as the region's most sophisticated, experienced, and well trained. Japan's continued alliance with the United States could have switched from being, arguably, a sign of weakness, to a point of strength, giving the nation a British-style "special relationship" with what will still be the world's leading power.

That is the potential. Now consider the alternative: What if none of this happens? If Japan remains reliant on high-productivity manufacturing, which already accounts for a diminishing share of its economy, it will struggle to earn its way and to bear the burden of its aging population. If Japan's universities choose to remain inward-looking and traditional, they will slide down the world's rankings. The country's technological lead will evaporate. The cost of an inefficient service sector will be a heavy burden, and the young will feel increasingly alienated. Other countries will take the lead in whatever institutions emerge. Worse, the region might become dominated and damaged by friction or actual conflict between the rising powers.

Japan could choose either future. Right now, the country is leaning more toward maintaining the status quo than embracing change and seizing the opportunity. The temptation following the tsunami will be to rebuild exactly as things were, rather than seizing new opportunities. With a weak economy, dysfunctional politics, and powerful vested interests opposing liberalization, it is proving difficult for the country to change direction. Inertia is hardly a compelling philosophy, but it is a comfortable one. Economic stagnation and the ever-present competition from China, however, will surely alter that dynamic. The rewards from change would be great. What Prime Minister Naoto Kan called for on March 12th could truly again be created: A New Japan.

IS JAPAN A FADING STRATEGIC ASSET FOR THE U.S.?

MICHAEL J. GREEN

FOR DECADES, US officials routinely described the alliance with Japan as the linchpin of American strategy in Asia. So President Obama raised eyebrows during the June 2010 G-20 Summit in Toronto when he referred to South Korea as "the linchpin" of US-East Asia strategy. Secretary of State Hillary Clinton caused a further stir in a speech before the Council on Foreign Relations in September 2010 when she "reaffirmed" America's bonds with close allies, listing Japan second after Korea.

When a Japanese questioner asked about these formulations, State Department spokesman P. J. Crowley tried to be reassuring, saying that Japan remained *"an anchor"* of regional stability. The response only compounded the impression that Japan's standing had slipped.

The Obama administration clearly values the US relationship with Japan. The president invited then-Prime Minister Taro Aso to be his first foreign visitor and Hillary Clinton made Tokyo her first destination as Secretary of State. But could these comments have been Freudian slips that revealed deeper anxiety about the value of the alliance with Japan?

For some 200 years, American strategists have viewed Japan as the critical determinant of US influence in the Pacific. In 1815 Captain John Porter of the USS Essex returned from the first US naval foray into the region urging his fellow officers to focus on Japan as a way station to China. Commodore Matthew Perry told audiences in New York after his own 1853 expedition to open Japan that the Japanese were superior in all respects to their neighbors and that the United States should seek an

Michael J. Green is senior adviser and Japan Chair at the Center for Strategic and International Studies in Washington, D.C.

"honorable and friendly understanding" rather than assume the patronizing role of "Christianizing teacher." President Theodore Roosevelt described himself as "fully alive to the danger from Japan," but sought a maritime alignment with Japan and Britain to maintain order in Asia and protect the sea approaches to the Philippines, Hawaii, and the West Coast. Even in the brutal depths of World War II, Japan specialists planning for the postwar era recommended restoring Japanese economic power to maintain stability and American access to the rest of Asia. During the Cold War, the US-Japan alliance became an indispensable bastion for containing communism—an "unsinkable aircraft carrier," in the words of former Prime Minister Yasuhiro Nakasone (1982–87)—that bottled up the Soviet Far Eastern fleet and ultimately helped the West prevail.

For every strategic argument in favor of a Japan-centered Asia strategy, however, other voices have called for one focused on China. During the early 1970s, Japan was shaken by President Richard Nixon's surprise opening to China and apparent relegation of Japan to second-tier status. Immediately after the end of the Cold War, presidents George H. W. Bush and Bill Clinton both pursued aggressive trade strategies against Japan as Americans began assuming that the greatest future threats would emerge from economic rather than security rivals.

In 1995, though, the Clinton administration shifted back to a Japan-centered approach to Asia. The aim was to engage China while hedging against its growing power through a stronger US-Japan alliance. Crafted during the Clinton administration by Assistant Secretary of Defense Joseph Nye and then expanded in the George W. Bush administration under Deputy Secretary of State Richard Armitage, this strategy continues to define America's overall approach to Asia. As Vice President Biden put it in September 2010, the road to China "goes through Japan." US officials deal directly with China all the time, of course; Biden's point was that the United States continues to regard strong ties to Japan as an indispensable element in the successful management of a rising China.

Despite this well-established bipartisan support for a Japan-centered strategy, the Armitage-Nye approach is also coming under new scrutiny in the United States because of questions about Japan's capacity to continue serving as an effective counterweight to China. People are asking whether the Liberal Democratic Party's fall from power in 2009 could prompt the beginning of de-alignment from the United States; whether Japanese diplomacy in Asia can overcome the burden of Japan's historical legacy; and whether Japan's fiscal and demographic challenges will lead to the further degradation of Japanese financial support for foreign aid, US bases, and Japan's own Self Defense Forces.

These are reasonable questions, but they have not yet led to significant changes in US strategy. For one thing, Japan has shown that it can restore its national power. Under the leadership of Junichiro Koizumi, prime minister from 2001 to 2006, Japan improved its rate of economic growth, and its foreign policy was unusually bold (some in Japan thought *too* bold), as he deployed Japanese troops to Afghanistan and Iraq. For another, US critics of a Japan-centered strategy in Asia have not offered a compelling alternative. One group of scholars and policy experts, including C. Fred Bergsten of the Peterson Institute for International Economics, World Bank President Bob Zoellick, and China expert David Shambaugh at George Washington University, have argued for something closer to a US-China "G-2" in which Beijing and Washington would take a leading role in managing the global and regional economic order. However, there is no historical precedent for a hegemonic power (i.e., the United States) surrendering preeminence to a rising power (China) that rejects its fundamental values. China's mercantilist economic policies, support for unsavory regimes, suppression of human rights, and heavy-handed approach to territorial disputes all complicate efforts by Washington to meet Beijing midway on questions of international norms and order.

A second group of American scholars, including Charles Kupchan at Georgetown University, has argued for moving from bilateral alliances toward multilateral security arrangements in Asia comparable to those the United States has in Europe, for example, NATO and the Organization for Security and Co-operation in Europe (OSCE). Such an alliance is also highly unlikely, given the deep skepticism, across

Grip and grin: How can they work together?
© Xinhua/Xinhua Press/Corbis

the region, that stability can be maintained absent the US "hub-and-spokes" of bilateral alliances centered on Japan.

A third group of prominent American theorists, including Christopher Layne of Texas A&M and scholars at the libertarian Cato Institute, have argued for an "offshore balancing strategy" in which the United States would withdraw militarily from Asia but manage the regional balance of power through diplomacy from afar, much the way 19th-century Britain managed European power politics without permanent military bases on the Continent. That choice also has little currency among policy makers in the real world. The Pacific is much larger than the English Channel—and the British strategy ultimately failed to prevent two world wars.

JAPAN'S STRATEGIC IMPORTANCE MAY ACTUALLY INCREASE WITH CHINA'S RISE.

In short, the Armitage-Nye approach is here to stay. There are efforts to supplement that strategy, such as the second Bush administration's strategic partnership with India and the Obama administration's embrace of South Korea and pursuit of closer relations with Vietnam, Malaysia, and Indonesia. Given China's rising power, such diversification is logical. Still, none of these bilateral relationships can substitute for the US-Japan alliance in terms of economic and diplomatic power, let alone as a base for a forward US military presence in Asia. From a US perspective, the US-Japan alliance is too big to fail and too important to replace.

On Japan's side, leaders from both main political parties have rejected the brief, disastrous effort of Yukio Hatoyama, the first prime minister (September 2009 to June 2010) from the Democratic Party of Japan (DPJ), to create more distance between the United States and Japan. Hatoyama's successor, Naoto Kan, has embraced the alliance, particularly in the wake of confrontations with China over the disputed Senkaku (Diaoyutai) Islands. And according to numerous polls, the public continues to place a high value on the alliance, with 75 percent or more expressing approval of it in the most recent surveys. For Japan, too, the US alliance appears to be an enduring fact of life.

Though the alliance is strong, it is not without problems. The most important of these is the issue of how and whether to realign US military bases on Okinawa. It was this, more than any other single factor, that took down Hatoyama. Nothing has been resolved since. The key question is whether Tokyo will be able to prevail upon reluctant local politicians to accept the construction of a new US helicopter base on the coast so that the US Marine Corps can close the existing base at Futenma and then move some 8,000 personnel to Guam. The overall effect would be to reduce significantly the US footprint, but the requirement to build a new facility has run into fierce local opposition. This opposition is not a reflection of "Yankee Go Home" sentiment in Japan, but rather a variation of the "not-in-my-backyard" parochialism that has vexed DPJ efforts to build dams, nuclear power plants, and other large-scale projects.

While Futenma is important, the fundamental issue for Washington is not the bases, but whether Japan can restore its national power. There appears to be an emerging consensus among the DPJ and the LDP that Japan needs to focus on growth through regulatory and tax reform, free trade agreements, and fiscal prudence. The political will to act, however, is sorely lacking, and Japan has endured a succession of short-term coalition governments. This is not a political environment that breeds bold economic decision making.

Even if politics stabilize, Japan is unlikely to grow more than 2 percent or so, given its mature economy and aging society. It will therefore not be able to rely on "checkbook diplomacy" to deploy its influence, as it did in 1991, for example, when it provided $13 billion to support the US-led effort in the Gulf War. Instead, Japan will be obliged to fashion strategies that do more with less—and it can.

FOR EVERY STRATEGIC ARGUMENT IN FAVOR OF A JAPAN-CENTERED ASIA STRATEGY, OTHERS HAVE CALLED FOR ONE FOCUSED ON CHINA.

Diplomatically, Japan has a number of cards to play. The first is Japanese "soft power"—or the ability to attract other nations' cooperation without resorting to force or economic assistance. In the 2008 Chicago Council on Global Affairs survey of soft power in Asia, Japan was second only to the United States in being perceived as having attractive political, economic, and cultural attributes. A number of Gallup/Yomiuri polls have demonstrated that Japan is more popular in Southeast Asia than either the United States or China. In the British Broadcasting Company's annual survey of the most respected countries, Japan has consistently come in first or second place.

The second diplomatic card Japan holds is the nation's democratic values, an attribute recognized by both the LDP and the DPJ. The DPJ, in particular, has made human rights a major subject of bilateral discussions. In the competition of ideas in Asia, democratic norms such as good governance, accountability, free expression, and the rule of law carry far more weight than the authoritarian development alternative championed by Beijing. Major powers like India, Korea, and Indonesia have affirmed the importance of open societies to Asia's future, while only repressive regimes like Burma or North Korea take refuge in Beijing's vision.

The third card is the potential for closer strategic relations with other maritime powers. In recent years Japan has signed security agreements with India and Australia that open the way for significant advances in naval cooperation, intelligence-sharing, and diplomatic coordination. These are important new strategic partnerships that complement the US-Japan alliance. The most important opportunity is with South Korea. That bilateral relationship continues to be burdened by the past, though there have been steady improvements in political, economic, and cultural relations, especially since the DPJ took power in Japan in 2009 and President Lee Myung-bak took office in South Korea in February 2008. A South Korea–Japan entente could transform Japanese strategic influence and stabilize Asia more broadly.

Japan can also apply smart power to its defense policy. Japan spends less than 1 percent of its GDP on defense, even though it lives in one of the world's most dangerous neighborhoods. Japan should increase that share, and also use its defense budget more wisely. One step would be to remove such anachronistic constraints as the prohibition on collective self-defense *(shudanteki jieken)*, or the ban on integration in the use of force by the United States *(buryoku koshi no it-taika)*, or the cap on overseas deployments for UN peacekeeping. Japan's defense spending would go further if it streamlined the Ground Self Defense Forces and shifted them away from Northern Honshu and Hokkaido and toward Kyushu and the southern front now threatened by Chinese air and naval expansion and North Korean missiles. Relaxing export regulations to allow greater international co-development of systems, for example, would give Japan much more bang for its yen.

New Japanese trade and development strategies could also enhance its power. South Korea has negotiated numerous free-trade agreements to create growth and cement strategic relationships; these now cover 35.6 percent of its trade. Hobbled by aging but politically pivotal agricultural lobbies, Japan's free-trade agreements cover only 18.5 percent. Japan also needs a development strategy that moves beyond the quasi-mercantilist infrastructure focus of the 1980s and the diffuse "human security" handouts of the 1990s. With a focus on aid effectiveness, donor coordination with other like-minded states, and public policy support for an expansion of the country's NGO sector, Japan could emulate the high-impact aid strategies of Australia and Denmark at a time when the developing world needs alternatives to China's more predatory style.

All of these steps are well within reach of an ambitious and politically skillful Japanese leadership. Will Japan produce such leaders? Today's messy politics are not necessarily a foreshadowing of what is to come; they could be the turbulent death throes of the 50-year-old LDP-dominated system. It is at least possible that the current political instability is transitional and not some default setting for Japan's political and strategic culture.

So back to the original question: is Japan a fading strategic asset? In economic terms, the answer is clearly yes. Japan will remain the world's number-three economy for some time, but its share of global GDP will continue to shrink.

In strategic terms, however, the answer is probably no. Indeed, Japan's strategic importance may actually increase with China's rise. Geographically, the Japanese archipelago sits athwart China's approach to most of the Pacific. That geography will matter more as the Chinese Navy and Air Force attempt to increase their ability to project power. Diplomatically, Japan's new security relationships with Australia and India will help the United States maintain a more positive balance of influence in Asia.

Too often, US officials think of Japan as the ATM for American diplomacy. Instead, they need to search for opportunities to work together and figure out how to best use Japan's considerable assets. History suggests that Japan is capable of transforming its institutions in the face of new threats and challenges. But it will take a new class of Japanese leaders willing to break free of current institutional and political manacles to fulfill that vision.

COPING WITH CHINA

KENNETH LIEBERTHAL

THREE RELATIVE CERTAINTIES will shape Japan's strategic options regarding China.

Economically, Japan will maintain a very high GDP per capita but likely will not experience strong GDP growth. Demographics dictate that its labor force will shrink and the number of elderly rise, increasing health and pension costs. Adding in the government's large debt overhang, the country will have limited room for major initiatives, such as substantially increasing the size of the Self Defense Force, that could raise its international profile.

Politically, factional divisions and weak institutions make it unlikely Japan will undertake the major reforms that could significantly enhance economic growth.

Socially, cultural norms will likely prevent Japan from turning to immigration in order to alleviate its serious demographic problems.

But three critical uncertainties also loom large.

1. How will China change?

Domestically, China's growth to date has relied on a model combining abundant cheap labor, lax environmental policy, public tolerance of increasing social inequality, and a global market willing and able to absorb Chinese exports. That model is no longer fully viable, and the country's capacity to make necessary changes in the next five years (during a period of political succession) is uncertain.

Internationally, China's relatively successful performance during the economic crisis has increased its influence; it is still struggling, however, to define its role.

Kenneth Lieberthal is director of the John L. Thornton China Center and senior fellow in foreign policy and global economy and development at the Brookings Institution.

The results to date are mixed at best: China's foreign policy has become more muscular, but its inclination to take on the responsibilities of a global power is much less evident.

2. How will the United States and China get along?

The United States faces severe fiscal challenges, but it should remain the world's strongest country for decades to come. Japan must consider two possibilities: that US policy will be forced to accommodate an increasingly multipolar world, with China emerging as a major force; and that the US relationship with China will become deeply antagonistic, raising threat perceptions on both sides.

THE LIST OF POTENTIAL FRICTION POINTS WITH A RISING CHINA IS TOO LONG TO ASSUME THAT SERIOUS TENSIONS ARE AVOIDABLE.

Some in Japan may be tempted to favor an exclusively pro-US policy as a way to enhance its strategic space if Sino-American tensions worsen. Such a choice would, however, likely prove counterproductive. Considering the importance of China to Japan's economic prospects, strategic antagonism toward Beijing would be a high-cost policy. But if Japan were to move too far from the United States, it would give China excessive leverage to bend Japan to its own priorities. Japan should instead hew to a pragmatic mix of policies.

Shall we dance?
© Kasuhiro Nogi/AFP/Getty Images

3. What will happen on the Korean peninsula?

The range of possible outcomes on the Korean peninsula remains extraordinarily broad. Within five years, Japan could face a nuclear North Korea with the capacity to reach any part of Japanese territory with its missiles; a North Korean collapse and warfare that weakens the peninsula and creates new strains between China and the United States; a united Korea that, while temporarily absorbed with the problems of unification, is recognized as a potentially major economic and military power; or something resembling the status quo, with the possibility that North Korea begins to reform slowly, remaining a viable enough state to keep the peninsula divided without becoming a direct nuclear threat.

After the next presidential election, in 2012, South Korea (ROK) might also adopt a far more accommodating "sunshine policy" toward North Korea. This approach could result in closer ROK–China relations and greater ROK–US strains, further complicating Japan's strategic environment.

Mapping a strategic direction

Given Japan's fiscal and demographic challenges, substantial investment in China should remain a critical part of its economic strategy—as should diversification involving India, Indonesia, and other countries. At the same time, however, Tokyo

Senkaku or Diaoyu? More than the name is in dispute.
© Sankei via Getty Images

should seek to minimize its exclusive dependence on China for critical resources, such as rare-earth metals, by finding new sources of supply or investing in production in other countries.

Japan should also attempt to leverage its excellence in the many managerial and technological areas (for example, energy efficiency) where China is weak in order to maximize Sino–Japanese economic interdependence. Such interdependence may reduce China's willingness to use unilateral economic and trade measures to pressure Japan. Even a faltering Chinese economy would continue to provide plenty of opportunities for Japanese investment—as long as anti-Japanese sentiment in China is held at bay.

The list of potential friction points with a rising China—including conflicting territorial claims in the East China Sea, differing concerns about North Korea, and maritime disputes—is too long to assume that serious tensions are avoidable. Japan should, therefore, promote the development of dispute resolution mechanisms with China to help fashion compromises on such issues as operationalizing the 2008 agreement on the East China Sea. It should also develop crisis-management mechanisms to prevent future incidents from escalating.

Such bilateral institutions will be important. But Japan's well-being relies on figuring out how to prosper in a dangerous neighborhood that it cannot dominate militarily. It should consider encouraging the creation of a regional security community, including China, Japan, the United States, and South Korea (and maybe North Korea, if it gives up its nuclear program). These countries include the world's largest economies, energy importers, and militaries in a region riven by territorial disputes, different political systems, and fraught histories. The region needs institutions that can contain the inevitable disputes before they run too hot.

A security community would fall far short of acting as an Asian NATO; that idea is inconceivable. After all, both Japan and South Korea are formal US allies, while China is not and does not want to be. Rather, the idea is to create a mechanism that can help to reduce the chances of conflict in northeast Asia. This group would focus on developing rules for routine naval and air operations, consulting on security perspectives and planning, promoting energy security, and working together on common—and especially nontraditional—security threats.

A very rough analogy might be to the Shanghai Cooperation Organization, which began in 2001 as a talking shop with China, Russia, and four central Asian countries and has gradually developed stronger institutional capacities and a more substantive agenda.

It will take time and considerable effort to develop a northeast Asia security community, so it is important to make a start. Japan should initiate direct conversations with the other countries. There is some history to build on, as bilateral and trilateral meetings are already a part of the landscape.

It is in Japan's interest to broaden and strengthen cooperation in northeast Asia and to include the United States. In a dangerous region—and in uncertain times—such institutions make everyone safer.

FORGING A PARTNERSHIP WITH CHINA

HITOSHI TANAKA

AS THE BALANCE OF POWER SHIFTS IN ASIA, China increasingly presents critical risks and opportunities for Japan's prosperity. Having lost its place to China as the world's second-largest economy in 2010, Japan is grappling with the question of how to interact with its increasingly assertive neighbor.

Indeed, in recent years, China's growing international profile has magnified the confidence it gained from rapid economic growth. During the global financial crisis of 2008–09 when Japan and other developed nations were mired in economic turmoil, China managed to achieve 10 percent annual growth by significantly expanding domestic demand. The subsequent successes of the 2008 Beijing Olympics and Shanghai Expo in 2010 added to China's assertiveness.

Yet, in 2009, the Chinese best-seller, *Unhappy China*, by a group of Chinese authors, portrayed a nation proud of its international contributions but deeply resentful of a perceived lack of recognition by the rest of the world.

At the same time, China's leaders remain acutely sensitive to growing dissatisfaction among ordinary Chinese over widening income gaps between the rural and urban populace as well as inland and coastal regions. Those gaps can only be narrowed through continued economic growth; to achieve that growth, China will need international cooperation in a range of sectors.

Even so, former leader Deng Xiaoping's policy of maintaining a low external profile clearly has been consigned to history. Highlighting the rising influence of the People's Liberation Army over domestic and international affairs, China has declared the South China Sea an area of "core interest," reinforcing its territorial claims while boosting its activities in the East China Sea.

Hitoshi Tanaka is chairman of the Institute for International Strategy at the Japan Research Institute.

China's military spending—and its arsenal—have grown steadily. All these factors have naturally fueled concern among neighboring countries, most of all Japan, about China's ultimate goals.

China's growing assertiveness manifests itself most clearly in its relationship with Japan. The government's patriotic education policies of the 1990s emphasized Japan's aggression in the first part of the 20th century and portrayed a valiant Communist Party driving back the marauders before taking its rightful place at the country's helm. The younger generation steeped in this curriculum harbors strong anti-Japanese sentiments. Their distrust of Japan has been fueled by the explosive growth in Internet usage; the number of Internet users in China is estimated to exceed 400 million and continues to grow at a rapid rate. Key Chinese Web sites seethe with patriotic anger, resentment that erupted into public protests first in the early 2000s over repeated visits by top Japanese officials to Tokyo's Yasukuni Shrine, which honors the war dead, and more recently over a diplomatic dispute concerning the Senkaku Islands in the East China Sea.

Both issues marked a sharp deterioration in bilateral relations between China and Japan. But the stark contrast in China's responses on each occasion reveals much about the shift in Beijing's official mindset.

At the height of the "Yasukuni Shrine problem," when then-Prime Minister Junichiro Koizumi enraged Beijing with his visits, the Chinese government took diplomatic measures such as suspending summit meetings and other high-level contacts, but did not touch bilateral trade and economic relations, an approach Chinese officials described as "cool politics, warm economics."

However, in late 2010, when the two countries locked diplomatic horns over Japan's detention of a Chinese boat captain in the Senkaku Islands region, China acted swiftly and ruthlessly. In official and unofficial moves, it suspended all manner of bilateral exchanges and halted exports of crucial rare earth metals to Japan (and subsequently to other markets). In other politically charged actions, China detained Japanese company employees, accusing them of espionage.

Yet, from the time China set out on the path of economic reform in 1978 until just recently, the country saw Japan as a necessary partner, one that provided more than $40 billion in government loans and supported China's infrastructure development. Through public- and private-sector programs, Japan also provided China with badly needed capital and technology. More significantly, Japan remained China's biggest trade partner throughout this period.

On the diplomatic front, Japan went to great lengths to prevent China's political isolation and worked to lift economic sanctions imposed by the Group of Seven (G-7) nations in response to Beijing's 1989 Tiananmen Square crackdown. It was Japan that immediately resumed bilateral contact at the top levels. As host of the 2000 summit in Okinawa for the Group of Eight (the G-7, expanded to include Russia), Japan contemplated inviting China to participate for the first time as a G-8 dialogue partner; and Japan was among the first countries to complete negotiations over China's accession to the World Trade Organization in 2001.

ジャイアントパンダ
Giant Panda
シュアン シュアン
Shuan Shuan

Panda diplomacy: cuddling up to Japan
Koichi Kamoshida/Getty Images

As a result of its ensuing international engagement and globalization, China has acquired many options, not least in its choice of trade partners. Japan has lost its position as China's largest trade partner to become its third-largest, after the European Union and the United States. For Japan, however, China has become the most important trade partner, with bilateral trade surpassing the total value of US–Japan trade in 2004. Since then, Japan's reliance on China as its largest trade partner has only increased, and significantly so in the wake of the global financial crisis.

While both sides would endorse the proposition that Japan and China maintain an important relationship marked by mutual reliance that benefits both countries, the power balance has clearly changed. Simply put, Japan is becoming less and less vital for China, while China is becoming more important to Japan. This trend is likely to continue. But what does it portend? As recent history has shown, in periods of diplomatic or economic success since the two countries established diplomatic relations in 1972, Chinese nationalist sentiment and conservatism has increased, and attitudes toward Japan have hardened.

Also, Japan fears that if domestic problems such as the income gap, pollution, and soaring inflation spiral beyond Beijing's control, the Communist Party administration could see external crises as a way to divert public attention, and that the ideal focal point for popular ire could well be Japan.

For Japan, the challenge of creating a constructive relationship with an increasingly emboldened China looks more daunting every day. What Tokyo needs is a comprehensive strategy to deal with China, one that will avoid damaging relations while expanding the opportunities for mutual economic benefit.

Japan's fundamental priorities should be to deter China from seeking to dominate the East Asian region and to build a multitiered framework to shift the country in a constructive direction.

States change and evolve. Japan, too, changed considerably in the process of rebuilding from the ashes of WWII to become the world's second-largest economy. Once widely regarded as a closed market in international trade circles, Japan proceeded with trade liberalization and deregulation in the 1980s. Meanwhile, pressure from the international community, especially the United States, spurred it to expand international cooperation and contributions to overseas aid programs and in key areas such as environment, energy, and infectious diseases.

Of course, Japan is a multiparty democracy that relies on the United States for security and shares Western values. China, however, does not share the values of a democratic industrialized nation. Rather, some might say it is adhering to its home-grown model of strong state regulation, and attaches little importance to friendly relations with the international community. Such critics would also argue that constructive pressure from the international community does not work. While this kind of debate cannot be dismissed, the only way China can achieve the economic growth it needs for domestic governance is by maintaining and expanding such mutually reliant relationships. Ultimately, then, China would seem to have little choice but to take the path of international collaboration.

But what kind of comprehensive strategy could lead to positive changes in China and a viable, multitiered framework?

First, it is imperative to build a strategic multilateral partnership in East Asia, the foundation of which should be the Japan–US alliance. Only the United States has the capability to deter China from regional hegemonic ambitions and to counter the expansionary influence of that country's vast military force. In this respect, the US military presence in East Asia will be more vital than ever, as will Japan's role as alliance partner and host to the bulk of US forces in the region.

But Japan needs to reconfirm the stability of the Japan–US alliance, which has been shaken by diplomatic disputes over the US troop presence in Okinawa. At the same time, the alliance should make fostering mutual trust with China a key priority. To achieve this trust, all three countries need a confidence-building framework that includes dialogue and such measures as defense exchanges and joint disaster-relief efforts.

SIMPLY PUT, JAPAN IS BECOMING LESS IMPORTANT TO CHINA, WHILE CHINA IS BECOMING MORE IMPORTANT TO JAPAN.

Also, Japan's regional partnerships must be strengthened, particularly with key member countries including Australia, India, South Korea, and the ten countries of the Association of Southeast Asian Nations, particularly Indonesia, Singapore, and Vietnam.

With Russia and the United States joining the 16-member East Asian Summit from 2011, greater integration of the East Asian region should also be pursued. It is not possible for countries of East Asia, with their different threat perceptions and levels of economic development, to strive for a union modeled on the European Union. However, stronger interregional relationships of mutual reliance are essential to enable more effective interaction with China. In the field of "nontraditional security," which includes natural disasters, piracy, drug trafficking, and terrorism, it is possible to envision a body for joint security cooperation with a focus on the East Asian Summit countries.

In the field of economic exchanges, in areas such as trade, investment, and labor mobility, East Asian countries have concluded bilateral economic partnership agreements with multiple countries. But why should there not be a multilateral partnership agreement for regional economic integration?

Such a formal arrangement would establish more effective, orderly economic relationships by liberalizing trade and investment and agreeing to certain rules for cooperation. For Japan, the top policy option is greater East Asian economic integration through such partnership agreements. Such agreements should also build on early moves to promote trans-Pacific cooperation, which would also focus on trade and investment.

Finally, as China steadily transforms from a regional to a global power, key countries must build a truly global cooperative relationship. In particular, top-level collaboration is essential between the European Union, Japan, and the United States. Anything less can be counterproductive. A few years ago, the European Union attempted to lift the international arms embargo on China, while Japan and the United States opposed the move. Many countries in Asia became increasingly concerned about China's aggressive maritime behavior, Sino–Japanese relations cooled, and Europe pressed ahead to strengthen its economic relationship with China while the United States moved to harden its attitude toward China.

Of course, even though geopolitical factors and specific national-interest priorities differ, there is growing international agreement that the "China question"—how to interact with this increasingly powerful and assertive nation—is critical to future global stability.

How to deal effectively with China is not a challenge just for Japan and the United States. The world needs true regional and global collaboration to achieve a win–win relationship between China and the international community.

HOW JAPAN CAN PROFIT FROM A RISING CHINA

VICTOR K. FUNG

SINCE CHINA'S OPENING to foreign investment, Japanese companies have achieved a remarkable record, at least as good as any other major foreign investor. Japanese companies, led by retailers, service providers, and a small number of manufacturers and industrial concerns, entered China early. It was China's accession to the WTO in late 2001, however, that kick-started foreign direct investment (FDI) and paved the way for the increasing integration of Japan's industry with China's.

From 1995 to 2008, Japan was China's second-largest source (after Hong Kong) of FDI. Cumulative Japanese FDI into China stands at more than $70 billion, covering some 42,400 ventures across a broad range of sectors. Today it would be unusual to find a major Japanese brand that is *not* doing much (and probably most) of its assembly or manufacturing in China. Numerous surveys show that Japanese businesses regard China as their most important investment destination.

And all this is just the beginning. I believe China is at a major inflection point in its development, and that deep and lasting changes are taking place in its export sector, consumer economy, and industrial structure. It is clear that investors in China will need analytics, foresight, and creative thinking to understand these changes and determine how to make the most of them.

Here are some of the changes and their implications for Japanese companies in particular, and how these companies might respond.

The end of low-cost China

China's export economy has been irrevocably recast by rising wages. In 2010, wages in the export manufacturing sector rose 20 to 50 percent, depending on

Victor K. Fung is chairman of the Li & Fung group of companies.

location, and are still rising. Many foreign investors watched closely in the spring and summer of 2010 as labor unrest played out at Foxconn, a Taiwanese assembly company, and other major manufacturing sites in the export powerhouse of Guangdong, center of the Pearl River Delta (PRD). While the specific issues varied, there were common themes: low pay, long hours, dull and repetitive work, and lack of career development.

R&D SPENDING IN CHINA COULD REACH $153 BILLION IN 2011, SURPASSING EVEN JAPAN.

With expectations rising, one-off wage increases failed to stem the discontent. Workers are demanding improved working conditions and benefits, and the law is increasingly supporting them. The Guangdong Provincial People's Congress has committed to accelerate wage rises, while giving workers collective bargaining rights across the board. Similar changes are taking place throughout the country. As China's working-age population declines while becoming better-educated, industries at the lower end of the skill ladder are seeing labor shortages in certain provinces.

All these factors are changing the calculus for global exporters, while creating potential for countries lower on the economic chain, including Bangladesh, Cambodia, Vietnam, and Indonesia. As manufacturing relocates, there will be shifts in the Asia-based supply chain. That, in turn, will drive demand for commodities, logistics, and distribution services.

The makings of an R&D center

A rise in wages is a disruption. It is also an indicator of China's progress. Where multinational companies once looked to China only to assemble or manufacture, now they also seek out the country's research and development skills. R&D spending in China could reach $153 billion in 2011, surpassing even the amount spent in Japan.

More than half of undergraduate degrees in China are in science and engineering, compared with only a third in the United States. Moreover, improvements in the quality of education and postgraduate opportunities are beginning to make these numbers relevant for the international business community. A decade ago, nine out of ten Chinese PhD graduates in the United States preferred to stay in the United States for work; today they are much more likely to return home.

All of these trends—rising wages, higher-skilled workers, and China's climb up the value chain—present opportunities. Japanese companies already possess world-class R&D expertise. Developing new forms of partnership is a logical next step.

A number of obstacles, however, including intellectual property rights (IPR) issues and fears of economic nationalism, have impeded investment into higher-end R&D. IPR protection is improving in China, as the authorities acknowledge its key role in spurring innovation. Pragmatic companies will see this as a good time to build a position that prepares them to take advantage of changing conditions.

The Outline of the Plan for the Reform and Development of the Pearl River Delta (2008 to 2020), drafted by the Chinese government's economic planning arm, the National Development and Reform Commission (NDRC), sets out the goal of moving the region from low- and medium-skilled export processing industries, to high-tech-, IT-, and R&D-intensive industries. In support of this goal, universities, educational institutions, and networks are being built; financial incentives are being established; and resources are being allocated to environmental protection and other quality-of-life issues.

Honda is revving up operations in the Pearl River Delta.
© Peter Parks/AFP/Getty Images

The PRD is the natural place to test China's burgeoning advanced technology capabilities. Guangdong already accounts for 17 percent of China's R&D personnel and 16 percent of the nation's total expenditure on R&D projects, more than any other province on both counts. The nation's leading patent registrant, Huawei Technologies, is located in Shenzhen, and in 2009, Guangdong accounted for 27 percent of the nation's patent applications. Japanese companies, led by those in the automobile and consumer electronics sectors, have a positive record of investment into Guangdong. Moreover, in an era of accelerating integration of China and Southeast Asia—driven by the signing of the China–Association of Southeast Asian Nations (ASEAN) Free Trade Area agreement in 2010—the PRD's geographical position makes it a natural candidate to connect the Chinese hinterland with the ten ASEAN economies.

Welcome, shoppers

With wages rising, it is not surprising that China's consumers are drawing the attention of global business. China consumes around $1 trillion a year (compared with about $10 trillion in the United States); by 2030, China's consumer spending could be $2.5 trillion. China's growth will affect not only its own domestic markets, but also global ones.

Consider tourism. About 50 million Chinese travel abroad each year; in the next decade, that number could rise to 110 million. That's good news for the Asian tourism industry in particular, because while the Chinese love to travel abroad, they prefer to explore neighboring countries first. Hong Kong is the most popular destination, where Chinese outspend the average tourist by 15 percent, followed by Southeast Asia. In Japan, China is the third-largest source of tourists; even so, Japan should step up its efforts to attract more. This effort will require tour agencies and businesses to address issues related to language, food, and local practices.

Higher domestic consumption in China also presents opportunities for Japanese companies, particularly in electronics, autos, and entertainment products. Adaptation and creativity—including working with local partners—will help to define success as the consumer market matures and segments.

New values

China is also undergoing a fundamental shift in how it values growth, which is not all about the headline number anymore. As China becomes more prosperous, it is also looking at such qualitative factors as social progress, environmental protection, health, and education. Specifically, China is aiming to reduce its carbon intensity (that is, carbon or carbon-equivalent emitted per dollar of output) by 40 to 45 percent by 2020. The national government is serious about this initiative and is creating new investment incentives and policy frameworks, while stimulating growth in renewable energies.

At the micro level, many Chinese enterprises are notoriously energy-draining, a legacy of rapid development, subsidized electricity, and lack of a well-developed environmental industry. The result is that China requires five to eight times more energy, depending on the industry, to produce a dollar of GDP than does Japan. Given Japan's track record in energy efficiency, partnerships in this area are logical. So far, though, there have been few. Again, a few small experiments could pave the way for action by both sides that achieves sufficient scale and scope to make a difference for the planet.

China has changed enormously over the past 30 years. But the biggest transformation lies ahead. I see a future in which China emerges both as producer and consumer, and one in which progress is measured not by numbers alone.

For those who are already heavily invested in China, such a future may appear threatening. I see it differently. I believe these changes will create even more opportunities for those ready to deal with the emergence of a new China—a China that is a knowledge partner and an equal in every way.

THE DIPLOMACY DEFICIT

PAUL BLUSTEIN

AKIRA AMARI HAD HAD ENOUGH. It was late in the evening of July 28, 2008, the eighth day of a marathon negotiating session at the headquarters of the World Trade Organization (WTO), in Geneva. Amari, Japan's minister of economy, trade, and industry, had flown to Switzerland to help end a seven-year deadlock in the global trade talks. But as the clock ticked well past midnight, Amari found himself locked outside the office of WTO director-general Pascal Lamy, waiting for a meeting of key ministers to begin. Inside Lamy's office, Amari's counterparts from Australia, Brazil, the European Union, the United States huddled in intensive discussions over the meeting's most contentious issues. Unable even to get answers about the meeting schedule, Amari was left for hours to cool his heels. When at long last the office doors swung open and Lamy emerged, Amari let him have it.

Amari, leaping to his feet and banging his briefcase for emphasis, assailed Lamy in Japanese as his interpreter, waving her arms and contorting her face, did her best to convey Amari's wrath. "Mr. Lamy, I am a minister in the Japanese government with a very large portfolio," Amari bellowed. "It is intolerable that I have been made to wait this long!" The racket prompted curious WTO officials to poke their heads out from nearby doors; some could barely conceal their mirth over the interpreter's histrionics.

Amari's middle-of-the-night meltdown reveals a lot about Japan's chronic power deficit in multilateral organizations. For a country that is so wealthy and so dependent on the economic and security architecture constructed after World War II, Japan plays a surprisingly modest role in shaping the policies of international institutions. Sometimes, as in the story above, it literally cannot get in the door.

Paul Blustein is a non-resident fellow in the global economy and development program at the Brookings Institution, and senior visiting fellow at the Center for International Governance Innovation.

All too often, Japan finds itself cast as the global equivalent of the late US comedian Rodney Dangerfield; it can't get no respect. This lack of heft is all the more surprising given the considerable talents of its professional diplomatic corps and the generosity of its government, such as the $100 billion Tokyo ponied up in November 2008 for the International Monetary Fund (IMF) during the depths of the global financial crisis. As hard as Japanese officials try, the country punches well below its global weight.

Why is this the case? Some of the reasons are of long standing. Japan's wartime history and the lingering animosity toward it in parts of Asia have made its policy makers uncomfortable with asserting themselves. Cultural and linguistic differences are another inhibiting factor, especially for Japanese cabinet ministers; they tend to have much less experience abroad than professional civil servants and diplomats. Even domestically, most Japanese political leaders, constrained by social mores and the imperatives of consensus building, shy away from aggressive leadership styles. Their reticence is all the more pronounced when they are in international settings.

Repeated bouts of economic recession and stagnation over the past two decades have sapped Japan's already-modest capacity for exerting influence overseas. The same goes for the repeated bouts of turmoil in government leadership, as manifested in the dizzying turnover of prime ministers—six since September 2006.

On the UN Security Council, there's no seat for Japan.
© Don Emmerti/AFP/Getty Images

Tokyo will pack an even feebler wallop the longer the economy's torpor persists, the deeper the political system slides into dysfunction, and the more the population shrinks.

Nowhere is Japan's relative weakness more evident than in the WTO. Along with Canada, the European Community, and the United States, Japan was once a proud member of the "Quad"—the four powers that from 1980 to 2000 basically made the rules for world trade. Their deals were almost invariably approved by other participating nations (provided, that is, that developing countries were granted major exemptions from abiding by the rules).

But by the turn of the millennium, with Japan having lost much of its economic mojo, Robert Zoellick, then the US Trade Representative, felt free to kick the Japanese out of the charmed circle as the Doha Round got under way, in 2001. Frustrated by what he perceived as Tokyo's defensive crouch on key issues and pointless speechifying by Japanese ministers at negotiating sessions, Zoellick formed a new power group with Australia, Brazil, the European Union, and India in 2004. Despite frantic lobbying, Japan was not invited. Only in 2006 did Japan begin to edge its way back into the inner sanctum, after it had appointed a trade minister with some capacity for engaging in give and take—the late Shoichi Nakagawa. For a while, Japan was relegated to a sort of second-class citizenship as a member of the "G-6" but not of a smaller four-member group (Brazil, the European Union, India, and the United States), where the real action was. Even after gaining formal readmission to the elite club of WTO powers, Tokyo's negotiating status never matched its economic stature—as the story about Amari's tantrum attests.

Back in Japan's economic heyday of the 1980s, it looked as though it would start exercising a proportionate amount of international clout. Tokyo insisted upon—and eventually got—a voting share on the boards of the IMF and World Bank that reflected its financial stake in those institutions and its number-two position in global GDP rankings. Japan was able to steer the World Bank, for example, toward publication of a report, titled "The East Asian Miracle," that credited Japanese-style government planning for some of the success of the Asian tigers. The report influenced World Bank advice to developing countries.[1] In the United Nations, Japan bid for a permanent seat on the UN Security Council, and Tokyo began dispatching members of its Self Defense Force on UN peacekeeping operations, albeit with rigid restrictions designed to prevent violations of the nation's pacifist constitution. In 1993, a Japanese policeman on a peacekeeping mission in Cambodia was killed in an ambush—the first such death since World War II.

But as the luster of the Japanese model faded, so did prospects that Japan would be a more forceful participant in international organizations. During the Asian financial crisis of 1997–98, Japan's objections to the discipline imposed by the IMF

---

1 Philip Y. Lipscy, "Japan's role in international economic institutions: Why does Japan have a greater voice in the World Bank than the IMF?" Paper prepared for "Japan and the World" conference, Yale University, March 9–10, 2007.

on neighboring countries had little effect on the organization's policies. Similarly, the country's efforts to create an Asian Monetary Fund wilted in the face of strong opposition from China and the United States.

Meanwhile, Tokyo's ambitions for a permanent seat on the Security Council languished. Japan joined forces in 2004 in the "G-4" with Brazil, Germany, and India, which were also seeking permanent membership; the four agreed to support one another's bids. The Chinese, however, were not about to allow their old wartime enemy in, and dozens of other countries sided with Beijing in rejecting the G-4. It didn't help that Japan's peacekeeping missions were kept from going anywhere they might come into harm's way; the death of the police officer in Cambodia, instead of helping the Japanese public accept the possibility of casualties in peacekeeping, only fortified the nation's allergy to going into danger overseas. The hundreds of Japanese Self Defense Force ground troops dispatched to southern Iraq performed ably but had to be guarded by British and Dutch forces, eliciting international scorn—and making it all the easier for Japan's foes in the UN to make their case that Tokyo is far from ready for the responsibilities of permanent membership on the Security Council.

A further blow to Japan's stature has come in the G-20's eclipse of the G-8 as the world's premier economic steering committee. Of course, all the G-8 members, including the United States, have had to face the reality that the "rise of the rest"— Brazil, China, and India, in particular—obliges them to share power they had previously arrogated to themselves. But this transition is especially poignant for Japan.

At a conference in Seoul, in advance of the 2010 G-20 summit there, Noriyuki Wakisaka of the *Asahi Shimbun* wistfully recalled how his newspaper used to dispatch about ten journalists to G-8 summits. "Although we often criticized the outcome, the summits were like annual festivities where journalists gathered and enjoyed seeing Japan's performance in the 'most privileged members' club' in the world," Wakisaka wrote in his conference paper. These days, he noted, the *Asahi* wouldn't dream of sending such a large contingent to a G-8 summit, given the group's increasing irrelevance. Although it is still too early to tell how Japan will perform in the G-20, China is the Asian member that commands the most attention, and South Korea adroitly capitalized on its 2010 chairmanship, offering initiatives on development and financial regulation that others accepted. (Japan's offers to host G-20 summits have been turned down—a minor setback, but worth noting.)

Along with the economic, geopolitical, and historical factors that diminish Japan's impact in international institutions, cultural and linguistic problems also loom large. While foreign-policy makers praise Japanese civil servants as exceedingly well-briefed, skilled in the diplomatic arts, and proficient in English, their eyes almost invariably roll when they are asked about the way Tokyo represents itself at ministerial meetings where politicians must do the talking. According to regulars on the diplomatic circuit, there does, unfortunately, seem to be some validity to the stereotype of a Japanese delegate whose idea of engagement is to drone through a statistics-packed briefing paper.

Japan sometimes gets exceptional representation, of course. Former UN High Commissioner for Refugees Sadako Ogata and former Vice Minister of Finance Toyoo Gyohten were both highly regarded. But the country simply does not have enough skilled diplomats; the result, informed observers say, is that the Japanese don't shape agendas or interact with other delegations nearly as effectively as they should. Defensiveness, in the form of a narrow focus on deflecting criticism, is another commonly cited trait. Although Japan is hardly unique in putting its national interest first—indeed, this is what diplomats are supposed to do—an oft-heard complaint is that its representatives devote too much effort to justifying what Japan is doing rather than articulating positive visions concerning global welfare.

EVEN AFTER GAINING FORMAL READMISSION TO THE ELITE CLUB OF WTO POWERS, TOKYO'S NEGOTIATING STATUS NEVER MATCHED ITS ECONOMIC STATURE.

Japan's political system exacerbates these weaknesses. A comparison with South Korea is instructive in this context. Its president can and often does appoint a well-qualified English speaker to represent the government at important meetings. In Japan, however, the prime minister often chooses trade ministers or even foreign ministers, based on patronage considerations—that is, the need to award posts to powerful factions within the ruling party. This is even more true when the prime minister has only a tenuous grip on power, as has been the case since 2006.

To give credit where credit is due, Japan deserves recognition for its efforts to play a constructive role in global organizations. The $100 billion loan it extended to the IMF was the first such contribution from countries with substantial currency reserves, and it was a major turning point in the nascent G-20's effort to bolster global recovery. Japan can also take pride in the success of its signature UN Commission on Human Security, which under the leadership of Ogata and Nobel Prize–winner Amartya Sen led to the creation of a UN trust fund, financed by Tokyo and dedicated to priorities such as protecting people caught up in violent conflicts. Japan also wins kudos for its skill at hosting international forums. According to Canadian scholar John Kirton, a leading authority on the G-8, "Japan is the only member to have consistently hosted successful summits, having done so on all of the five occasions [1979, 1986, 1993, 2000, and 2008] when it has been put to the test."[2]

One institution in which Japan has achieved significant influence is Asia-Pacific Economic Cooperation (APEC). But in important respects, that influence has not been positive. In the early 1990s, APEC set a goal of achieving free trade and investment in the region by 2020. The target, though unrealistic, was at least in the right direction. Tokyo scuttled the initiative in 1998, when Japanese leaders, anxious to protect the domestic fishery and forest products industries from foreign competi-

2   John Kirton, "A committed contributor: Japan in G-8 and G-20 governance," paper prepared for an international workshop on "Japan (Still) Matters: What Role in the World," Sheffield University, April 30– May 1, 2009.

tion, blocked a proposal to phase out tariffs in nine key areas. Cut off at the knees, APEC has become a glorified talk shop.

The Asian Development Bank is where Japan exerts the most constructive leadership. The country prides itself on being a founding member of the institution; it holds more than 15 percent of the capital stock—equal to that of the United States—and all of the ADB's eight presidents have come from the Japanese Finance Ministry. In turn, they have appointed ministry colleagues to powerful management posts. The current president, Haruhiko Kuroda, has advocated greater integration and cooperation among Asian countries, in both trade and finance (with numerous exceptions, of course, for critical domestic industries). Tokyo's power within the ADB is one of the reasons Japan can legitimately claim some of the credit for Asia's economic development.

Still, the Rodney Dangerfield syndrome plagues Japan, raising two questions: does Japan's treatment matter, beyond the damage inflicted on the egos of its policy makers? And if it does, what can Tokyo do about it?

Japan could just shrug off this power shortage. After all, if countries such as Australia, Canada, Singapore, Sweden, and the United Kingdom punch above their weight, then logically some countries have to do the opposite. There's a reasonable case for Japan to adopt the view that its destiny simply isn't to exercise international power. Perhaps it would be better off concentrating on using its resources to support initiatives taken by others—the $100 billion loan to the IMF being a perfect example.

The problem with this way of thinking, however, is that Japan has an enormous stake in the health of the multilateral system. With its export orientation, it relies on a robust WTO to protect the rule of law in international trade, and its economic recovery depends on the financial health of nations around the globe—which in turn entails successful international institutions. Japan's national security may be anchored in its alliance with the United States, but with its pacifist public to consider, Tokyo also attaches huge importance to the UN as the legitimate authority for dealing with global threats. Japan badly needs effective global governance and cannot afford to sit back forever while others take the lead.

To enhance Japan's clout, there is no substitute for revitalizing the economy, overcoming the nation's political paralysis, electing strong leaders, and promoting better understanding of foreign cultures. These things take time, of course, and none is inevitable. If revitalizing the economy was easy, after all, Japan would have done it by now. That said, there are things Japan can do.

At the very least, policy makers should be much more mindful of the need to put the nation's best foot forward at international gatherings. For starters, when it comes time to appoint ministers with international portfolios, picking top-quality individuals should take priority over faction-balancing. Prime Minister Naoto Kan has shown that he is willing to break with the hoary tradition of handing out ministerial posts like consolation prizes to rival factions. Let us hope that this is one step on the path toward healthier domestic politics and a more self-confident international stance.

More important, Japanese leaders should pluck up their political courage and embrace policies that will strengthen their country's leadership credentials. In the WTO context, this approach would mean advancing offers to cut agricultural trade barriers drastically rather than continuing the age-old strategy of waiting until the last minute to make grudging concessions. In the UN context, it would mean allowing the dispatch of Self Defense Force troops on much more perilous peacekeeping missions than before. In the G-20, it would mean resisting the pleas from business executives to intervene in currency markets and instead taking measures that blaze the way toward rebalancing Asia's excessively export-dependent economies.

These ideas are easy for a foreigner to propose—and very tough for Japanese politicians to accept—but they are in Japan's long-term national interest. If Tokyo fails to move in this direction, Japan will have only itself to blame when it can't get no respect.

CHAPTER SIX: RETOOLING THE ECONOMIC ENGINE

© Illustration by Tatsuro Kiuchi

THE ROAD AHEAD FOR JAPAN'S CAR INDUSTRY

PAUL J. INGRASSIA

WHEN JAPAN'S CAR COMPANIES invaded the United States in the 1970s, the market was ripe for the plucking. As US consumers began turning to small cars after the 1973 oil crisis, Detroit responded with the Chevrolet Vega, the Ford Pinto, and the AMC Gremlin. The Vega's engine leaked oil; the Pinto's gas tank exploded on impact; and the Gremlin had a pug-ugly, chopped-off shape that led to the memorable joke: "What happened to the rest of your car?"

Little wonder that Japan had its way with Detroit for most of the next 35-plus years. Honda, Nissan, and Toyota became the symbols of Japan's postwar economic miracle and continued to thrive even after its bubble economy collapsed in the 1990s. But lately the Japanese auto industry has had its own troubles, and the question is whether this is a rough patch or a sign of long-term decline. In the United States, the reputation of Toyota, once the gold standard for quality, has been sullied thanks to massive recalls and allegations of safety defects. In China, Honda has become the poster child for labor unrest. Some of the smaller companies, notably Mitsubishi and Suzuki, have suffered significant setbacks. Suzuki's US sales, for example, plunged some 50 percent for the first nine months of 2010 (on top of a 54 percent decline in 2009). And the entire industry is worried—with good reason—about the Chinese and the South Koreans.

So are the good times over? To answer in classic Japanese style: Yes and no. The industry will struggle in the near future, and some of the weaker players might not survive as global companies. But most of Japan's automakers have substantial underlying strengths that will allow them to prosper in the long run.

Paul J. Ingrassia has written about automobiles and the auto industry for 25 years.

The problems

The biggest immediate issue is the strength of Japan's currency. Since June 2007, the yen has appreciated more than 30 percent against the US dollar, making Japanese exports more expensive. This trend is more problematic for some companies than others. Of Honda's US sales, only 9 percent are cars exported from Japan. But for Toyota, that number is about 40 percent. For every yen that the Japanese currency increases beyond 90 to the dollar, the company loses 30 billion yen, or about $355 million. In 2010 Suzuki went so far as to delay the launch of its updated subcompact, Swift, because it couldn't earn a profit at prevailing exchange rates.

At the same time, global competition is getting tougher. The world's fastest-growing major car company is South Korea's Hyundai, which has gained a reputation for high quality and is moving into luxury cars. Ford has staged a remarkable turnaround, and Chrysler and General Motors have new leases on life, thanks to their bankruptcies and bailouts by the US and Canadian governments. And Germany's Daimler has rebounded after shedding the albatross of pre-bankruptcy Chrysler.

Another problem is the state of Japan's domestic market. Auto sales plunged in most major markets in 2009, but it marked the fifth straight year for Japan. That streak reflects the country's severe structural issues—the developed world's highest national debt (as a proportion of GDP) and fastest-growing elderly population.

The government aims to average 2 percent growth for the next decade. It's a modest enough goal but one that Japan has achieved only five times since 1992, according to the International Monetary Fund (IMF). Little wonder, then, that Honda has delayed opening its newest Japanese plant until 2013, while Yachiyo Industries has canceled plans for a new factory to build mini-cars for Honda.

On top of everything else, Japan's car companies must contend with the fact that they simply cannot maintain the same rates of growth in some of their major markets. From 1978 to 2008, Honda's US sales, for example, rose fivefold, to 1.4 million vehicles. It cannot grow that fast again in the United States.

Can the Chinese market fill the gap? Rich opportunities exist there, of course, with auto sales growing 40 percent a year; in 2009, 13.6 million vehicles were sold, 10 million of them passenger cars. But J.D. Power, the car consultancy, expects Chinese companies to command 45 percent of their home market by 2017, up from just 18 percent in 2000. If that's true, it will limit the growth prospects for Japanese companies.

So that's the gloomy picture, painted in foreboding hues. There is a brighter side, however, and it would be foolhardy to dismiss the Japanese as Edsels-in-waiting.

The possibilities

For starters, Japan's automakers have dealt successfully with the strong yen before. It happened in the mid-1980s, after the Plaza Accord caused the Japanese currency to double against the dollar. The situation recurred in the mid-1990s, when the yen hit 85 to the dollar, about where it was for much of 2010.

Japan is, and is likely to remain, a major auto exporter.
© Robert Gilhooly Photo

The Japanese responded by slashing costs and by increasing production outside the country, a playbook that's now being pulled off the shelf. Next year, for example, Toyota will open a new factory in Mississippi that had been put on hold because of the financial crisis.

Another strong suit for Japan's car companies is their formidable technological prowess, both in manufacturing and product engineering. It's a trite but true saying: while US kids want to be lawyers or hedge fund managers, Japanese youngsters aspire to be engineers.

Thus Toyota was the first to bring a gas-electric hybrid to market and has made the Prius the world's best-selling hybrid. In 2012, Toyota will launch a "plug-in" Prius that will run almost entirely on electricity, with a tiny gas engine that will recharge the batteries if necessary instead of directly powering the vehicle at highway speeds, as the Prius's engine now does. The current Prius gets 50 miles a gallon, but the plug-in might get double that or more. (GM's Chevy Volt is also a plug-in hybrid.)

The Chinese and South Koreans certainly will mount bids for global leadership in automotive technology, but for now Japan's position remains enviable. The plug-in Prius will be one of six new hybrid or all-electric cars Toyota will launch in the next two years. The company's much-publicized and costly quality woes in the United States stemmed from overaggressive capacity expansion, not technology lapses.

Japan's engineering expertise is especially strong in small cars, critical models for the emerging automotive markets where the greatest growth prospects lie. This alignment bodes well for most Japanese companies, not just the "Big Three" of Honda, Nissan, and Toyota.

Maruti Suzuki, for instance, is the largest auto company in India, where it has introduced a new line of cars that run on compressed natural gas. The Japanese also dominate Southeast Asia, a region of 500 million people that often gets overlooked amid the focus on the BRIC nations.[1]

As for China, it's far from certain that domestic car companies will grow at the expense of the Japanese, despite the J.D. Power forecast. In fact, the market share of Chinese-made cars has remained stuck at about 30 percent for the past three years.

IT WOULD BE FOOLHARDY TO DISMISS THE JAPANESE AS EDSELS-IN-WAITING. China's car companies excel at low-cost production, but they still fall short on the quality and high-tech features that the country's increasingly demanding car buyers want. Although the Chinese have improved the quality of their products in other industries, cars are especially complex and demanding products. And with their home market expanding so quickly, Chinese automakers remain focused on boosting production as opposed to increasing sophistication.

The Chinese market offers insight into the broader challenge in the BRIC countries. The Japanese aren't market leaders in any of them with the exception of Suzuki Maruti in India, which has nearly as many sales there as its next three competitors (Tata, Hyundai, and Mahindra) combined.

Unlike Suzuki, which has been a small-car specialist for decades, Japan's Big Three tend to focus on cars with fatter profit margins and higher prices than many emerging-market customers can afford. In most of these markets, the Japanese also lack the production cost advantage that powered their growth in developed nations.

After a slow start, however, the Japanese are gaining strength in the BRIC countries. Brazil's overall car market—where Fiat, Volkswagen, and GM are the top three players—more than doubled from 2000 to 2009. But the sales of Nissan (in partnership with Renault) and Toyota more than tripled during that time, and Honda's surged more than sixfold.

In Russia, the weakest BRIC country for car sales, the market plunged 50 percent in 2009. But the Renault-Nissan alliance remains locked in a virtual three-way tie for second place in sales (with GM and Hyundai), after industry leader Autovaz.

Similarly, the US market presents the Japanese with some unusual new challenges—specifically, the new labor contract that allows Chrysler, Ford, and GM to hire workers at lower wages. This "two-tier" wage system, however, might not be as much of a competitive advantage for Detroit as advertised. The sluggish US economy means more autoworkers are delaying planned retirements, leaving less opportunity to hire lower-paid workers.

---

1 Brazil, Russia, India and China

In addition, Detroit's most important labor problem hasn't been wages but complex job classifications, featherbedding work rules, and the mind-set that underlies them. The UAW's national contract with the Detroit companies is as big as a small phone book, and each factory has its own local agreement as well. Even with the recovery from bankruptcy, little of that has changed. It's likely that being nonunionized will continue to be a competitive advantage for Japanese car factories in the United States.

The prediction

It's simplistic to consider Japan's automakers as a single bloc, because the disparities among them are striking. Honda, Nissan, and Toyota are strong global players and are likely to remain so, even though in today's global auto industry no company or group of companies can dominate in every market.

Mitsubishi Motors, however, wouldn't be alive today if it hadn't been rescued a few years back by the Mitsubishi Group. Both Mitsubishi and Suzuki should pull out of the US market, as Isuzu did nearly two years ago. With weak sales and bland images there, both would be better off focusing on other markets where they have stronger positions and better opportunities. Global auto production is expected to rise from 70 million vehicles in 2010 to 93.5 million vehicles in 2016, with most of the growth coming from China and other emerging markets.

The lessons of history are important. Back in 1994, when the yen was strong and Detroit was cashing in on America's SUV boom, predictions that Japan's car companies had peaked were common. "I don't think they'll regain the share of the US market they once had," a Jardine Fleming analyst said at the time. "It's a case of damage limitation."

Just a decade later, however, the Japanese actually surpassed Detroit in US market share. So it's worth remembering why that prediction, which came as the Japanese economy was sagging into a postbubble malaise, was so wrong.

What happened was that Japan's car companies reacted. They cut costs and moved quickly to correct their mistake in missing the US market's truck boom. They also launched new luxury brands, one of which, Toyota's Lexus, now vies with BMW and Mercedes-Benz for the top spot in US luxury sales. And around the world, the Japanese used their manufacturing efficiency to produce profits that they plowed back into product development. Nissan's remarkable revival a decade ago stemmed from a corporate and product overhaul that nobody predicted.

Many of the same trends are evident today. Toyota has stopped denying its quality problems and is moving to address them. Fuji, which makes Subaru cars, is a global leader in light four-wheel-drive vehicles. Mazda enjoys a reputation for sharp styling and performance.

The gloomy predictions of the '90s about the future of Japan's auto industry proved flat-out wrong. Today's doomsayers would be wise to remember.

FINDING THE PERFECT BLEND

HOWARD SCHULTZ

STARBUCKS OPENED ITS FIRST STORE in Japan in August 1996, in Tokyo's Ginza district, just around the corner from the Matsuya department store. It was a big step for us—our first attempt to operate outside North America—and one that many experts advised us not to take. In the United States and Canada, our brand had become a household word. But Japan already had an established coffee culture. In Tokyo, we found coffee shops on nearly every corner; one national competitor boasted hundreds of outlets.

Many of the retail and marketing specialists we consulted in preparing for our Japan debut seemed to think we were out of our minds. The Starbucks business model was all wrong for Japan, they told us. For starters, our "no smoking" policy would have to go. Never mind that the policy was one of our core operating principles (smoke gets absorbed by roasted beans, damaging the taste and the quality of the coffee). Japanese coffee shop customers, the experts insisted, were mainly middle-aged men, who wouldn't care about the ambience or even the quality of the coffee—and wouldn't set foot in a Starbucks if they couldn't smoke. The experts also told us no self-respecting Japanese would be seen carrying a beverage onto the street.

We listened politely to all this wisdom—and then pretty much ignored it. Instead, we stuck to our values and followed our instincts. I remember setting out with trepidation that morning for the opening of the Ginza store. The heat was unbearable. The ribbon cutting was scheduled for 7:30 AM; by 7:15 AM it was sweltering. I wondered if we'd get any customers at all. But as I approached the entrance, I did a double take. On the sidewalk in front of our green logo stretched a line of nearly 50 people. I was so surprised that for a moment I worried some misguided

Howard Schultz is chairman, president and CEO of Starbucks.

Queue for brew: Starbucks opening day in Ginza, August 1996.

© Starbucks Japan

staffer had hired ringers to stand in line as a marketing ploy. But these were not ringers. They were real people with real enthusiasm for Starbucks.

Our first customer was a young man in his 20s, who looked as if he'd camped out overnight. Weary but exhilarated, he ordered a tall latte in almost perfect English. Throughout the day customers came: men in dark business suits, women with elegant silk scarves, students with backpacks—all queuing patiently in the unforgiving summer heat. Some even ordered Frappuccino, a blended coffee drink we'd introduced only recently in the United States. I watched with satisfaction as customer after customer marched out the door, drinks in hand.

That day laid the cornerstone for Starbucks' global expansion. We now operate more than 17,000 outlets in 55 countries, roughly a third of the stores outside the United States. Japan remains our largest overseas market by sales (more than $1 billion a year, out of total revenues of $10.7 billion) and number of stores (more than 900). The country continues to play a crucial role in our worldwide strategy.

Our experiences in Japan have helped us to develop a host of globally successful products, for example, the Coffee Jelly Frappuccino, a beverage that has proved hugely popular, particularly in Asia. And because Japanese consumers are such avid drinkers of instant coffee—the market for retail instant coffee in Japan is some $3 billion, more than double the size of the US market—we see vast potential for products like Starbucks Via Coffee Essence, the soluble coffee line we introduced in Japan in 2010 and that now accounts for more than $100 million in sales in the United States. Green tea lattes were also inspired by Japan, then made their way to the US and other markets.

Of course we have faced our share of challenges. In 2002, just after we'd raised $149 million in a Japanese IPO, our expansion drive ran ahead of our ability to deliver to customers the type of experience they sought. Our Japan business slipped into the red and year-on-year same-store sales declined for several years. The shares of Starbucks Japan, a joint venture with Japanese retailer Sazaby League, fell more than 70 percent. We were forced to close some stores, cut our dividend, and reexamine our cost structure.

But even in the difficult years, we kept faith in the long-term promise of Japan. We reexamined our business model. We made an exhaustive analysis of what was working, and what wasn't. We sought to identify a few important things we could do differently.

Among the changes we introduced was Starbucks Discoveries, a ready-to-drink product developed exclusively for Japanese customers with our local partner, Suntory. Since it was first distributed through Japanese convenience stores in 2005, Starbucks Discoveries has proved an extraordinary success and paved the way for integration of our consumer packaged goods into the larger Starbucks brand. We also changed our menu to adapt to Japanese tastes, bringing in fresher food and trying out items like steamed buns. All of these efforts will help us as we continue to expand in Japan and in other markets in Asia.

> **YOU CAN'T GET OUT OF TROUBLE BY TRYING TO NAVIGATE WITH A DIFFERENT MAP. YOU HAVE TO BE AUTHENTIC; YOU HAVE TO BE TRUE.**

Throughout this period of examination and experimentation, we held fast to our core values: our love of coffee; our passion for ethically sourcing the world's finest coffee beans and roasting them with care; our respect for our employees (or partners, as we prefer to call them); our commitment to make a human connection with our customers; and our dedication to being engaged in our communities.

Crises—and opportunities

Perhaps because Japan is such a critical part of Starbucks' global operations, I'm often asked: What are Japan's prospects? What might Japan do to bolster growth?

I recognize, of course, that it's far more complicated to manage a country than a company. Still, I can't help thinking that perhaps in some small way, our experiences in coping with adversity might have relevance for Japan. At the very least, the lessons Starbucks learned in Japan in the early part of the decade helped us weather even bigger problems globally at that decade's end.

For most of our history, Starbucks has thrived. Year after year, we opened more stores and hired more people. Sales and profits soared. We became infatuated with expansion. Everything we did more or less worked, producing a level of hubris that caused us to overlook what was coming. Lacking much competition, we lost sight of the importance of pursuing transformational, market-changing innovations. Gradually, we grew complacent.

By 2007, the company was in trouble. In January 2008, when I returned as CEO after a seven-year hiatus, I discovered things were worse than I thought. We had to admit to ourselves that we had failed our partners and our customers. It was a very, very difficult time. There was tremendous pressure to change the strategy and business model of the company.

And then came the financial crisis, which brought seismic changes in consumer behavior. In our customers' efforts to economize, they visited our stores less frequently, particularly during peak hours and weekends. With gas hitting $4 to $5 a gallon in the United States, people's habits changed, and sometimes on weekends we didn't make enough sales to justify the labor. Spending at Starbucks became a kind of symbol for consumer excess. We'd never experienced anything like this downturn of business. And the blogs began to weigh in, too: "Starbucks' days are numbered," one said, and it was not alone.

As the downturn raged, we reassessed our model, just as we had in Japan after 2002. We resolved to do a few key things differently, such as embracing social media and integrating our retail and grocery channels in much the same fashion as we had done in Japan.

But for the most part, instead of charging off in a completely new direction, we focused on our traditional strengths: coffee, the coffee house experience, innovation, and our people. We reduced operating expenses even as we raised our quality standards. And this strategy worked. We finished our most recent financial year with record operating income ($1.4 billion), up more than 150 percent from the previous year.

Capturing the future through the past

The point is that, in both Japan and the United States, when the going got tough, Starbucks coped, in part by *not* changing the culture of the company. The lesson I learned is that you can't get out of trouble by trying to navigate with a different map. You have to be authentic; you have to be true.

There is relevance here for Japan. In coping with its challenges, I believe Japan should hold fast to its core values, but be willing to do some things differently. It seems clear to me, for example, that Japan could do a lot more to encourage entrepreneurialism and create new work opportunities for women. These strategies have certainly worked well for Starbucks. Our female partners have proved extraordinarily talented and dedicated; women account for one in every two store managers in our Japanese business.

The strength of Japan's traditional values is extraordinary. The key to the country's revitalization, I believe, is for it to rely on the attributes that were the foundation of its modern greatness: a strong work ethic; attention to quality, detail, and precision; and a passion for innovation. I have long marveled at the commitment the Japanese people bring to tasks large and small, and at the ethos of cooperation that prevails in the workplace.

As Japan charts its course, it must preserve these essential virtues in a manner that leaves room for entrepreneurialism and healthy risk-taking. Japan's success is not assured, but the foundations for that success are solid.

FROM THE MIDWEST TO THE FAR EAST

BOB MCDONALD

WELL INTO THE 1980S, Procter & Gamble (P&G) had a distinctly Midwestern American sensibility. We focused on the US market, which we understood thoroughly and where most of our business resided. While most of our consumers were female, almost all of our leadership was male.

Over the past 20 years, however, P&G has transformed itself into a truly global, more diverse—and, not coincidentally, more successful—company. In fiscal 2010, 58 percent of our $78.9 billion in net sales came from outside North America and 34 percent from developing markets. P&G has stayed true to its historic values, and we are still based in Cincinnati, Ohio. But in many important ways, we have reinvented ourselves.

Leading a country is, of course, a lot harder than leading a company. The comparisons are necessarily limited. And yet I think P&G's journey offers some useful signposts not only for Japanese companies, but also for Japan itself. The key lesson is that you can't predict the future; you have to learn and adapt and not be afraid of the unfamiliar.

P&G was late to globalization and slow to grasp the importance of diversity to global success, particularly in innovation. But the leadership of the company recognized that if we wanted to reach our growth goals, we had to go outside the United States, and we then very methodically set out in that direction. With the acquisition of Richardson-Vicks in 1985, we got a regional footprint in Asia for the first time. That footprint was still small when I came to the region in 1991. Now we're one of the leaders, if not *the* leader, in many Asian markets. In Japan, which we entered in 1973, we are increasing market share on 90 percent of our products.

Bob McDonald is chairman, president and CEO of Procter & Gamble.

Creating global leaders

In 1989, when I was asked to go to Canada for my first international assignment, my reaction was, "What did I do wrong?" At the time, an assignment outside the United States was not considered a good career move; staying with the US organization was the priority. Eventually, I went to Japan, Belgium, and the Philippines before returning to the United States some 14 years later. And far from a career killer, that international experience was one of the key factors contributing to my being considered for CEO in 2009.

AT P&G, IT IS A GIVEN THAT OVERSEAS EXPERIENCE IS GENERALLY A PRE-REQUISITE FOR THOSE WHO WANT TO RISE TO SENIOR LEADERSHIP.

Now at P&G, overseas experience is generally a prerequisite for those who want to rise to senior leadership roles. In some Japanese companies, the reality is just the opposite: there is a concern that once you leave the country, you become divorced from your home culture and away from the perceived heart of the business. There are many countries, Japan and the United States included, where individuals are simply unwilling to move, believing that their children will grow up outside the mainstream or that their own career prospects could suffer from venturing off the prescribed path. But I believe that the acid test of leadership is to be effective globally, not just in your own country. At P&G, we make a point of sending our rising Japanese stars overseas as early as practical. We want them to learn the trade in Japan and to see the company and its culture in global terms.

This kind of career development is a long-term process. Because we are planning two or three moves ahead, it requires a degree of deliberateness that most companies don't have. But it works for P&G because we do almost all our promotion from within, as do many Japanese companies.

Managing global brands

Some Japanese consumer-products companies have found it difficult to understand the US consumer because these companies are not immersed in the culture. In 1989, for example, one consumer-products company's first entry in the United States was an effervescent bath tablet that created a sauna effect. Any American—or anyone who had spent much time in the United States—would have said, "That's not going to work. Most Americans take showers."

P&G has made similar mistakes, of course. In 1973, we introduced All Temperature Cheer laundry detergent that could be used in hot, warm, or cold water. We failed to consider that Japanese people pumped their bath water into the washing machine; there was really only one temperature. That disaster played a role in the company's loss of something like $200 million in our first few years in Japan. But we learned from these mistakes. Our brands are now global, and so is our decision making.

Managing global brands is a crucial issue, given the increasing importance of emerging markets like Brazil, China, and India. It is not enough to simply repackage a product that's effective in Japan; sometimes you have to rethink it. In the Philippines, where I lived from 1991–95, P&G introduced Downy Single Rinse fabric conditioner. Instead of taking five loads of water to rinse the suds out of clothes, Downy Single Rinse required only one. Water can be expensive in developing countries, and the service erratic. Doing one rinse instead of five saved money and aggravation; the product paid for itself in one use. The ability to search out and identify deep consumer insights and then adapt technologies or services to meet those consumer needs is a critical component to global success.

You are going to develop that kind of nuanced consumer knowledge only if you are thinking of the world, not just a single country or an individual consumer group. That's why many Japanese companies have embraced the concept of searching for leadership from outside Japan, and encouraging more Japanese people to venture outside themselves.

Promoting innovation

Some experts now believe that Japan's declining population will pose a challenge to the nation, which is fighting to energize its economy. Some have suggested that immigration may be a solution to this issue and Japan can look to many other countries for examples of the good and the bad in immigration policies. There is no doubt that immigration brings in diversity and that diversity is a critical component of innovation.

In some respects, of course, Japan is incredibly innovative. Look at its car and electronics industries and how its consumers flock to new ideas. Insularity, however, will stifle innovation. P&G knows this from experience. Historically, we preferred to develop everything ourselves. In 2000, we established a goal that half of new innovations would come, at least in part, from outside the company. We're now well above 50 percent. In fact, it's hard to find any new innovations that don't include some participation from an outside firm or partner. We call this model "Connect & Develop," and it works.

We will partner with competitors, consumers, entrepreneurs, academic centers, and inventors; all can offer suggestions through our Web site. Right now, for example, we are working with a supplier whose scientists in Europe are good at Chemistry A, while our scientists in the United States excel at Chemistry B. For the purpose of a given project, we have co-located in a given lab in order to develop a chemistry that allows us to reduce the use of a key ingredient by 35 percent. We know that this supplier could well be working on other projects with our competitors; but we also know that this project is good for both the supplier and us.

You have to become comfortable working alongside outside individuals and companies where a common language or culture are not shared or fully understood. We have worked hard to develop Japanese partners on some of our technologies and, of course, we would welcome more such partnerships.

Balancing tradition and change

I'm encouraged by the Japanese young people P&G recruits. They are willing to take initiative, partly because those who join us have opted for a multinational career experience. But we also invest heavily in training and are willing to give these young recruits significant responsibilities early in their careers. We try to make sure younger employees have a voice in meetings and decisions. We want to avoid stifling their enthusiasm through deference to seniority and hierarchy.

When I was working in Japan, I tried to demonstrate that I wanted criticism; I wanted negative feedback; and I wanted this feedback to be routine. I didn't want to hear the truth in bars after working hours; I wanted to hear it in the office. In Japan, I became keenly aware of the difference between *tatemae*, or "façade" (the way people believe they are expected to act), and *honne*, their true feelings, (which may be hidden). I wanted my Japanese colleagues to bring their *honne* to the office.

This openness is part of the P&G culture, and it is an important part of our training. In turn, we need to be forthright, too. One of the things I tell young Japanese is that there are many learning opportunities outside Japan. If these workers want to help their country, and their own careers, they need to embrace these opportunities.

At P&G, our mission is to touch and improve the lives of consumers around the world. We have strong values, leadership, and ownership. We are passionate about winning trust and keeping it. Those things have not and will not change. But we are willing to change everything else. This combination of core values and flexibility has been the foundation of our global success.

Japan also has core values that it cannot and should not change. However, it is also important to have flexibility. Japan has demonstrated this ability over the centuries and reaped the rewards of success from these endeavors, the Meiji Restoration being a remarkable example of offering an open hand while keeping traditions very much alive.

In the 1990s, I attended many meetings in Japan at which all the leaders appeared to be white-haired men and the only woman in the room was serving tea. P&G once operated much the same way. But over the past two decades, P&G has successfully integrated many more non-Americans and women. Among our 13 group presidents, for example, four are women and more than half were born outside the United States.

Without our cultural transformation, in both our business and our people, P&G today would be a less prosperous, successful, innovative, and interesting company. If we had kept to our Midwestern roots, which had served us well since our founding in 1837, we might well have become globally irrelevant.

That is a risk Japan—and many other countries—cannot afford to ignore.

ADVICE FROM JAPAN'S MOST POPULAR CEO

KENSHI HIROKANE

IN A CORPORATE CULTURE where even small missteps can have devastating career consequences, Kosaku Shima is an improbable success. Soon after he joined Hatsushiba Electric, a giant consumer electronics manufacturer, he became romantically entangled with a subordinate, destroying his marriage. As he rose in seniority, he developed a reputation for speaking his mind and challenging superiors. Late in his career, he sided with the losing faction in a key battle for control of the company, resulting in his exile to a foreign subsidiary.

And yet, despite those indiscretions—or perhaps because of them—Shima became president and CEO in 2008. He promptly launched an aggressive program to transform Hatsushiba into a global conglomerate. Shima, now 63, is handsome, hardworking, and loyal in his personal dealings. Decisive in business and fluent in English, he is, by all accounts, Japan's most admired chief executive.

If only he were real. But Shima is the creation of Kenshi Hirokane, a former salaryman who left a secure job at Panasonic to become an author and illustrator of manga (comic-book novels). Shima first appeared in 1983 in a short story about office romance, "Lipstick on the Collar." Readers loved the realistic depiction of corporate life, and Hirokane was quickly invited to feature Shima as the main character of the manga series, Kacho Shima Kosaku (Section Chief Kosaku Shima). Shima has remained a Japanese manga icon ever since.

Over the years, Hirokane's storyline has followed Shima up the corporate ladder, from kacho to bucho (division chief) to jomu (managing director) to senmu (executive director). In 2008, when Shima was named shacho (president), Japanese newspapers reported

---

Kenshi Hirokane is a manga creator whose work includes Hello Hedgehog and Like Shooting Stars in the Twilight.

Man at work: Company President Kosaku Shima in Shanghai.
© Kenshi Hirokane / Kodansha (PRESIDENT SHIMA KOSAKU)

his promotion almost as if it were straight news. The Shima series has sold more than 30 million copies in book form, and spawned two films.

Hirokane's account of Shima's rise includes its share of fantasy, and perhaps more than its share of sexual intrigue. But the broad contours of the narrative also hew closely to the ups and downs of the Japanese economy. During the boom years of the 1980s, for example, Shima works too hard and neglects his family. His personal and professional experiences reflect the assumption shared by so many Japanese managers during those years that Japan would keep rising and the West would decline. As section chief, Shima is sent to Hollywood to oversee the acquisition of an American movie studio. He gets mugged in Los Angeles, his American-made rental car breaks down, and he supervises an effort to blunt US protectionism by hiring former US congressmen to lobby for Hatsushiba in Washington. But the stories are nuanced; many of Shima's senior colleagues at Hatsushiba are depicted as arrogant and insensitive to American concerns about lost jobs, while Shima himself seems conflicted.

After Japan's financial bubble imploded, Hirokane used the Shima saga to consider Japan's own shortcomings. In many episodes, he sends Shima into battle with entrenched senior executives who run their divisions like feudal fiefdoms, obsess over factional rivalries, and neglect their obligations to ordinary workers. A common theme is the heavy toll that corporate decline exacts on individual Japanese.

Young Shima

The final three months consist of hands-on sales training at an affiliated retailer. Known as an "apprenticeship," this training includes sales, delivery, handling complaints, and making repairs in the field.

R: "Good day, I'm from Trust Electric."
Graduates in science and the liberal arts, as well as those who came out of graduate school, all undergo the same training.
L: "Good day, young man! The washing machine is on the fritz. Can you take a look?"

Repairs are the most demanding, especially for liberal arts graduates. With home appliances such as washing machines and air conditioners, graduates are usually able to follow the wiring diagram, but AV equipment presents an insurmountable challenge.

© Kenshi Hirokane / Kodansha (YOUNG SHIMA KOSAKU)

By 2005, when Shima becomes managing director, Hatsushiba has been overtaken by rivals in China and South Korea, and lifetime employment has become an empty promise. Shima speaks bluntly about such failings, gets caught in the crossfire of a management power struggle, and is left to languish at an obscure affiliate. When he is

Section chief Shima

"It's impressive, isn't it? That's the biggest signboard on Hollywood Boulevard."

"Here's another."

R: "And another one."
L: "And here on Oldera Street, we've donated 50 beach umbrellas emblazoned with the HATSUSHIBA name."

rehabilitated and installed as president, Shima champions a bold merger with a weakened domestic rival and leads a drive to raise the company's profile in global markets.

Hirokane, who writes and illustrates each episode himself, is a stickler for detail. In researching the series, he has traveled extensively in the United States, Europe, and, more recently, China, India, and Vietnam. He works hard to weave current events into his plotlines and in some cases actually seems to anticipate the news. For non-Japanese speakers, Kodansha International's three-volume bilingual edition of the Shima series, featuring selected episodes in English and Japanese, is an engaging primer on modern Japanese corporate life.

Hirokane's penchant for realism notwithstanding, The Economist has argued that Shima, a risk taker who recognizes the importance of the global economy, could not exist outside a manga. "Such independent-minded individuals are anathema to corporate Japan," the magazine contended. "Mr. Shima is, in other words, the antithesis of a Japanese manager."

Hirokane disagrees. In a November 2010 interview with McKinsey's Asia Editor, Clay Chandler, he insists that Shima and his management methods are quintessentially Japanese. Below, Hirokane discusses what real Japanese managers might learn from their cartoon hero.

McKinsey: Why did you create a manga about the life of a middle manager?
Hirokane: For three years after graduating from university, I was a salaryman. Being a manga artist had been my dream from a very young age. But I didn't think there was any chance of that dream ever coming true, so I got a proper job instead. I was a "baby boom" kid, one of the generation born immediately after the war [in 1947]. When we entered the workforce, the economy was thriving, so getting a job with a big company was a lot easier than trying to become a manga artist. Looking back, I realize that those three years as a salaryman were an invaluable experience that taught me

about the realities of business life. Later, I drew on those experiences when I tried my luck at *manga*.

I started the *Kosaku Shima* series in 1983. By that time, I'd already had some success as an artist. I'd won the Best New Manga Artist prize in 1974, made my debut in the magazine *Big Comic,* and had launched a popular series called *Human Crossing ("Ningen Kosaten").* Shima began as a one-off piece about office romance. But the response from readers was so enthusiastic, I was able to turn it into a series.

McKinsey: *But the storylines for Shima range far beyond office romance.*

Hirokane: I decided that even though Shima's story was a *manga,* it should depict the business world in a realistic way. So the storyline is half entertainment and half real-life information. One of the things that makes Shima unique is that he ages in real time. He was 35 years old when the series launched. Each year in the real world he has aged another year in the story. Over the course of the series, he's gradually come up in the world.

McKinsey: *How has Shima's career been affected by the ups and downs of Japan's economy?*

Hirokane: I try to show the Japanese economy as it is the moment I am writing. Shima's "section-leader" period corresponds with the exuberance of the bubble economy. He spends a lot of time traveling overseas and is a kind of "super-salaryman." The series was

"Look! Even here in Beverly Hills, where there's no place for advertising, we've managed to imprint our name!"

R: "But . . . is that OK? Isn't there a backlash if you overdo it? At a time like this, when Japan-US relations are at a low point . . ."

L: "Shima, that's how government officials think. Private citizens don't think like that."

"People will buy if the products are good and the price is reasonable. You won't find many fools concerned about the US economy who are willing to pay more to buy made-in-the-US products. This country is based on free competition. Here, capitalism is far more entrenched than in Japan."

R: "OK..."

L: "Soon the yen will be valued at 100 to the dollar. Now, while the yen is high, we should work on exporting our image."

© Kenshi Hirokane / Kodansha (SECTION CHIEF SHIMA KOSAKU)

discontinued for a while [it was irregularly published between 1992 and 1998]. But after the bubble economy ruptured and Japan entered recession, we brought Shima back as department manager. At that juncture, Shima was seconded to a subsidiary,

President Shima

"Suddenly, almost before we realized, our name value has declined. It's payback for our reluctance to compete on the world stage."

"At present, overseas sales account for 49 percent of Hatsushiba revenues; at Korea's Somsang, that figure is 80 percent. We're no longer competing against our fellow Japanese manufacturers. Our rival is Somsang in Korea."

where he experienced business in a completely different sector.

McKinsey: *In the latest installment, Shima makes a strategic decision that seems to anticipate real events.*
Hirokane: In "President Kosaku Shima," he launches a new brand and negotiates a merger with another big electrical equipment manufacturer. This was a case of reality imitating *manga*. After I published the story, Matsushita Electric Industrial changed its name to "Panasonic" and Panasonic acquired Sanyo Electric as a subsidiary.

In writing the storyline for Shima, I've never tried to make prophecies about the future of Japanese companies. But I've been watching the Japanese economy for a long time and developed something of a sense for what is likely to happen in the near future.

McKinsey: *How do you come up with the material for your stories?*
Hirokane: I do a lot of research. In preparing for "President Kosaku Shima," I visited with a number of chief executives, many of whom run listed companies.

McKinsey: *Shima is charismatic, handsome, popular with women, fluent in English and willing to make bold business decisions. Is he meant as a role model?*
Hirokane: I don't think of Shima as a particularly charismatic CEO. He is more the consensus-building type. Most of the Japanese managers I have met are that way, too. In a sense, Shima epitomizes the classical Japanese manager. The Japanese tend to dislike absolute authority. When such figures emerge as leaders at major companies, they are often overthrown. I think one of the things that sets Japanese society apart is the ease with which top leaders change. Japan's prime minister represents the ruling party in the legislature, but he is immediately replaced if something goes wrong.

McKinsey: *Should Japanese CEOs adopt a bolder leadership style? Would that help Japanese companies compete more effectively against rivals from China or South Korea?*
Hirokane: US business magazines often write about how Japanese managers can't take risks. There may be a certain amount of truth to that. When you head a com-

"Within the next five years, we want to bring our overseas revenue share up to 60 percent. To do that, we need to build a world-class brand!"

"Think global!!"

© Kenshi Hirokane / Kodansha
(PRESIDENT SHIMA KOSAKU)
Translator, Julia Nolet

pany with 300,000 employees, it is difficult to make risky decisions. There are too many stakeholders: your employees, their families, your suppliers, customers, and subcontractors. The first-generation owner-manager who built the company may be able to take such risks, but responsibility weighs much more heavily on a "salaryman" president. Shima is definitely a salaryman president. His story is meant to depict the real world, not some fantasy.

But it's true that Japanese companies are paying the price for their failure to be more adventurous. In the 1980s and 1990s, when Japan's economy was booming, Japanese companies never really moved out into the world at large. By the time Japanese consumer electronics companies woke up, the global market was ruled by Korean manufacturers like Samsung and LG. The products offered by Japanese manufacturers fell victim to the "Galapagos Syndrome" and no longer conformed to world standards. This is now a very serious problem.

McKinsey: *In a speech broadcast to employees around the world, President Shima declares "Think Global!" the new corporate slogan and asks everyone to repeat it with him. Why did you choose that message?*
Hirokane: I chose it because I believe that if we fail to break out of our current situation, we face a bleak future—not just Japanese companies, but the country as a whole.

McKinsey: *Recent episodes have focused on Japan's complex relationship with China. How should China figure in Japan's effort to go global?*
Hirokane: We need to rethink the notion that China is virtually the only destination for international expansion. In years past, China's leaders have encouraged inflammatory anti-Japanese ideas in the nation's education system. The generation that received that education is now at the helm of Chinese society. I think it will be difficult to expect Chinese who grew up exposed to that kind of education to show much sympathy for Japanese products and services. Look what happened in the 2010 Asian Games in Guangzhou. During the opening ceremony, there was virtually no applause for the Japanese team. I think we need to diversify out of China by shifting production facilities currently located in China to elsewhere in the region, such as to Vietnam, Indonesia, Pakistan, or India.

McKinsey: *Why aren't more Japanese companies doing that?*
Hirokane: One of the biggest challenges for Japanese companies is allowing local subsidiaries to be managed by local staff. One of the biggest differences between Japanese and Western companies is that when they set up operations overseas the Japanese companies will usually station three or four Japanese as the top managers. Western multinationals are more willing to delegate to local managers.

McKinsey: *What's next for Kosaku Shima? Is it possible he'd be asked to take over as chairman of Keidanren [Japan's influential employers' federation]?*
Hirokane: I get asked that question by a lot of readers. Typically the president of a large manufacturer holds his position for six or seven years. Shima was appointed president at the age of 60. So naturally, in another three years or so, he will move on to the role of chairman. If the circumstances are right, he might be a good candidate to lead Keidanren, but that would give the storyline an undeniable whiff of politics. At this stage, I am still unsure whether that would work as a *manga*. The idea is still a little hazy in my mind. But it's something to think about.

THE SKY'S THE LIMIT

GERARD J. ARPEY

AT AMERICAN AIRLINES, we believe Japan is, and will continue to be, one of the world's most important aviation markets—and we're backing up our belief with action. This year alone, we are launching an industry-changing joint business with Japan Airlines (JAL) as well as new American service between New York's JFK and Tokyo's Haneda Airport.

While some pundits have expressed doubts about Japan's economic prospects, from our perspective, investing time, energy, and capital in Japan is an easy decision. Japan is the third-largest economy in the world. Passenger traffic between the United States and Japan dwarfs traffic between the United States and other Asian nations, and will continue to do so for years to come.

Our increased presence in this critical market has been a long time coming. It has been nearly a quarter century since our inaugural service began between Dallas/Fort Worth International Airport and Tokyo's Narita International Airport. In the years since, we have grown our Japan service in a number of ways. Today, we also serve Narita from New York, Chicago, and Los Angeles. But the fact is, because of the restrictive aviation agreement between our two countries, we were unable to grow as much as we would have liked. Happily, the United States and Japan signed an Open Skies agreement in October 2010, allowing airlines to determine which airports they want to serve and how many flights they want to operate on each route.

One of the most positive results of the liberalized aviation regime is the opening of Haneda Airport to international long-haul flights. The airport's new international terminal is beautiful, and much closer to central Tokyo than Narita is. Haneda is

Gerard J. Arpey is chairman and CEO of AMR Corp. and American Airlines.

also JAL's principal hub for domestic operations, and will ultimately allow travelers from New York or anywhere else to connect more easily to points within Japan.

Of course, from our perspective the most exciting Japan-related development in years is our landmark joint venture with JAL. Having competed vigorously with each other across the Pacific for many years, American and JAL have begun to collaborate on scheduling and pricing our services, and now share the revenues we generate together. (The United States and Japan granted antitrust immunity to our venture in 2010, allowing us to go forward with these changes; earlier, cooperation between our airlines was limited to operations such as code-sharing and frequent-flyer programs.) This venture will boost American's presence throughout Asia tremendously, given the size and quality of JAL's Asian network. This is a big deal for us because, for many years, the aviation agreement between the United States and Japan prevented us from competing aggressively across the Pacific with other US-based carriers. The result is that we're still not very big in the Japan–United States market compared with our competitors. Our hope and expectation is that the increased competition created by our joint venture will lead to more and better options for consumers, which will in turn spur greater travel and overall economic activity.

Haneda's international terminal brings the world closer to Tokyo.
© Yoshikazu Tsuno/AFP/Getty Images

The greater global connectivity we will create by effectively merging the networks of American and JAL will be enormously powerful. But one thing we have learned over the years is that truly effective alliances are about a lot more than dots on a map. The opportunity to share knowledge has both carriers excited. At the beginning of 2010, I committed to JAL's chairman, Dr. Kazuo Inamori, and its president, Masaru Onishi, that American would open its doors and share our management tools and proprietary models. In the last year, executives and hundreds of employees from both sides have exchanged ideas and information at our headquarters near Dallas, Texas. And, in the same spirit, JAL has been **THE US-JAPAN ROUTE IS THE LARGEST AVIATION MARKET BETWEEN NORTH AMERICA AND ASIA.** helping us to improve in such areas as providing authentic Japanese hospitality. In the near future, we're hoping to have true job exchanges, where JAL or American senior managers are assigned to work for the counterpart airline, something we already do with our partners across the Atlantic, British Airways and Iberia.

We are optimistic, not just about our partnership with JAL, but about Japan's future, both as an air travel destination in its own right, and as one of the world's premier international gateways. We see pent-up travel demand, from both Japanese and other overseas tourists. Japan is a wonderful cultural and historical destination, as I rediscovered myself on a recent visit to Kyoto, one of the most remarkable cities in the world.

Air travel in general, and connecting hubs in particular, are incredible drivers of economic activity. That said, it's important to remember that the demand for air travel is elastic: no matter where in the world you are, if governments tax air travel too heavily, impose unreasonable airport departure charges, or limit competition for airport handling services, those costs get passed on to the consumer. Those added costs can discourage many people, especially price-sensitive leisure travelers, from taking to the skies.

Just as we and our Japanese partner must remain cost-competitive to survive in the airline industry, Japan, to sustain its rightful place as a premier global gateway, will need to ensure its cost competitiveness vis-a-vis other countries on these fronts. The country has a tough challenge, but the incentive to meet it is strong and clear.

Given our burgeoning partnership with JAL, our new service to Haneda Airport, the size of the Japanese economy, and the nation's geography as a connecting point between countries, American Airlines is bullish on Japan. We are happy to be increasing our presence there, and we look forward to playing a bigger role in the years to come.

SEE THE BIG PICTURE, MIND THE DETAILS

MASAHIRO SAKANE

IN THE MANUFACTURING SECTOR, we have entered an age of all-out, global competition. Komatsu is a global company, with a worldwide distribution network and major production centers in 11 countries. I lived eight years in the United States. I was appointed president and began to oversee management of the worldwide group in 2001. My experiences have helped me identify some of the challenges facing Japanese companies as they strive to become more global, and develop some ideas about how those problems can be solved.

Every country has its strengths and weaknesses. The key to prevailing in global competition is to be able to integrate the different strengths of each country. For example, it is difficult to find talented people in the manufacturing unit of Komatsu America. Top talent in the United States generally prefers jobs in marketing or finance, and those people who work in manufacturing tend to be unmotivated. By contrast, the Japanese understand the importance of manufacturing, and many see it as a desirable destination. Our solution has been to let Americans serve as CEOs and plant managers, but capitalize on our country's technology strengths by sending Japanese workers in as assistants and production engineers. Thus, one task for managers is to understand the strengths and weaknesses of different countries and different people, and use those strengths to achieve the highest possible productivity.

For us, the important thing is that everyone who works in the Komatsu Group shares the same sense of values. To that end, we have created a book called *The Komatsu Way*; we give it to all of our employees. The book has two primary sections, one on top management and one on *monozukuri* (manufacturing). The first section stresses the importance of an active board, proper communication, adherence to

Masahiro Sakane is chairman of Komatsu.

rules, confronting risk immediately, and training successors.

To ensure proper communications, the president of Komatsu holds a meeting for all head office staff twice a year, on the day after we close our books for the financial half year. Typically, these meetings run for about 90 minutes. The president describes the status of the company, and outlines challenges and targets for the next term. He then takes questions from employees. The sessions are videotaped and translated into English for distribution to group companies around the world over our intranet.

Moving earth in many markets.
© Dimas Ardian/Bloomberg via Getty Images

The communication effort doesn't stop there. The president also talks to Komatsu suppliers and distributors around the world. The CEOs of Komatsu China and Komatsu America also hold the same kind of meeting. The tenor of these sessions is not "do this, do that": rather, our goal is to communicate clearly to everyone and create a sense of joint ownership. I am confident this practice translates directly into many of Komatsu's core strengths.

Another of our strengths is the fact that we have local people heading up seven of our 11 major production centers worldwide. It is perhaps a truism that you can only maximize the strengths of local countries and people when management itself is localized. But the fact is that, while Japanese companies are good at creating local subsidiaries, they often fail to train local people to run them. Even if these companies headhunt a local manager, the person often performs poorly.

Komatsu first moved into the United States in 1970, and until 1988 the top managers of the local subsidiary were Japanese. It was only when we created a joint venture with Dresser Industries, a Texas company, that we finally appointed an American manager. Five years later, that company became a wholly owned subsidiary, and it has been managed by local people ever since. Likewise, the general manager of Komatsu China is Chinese. He has worked at Komatsu for 27 years. Training top managers requires either a lot of time, a merger with a local company (i.e., purchasing time with money), or both of those things.

We approach recruiting local staff by picking a local company as a benchmark. If you offer potential managers compensation on a par with your benchmark, you will be able to recruit talented people. For several years the top manager at Komatsu America was paid more than I was. The top manager at Komatsu China also is compensated very highly for China. Our principle is not to compare compensation overseas against what is paid by Komatsu in Japan. Rather, our objective is to recruit talented local people.

People who would lead global companies must do at least four things: understand the changes that are taking place in the world; understand the strengths and weaknesses of their own organizations; think about the value of their company; and train people able to provide solutions. It is particularly important to reexamine the corporate value as we attempt to rebuild and adapt to the global economy since the "Lehman Shock."

We define corporate value as the "total sum of trust given to us by society and all stakeholders." That includes the people who create corporate value at Komatsu (employees, suppliers, and distributors) as well as people who measure Komatsu's ability to realize its corporate value (shareholders, financial institu-

IN SEVEN OF THE 11 COUNTRIES WHERE KOMATSU HAS COMPREHENSIVE OPERATIONS, INCLUDING GERMANY, CHINA, AND THE US, THE TOP MANAGEMENT IS LOCAL.

tions, the media, and society at large). It also includes the people who both create *and* measure corporate value. This is the most important group of all: our customers.

We rank our customers on a scale of 1 to 7, with those ranked 7 being our most loyal customers. Level 7 customers trust us implicitly. Building such close relationships of trust with our customers is vital to increasing our corporate value.

Global leaders must understand how the world is changing. One cannot rely just on reports from subordinates. As a manager, one must get out, walk around, and see things with one's own eyes. We have a phrase in Japanese that roughly translates as "see the big picture, but mind the details."

As I look around the world, I see increasing urbanization in emerging economies with large populations, which is accelerating the pace at which people become economically affluent. This urbanization gives rise to four challenges the world will need to address: resources and energy, food, water, and the global environment. In light of the needs of the growing population of Africa, I would add "health care" as a fifth challenge.

At Komatsu, our business is directly related to resources and energy. While we have no direct relationship with food and water, we can make contributions to the field of agriculture. In the area of global environment, I currently serve as the chair of the environment and safety committee at the Nippon Keidanren. Komatsu has long considered this issue a top-priority issue, and three years ago became the first company in the construction equipment industry to market a hybrid hydraulic excavator, which we now sell in Japan and China.

At the same time, microperspectives are also important to the understanding of change. For example, the construction industry in China rejects machinery unless it offers both high quality and high performance. Construction deadlines are extremely strict in China, and delays incur far stiffer penalties than they would in Japan. The people on the ground are not satisfied with equipment unless the manufacturer is willing to come immediately and repair it should it break down.

To deal with this requirement, we have installed GPS equipment on approximately 70,000 of the machines we have sold in China. Their sensors transmit radio signals monitored in Shanghai, so we are able to grasp what is happening with all of our equipment. The system knows which engines are running, which have proper hydraulic pressure, which have the right fuel, and even which of our dealers have inventory piling up. Our top manager in China understands our "quality-oriented" philosophy. And that is why ours are the products of choice in China.

Naturally the development of human resources is a key point for any company. In 1970, Komatsu created a program allowing talented young employees to study abroad. Every year between five and ten of our people are enrolled in MBA courses at top universities around the world. We also have our own internal business school. This program provides training to selected employees between the department head and division general manager ranks. The head office controls all of their assignments. If participants in the program have not had an overseas posting, we work actively to place them in one. Komatsu currently has 32 board members and officers, of whom 25 either have been posted abroad or have studied abroad. Our young employees are enthusiastic about positions overseas, because a foreign posting is seen as an advantageous career path.

One thing that distinguishes Komatsu from other Japanese companies is that many of the people in our Human Resources division have also lived overseas. The first board member sent to Komatsu China to serve as an adviser to the CEO was the director with responsibility for human resources for Komatsu worldwide. He focused on human resources and labor relations at our local subsidiary. We have a plant in the town of Jining in Shandong Province, and much of his time was devoted to making an accurate determination of proper wage levels for the workers there, checking the quality of the food served in the employee cafeteria, and minimizing the gap in wages between our employees and those of our suppliers. I consider it essential for HR people to have international experience.

Another important aspect of human resources development is motivating midlevel managers. Before he became CEO of Nissan, Carlos Ghosn came to Japan as an executive with Michelin Tires. He toured Komatsu and later wrote about how our young employees were free to voice their opinions and ideas, and how typically Japanese he felt that to be. Interestingly, when Mr. Ghosn moved to Nissan, he began advocating top-down management. I attended one of his speeches and told him that, while he was probably right about Japan lacking top-down power, I also felt that if you overemphasized top-down power, you risked creating a class of passive midlevel managers who just sit around waiting for orders. I reminded him that when he toured Komatsu, the young people he had praised were midlevel employees.

I think the midlevel is the source of Japanese companies' strength, and holds the key to our future. If the midlevel is to have some power, top management must not go too far in its instructions. The job of senior executives is to identify the broad challenges. The job of midlevel employees is to come up with products and services that address those challenges. In manufacturing, a company in which the midlevel does not function properly will never be strong.

At Komatsu, we seek a proactive, transparent culture with strict adherence to business rules. When I first became president I said to our employees, "There will always be mistakes and improprieties. It is human to make mistakes, and society's standards are always changing, so improprieties will never entirely disappear." We punish people who conceal mistakes and improprieties far more heavily than people who commit them.

That is why we require Komatsu leaders around the world to give us the bad news first. During the first week of each month, all operational managers are required to provide the president with a flash report of results for the previous month. The space for the bad news is right at the top. They must also fill in the date on which the news occurred. Those who fail to report bad news immediately risk severe consequences. I believe we are one of the rare companies to have this system, but I am confident this standard will eventually be adopted around the world. With this rule as a shared value, I believe Japanese companies can achieve astounding growth in the world at large.

JAPAN, THE ASIAN PIONEER

PETER LÖSCHER

JAPAN OCCUPIES A UNIQUE and central place in world culture and the global economy. Japanese concepts have transformed art and music, fashion, and food. Japanese practices and technological achievements have redefined the way we live, work, and do business.

Most of us, in light of these profound influences, have clear mental pictures of Japan. We all know the automobiles and consumer electronics that Japan exports. When we think of the country itself, the images that most often come to mind are the dynamic and futuristic urban scenes of Tokyo-Yokohama, the awesome splendor of Mount Fuji, and the tranquil beauty of Japanese gardens and pagodas. We know Japan—or at least we think we do.

One of the challenges in business is to reexamine situations we think we already know, and to anticipate what will happen next. Of course this challenge is not limited to business. Politicians, city planners, even athletes grapple with the same question: What's going to happen next? Good information is essential, but there is also a certain degree of instinctive decision making involved. The Argentinean soccer star Lionel Messi put it best. He once said that the secret to his success was that he didn't run to the ball, but to where the ball was going to be.

For me, this essay is a chance to look at Japan—a country with a remarkable past and breathtaking record of achievement—and try to anticipate where the ball is going. My family and I lived in Japan for three years when I headed the Japanese operations of a global pharmaceutical company. Our memories of that time are strong. I try hard to maintain my ties to Japan. Japan was one of the first overseas markets I visited when I became chief executive officer of Siemens, the world's

Peter Löscher is president and CEO of Siemens AG.

biggest sustainable infrastructure company, not only because I find it a fascinating country but also because I believe its success in the years ahead can point the way for many other economies in the world.

Partly because of its geographic status as a resource-poor island nation, Japan has developed differently from many other nations. Of necessity, it has always been a pioneer: lacking in oil or other natural resources, Japan became a world leader in energy efficiency. With a large population but a limited supply of habitable land, Japan devised innovative approaches to urban design and transportation. Japan's commitment to science made it a world leader in technology, a position it has held for more than half a century. All these factors reflect a willingness to think creatively, to develop unique solutions based on a realistic assessment of the situation.

I BELIEVE JAPAN WILL EMERGE AS A LEADER IN FIELDS LIKE RENEWABLE ENERGY AND ENVIRONMENTAL PROTECTION.

As we look to the future, Japan—and the world—must adapt to three megatrends: urbanization, demographic change, and climate change. The Japanese are further along in thinking about these issues than the people of many other societies. On urbanization, the Tokyo metropolitan area, with a population exceeding 35 million, is the largest megacity in the world. Its development can serve as a model for fast-growing cities in emerging markets. On demographic change, Japan has a rapidly aging population that requires medical care and comfortable surroundings to live in. Both Japanese industry and academia have been working on ways to address this issue. On climate change, the Japanese recognized and embraced the concept of sustainability long before it became fashionable.

In the decades ahead, Japan's skill at managing resources and harnessing energy will become increasingly valuable. I believe Japan will emerge as a leader in fields like renewable energy and environmental protection. Many Japanese companies are already working on technologies for cleaner and more efficient power generation and transmission, better lighting, and more efficient use of electricity, especially in buildings. These technologies are good not only for the planet, but also for business, as the experience with our environmental portfolio shows. This initiative generates €28 billion in revenue—roughly a third of Siemens' total revenues. Within the next three years, we expect this figure to climb to €40 billion.

Other areas where Siemens sees tremendous growth opportunities for Japan are improved energy storage technologies to promote mobility and smart grids, and advanced medical diagnostics. Japan continues to excel in research and development in robotics, material science, LED technology, and photovoltaics. Siemens is active in most of the fields mentioned and we have been doing business in Japan for more than 120 years. The opportunities for partnership and collaboration are vast, and I am hopeful that by working together with our Japanese partners, we can contribute to further progress on these fronts.

Countries with a history of adapting quickly—moving to new manufacturing processes or business models, and aggressively pursuing new markets—will thrive in today's more competitive, globalized economy. But the converse is also true: countries and companies that cling to yesterday's practices will find the coming years very difficult. For example, Siemens was for many years a world leader in telecommunications. Our mobile phones were among the most advanced in the world. But in some ways we had become too specialized, catering to niche markets. Over time, this specialization proved more harmful than helpful. Japan has experienced a similar phenomenon.

The key to success in the decades ahead is to look not just at the quality and sophistication of one's products but also at the breadth and diversity of one's markets. Prospering in those markets, especially in the fast-growing emerging countries, will require people with a broad knowledge of other languages, who have studied abroad, and who are open to new ideas. At Siemens we work hard to encourage our employees to work abroad. Countries can, and should, encourage such activities as well. Only then will we be on the side of the innovators and pioneers.

I have always admired Japan's pioneering spirit and history of overcoming obstacles. I have great respect for the Japanese government's New Growth Strategy, which sets out clear policies and targets. I am impressed by the confidence and dexterity of Japan's new generation of business leaders. These factors all point in one direction: a new era of stability, prosperity, sustainability, and success, with Japan as the Asian pioneer.

REMEDIES FOR JAPANESE HEALTH CARE

LUDWIG KANZLER AND AKIRA SUGAHARA

ON THE SURFACE, the Japanese health care system seems robust. The country's National Health Insurance (NHI) provides for universal access. Japan's citizens are historically among the world's healthiest, living longer than people anywhere else. Infant mortality rates are low, and Japan scores well on public-health metrics while consistently spending less on health care than most other developed countries do.

Yet appearances can deceive. Our research indicates that Japan's health care system, like those elsewhere, has come under severe stress and that its sustainability is in question. The conspicuous lack of a way to allocate medical resources makes it increasingly hard for patients to get the care they need, when and where they need it. The quality of care varies markedly, and many cost control measures have actually damaged the system's economics.

Meanwhile, demand for care keeps rising. For a long time, it was dampened by the good health of Japan's population—partly a result of factors outside the system's control, such as the traditionally healthy diet. But rates of obesity and diabetes are increasing as people eat more Western food, and the system is further strained by a rapidly aging population: already, 23 percent of Japan's citizens are 65 or older, and by 2050 almost 40 percent may be. Advances in treatment are increasing the cost of care, and funding mechanisms cannot cope.

Japan must act now to ensure the sustainability of its health care system. It must close the funding gap before it becomes irreconcilable, increase control over the supply of and demand for services, and change incentives to promote high-quality, cost-effective treatment.

Ludwig Kanzler is a partner and Akira Sugahara is a senior partner in McKinsey's Tokyo office.

Exhibit
Four factors influence the projected increase in Japan's health care spending, trillion yen

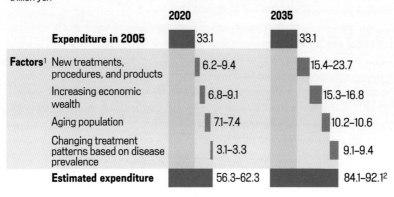

		2020	2035
Expenditure in 2005		33.1	33.1
Factors[1]	New treatments, procedures, and products	6.2–9.4	15.4–23.7
	Increasing economic wealth	6.8–9.1	15.3–16.8
	Aging population	7.1–7.4	10.2–10.6
	Changing treatment patterns based on disease prevalence	3.1–3.3	9.1–9.4
Estimated expenditure		56.3–62.3	84.1–92.1[2]

[1] Estimates for each factor are weighted for combined effect of all 4 factors proportionate to the size of that factor.
[2] Figures do not sum to totals, because of rounding.
Source: McKinsey & Company analysis

Japan's challenges

Several unique features of this health care system, which provides universal coverage through more than 4,000 public and private payers, underlie the issues facing Japan. All residents must have health insurance, and it covers a wide array of services, including many most other health systems don't.

Access to treatment is virtually uncontrolled. Patients may consult any provider—primary care or specialist—at any time, without proof of medical necessity and with full insurance coverage. Similarly, Japan places few controls over the supply of care. Physicians may practice wherever they choose, in any medical area, and are reimbursed on a fee-for-service basis. There is also no central control over the mostly privately owned hospitals. All these are important reasons for Japan's difficulty in funding its system, balancing supply and demand, and providing quality care.

Funding the system

Japan's health care system is becoming more expensive. In 2009, the NHI cost 35.3 trillion yen ($377.1 billion at the 2009 average exchange rate), or 7.4 percent of GDP.[1] By 2020, our research indicates, that could rise to 62.3 trillion yen, almost 10 percent of GDP, and by 2035 it could reach 93.6 trillion yen, 13.5 percent of GDP. Admittedly, the current outlay—low by international standards—is projected to grow only to levels the United States and some European countries have already

---

1 The 7.4 percent figure includes only medical care provided through Japan's health system. The country's total spending on medical care claimed 9 percent of GDP in 2009.

reached. Yet funding is a challenge, for Japan has by far the OECD's[2] highest debt burden, a rapidly aging population, and a stagnating economy.

Why costs are rising. Four factors explain the projected rise (exhibit). By 2035, new treatments, procedures, and products will account for about 39 percent of it; the country's growing wealth, which encourages people to seek more care, for 28 percent; and the aging population for 17 percent. The remaining 16 percent will result from shifting treatment patterns required by changes in the prevalence of different diseases.

Japan can do little to influence these factors—for example, the aging population. Delays in the introduction of technologies would be medically unwise and politically unpopular. Yet unless financing mechanisms change, the system will generate no more than 43.1 trillion yen in revenue by 2020 and 49.4 trillion yen by 2035, leaving a funding gap of 19.2 trillion and 44.2 trillion yen, respectively.

Further compounding matters is Japan's lack of central control over the allocation of medical resources. No central authority has jurisdiction over hospital openings, expansions, and closings or oversees the purchase of expensive medical equipment.

No easy answers. Japan must increase the system's funding, cost efficiency, or both. Traditionally, it has relied on insurance premiums, copayments, and government subsidies to finance health care and has controlled spending by repeatedly cutting fees to physicians and hospitals and prices paid for drugs and equipment. That has helped Japan hold growth in health care spending to less than 2 percent annually, far below that of its Western peers. If, say, Japan increased government subsidies by raising the consumption tax, the rate would have to reach 13 percent by 2035. But the country went into a deep recession in 1997, when the tax went up to the current 5 percent, from 3 percent. Similarly, a large spike in insurance premiums would increase Japan's labor costs and damage its competitive position. Soaring copayment rates would undermine the very concept of health insurance—the rate is already 30 percent.

Mismatched supply and demand

Japan combines an excess of some health resources with massive overutilization—and shortages—of others. On average, the Japanese see physicians almost 14 times a year, three times the number of visits in other developed countries. What's more, the average length of a hospital stay is two to three times as long in Japan as in other developed countries. Demographics, the severity of illnesses, or other medical factors can't explain these differences.

In fact, the country's health system inadvertently promotes overutilization. There is evidence that physicians and hospitals compensate for reduced reimbursement rates by providing more services, since the system doesn't limit the supply of care comprehensively. Japan's physicians can bill separately for each service—for example, examining a patient, writing a prescription, and filling it. The system also rewards hospitals for serving larger numbers of patients and for prolonged lengths of stay, since these costs are not strictly controlled.

2 Organisation for Economic Co-Operation and Development.

Quality of care

Given the system's lack of controls over physicians and hospitals, it isn't surprising that the quality of care varies markedly. Among patients with Japan's most common form of cancer—of the stomach—the five-year survival rate is 21 percent lower in Kure than in Tokyo, for example. Four factors help explain this variability.

First, Japan's hospital network is fragmented. Research has repeatedly shown that outcomes are better when the centers and physicians responsible for procedures undertake large numbers of them. Because Japan has so many hospitals, few can achieve the necessary scale.

JAPAN'S HEALTHCARE SYSTEM IS STRONG AND EFFECTIVE, BUT AN AGING POPULATION WILL PUT ENORMOUS PRESSURE ON IT.

Second, Japan's accreditation standards are weak. Doctors receive their medical licenses for life, with no requirement for renewal or recertification. No central agency oversees the quality of training or the criteria for board certification in specialties.

Third, the system lacks incentives to improve the quality of care. Japan has few arrangements for evaluating the performance of hospitals; for example, it doesn't systematically collect treatment or outcome data and therefore has no means of implementing mechanisms, such as pay for performance, promoting best-practice care.

Finally, the quality of care suffers from delays in the introduction of new treatments. Specialists are too overworked to participate in clinical trials or otherwise investigate new therapies. And because the country has so few controls over hospitals, it has no mechanism requiring them to adopt improvements in care.

Specific reforms to consider

To ensure the system's sustainability, Japan should carry out reforms to reduce the supply of and demand for health care; to encourage high-quality, cost-effective care; and to increase funding. Many reforms would address multiple challenges. Japan could begin to address concerns about the quality of and access to care, for example, by more closely regulating how physicians train and where and in which areas of medicine they practice. In addition, it could implement stricter accreditation requirements for specialists and primary-care physicians (family practice would become a specialty) and require recertification or continuing medical education.

Japan could also realign the system's incentives to encourage high-quality, cost-effective care rather than the overdelivery of services. One possibility would be moving away from uncontrolled fees for services in primary care, perhaps by using capitation (in which doctors are paid a fixed fee per patient) for some things. It could also implement a strict diagnosis-related system for hospital reimbursement.

Yet payments to hospitals may have to be raised to make practicing in them more attractive. Financial incentives could also encourage hospitals, especially subscale ones, to merge or specialize, or to abandon acute care and instead become long-term, rehabilitative-, or palliative-care providers. Japan could combine financial incentives and volume targets to encourage greater hospital specialization, so that low-volume centers wouldn't perform high-risk procedures. Similarly, the country could use incentives and controls to lower demand for health services—for example, by eliminating coverage for diagnostics and treatments that are medically unnecessary. Of course, Japan should ensure that new controls generate value and don't inadvertently undercut best practices. Rather than using across-the-board cuts to reduce pharmaceutical spending, for example, the use of generics could be further encouraged, freeing up funds for innovative treatments. And Japan could replace across-the-board fee cuts for physicians with pay for performance, rewarding high-quality care and penalizing poor or inefficient care.

Finally, Japan must find novel ways to generate additional health care financing. It could follow the example of Germany and Switzerland by allowing patients to pay extra for access to certain services—for instance, consultations with top specialists, coverage for diagnostics, and treatments not deemed strictly necessary. Combined with greater cost efficiency and increased insurance premiums, copayments, and subsidies, this approach could help ensure the system's sustainability.

Getting reform going

Health system reform is daunting, and many countries have difficulty determining where to begin. In our work with other health systems, we identified seven steps that Japan should consider pursuing.

First, the country could have its leading physicians undertake a comprehensive, well-funded review of the health system. Such a review would help Japan achieve consensus on the system's most pressing problems and improvements and encourage people—especially other physicians—to accept the necessity of change. More important, the review could set clear targets for the health system.

Second, Japan could establish independent regulators for its health system. One agency could oversee hospitals and require them to report regularly on treatments and outcomes. Another could oversee physician-training programs and raise accreditation standards. Like central banks, these agencies could act as politically independent forcing devices. France and the United States provide good examples of how independent regulators can ensure the quality of physician training and hospital care.

Third, Japan could change its payers' role by giving them more power. They could be authorized to adjust reimbursement formulas to encourage cost-effectiveness and care quality, to demand outcome data from providers, and to reject bills for any service that is medically unnecessary or doesn't provide enough value for money. As an incentive to push useful reforms, payers could be allowed to benefit financially from successful ones. In addition, they could be permitted to compete with one another—competition promotes cost-effectiveness.

Fourth, Japan could identify and implement short-term operational improvements that produce immediate, demonstrable benefits. Such quick wins would build support for the overall reform effort, especially for some longer-term or politically contentious changes. The country already has examples it could implement more broadly: several regions markedly reduced ER utilization through relatively simple measures such as a telephone consultation service combined with a public education campaign.

Fifth, to test potential reforms, Japan could conduct a series of well-selected pilots, which would be organized strategically and undertaken regionally to ensure that ideas are tested in a range of settings and help build support. A central organization would oversee and monitor the pilots and then roll out successful ones across the country.

Sixth, as the health system realigns its incentives, it could systematically link them to results, not activities. If the country wanted to reward primary-care physicians who improved their patients' cardiovascular health, for example, blood pressure and cholesterol-level reductions could be the metric, not the number of office visits or prescriptions written.

Finally, if Japan reforms its health system, it should communicate regularly with all stakeholders, including the public, so that they fully understand why change is necessary and what it will include. Even the best reform program fails without sufficient buy-in.

• • •

Japan confronts a familiar and unpleasant malady: difficulty in providing its citizens with affordable, high-quality health care. Yet by making the right choices, it can control the health system's costs without compromising access or quality.

A LOW-COST DRUG PRESCRIPTION

SHLOMO YANAI

JAPAN'S HIGH-QUALITY HEALTH CARE SYSTEM is under pressure, stressed by an aging population straining its resources and calling into question its sustainability. As a result, all stakeholders in the system must look for ways to control costs.

One way to do that is aggressively to pursue the shift from brand-name drugs to generic ones. Of course, as chief executive officer of Teva Pharmaceutical Industries, the world's biggest producer of generic drugs, I (and our company) have a vested interest in this change. But so do Japanese consumers and taxpayers. The cost savings accruing to more use of generics in Japan are potentially enormous: if the market share of generics reached 50 percent, the government health system would save huge amounts every year.

Until recently, Japan put up a "Keep Out" sign to generic drug producers, in part through strict rules of registration. As a result, in 2007, generics accounted for less than 20 percent of the pharmaceutical market in Japan, compared with 70 percent in the United States and 65 percent in the United Kingdom. Discouraging generics forced health providers and consumers to pay higher prices; it also hurt Japanese drug producers, who lacked the incentives to compete in an industry in which they might have thrived.

In 2008, though, the environment began to change. Acutely aware of the need to control healthcare costs and to foster innovation, the government set an ambitious target of 30 percent penetration by 2013. Teva Pharmaceutical Industries saw this target as a window of opportunity. In late 2008, we made our first deal in Japan—a 50-50 strategic partnership with the pharmaceutical unit of the Kowa Company— and now we see the country as a large and growing market.

Shlomo Yanai is president and CEO of Teva Pharmaceutical Industries.

The 30 percent target is ambitious, but the government has pursued it methodically with a series of well-crafted regulatory and administrative changes. Japanese health officials, working in partnership with major hospitals, have sought to raise awareness among opinion leaders and patients of the advantages of generic drugs. They have also introduced significant financial incentives to pharmacies in order to reach the 30 percent target, changed administrative procedures making it easier for physicians to prescribe generic drugs, and sought to separate the tasks of prescribing and dispensing drugs to minimize incentives to recommend more costly medications.

Since 2008, the market share of generics has risen to 20 percent, from 17 percent, so the effort appears to be working. Will Japan hit the 30 percent target? That is not clear. But I believe that there is no going back. The unprecedented demographic situation in Japan, and the number of people who will need medications for chronic conditions, require society to embrace the idea of high-quality generic pharmaceuticals. There is another dimension, too. Given the excellence of Japanese manufacturing, it is not difficult to imagine Japan's pharmaceutical companies becoming global leaders in generics.

That said, Japan has a long way to go. In particular, generics still have a poor image in the country, whose consumers are famously brand-oriented. For the generics strategy to succeed, the government needs to do more. For example, it should eliminate the right of physicians to block the use of generics and start a promotional campaign to increase public acceptance.

I am more optimistic than many others about Japan's future. I have seen how Japan can make a decision, set a goal and take actions to reach it. I believe this kind of thoughtful deliberation can help the country meet its many challenges. I also believe Japan has accepted that its future lies in economic openness and less heavy-handed management. Generic drugs cannot cure Japan's economic woes, but the government's policies toward these products are, at least, a useful example of how to deal with some of the symptoms.

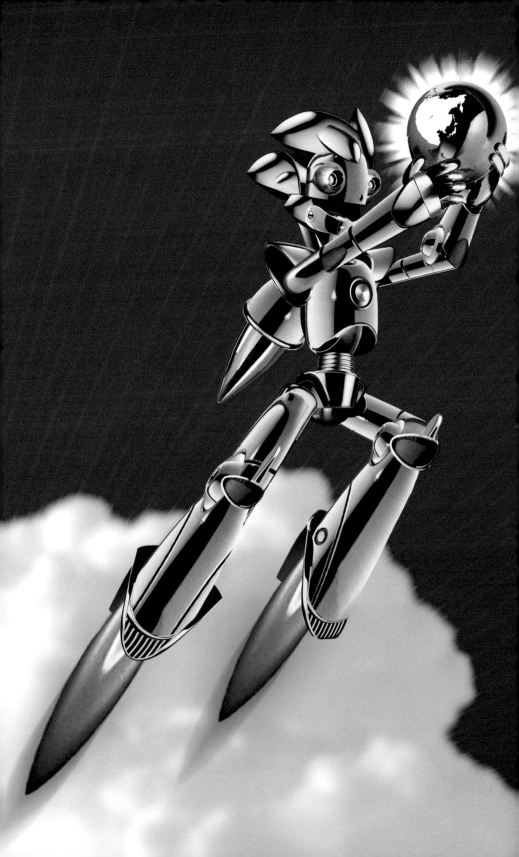

CHAPTER SEVEN: REVITALIZING TECHNOLOGY AND INNOVATION

© Illustration by Eddie Guy

ESCAPE FROM GALAPAGOS

WAICHI SEKIGUCHI

AN UNLIKELY PRODUCT NAME—Galapagos—was bestowed on the tablet personal computer launched in December 2010 by Sharp, one of Japan's largest consumer electronics makers. The moniker was a reference to the islands off the Ecuadorean coast whose unusual flora and fauna inspired Darwin's theory of evolution. Sharp said it chose the name deliberately to emphasize the fact that the device was meant to stand apart from global standards and was uniquely "evolved" for the Japanese market. This Galapagos tablet was to be so utterly Japanese that foreign manufacturers would be unable to mimic it.

The name, and the product itself, highlight the direction that Japan's IT industry has traveled in recent years, thanks to peculiarities of the nation's technology and industrial structure. The upshot of this trend is an industry mired in difficulty, with serious implications for Japan as a whole.

Japan's consumer electronics companies are justly renowned for producing high-quality products with advanced functionality. And yet, outside their home market, Japanese makers increasingly find themselves on the defensive, struggling to retain market share across a range of product categories, including mobile phones, personal computers, automotive navigation systems, and portable music players.

In the analog age, Japanese manufacturers dominated the global consumer electronics market. The product that became that era's iconic symbol, the Sony Walkman, was conspicuously "Made in Japan." The digital age, symbolized by the Internet rather than any one device or product, has wrought dramatic change; US companies like Microsoft, Apple, and Google now lead in technology and services. Even in the market for mobile telephones, Mitsubishi Electric and the other Japa-

Waichi Sekiguchi is a senior editorial writer for the Nihon Keizai Shimbun *newspaper.*

nese companies that enjoyed high shares in the US market during the analog age have virtually disappeared from the scene overseas.

What went wrong? And how can Japan's vaunted high-tech companies avoid the atrophy that may befall them if they remain stuck in the Galapagos Syndrome? The use of the word "Galapagos" to describe the self-imposed seclusion of Japanese manufacturing dates to 2007. That is the year when people began to take serious note of the fact that Japan's share in the global market for mobile handsets had tumbled, while that of Korea's Samsung Electronics had surged. The term is laden with irony, because although many of the species on the Galapagos archipelago are somewhat backward in an evolutionary sense, Japan's high-tech firms have stayed ahead of the pack—often with detrimental side effects.

Take mobile phones, where the Galapagos Syndrome is particularly apparent. Japanese manufacturers began equipping mobile handsets with dazzling new functions as far back as 1999, when NTT's DoCoMo subsidiary launched i-mode, the world's first service that enabled consumers to send and receive e-mails, and view some Internet sites, as they carried their phones from place to place. In 2004, the Japanese began enjoying the convenience of *osaifu keitai* (wallet phones), using a Sony "contactless" chip technology so that a simple swipe of a phone near a card reader would effect a purchase. Another huge advance—watching TV on a handset—came in 2006, thanks to a technology called One Seg Broadcasting that took a small segment of digital broadcasting airwaves for use on mobile devices. Still more functions followed, such as infrared communications and global positioning systems (GPS), that set Japanese handsets on a different evolutionary track from the rest of the world.

ALTHOUGH JAPANESE INDUSTRY STILL SHIPS AN ENORMOUS PORTION OF ITS PRODUCTION OVERSEAS, THE EXPORT-OR-DIE MENTALITY TOOK A DRUBBING IN THE 1990S.

All the while, Japanese manufacturers were paying scant heed to their handsets' lack of viability outside of Japan. One major reason for their complacency was the structure of the country's distribution system. Typically, Japanese carriers like DoCoMo and KDDI (au) purchased and resold all of the phones that a manufacturer produced—and with the sizable Japanese market to supply, there was plenty of profit to go around. Only a handful of manufacturers, led by Kyocera and Sanyo Electric, even bothered with international markets. The result: all Japanese handset makers combined claim only about a 5 percent share of the global mobile handset market, according to figures for 2009 and 2010 (and most of that 5 percent consists of the Japanese market itself). Market leadership has been ceded to non-Japanese handset makers, notably Finland's Nokia, which holds a share of nearly 40 percent, and Samsung, which claims a 20 percent share. It is no coincidence that the Finnish and Korean domestic markets are much smaller than Japan's, which is one reason why those two firms are so much more fixated on global sales than their Japanese rivals.

About five years ago the Ministry of Internal Affairs and Communications (MIC) began waking up to the gravity of the situation. The ministry changed mobile subscription rules so that users could switch freely between carriers. The aim was to force down stubbornly high usage charges, and squeeze domestic profits, thereby motivating handset manufacturers to seek income in international markets.

The first step was the 2006 introduction of "mobile number portability" (MNP), which allowed consumers to keep their phone numbers when switching carriers. MIC also used its administrative guidance powers to force a review of the sales rebates that telephone carriers gave retailers to keep handset prices low for consumers when they signed up for mobile telephone service. As long as sales rebates made it possible for the carriers to attract consumers with "zero yen phones," the overly cozy relationship between carriers and manufacturers would continue. And Japan would remain stuck on Galapagos.

Technology issues also contributed to the Galapagos Syndrome in the mobile phone market. When car phones, the predecessor of mobile phones, first emerged, NTT enjoyed a monopoly on the market, and even after the advent of fully mobile phones, NTT's DoCoMo continued using a proprietary digital technology called PDC. With European and American makers using different technologies, foreigners coming to Japan found that their mobiles wouldn't work—and the Japanese, whose mobiles wouldn't work when they traveled overseas, were surprised to discover that the ones they rented abroad worked in a number of countries. Coming under intense criticism for the closed nature of its technology, DoCoMo joined with the European industry, which used a standard called GSM, to spread the next-generation technology called W-CDMA as a world standard for phones designed for use by international travelers. However, the Japanese industry still wasn't going far enough to embrace standards elsewhere. Japanese firms had little proficiency at making GSM-equipped phones, because they couldn't sell such phones in their domestic market. These technological problems have mostly vanished with the advent of later-generation phones, but a lot of damage was done to the global market position of Japanese companies in the meantime.

Automotive navigation systems are another uniquely Japanese world. The most advanced systems can sell for as much as 300,000 yen—well above the price of a Nano car from India's Tata Motors. Several factors have contributed to this high price level. Most importantly, with all of Japan's narrow roads and tunnels, the density and complexity of the nation's highway grid requires GPS capable of extraordinary precision and the communication of minutely detailed information to drivers. By contrast, in Europe and North America the market trended toward portable navigation devices (PNDs) with simpler functions and greater portability. Prices differed by an order of magnitude from those offered in Japan. Once again Japanese navigation devices were world-beaters in terms of technological sophistication, but the extra functionality was simply overkill for non-Japanese consumers, and Japanese manufacturers of PNDs never made a serious bid to dominate the global market.

Smart cards—used in Japan for buying everything from train rides to vending-machine drinks to rice balls at convenience stores—offer yet another case study of the

Perfectly evolved for life on Galapagos—but could he survive on another island?
© Jim Ballard/Photographer's Choice/Getty Images

THE NEW JAPANESE BUSINESS MODEL SHOULD BE ONE IN WHICH COMPANIES PICK THEIR BATTLES MORE STRATEGICALLY AND AIM TO CREATE NEW MARKETS RATHER THAN PLAYING CATCH-UP IN A LOT OF DIFFERENT SECTORS.

Galapagos Syndrome at work. In global markets, there are two standards ("Type A" and "Type B") for such cards, which consumers buy with prepaid amounts so that they can effortlessly use card readers to make purchases. In Japan, however, Sony has championed a third technology called "FeliCa" that achieves higher processing speeds. This system was adopted by JR East Japan for its popular "Suica" electronic railway tickets, making Sony's approach the de facto standard in Japan. Although there are a number of Japanese brands for e-money and mobile ticket sales—services like "Edy" and "Pasmo"—all use the Sony technology, and are incompatible with smart cards in other countries.

Above all, the Galapagos-ization of Japan's IT industry is traceable to a fundamental shift in the nature of technology, in which networks—especially the Internet—began to dominate individual products in importance. Japanese firms were unsurpassed at making stand-alone products such as televisions, VCRs, and camcorders, which can be sold anywhere in the world. Indeed, Japanese companies still reign supreme in a number of global markets for such products, prime examples being Toyota in automotive vehicles and Canon in cameras. But over the past decade, as high-speed Internet service has become available to the overwhelming majority of consumers in the advanced world, stand-alone excellence is no longer sufficient for many electronic items. The performance and value of these gadgets depends most on what they do when plugged into a larger network. Grand design is the forte of American IT companies, which have shown they have an edge over Japanese competitors in figuring out what consumers want and need in the networked age. Moreover, the creation of such systems in Japan is often hampered by legal and technical problems; for example, very strict copyright laws have tightly limited the distribution over the Internet of music and video programming. All these factors accelerated the retreat of Japanese IT firms from the global fray, and intensified these companies' preference for focusing on the market they know best.

Beyond that, Galapagos-style outcomes sometimes stem from very un-Japanese miscalculations by industrial planners in Tokyo, combined with equally un-Japanese lapses in corporate offices. Digital TV offers the clearest manifestation of this problem. The broadcasting of digital programming began in Japan in 2003, five years after the United States and the United Kingdom, so Japanese broadcasters were able to incorporate newer technologies. The standard, known as Integrated Services Digital Broadcasting-Terrestrial (ISDB-T), was uniquely Japanese, leading to a broadcasting system at odds with the rest of the advanced world. Anxious to keep ISDB-T from being a Japan-only standard, Japanese bureaucrats at MIC successfully lobbied Latin American countries like Brazil to use it. But even the adoption of Japanese technology in these markets does not appear to have produced an increase in sales for Japanese television manufacturers. In an embarrassment for the Japanese industry, Korean TV and broadcasting equipment makers have reaped the greatest gains in Latin American markets that adopted the Japanese standard. Samsung in particular, recognizing in 2008 what direction Latin American governments were heading, outhustled the Japanese in getting the proper television sets to local markets, establishing a dominant position before Japanese manufacturers arrived.

Another reason for Japan's Galapagos Syndrome may have to do with changes in the attitudes and priorities of managers. One of the most important duties of Japanese companies during the 1980s was to export, whether the product in question was autos, steel, machine tools, or electronic goods. Although Japanese industry still ships an enormous portion of its production overseas, the export-or-die mentality took a drubbing in the 1990s when the United States confronted Tokyo over its structural trade surplus and, in negotiations such as the "Structural Impediments Initiative" and "US–Japan Framework Talks," demanded that Japan Inc. concentrate on expanding and cultivating the domestic market.

The generation at the forefront of domestic sales during that period has become today's top management. These executives took to heart, at least to some extent, the message that their top goal must be to prevail in domestic competition. And nowhere is that message more true than in the IT industry, where so many other factors are inhibiting Japanese firms from winning overseas; the change in the industry's mindset might be described as making a virtue of necessity.

Self-imposed seclusion extends to the country's engineers, too. During the analog age, international standards were determined in intergovernmental negotiations, such as those fostered by the International Telecommunications Union (ITU), which set the direction for many new technologies. In the Net age, voluntary conferences of engineers, like the World Wide Web Consortium (W3C) and Internet Engineering Task Force (IETF), make the decisions. These groups do not necessarily have the same "one person, one vote" rules found in international institutions. A country or company that wants its technology adopted as the international standard must lobby proactively and aggressively. The Japanese have never been particularly good at foreign languages and have fewer opportunities to attend international conferences because companies and universities are cutting back on foreign travel. This seclusion has put the country's executives in the backseat when it comes to technology standard-setting.

In the past, it was not uncommon for Japanese scholars to go to the United States and other countries, study under leading researchers there, and become involved in local research projects. Recently, however, researchers and engineers have shown a strong tendency to stay within their domestic cliques. An analysis by Professor Hiroyuki Chuma of Hitotsubashi University, who has closely studied research citations by engineers from various countries, shows that in terms of technology exchange with foreigners Japanese engineers are more isolated than their counterparts in Korea or China.[1] With technology directions being set by gather-

1 RIETI Policy Discussion Paper Series 10-P-015, November 2010, http://www.rieti.go.jp/jp/publications/pdp/10p015.pdf (in Japanese).

ings of researchers, the Galapagos Syndrome on the human side may emerge as a much larger problem in the future.

Obviously, escaping from Galapagos won't be easy. A few straws in the wind indicate that the Japanese IT industry is mobilizing itself to do so. One example is a recent announcement by Toshiba that it will offer a tablet device in the US and European markets to compete with Apple's iPad. But much bigger steps are in order.

I am a member of a group called the Research Council on International Competitiveness in IT, more commonly known as the "Beyond Galapagos Study Group," and sponsored by the nonprofit Broadband Association of Japan. We recently offered a series of recommendations for three sectors suffering from Galapagos Syndrome: communications, electrical equipment, and content.[2] In my view, the following measures are most essential:

1. Business models in the industry must change, with the aim of eliminating the Japanese tendency to in-source and integrate vertically. That model worked wondrously well when global competition revolved around individual products and the winners were the companies that made the best products at the cheapest price. But it makes much less sense in the world of digital electronics where the network is king. Now the companies coming out on top are the ones creating new markets that enhance the power of the Internet—Google in search engines, for instance, or Cisco in network technology. Japanese companies, with their penchant for trying to make everything in the hope of making it better than anyone else, end up spread too thin, then find themselves undercut by Korean firms' superior manufacturing efficiency. The new Japanese business model should be one in which companies pick their battles more strategically and aim to create new markets, rather than play catch-up in a lot of different sectors.

2. Japan's IT companies must create systems and organizations able to shape and influence international standards. Technical standards in the digital age are determined by international "salons" of engineers. The standards that these engineers agree upon are ultimately ratified by the International Organization for Standardization. Japan must develop professionals capable of selling the country's excellent technologies to global counterparts and forging consensus around those technologies in international standards negotiations. Japanese companies now have intellectual property professionals on staff as part of a new emphasis on IPR strategy, but there are few professionals in international negotiations.

3. International staff is crucial. Creating networks of like-minded engineers in the international community requires more than just specialist technology and creativity. Also essential are the international sensibilities required to transform technology and expertise into global standards. To acquire these

---

2 For the study group's recommendations, see http://www.npo-ba.org/public/20090928dr.pdf (in Japanese).

sensibilities, employees should get international experience at an early stage in their career, either as students or in foreign postings. Among other things, they need opportunities to polish their abilities in English, Chinese, and other languages. It is also vital for Japanese companies to recruit talented staff from overseas and put them in positions of responsibility within their organizations.

4. Japanese managers must reexamine their own attitudes and motivations. More than a few managers attribute the poor performance of Japanese industry to factors such as the strong yen or high corporate income taxes. But the fact is that exporters are no longer as vulnerable to the exchange rate as they used to be because they have moved much of their production overseas. Indeed, the strong yen should be mostly positive for companies that depend on China and other foreign markets for their parts and materials. And while it is true that countries in Asia and elsewhere have lowered their corporate income taxes, Japanese companies were in the past able to work with tax rates as givens and still compete head-on with foreign rivals. Rather than excuses, what is required is the formulation and implementation of international strategies.

5. The Japanese government must do more. The most essential measures are to push forward with deregulation, and scrap outdated legal systems that are unsuited to the digital age. A case in point: copyright law. There are no serious Japanese competitors to Google in the search service sector, in part because Japan deemed scanning a copyrighted work—books, publications, websites, and the like—a de facto crime. Until copyright law was amended in 2010, data-search centers operating in Japan were severely limited in what kind of information they could input for use in searches.

If new information services are to flourish in Japan, policy must change to eliminate domestic restrictions and constraints, and to foster an environment that gives companies the freedom to create new business models.

Opinions may differ on whether these recommendations are best. But there can be no doubt that Japan's economy faces tough times if the nation's information technology companies fail to escape from Galapagos. Even though it may matter little that Japan has lost its position as the world's second-largest economy, it will matter a lot if Japan slips from its No. 2 spot in technology and market sophistication. With the country's advanced telecommunications infrastructure and a younger generation adept at using network technologies, Japan has many natural advantages, which it should exploit so that technology historians one day look back at the Galapagos Syndrome as a brief and curious phase in the nation's industrial development. Now is not the time for Japan to resign itself to anything less.

THE T-SHIRT AND THE KIMONO

SENAPATHY GOPALAKRISHNAN

THE JAPANESE CONSIDER THEMSELVES to be an "island nation." Geographically, of course, this is true—Japan is an archipelago. But the term also describes Japan's service sector, which is an island unto itself. Not a single non-Japanese multinational can claim a leadership position in the services business in Japan. The reverse is also true: no Japanese company leads in such major service industries as IT, commercial banking, investment banking, insurance, airlines, software, travel, or hotels.

The problem is not poor quality; every visitor to Japan carries memories of being exquisitely tended to by polite, well-dressed people in hotels, airports, taxis, and the famous bullet trains. Moreover, Japan has exemplary service businesses in its domestic market, including speedy and reliable broadband mobile networks. So why has it proved so difficult for Japan's service industry to succeed overseas?

Home, sweet home

Japan's economic system is a curious blend of a market-led economy and socialist principles, including strong government guidance. In many sectors, including IT, three to five companies collectively dominate the market. While these companies compete intensely, they also collaborate when required—for example, to keep out new competition—and their profit margins are similar.

Unfortunately, this model has downsides when taken beyond Japan. For one thing, the system can be slower to change and adapt to circumstances; by its nature, it is inwardly oriented and exquisitely attuned to Japanese social mores. Given that

Senapathy Gopalakrishnan is CEO and managing director of Infosys Technologies.

Japan is homogeneous in terms of culture and language, all the players—government officials, executives, and salarymen—understand how to work together. That kind of knowledge doesn't translate anywhere else.

Moreover, the high quality typical of services in Japan requires a significant human component. Consider ATM terminals in bank branches. These machines are reliable and easy to use, but there is almost always a human on hand to help, too.

IN SERVICES, JAPAN CREATES ONLY 38 PERCENT AS MUCH VALUE AS THE U.S., WHICH PUTS IT IN THE BOTTOM THIRD OF THE OECD.

Similarly, almost never do consumers in Japan call a company and hear a computer tell them to "Dial 2 for more information." They will get another person. Undoubtedly, this system makes life more pleasant; it also raises costs. And it creates a set of norms that are difficult to export.

So it is not surprising that among the Organisation for Economic Co-operation and Development (OECD) nations, Japan's services productivity is low. One metric the OECD uses compares its members to the United States in the amount of GDP produced per hour worked. In services, Japan creates only 38.2 percent as much value as the United States, a figure that puts Japan in the bottom third behind all of Western Europe (except Greece and Portugal), and not much ahead of Slovenia (33.9 percent).

The limits of oligopoly

A classic example of a high-cost, low-productivity sector is IT services. The top five companies hold about half the market share; the top 20, more than 75 percent. Having carved up the domestic market to their satisfaction, the powers-that-be have no major incentive to change, and the smaller companies are in no position to force the issue, since they depend on the big ones for their survival. Such an oligopoly is comfortable for the insiders, but it does not encourage innovation.

On the flip side, it is difficult for anyone else to break into what is, in effect, a closed system. With the possible exception of IBM, which for all practical purposes operates as a Japanese company, there is not a single non-Japanese company among the country's IT leaders. Among other major IT consumers, including China, the United States, and to a lesser extent Europe, the IT services market is much more fragmented, and therefore more competitive, dynamic, and, in a sense, vulnerable. In Japan, it is almost unheard of for a newcomer to topple an incumbent; elsewhere, challengers are constantly nipping at the leader's heels.

The IT industry in Japan employs about 800,000 people (average age: 37) and the average annual salary is more than $70,000. Up to 80 percent of annual IT spending goes toward maintaining and operating existing systems (compared with no more than 60 percent in the United States). That leaves only a small share of IT budgets to be spent on new projects and initiatives. Most of the best-paid and most-experienced people are not contributing to next-generation systems, but are overseeing routine maintenance and operations.

Kimono: Beautiful, expensive, and not for everyday use.
© Justin Guariglia/National Geographic/Getty Images

Why? An obsession with perfection and systems completeness can lead to cost overruns as a result of opaque, often unspecified requirements. These characteristics also make sending IT services offshore more difficult; it is far easier for clients and service providers to clarify such ambiguities if they are in the same place, speaking the same language. These projects tend to be highly stressful and often end up losing money.

Quality is crucial, of course, but the cost to reach the final fraction of a percentage point of reliability can be high, in terms of both money and time. IT service providers in Japan, unlike those other countries, do not place a premium on innovation and speed. Foreign service providers seek out "good enough" solutions and put their most experienced and capable people to work on new initiatives that help their organization grow and stay competitive. That is likely to add more value than making sure the lights are on.

Take the analogy of the T-shirt versus the *kimono*. A T-shirt can be bought for less than the price of a Big Mac, thrown on, and tossed away. A *kimono* is a special purchase; it's expensive and requires precise knowledge and at least two people to be worn correctly. There is a place for the *kimono*, but on a day-to-day basis, the T-shirt is darn useful. Japan's IT service industry lacks a drawer full of T-shirts.

Another important reason for the lack of Japanese leadership in services is the inability of the country's businesses to create global standards. The traditional Japanese economic model was "inside-out," that is, companies created products and services that met local needs. Only after succeeding at home would these companies go on to test overseas markets. This strategy worked in products, but it has failed for services. Worse, it has propagated a "Japan is unique" ethos.

Absorbed in the Japanese paradigm, the IT service industry has tended to think in terms of domestic rather than global standards. A Japanese standard can certainly be useful and of high quality, but has limited value if it fails to become a global standard. For this reason, no global operating or database management system has ever come out of Japan. In fact, all of Japan's major IT manufacturers created hardware and software that emulated IBM mainframes. The telecoms industry is another classic example: there is great technology and great service—but the phones work only in Japan.

Japan's choices

What, then, should Japan do?

1. *Try an "outside in" model.* Japanese companies should experiment with succeeding in another market, and then use that experience to launch both at home and globally. One example from outside IT might be for a Japanese car company to go into India or China with the goal of creating a $5,000 hybrid. This product would certainly reveal ways to make such cars less expensive everywhere. Recently, General Electric (GE) developed a low-cost ECG machine in India and then took it to the global market. GE was able to create new markets for this product because of the machine's lower cost and ruggedness.

2. *Embrace IT as a key element of corporate strategy.* Of course, information technology is embedded in many Japanese companies, but acquiring technology, of itself, is not enough. Corporate leaders must move away from seeing IT as a cost center and instead consider it a center of business innovation and competitive advantage. CEOs should be asking: how do I leverage emerging technologies to create new business models? And how should I change our existing business processes to make them more competitive?

WITH THE POSSIBLE EXCEPTION OF IBM, WHICH FOR ALL PRACTICAL PURPOSES OPERATES AS A JAPANESE COMPANY, THERE IS NOT A SINGLE NON-JAPANESE COMPANY AMONG THE COUNTRY'S IT LEADERS.

To answer these questions, a professional chief information officer (CIO) is a must, particularly since so many business leaders at or near the top in Japan lack tech savvy. An expert CIO can offer an informed perspective on the entire value chain, including which pieces of it can be disrupted by new technologies. In too many Japanese companies, though, the concept of the CIO is still nascent. The senior person responsible for IT systems is often doing the job on rotation and has limited IT experience.

Companies should also seek to create a tech-literate workforce—and not only in Japan. With so much skill available around the world, it makes sense to bring this talent into the corporate fold. We understand that this may sound self-serving, considering Infosys's position as a global leader in the outsourcing of IT services. The fact remains, though, that outsourcing can be not only more efficient and less expensive than trying to do everything in-house, but also a way of importing new people and ideas. If Japan wants to create a global model for services—and this should indeed be its goal—outsourcing has to be part of that model.

3. *Create a new pool of talent.* Japan's postwar success has created its own di-lemma. The country is so prosperous and pleasant that younger people have no real incentive to absorb another culture, and jobs are still available for the most talented. But that kind of complacency carries real consequences in the form of opportunities lost. It is part of the reason that Japan lacks an innovation ecosystem with the vibrancy of Silicon Valley or Bangalore.

Japan should create an independent university, truly global in nature, focused on computer science and software engineering, and aim to make this institution the world's best in ten years. This university should have international partnerships—the United States and India are natural sources of expertise—and the curriculum should be in English. Faculty should be recruited from all over the world and half the students should be from outside Japan. Such a university would bring in talent that understands software engineering, global business, and the importance of open standards. This institution would also bring in energy and ideas and help to nudge Japan closer to the best thinking on subjects such as the use of venture capital, and the role of failure in entrepreneurism.

Japan's choice

Japanese society is similar to a mainframe computer—a monolithic, ordered, and tightly controlled system. The United States and other, more individualistic societies have an affinity for the distributed, fast paradigm of modern technology.

In a sense, this difference describes not only Japan's present, but also its future. Japan can continue to favor a closed, highly integrated model that works well—but only in Japan. Or it can try a more networked, open model that is susceptible to greater competition—but also has greater upside.

That choice, and how quickly Japan makes it, will shape the nation's destiny.

REBOOTING JAPAN'S HIGH-TECH SECTOR

INGO BEYER VON MORGENSTERN, PETER KENEVAN, AND ULRICH NAEHER

FOR MANY DECADES, Japan's high-technology companies, nourished by innovative products and prominent consumer electronics brands, were the envy of the global sector. But that is rapidly changing. More recently, these companies have been losing ground around the world, undermined by a reluctance to make the aggressive moves and hard choices necessary to compete in new markets and against emboldened attackers.

Recent McKinsey research shows that Japanese high-tech companies lost a decade between 2000 and 2010 (Exhibit 1) and on current trajectory could see their global market share drop by 20 percent from 2008 to 2013. That represents a cumulative loss of more than $30 billion in potential revenue. Japanese companies have a global presence and reputation, but most remain surprisingly dependent on Japan's domestic market for revenue, while struggling to capture a reasonable share of dynamically growing emerging markets. Our analysis shows that Japanese high-tech companies, as a group, still generate more than 50 percent of their sales in the home market, growing by a mere 1 percent annually, compared with growth of 5 to 10 percent in the developing world and 2 to 3 percent in other developed markets. As a result, Japanese companies will see their global market share decline rapidly even if they successfully defend their current share in each market.

But the situation is potentially worse. Japanese companies are also losing share in major products within key geographic markets. Between 2005 and 2009, these players' share of LCD-TV unit shipments grew to 100 percent, from 96 percent, in Japan but fell to 30 percent, from 40 percent, in North America. Also, total unit-vol-

Ingo Beyer von Morgenstern is a senior partner in McKinsey's Shanghai office; Peter Kenevan is a partner in the Tokyo office, where Ulrich Naeher is a senior partner.

Exhibit 1
Japanese high-tech players experienced a lost decade between 2000 and 2010.

Revenue; index: revenue in 2000 = 100

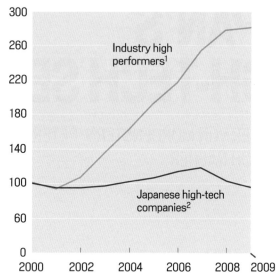

Operating profit margin, %

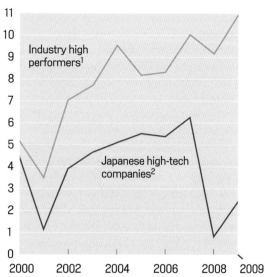

[1] Average of revenues for Apple, Acer, Cisco, HP, Lenovo, LG and Samsung.
[2] Average of revenues for Canon, Fujitsu, NEC, Panasonic, Sharp, Sony and Toshiba.

Source: Annual reports; Bloomberg; Nikkei Financial QUEST

ume growth in Japan during this period was very small relative to growth in North America and elsewhere. The pattern is similar for a number of other products, such as servers—success in Japan but failure abroad. For PCs and mobile phones, share declined even in the critical Japanese home market.

In addition, Japanese companies have almost no position in the critically important software and IT services markets outside of Japan. As a result, they will probably miss out on almost half of the absolute expansion in the global high-tech market between 2008 and 2013. Most of the growth will come from the United States and Europe, where Japanese companies have a limited presence. Market share changes little in these incumbent-dominated geographies, and most major movements that do occur reflect large-scale mergers and acquisitions. Unless Japanese companies join the party, they will be locked out of some of the most attractive growth and profit opportunities.

As a result of focusing on the wrong geographic markets and losing share within many of them, Japanese companies are sliding down the ranks of the leaders in units sold across a range of product sectors. In 2004, these companies held the number-one and -two spots in LCD TVs, but by 2009 their South Korean rivals Samsung and LG had taken a commanding lead. Similarly, Japanese companies occupied three of the top five slots in the global PC market in 2004, but only one in 2008. This rapid loss of leadership in important product categories in consumer electronics may be disastrous in the context of the winner-takes-all dynamic of the high-tech sector, where the top one or two players in each submarket tend to capture all the value.

Models for success

So what can these Japanese companies do to regain their edge? We looked closely at more than 20 global high-tech leaders to understand the sources of their success— category growth, market share gains, or M&A. We found four distinct models that Japanese companies could pursue (Exhibit 2).

World-class operators

Some companies win by identifying fast-growing product categories and geographic markets and grabbing share through an intense focus on operational excellence. They constantly apply lean-production techniques to manufacturing, the supply chain, and go-to-market operations and move as much of the value chain as possible to local markets. They also pursue dominant scale in their target markets by investing massively in capacity (for example, in semiconductor manufacturing).

Between 1999 and 2009, the companies in this group generated total revenue growth of 15 to 20 percent a year, on average. Roughly half came from underlying market growth in the categories in which they compete (portfolio momentum) and half from market share gains. There was limited M&A. This group's profitability fell over the period as competition intensified and markets shifted to the developing world's more value-oriented customers, but the leaders continue to deliver operating-profit margins by 5 to 10 percent a year. Acer, LG, and Samsung are examples of leading companies in this category.

Category creators

The small number of companies in a second group shape new markets for themselves by developing and marketing innovative products and services. Above all, they emphasize creative design and engineering talent. From 1999 to 2009, these companies generated revenue growth of 20 percent or more a year, almost entirely though category growth. Successful category creators are also very profitable—those in our sample delivered an average of 15 to 20 percent annual operating profit during the period of our analysis. Many Japanese companies started out as category creators, but most were heavily hardware driven and had lost their innovative edge well before the period of our research. Today's category creator concepts emerge primarily from the nexus of hardware, software, and services, and Japan lags behind global competitors. Apple, Google, and Research in Motion (RIM) are well-known companies pursuing this model.

Exhibit 2
In pursuing growth, Japanese high-tech companies can look to any of four distinct models for success.

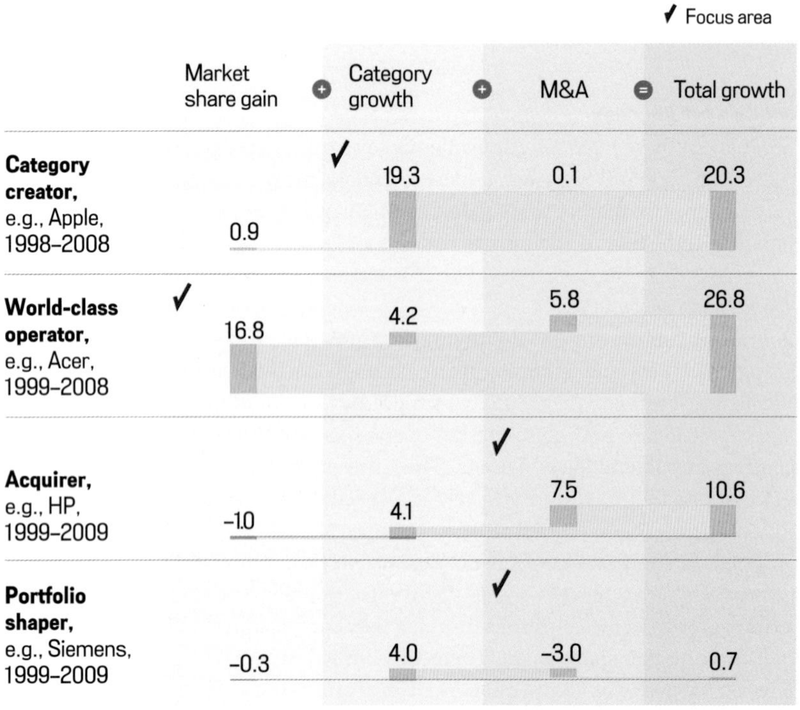

✓ Focus area

	Market share gain ⊕	Category growth ⊕	M&A ⊖	Total growth
Category creator, e.g., Apple, 1998–2008	0.9	✓ 19.3	0.1	20.3
World-class operator, e.g., Acer, 1999–2008	✓ 16.8	4.2	5.8	26.8
Acquirer, e.g., HP, 1999–2009	–1.0	4.1	✓ 7.5	10.6
Portfolio shaper, e.g., Siemens, 1999–2009	–0.3	✓ 4.0	–3.0	0.7

Acquirers

Another group of companies don't neglect underlying organic expansion but also aggressively pursue M&A to buy growth platforms in interesting product and geographic market segments. They do multiple deals each year and skillfully identify, acquire, and integrate promising companies both large and small. During the ten years from 1999 to 2009, these companies generated revenue growth of 10 to 12 percent a year, with the majority coming from acquisitions and the remainder from a mix of portfolio momentum and market share gains. Annual operating profits were relatively stable over the period, at 10 to 20 percent. This group includes many US companies, such as Cisco Systems and Hewlett-Packard.

Portfolio shapers

The companies in our last group emphasize profitability over growth and actively pursue both acquisitions and divestitures. They take a rigorous and disciplined approach to corporate-portfolio strategy, actively shaping their areas of business focus. Like the acquirers, they do multiple deals each year and have well-developed M&A-related skills and capabilities. Between 1999 and 2009, the companies in our sample generated revenue growth of only 1 percent a year, as the shrinkage of divestiture-related sales largely canceled out portfolio momentum and acquisition-related growth. Profitability grew substantially, however: over the period, most of these companies increased their annual operating-profit margins by five to ten percentage points. This group includes a large number of European and US companies, including IBM and Siemens.

What it will take to win

The leading Japanese technology companies in our sample appear to lack the strategic clarity and management willpower to pursue any of the winning strategies effectively, so they are falling behind in every kind of growth. Most tend to rely on moderate category expansion, fail to streamline their business portfolios, lose market share in core businesses, and do only a few (and domestic) M&A deals (Exhibit 3). From 1999 to 2009, the Japanese companies achieved average annual revenue increases of only 2 percent, because market share losses cancelled out category growth gains. Profitability—already low at an average of 2 to 3 percent in 1999—fell further during the period. Most players ended up in the 1 to 2 percent range in 2009.

Senior managers of Japan's high-tech giants urgently need to break out of their current strategic and operational inertia and take the bold steps required to leave a legacy of healthy global champions for succeeding generations. All the success models that global rivals use are possible for Japanese companies, but each of them must make its own hard choices.

Seeking the operational edge

Japanese companies that pursue market share gains and operational excellence must shift focus to growth markets, cut costs, and increase efficiency across the

Exhibit 3

Most Japanese technology companies rely on moderate category growth
and make few M&A deals.

Average annual revenue growth, 1999–2009, %

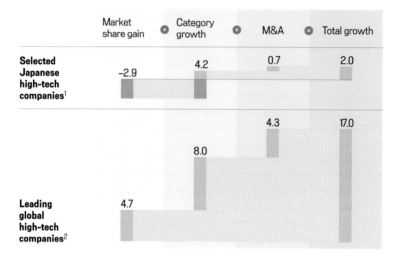

	Market share gain	⊕	Category growth	⊕	M&A	⊜	Total growth
Selected Japanese high-tech companies[1]	-2.9		4.2		0.7		2.0
Leading global high-tech companies[2]	4.7		8.0		4.3		17.0

[1] Average for Canon, Fujitsu, NEC, Panasonic, Sharp, Sony, Toshiba, Fujitsu and NEC.
[2] Average for Acer, Apple, Cisco, HP, LG, Lenovo and Samsung.

value chain. McKinsey & Company analysis shows a correlation between market success and commitment to emerging markets (for example, the level of localization in value chains and product portfolios). Most Japanese companies operating in emerging markets have been content to take a passive go-to-market approach, relying on scaled-back developed-market products delivered through venerable but underperforming distributor networks.

To compete effectively, these companies will need to build up their local organizational capabilities and become insiders in the markets they are targeting. At the top of the list is improved local R&D and product design to address the needs of customers in emerging markets at attractive price points more effectively. In addition, companies should strengthen relations with regulators and government officials to understand and navigate local constraints more successfully. Downstream, these companies must develop multichannel go-to-market models, including call-center and Web-based operations, and they will need to review, restructure, and better manage their distributor networks in the developing world.

Achieving sustainable cost-competitiveness will require Japanese companies to restructure their operations across the value chain by outsourcing and offshoring key functions and maximizing the efficiency of the remaining operations in Japan. In some cases, they should even consider offshoring the headquarters of business units to shorten decision-making processes and expose senior managers to local market conditions. All these changes will probably require headcount reductions in Japan, but they will be necessary to stay competitive with foreign rivals. Many Japanese technology executives we speak with understand the necessity for these measures. Some have begun to move quietly in this direction, but Japan's high-tech giants must do much more to get back in shape.

JAPANESE HIGH-TECH COMPANIES STILL GENERATE MORE THAN 50 PERCENT OF THEIR SALES IN THE HOME MARKET, GROWING BY A MERE 1 PERCENT ANNUALLY, COMPARED WITH GROWTH OF 5 TO 10 PERCENT IN THE DEVELOPING WORLD AND 2 TO 3 PERCENT IN OTHER DEVELOPED MARKETS.

Innovation renewal

Companies seeking to regain innovation leadership and create new product categories must break free of their current hardware-centric models and find ways to collaborate within and outside the organization. The digitization of the electronics industry means that hardware is commoditizing much more quickly than in the past, while software capabilities are becoming more important than hardware-engineering ones. Today, successful and sustainable innovations usually originate in superior customer insights and creative business models rather than technical breakthroughs.

But ramping up software capabilities quickly will be a challenge, both in the time needed to reach scale and in gaining access to top talent. Here we believe acquisitions of companies offering software solutions or specific customer applications could make sense. Similarly, building a portfolio of alliances on themes such as "smart" electricity grids, health care supported by mobile devices, or cloud-computing services could help jump-start innovation. In addition, Japanese companies seeking a second wind in innovation will probably also need to revamp their human-resources policies by introducing differentiated incentives and rewards to attract, motivate, and retain creative, talented staff.

Many Japanese high-tech companies have their roots in the category creator model. But they have moved far away from it in culture and mind-set and may find it difficult to recapture the magic organically. That's why we believe M&A will play a key role for companies choosing this path.

A growing need for cross-border deals

Japanese companies seeking growth through large-scale acquisitions will need a bolder approach to M&A, pursuing and completing deals that "move the needle." To do so, it will be necessary to aim for bigger targets that would have a strong strategic, operational, and financial impact, as well as bid aggressively to win. Since most Japanese companies share similar strengths and limitations, most of these transformational deals will, by definition, be cross-border. To compete effectively for such high-profile deals, Japanese companies must upgrade their internal M&A

skills, including faster decision making to enable quicker responses in the tricky world of deal negotiations.

Once a transaction closes, Japanese high-tech managers should act much more quickly and systematically than they have in the past to integrate the acquisition and actually capture synergies. Finally, Japanese acquirers will need to introduce more open and transparent governance structures and processes in areas such as the appointment and evaluation of C-level management to integrate world-class executives from acquired companies and to provide suitable incentives. The acquirer strategy will probably be a form of shock therapy for Japan's inward-looking giants, but successful serial acquirers such as HP have shown that significant rewards come with the risks.

Profiting from active portfolio management

Companies that choose to shape the portfolio for profitability rather than growth will need to rethink hypothetical but unrealized synergies between businesses and overcome internal resistance to divesting underperforming units. As a start, these companies should introduce a more rigorous performance-management culture, supported by world-class managerial-accounting systems and processes, to create clarity on expectations and actual performance across their businesses. Then they will need to use this transparency to break through the emotional and cultural barriers to identifying and selling noncore assets—for example, white goods or semiconductors, depending on the company.

Like the acquirers, the portfolio shapers must upgrade their M&A skills significantly to ensure that they can complete deals in a timely manner while simultaneously maximizing the value created. Although the portfolio shaper strategy could deliver a lot of low-hanging fruit to most large Japanese tech players, it is in many ways the most challenging model to follow, requiring hard-nosed leadership willing to break long-standing internal taboos and to part with old friends. In some cases, the early stages of this strategy could end up shrinking a company as large underperforming assets are converted into smaller emerging businesses with better returns.

● ● ●

We feel confident that Japanese companies still have the underlying assets and capabilities to compete globally. They can succeed under any of these models—provided that management sets clear strategic priorities and takes responsibility for making and executing hard yet necessary decisions. Competitors are moving very quickly, however, so the time to act is now.

WHAT JAPAN CAN LEARN FROM SILICON VALLEY

TOMOKO NAMBA

IN JAPAN, we take tremendous pride in *monozukuri*, our ability to make things. Whether crafting objects in small numbers or manufacturing them on a large scale, Japanese producers are famous for efficiency and quality. In many manufacturing sectors, Japanese companies are world leaders. And yet, in my industry, the Internet, no Japanese company has emerged as a global leader.

I often wonder why this is so. One reason, I think, is that in the Internet, things change so dramatically and at such a rapid pace. Consider the changes we've seen in the Internet during just the past three years. In the category of global Internet access, the market share of Yahoo and the Microsoft Network, which used to be dominant players, has declined significantly. Google's share has stayed about the same. Meanwhile Facebook, YouTube, and Twitter have experienced tremendous growth. In other industries—steel, for example, or beer—market changes of that magnitude take far more time: 20 years, or maybe even a century. By comparison, what has happened in the Internet is astonishing: we've witnessed a complete transformation of the industry in just three years.

To thrive in this kind of an environment, companies have to be able to move fast. You have to be able to make big decisions at lightning speed. You have to excel at strategy and execution. There's not that much regulation, and privileged access to natural resources isn't a major issue, which means that a newcomer with a good idea, who can make strategic decisions and implement them quickly, can become an industry leader in a very short period of time. Similarly, if you're already a market leader, and get it wrong, you can lose everything overnight. This

Tomoko Namba, a former McKinsey partner, is the founder and CEO of DeNA, one of Japan's largest mobile-game companies.

Go West, young gadget-lovers and entrepreneurs.
© Ryuhei Shindo/Taxi Japan/Getty Images

environment isn't one that plays to Japanese strengths.

In Silicon Valley, start-ups are built for speed. There might be a group of six or eight people—say, two from the United States, two from India, one from China, one from Russia—and they can decide in six hours to set up a programming game development center in India.

At a typical Japanese company, deciding whether to start thinking about something like that would take six months. For good ideas to work their way up the corporate hierarchy takes forever. Someone has to initiate the discussion, then solicit input from everyone about the idea, and then the person who proposed the idea has to be 200 percent prepared before he or she considers taking it to top management. Getting everything perfect can take months. And when the idea is finally presented to top management, nothing really happens right away. Japanese executives don't like to make quick decisions. What they typically say is, "Well, why don't we keep examining this?"

Of course Japanese start-ups can make decisions faster than larger, established companies. But Japanese start-ups are reluctant to venture overseas. One problem is the lack of diversity. In Silicon Valley, US-born Americans tend to be in the minority among founders; for leaders in these companies, it's natural to think of other markets. But the leaders of Japanese start-ups are overwhelmingly Japanese. Few have global experience. And for Japanese start-ups, usually the investors are all Japanese, too, and will push new Internet ventures to turn profitable in the Japanese market first before they think of expanding beyond Japan. Venture capitalists in Japan would hate to see the goal of being number one globally on the first page of a presentation; in the United States, though, the VCs would be worried if the top management lacked that ambition.

THE INTERNET IS NOT AN ENVIRONMENT THAT PLAYS TO JAPAN'S STRENGTHS.

I founded DeNA in 1999 and our business model was, for quite some time, inward-looking. Even now at DeNA, many of our top Japanese managers don't speak English and don't like to leave Japan. But with $1 billion in revenues (and $4 billion in market cap) we feel strong, and it is a natural aspiration for us to go beyond our borders.

We bought a US mobile-gaming company, ngmoco, for $400 million in October 2010, and we are looking to acquire more such companies. This acquisition made a significant difference to our company. Even though we were really big in Japan, and among the biggest in the world, top-notch players in Silicon Valley did not see us as a partner. Buying ngmoco changed that impression.

Could we have made a foreign acquisition earlier? Yes, but we were busy trouble-shooting and growing domestically. This is typical. Japan is just the right size to make it profitable to operate strictly domestically. The United States could be like that, too, because it is three times bigger, but if you succeed in the United States in this industry, it's very easy to win in other places. That is not the case in Japan, where too often the emphasis on domestic competition blocks the rest of the world from view.

That's one of the reasons why I wanted to add the ngmoco management team. A third of our staff is working overseas now, and we hope to generate half of our revenues from overseas by fiscal 2014. On a personal level, I'm spending a week every month in Silicon Valley and making connections. This time spent in California enables me to make decisions on the spot—something Japanese CEOs hardly ever do.

There's no comparison between the energy level in a place like Silicon Valley and that in Tokyo. I do not think Japan encourages or respects entrepreneurs. In Japan, the way small businesses are set up—with limited capital and entrepreneurs personally liable for bank loans—affords a very narrow chance of success. In Silicon Valley, entrepreneurs get not only a second chance, but also a third chance, and sometimes even a fourth chance. In Japan there is no second chance; if the business fails, you will never be able to borrow again. If you fail, you are a failure.

THE LEADERS OF JAPANESE INTERNET START-UPS ARE OVERWHELMINGLY JAPANESE. NO ONE HAS GLOBAL EXPERIENCE.

The venture capital system in Japan is also weak. In the heady days of 1998–99, there were, in fact, many VC-backed start-ups. I later went back and looked at these contracts, many of which had a provision that if the start-up did not complete an IPO within two years, then the founder had to buy back all the shares. With provisions like that, venture capitalists aren't putting up risk money; effectively, they're investing risk-free. When the market crashed and it became almost impossible to do an IPO, many companies went out of business because of that one provision.

Attitudes in Japan and Silicon Valley are different, too. The deal for ngmoco was a good one for both sides, and when I went to visit many places with Neil Young, the CEO of ngmoco, everybody said congratulations. Neil was so proud. But if that deal had happened in Japan and I was head of ngmoco, people would have said, "You sold your company. You were bought by someone." They would see me as a failure.

How can Japan change this culture? The quickest way is to invite great people from all over the world to Japan. If Japan can't change organically, we have to get in some entirely new blood to lead these changes for us. Singapore is changing in this way and the US Congress is also looking at giving more visas to entrepreneurs.

The year after I founded DeNA, a venture capitalist in Japan—pretty much the only truly professional one operating here at the time—took me to Silicon Valley and forced me to make presentations to all these VC firms. I didn't do so well, but I got a sense of how people did business. We couldn't get an appointment at Kleiner

Perkins, the most famous venture capital firm, but my VC drove me out to their offices on Sandhill Road anyway. We parked in front of the building, and the VC proceeded to give me a 20-minute speech "Beyond these doors Netscape was born, and beyond these doors...." He went on and on. There were four of us in this tiny little car, and he was practically giving me a full presentation. The windows started to fog up. I remember thinking, "Okay, okay, but can we just get some air?" But he was really passionate, and eventually I began to understand. I tried to bring some of that excitement back to Japan with me. These days, I can visit Kleiner Perkins any time, but I will always remember that speech.

In Japan, we need the right rules and regulations. We need more venture capitalists. We need a better ecosystem. We need to bring in more new people. But I think what Japan needs most right now are some good examples of success. We're trying to be one of those examples at DeNA. We want to send a message to young Japanese with talent and ambition that it's a great thing to start a business; that it's okay to take risks; that Japanese Internet companies really can move fast. And we want to send a message to the world that a Japanese Internet company can be a global leader.

STAYING IN THE GAME

KEIJI INAFUNE

TEN YEARS AGO, the Japanese game industry was No. 1 in the world: Japanese companies created over half of the 50 best-selling game titles. In 2002, we claimed about 50 percent share of global revenues. Not any more. Nintendo continues to be wildly successful; otherwise, there are now only a few Japanese games in the top 50, and Japan's share of the $60 billion global game industry has fallen to 10 percent.

We've forfeited our lead in technology; Japanese game technology is now at least five years behind that of competitors in the United States. And our approach to content has not changed much in the last decade. The technical quality and the user interfaces have improved some, but the ideas, the game play, and design are basically the same. There's not enough originality.

Look at *Dragon Quest*, which was Japan's best-selling game in 2009. The content hasn't changed that much from when it was introduced in 1986; it even uses the same characters. Now compare *Call of Duty*, developed by California-based Activision and currently the world's most popular video game. The look and design are completely different from the original version released in 2003. The technology has raced ahead and gives the player a real feeling of being in the middle of a battlefield.

So we—meaning Japanese game creators, company management, users, all of us—have to admit that Japan has fallen behind. If we fail to acknowledge this, we will not be motivated to learn from the United States, the current leader, and to change.

Many factors have contributed to the Japanese game industry's loss of global leadership. But I think there are three big reasons: game creators are like salary-men, the costs and risks of game creation are increasing, and Japan doesn't know

Keiji Inafune is CEO of Comcept, a creator of video games, and former head of global R&D at Capcom, an Osaka-based video game developer.

how to compete in overseas markets. One of the most fundamental problems is the way Japanese game companies are organized. They tend to be structured like any other big Japanese company. The key managers join for life and advance by seniority. Even the game creators think like salarymen, not

JAPANESE GAME TECHNOLOGY IS NOW AT LEAST FIVE YEARS BEHIND THAT OF COMPETITORS IN THE US

that differently from bureaucrats. These salarymen don't have to take risks. They're not interested in working hard. Month in and month out, they can count on a steady paycheck as long as they avoid making mistakes. No one is motivated to generate ideas or try new things.

In the West, game creators are often independent. They get evaluated and rewarded according to their results. In-house game creators change companies regularly. The model is similar to that of Hollywood, where people jump from project to project depending on what talent is needed where. A director will work with one set of actors or a certain team of special-effects experts for one film, and with a completely different group for his next film. Japan's game industry is more like the old Hollywood system, where players were under exclusive contract to a particular studio.

Japan's game industry tunes out global trends.
© Tomohiro Ohsumi/Bloomberg via Getty Images

What's interesting is that over time, the Japanese movie industry is becoming more like Hollywood of today. I believe the economics of Japan's game industry will eventually force it to follow that pattern. But for now, we're stuck in the past.

EVEN GAME CREATORS THINK LIKE SALARYMEN. THEY DON'T HAVE TO TAKE RISKS. THEY'RE NOT INTERESTED IN WORKING HARD.

For game companies, retaining the traditional Japanese corporate organizational structure is a huge liability because such a structure restricts the ability to hedge risk. In the past, creating a new game title cost about 200 million yen, but these days, producing a successful game can cost more than 10 times that. The cost of failure has gone way up. "Shooter" games like *Call of Duty* are hugely popular outside Japan. But they're expensive to develop, so Japanese game companies have shied away from them. The obvious solution is for a Japanese game company to team up with an experienced US game developer who knows how to create a shooter game, and thereby minimize the risk of failure. But Japanese companies won't do that; instead, they insist on working only with their own in-house game creators.

So for now, the Japanese game industry is trapped in a vicious cycle. The global industry is changing drastically. The technology, especially from the United States, is racing ahead, and production costs are soaring. But Japanese companies won't adapt. They don't know how to collaborate with outside partners. They're oblivious to what's happening overseas. And they're still trying to develop hit games on the cheap; they are reluctant to invest the billions of yen required.

In the past, Japanese makers could get away with ignoring overseas competition because of the size of the domestic market, and because Japanese players weren't all that interested in games from overseas. But now the Japanese market is shrinking. And the smaller Japan's home market, the less Japanese companies have to invest in games that might be competitive outside Japan. In Korea, where the domestic market is smaller, the game industry recognized from the start that it would have go global to survive. Now they're ahead of us in many ways. So what first looked like an advantage for Japan's game industry—a large domestic market—has proved a handicap.

Of course, Americans still buy some Japanese games. There are many fans of, say, Super Mario, guys in their 30s and 40s who like it because they've been playing it since they were 10 and it gives them a feeling of nostalgia. But for young kids, who are just discovering games, Japanese titles don't have much to offer.

For the most part, games created for the Japanese market aren't successful outside Japan. There is a different sensibility between gamers in the the US and Japan. If you look at US games, the lead character is often nontypical. He might be bald, or some bearded old guy. In Japan we would never have a nonstandard lead character; we have a kind of cliché image of a hero or heroine. Also, overseas games are often more aggressive, with lots more violence and blood, than Japanese games.

Why? Because Japanese game developers aren't familiar with other cultures, and so far have had little incentive to learn. We find it difficult to understand these nuances. At Capcom, I argued for years that we should try to develop games tailored exclusively for Western markets. One of our early efforts was *Shadow of Rome*, which was a game involving battling gladiators. It was the right idea, but we went too far. There was a lot of hacking off of limbs; it was just too bloody. What we learned was just adding a lot of violence is not enough to make a successful game.

So we tried some variations. Eventually, I came up with *Dead Rising*, which was the same concept but involved battles with zombies instead of human gladiators. In some ways it's even gorier than *Shadow of Rome*: not only can you slice off zombie arms but, if need be, you also can pick up a severed zombie arm and fight with it. But changing from gladiators to zombies made all the difference. It was a subtle change—to the extent that zombies can be subtle—but it worked. And it worked because we took the time to figure out what non-Japanese users would accept.

Mergers and acquisitions can help Japanese game companies to acquire the technology and cultural know-how to thrive outside their home market. But these factors are only part of the solution. You can't just buy a company and say, "Okay, now we can make good games." You need to be able to retain and motivate people at the company after you've acquired it. And you need to study how people in overseas markets live, how they think, how they talk, how they play games, what motivates them to improve their game skills.

In sum, for Japanese game companies to regain their global competitiveness, they will need to invest more creatively, act less like bureaucrats, and do a better job of understanding other cultures. But even in a creative sector like games, it's hard for large, established organizations to change. Last year, after 23 years at Capcom, I decided to follow my own advice about taking risks. I left the company and have decided to strike out on my own. I want to try to change the industry. And I felt that I didn't want to end up being known only as "Capcom's Inafune." Instead, I want to build my own brand. Think of Steven Spielberg. He's not "Universal's Steven Spielberg." He's just Steven Spielberg, even though he started with Universal.

It may be too late—or too hard—to tackle the US market at this point. The next big market is China. There I see many opportunities. My sights are on Asia.

THE NEXT CHALLENGE FOR JAPAN'S ENTREPRENEURS

ALLEN MINER

THE CONVENTIONAL WISDOM is that Japan is a land of salarymen who lack the spirit of invention and entrepreneurship the country needs to break out of its economic doldrums. In fact, for more than three decades, Japan has been the most inventive country and population in the world, and over the last decade, the environment for start-ups has improved markedly. Entrepreneurship has flourished. Japan's challenge—and opportunity—is to globalize its innovation economy.

Japan leads all other countries in patents granted, according to the most recent data from the World Intellectual Property Organization (WIPO). Japanese residents earned 151,765 patents in 2008, almost double the 77,501 patents granted to residents in the United States, the second-most inventive country. Since first passing the US in 1977, Japanese, who number less than half of the US population, have earned almost 1.5 times as many patents as Americans.

Japan demonstrates global patent leadership across the board: electrical engineering and energy, transport and telecommunications, chemistry and polymers, optics and semiconductors, nanotechnology and machinery, furniture and consumer goods. In the 35 technical areas in which WIPO classifies patents, Japan was first in 26 of them; second to the US in another eight; and third, behind the US and China, in the remaining one (pharmaceuticals). Japan's R&D investment as a percentage of GDP is among the highest in the world and is growing faster than the percentage in the European Union or the US.

Those are the general trends. Now look at the specific area of non-PC-related computer technology: lifestyle IT items such as game machines, digital cameras,

Allen Miner is the founder/chairman and CEO of SunBridge Corporation.

car navigation systems, and smartphones—consumer products that include a CPU, memory, and software. That's where the bulk of the growth is in the IT industry today. The first commercially successful products in each of these categories were created in 1990s Japan, and a substantial portion of the underlying technologies and components are also made in Japan. Japan has established an ecosystem for entrepreneurs to start companies that tap into these IT innovations, and, in fact, a number of substantial domestic companies have been launched around lifestyle IT.

True, much of Japan's patent creation is taking place in large corporate labs. But that does not mean Japan lacks individual initiative. I've spent a great deal of time in these labs, and have an informed sense of the breakthroughs they have produced. What I have found is that even within big companies, innovation tends to have a highly individual dimension; it is often the result of the creativity of a person who is iconoclastic and comfortable on the edge.

The first Internet-enabled phones, console and online gaming, and the blue-light laser, for example, all began with a passionate individual willing to challenge the corporate status quo. Then a large number of people, both inside and outside the corporation, took those innovations and built products and businesses around them.

History lessons

Company formation, entrepreneurialism, and risk taking are nothing new in Japan. Of the world's 32 oldest companies, founded between the years 705 and 1192, 19 are Japanese, including the four oldest.

Historically, entrepreneurialism has been especially common during periods of great change and necessity. The postwar period, for example, saw the creation of Sony, Honda, Nintendo, Omron, and other iconic names. Recognizing that Japan was entering another period of change and necessity, in the mid-1990s, the Ministry of Economy, Trade and Industry (METI) began a systematic effort to encourage entrepreneurism. METI conducted study tours of Silicon Valley, interviewed famous US venture capitalists, and studied the legal framework between VCs and start-ups. As a result, the Japanese government completely revamped the commercial code in 2002 to make it easier to start and finance companies.

For example, when SunBridge started investing in Japan in 2000, to form a company you had to pay $100,000 in equity capital. You either had to borrow the money, line up a financer, or be rich already. Once the company got started, there was no structure for issuing stock options to motivate employees. METI addressed all these matters.

A decade ago, investment was available for companies so well-established that they were ready to go public. Few VCs invested at the seed stage in Japan, nor was there an infrastructure of knowledgeable law firms, accountants, consultants, and others to deal with companies at that stage. Between 1998 and 2000, though, the Mothers Stock Market, the Hercules Stock Market, and NASDAQ Japan all opened for business. These exchanges targeted younger companies. For the first time, VCs could invest in start-ups with a reasonable expectation that those companies would be able to go public and that the VCs could therefore exit their investment within the ten-year life of a fund. This expectation created the conditions for profitable seed investing, and support at this stage significantly increased. VCs such as SunBridge began addressing and dealing with all of the issues surrounding the process of taking a business from an idea, to a small team, to a growing and viable entity.

FROM 2000 TO 2004, JAPAN WAS ONE OF THE WORLD'S LEADERS IN THE FORMATION OF YOUNG, HIGH-GROWTH COMPANIES.

At the same time, innovators at Japan's universities began to peek out from their ivory towers. Japan's universities had long disdained MBA programs or the idea of teaching entrepreneurship. So in 2001, METI and the Education Ministry announced a joint goal to spawn a thousand university-affiliated start-ups and established technology licensing offices to promote more entrepreneurial activity around the universities and to leverage the basic research done there into support of more commercial innovation.

All this change was happening against the backdrop of the "lost years" of economic stagnation. So long and so painful was this relative decline that major companies such as Toshiba and NEC were forced to make massive layoffs. At the same time, the extraordinary growth of the Internet and mobile Internet was creating huge new opportunities. For the first time in postwar history, young Japanese entering the workforce had a meaningful choice. They could seek to do as their fathers had done—that is, join a large, prestigious corporation, albeit knowing that lifetime employment was no longer guaranteed. Or they could jump into the entrepreneurial world that offered even less security, but more opportunity. Many chose the entrepreneurial option.

In the early 2000s, Japan became one of the world's leaders in the formation of young, high-growth companies. By 2006, I began to see Japanese starting their second or third companies and referring to themselves as "serial entrepreneurs."

A few years ago, I did some research to identify which countries had recently produced the most high-growth start-ups. I considered companies that were formed after 1997, were public by 2007, and had at least 50 percent annual revenue growth from 2005 to 2007. The leaders were China, India, and the US. Japan came in fourth. But in relative terms, Japan and the US were very close: Japan, about half the size of the US in GDP terms, had about half as many high-growth start-ups. Even more interesting is that Tokyo, the city with the most Fortune 500 headquarters, was also the metropolitan area that produced the most high-growth start-ups, with ten. (Silicon Valley had six and Shanghai, four.)

Entrepreneurship, Japan-style

Recent winners of the Kigyoka Prize for Entrepreneurial Excellence have founded companies like Pia, Plus, Culture Convenience Club, Softbank, and Nidec. Each of these is a $1 billion to $6 billion company. Most were built by entrepreneurs in their 20s and 30s who shared key characteristics with their American equivalents: force of personality and a willingness to challenge the status quo. There are also a number of well-known-in-Japan Internet companies, from the $3 billion e-commerce company Rakuten to DeNA, Cyberagent, and Mixi (essentially the Facebook of Japan). All are run by aggressive, dynamic CEOs and they have produced the kind of investment returns for their angel and VC investors that would have made any Silicon Valley player proud.

Given the evidence that entrepreneurialism is alive and well in Japan, why isn't this success better known? One answer is that other than Nidec, which supplies a huge proportion of the world's hard-disk motors, few of these companies have meaningful operations outside of Japan. By contrast, look at some of Silicon Valley's stars. Within ten years of being formed, Google, salesforce.com, Netsuite, and RightNow all had significant international operations. And while Tokyo might have more high-growth start-ups, Silicon Valley creates bigger ones. Every few years, it seems, an amazing world-changing success story flies out of northern California. Those are the companies we all pay attention to, and that give the Valley its reputation.

EVEN MORE INTERESTING IS THAT TOKYO LED THE METROPOLITAN AREAS THAT PRODUCED THE HIGHEST NUMBER OF HIGH-GROWTH STARTUPS, WITH TEN. SILICON VALLEY HAD SIX; AND SHANGHAI HAD FOUR.

Japan lacks this star power. The key questions for Japan, then, are: How can the country globalize its tremendous innovation and domestic business success? Why do today's entrepreneurs, unlike their postwar forebears, build innovative, highly successful domestic companies and then stop short of going global?

The answer to the second question, I believe, is "the missing middle." There has always been a group of later-stage investors who want to be the last money in before the IPO. Because of the changes in the late 1990s and early 2000s, seed-stage capital is also now available. But, when compared to Silicon Valley, midstage growth capital is still conspicuously lacking.

The typical Japanese company at IPO on the Mothers or Hercules Exchange has somewhere between $15 million to $30 million in sales and $1 to $2 million in net profits. Its growth is good; the business model proven; the product successful. In the US, a company that size would raise $10 million or more from VCs in a midstage growth round to establish a global sales force and to continue aggressive R&D to strengthen its platform for additional growth. US venture capitalists are quite comfortable with a company operating at a loss as long as they believe that aggressive investment will accelerate growth and create a better outcome. That better outcome usually includes international success.

In contrast, public equity investors, especially in Japan, expect predictable growth and increasing margins. Once companies go public, then, they are locked into the pre-IPO condition of the business. Only organic growth is expected. Consequently, most of the Japanese companies that went public in the last decade, particularly the smaller ones, dropped into a lower rate of growth after the IPO. In effect, "the missing middle" is another way of saying that companies in Japan go public too soon, at the expense of longer-term growth.

What is the alternative? At SunBridge, we are advising Japanese companies to ignore the investment bankers and wait to go public. Reinvest profits; raise private capital; and jump-start international expansion in the US first. We are also talking to the Japanese government and VC industry about the need to fund global expansion. And we are introducing Japanese companies with global prospects to internationally-minded VCs in Silicon Valley. The pitch is relatively easy. These companies have a proven technology, a commercial product, demonstrable market traction, and established revenues and profits.

But it is not easy for Japanese companies to make it in Silicon Valley. In Japan, because there is less venture capital and a smaller market, there is also less competition. Where 30 to 40 mobile game companies started in the Valley when Java phones were introduced, maybe four or five formed in Japan. If you're competing among dozens, and win that competition, you've got a huge head start on establishing global dominance. In Japan, the likelihood of survival is higher, but the natural-selection process is less intense. What needs to happen, then, is for Japanese entrepreneurs, boards, and investors to focus on how to become globally competitive against Silicon Valley rivals.

In addition, Japanese companies often provide a high level of client-funded customization. This process leads to happy customers and moderate organic growth. But inefficient R&D spending and scalability issues surface when the company attempts to sell into larger markets with more diverse customers. By contrast, Silicon Valley companies typically focus from the outset on a universal, scalable, best-in-class product that requires no customization for new buyers and little localization for new markets. Midstage funding to develop similarly generic but world-class products will enable Japan's globalization efforts.

Change and necessity, again

Japan is entering another period of change and necessity. Change comes from the fundamental shift in the computer and IT industries from legacy software and hardware systems to cloud computing. There is also the accelerating shift to mobile computing and focused global attention on "clean tech," both areas in which Japan is a world leader. Necessity comes from changing demographics. With the country's population shrinking, Japanese companies will be required to look abroad for growth.

I am confident that Japan can navigate its way through this new era. After all, it has done so before. In the 1990s, the Japanese government, VC industry, and universities considered what needed to be done to spur entrepreneurship. Their efforts worked remarkably well. Now the discussion is about how to reach the next level. It is the right conversation, at the right time. That is why I expect Japan to meet the challenges ahead, continue its innovation leadership, expand its entrepreneurial base, and create more and truly great global companies.

EXPANDING JAPAN'S SOCIAL CAPITAL

WILLIAM H. SAITO

IN THE 1980S, people engaged in "Japan bashing." In the early 2000s, the conversation was about "Japan passing." And now the consensus is "Japan missing."

In the past two decades, the country's once-vocal critics have fallen silent, largely because the world is no longer interested in Japan (with the possible exception of *manga* and *anime*). The sad truth is that Japan is becoming increasingly irrelevant, even though it is still one of the world's biggest and strongest economies. The country deserves more attention than it receives.

Japan bashing was never useful. But there is value in constructive criticism, especially if it offers a carefully considered examination of the issues or characteristics that may be holding the country back. I have spent my career in and around venture businesses, as an entrepreneur, an investor, and a judge of venture competitions worldwide, and I've developed some strong views about what works and what doesn't in growing young companies. Some of the problems I see in Japan today are social capital issues that must be addressed if the country is to experience the growth of a vibrant economy.

My recommendations might seem unusual, coming from someone with a technological background. But one thing I have learned from my career is that sometimes an indirect route is the best way to bring about the kind of change that is needed. Here are three paths I believe Japan might follow in order to invent a more promising, more dynamic future.

1. Build global social capital

My experiences in managing and evaluating many business ventures—from high-tech start-ups to established global competitors—have convinced me that

William H. Saito is an expert in the fields of encryption, authentication and biometric technology.

certain characteristics for success are universal. Among the most important is a sense of perspective.

The broader a person's outlook and experience, the better he or she will grasp changes, understand opportunities and challenges, and perceive market relevance. How does one gain such a perspective? One way is to read and study about different aspects of the world, and Japanese people are adept at that. From my teaching experiences at universities both in Japan and overseas, I have had a chance to observe hundreds of students. I have found Japanese students to be extremely bright and well-informed. And yet, something important is lacking. There's a huge difference between accumulating knowledge about the world and experiencing it firsthand.

Japanese students have a far narrower range of experiences than their counterparts in the United States or Europe. In the West, when young people go off to university, they often find themselves thrown together with people from vastly different religious, ethnic, cultural, and ideological backgrounds. They are exposed to a variety of studies and perspectives, both in and out of the classroom. Moreover, the general education courses required at most US universities are designed to broaden students' perspectives early on so that they will make informed choices about their major field of study and, eventually, their careers.

SOCIAL HOMOGENEITY HAS MANY ADVANTAGES, BUT THE DEVELOPMENT OF BROAD, VISIONARY THINKING IS NOT ONE OF THEM.

In contrast, Japanese universities attract few foreign students, and few Japanese students study abroad. This in itself is a problem. Also, Japanese students generally choose and then focus on their field of specialty early in their academic careers, so that four years at a Japanese university, however prestigious or difficult to enter, does not represent the same kind of stimulating, personally broadening experience that students in other developed economies encounter. Even at Japan's best universities, too many students lack key qualities possessed by their counterparts (and in today's interconnected world, their future rivals) from other countries. Japanese students memorize large quantities of raw information without exposure to the sort of creative problem solving that is further developed, challenged, and tempered by numerous encounters with people of different backgrounds.

Japan is certainly not homogenous in the sense that all its citizens think or act alike. But in important ways, compared with much of the rest of the world, the country's population seems homogeneous. While homogeneity has many advantages for society, the development of broad, visionary thinking is not one of them. In my dealings not only with Japan's university students, but also with the country's corporate executives, politicians, and government officials, I find, to my frustration, that a lack of cultural interaction has created intellectual myopia. For example, when I showed a newly released iPhone to the president of a major Japanese electronics maker, he was totally unimpressed: "Our phones have most of the same functions if not more." The idea that a cell phone was more than the sum of its parts, that it could be a platform for a myriad of independent applications, or that his company should be developing value-added platforms that would attract people from all over the world to create software and services to run on his company's products, simply did not reach him.

Traveling almost constantly, I find great value in immersing myself in foreign cultures and ways of thinking. The goal is not to mimic any particular culture or society, but to learn from them all. The more intellectually (and culturally, philosophically, and spiritually) diverse your environment, the greater the potential to grow as an individual and the more value you can bring to any company or organization. In a globalized world, this outlook constitutes essential social capital—and it is missing in Japan.

In the 1860s and 1870s, the Meiji oligarchs sent some of their "best and brightest" on overseas missions to learn about the world outside Japan. The famous Iwakura Mission included both government ministers and university students, and many of the students (including several women) stayed on in foreign countries to continue their studies. The government understood that gaining firsthand experience and perspective on the world was essential to Japan's survival.

To reclaim a global perspective, Japan's future leaders must expand their comfort zone. The ideal time to start doing so is during their university years. The first step would be for the government to partner with other stakeholders to finance and promote scholarships for study abroad. For this approach to have the desired effect, private industry also has to adapt by changing traditional hiring practices, for instance, expanding the strictly defined hiring season and eliminating the stigma of *chuto sayo* ("in between" hiring into a company). Society, too, must change. For example, many Japanese parents discourage their children from taking up such opportunities. When I offered two promising students four-year scholarships abroad, both declined the offer at the urging of their parents. I found this refusal an eye-opening experience.

The world outside can look frightening to those who have not been there. A more important consideration for these parents was the fear that anything that separates their child from the peer group creates a competitive disadvantage later when that child is up for a promotion. And the way things work in Japan now, these parents are right. That assumption needs to change. I believe that nothing will produce a higher "return on investment" for Japanese universities, companies, and government organizations than a steady flow of new, globally minded talent.

2. Encourage a culture of empathy through volunteering

At my high school in California, every student had to perform 100 hours of community service in order to advance to the next grade level. The focus was not on impersonal activities like cleaning up a park, but on providing meaningful service to the less privileged people in our community. Volunteering to help people instills the idea in young minds that "giving back" to society is a natural part of life. Young people discover that volunteering pays rich dividends in community appreciation, self-esteem, compassion, humility, and gratitude. Equally important, they learn that asking for help is nothing to be ashamed of.

Japan would benefit from such a program for a number of reasons. First, it would help young people learn empathy for others, and thus grow into compassionate adults. Second, it would lead people of all ages to reflect on their own strengths and weaknesses. And third, it would teach people to ask for help when they need it and both give and receive assistance from others as a matter of course.

A broader, deeper culture of empathy could also help to energize the business environment. One of the main reasons so few venture businesses appear in Japan and far fewer succeed is that people in established companies, in banks, and so on, feel no sense of responsibility toward, or even kinship with, individuals who build their own businesses. Reaching out to help others is essential to help a venture business succeed, just as employees willing to help each other inside a start-up company are essential to its success. Many Japanese are too concerned with their own department, their own company, their own clients. The empathy response to help others, especially those who are somehow disadvantaged, is just not there. This characteristic is evident not only in the lack of support for venture business but also in the abysmally low level of philanthropy in Japan.

Conspicuously absent on Japanese campuses: non-Japanese students and faculty.

© Tomohiro Ohsumi/Bloomberg via Getty Images

Empathy is important because it applies directly to a nation's ability to germinate and cultivate new businesses: start-up companies are all disadvantaged. Venture businesses are handicapped by a lack of experienced management, lack of access to capital, and lack of ability to attract talented employees. Ventures succeed when people in the business community see the potential of such companies and offer different kinds of assistance to help them grow.

While the effects of a large-scale volunteer program are impossible to estimate, one result would certainly be an increase in personal empathy, a greater feeling of kinship with and responsibility to help others in need. Businesspeople would feel more inclined to help rather than hinder others, both within their companies and in the business community at large. In this sense, the growth of venture business—which I see as essential to invigorating this economy—will rely at least as much on individual and corporate assistance as on government support. So, as volunteerism promotes empathy, it not only "humanizes" society but indirectly helps to energize the economy.

3. Break through the glass ceiling

In a future in which business will be under extreme pressure to eliminate waste and increase efficiency, it's hard to see how Japan can continue to underutilize half its population: women. The higher ranks of corporate Japan, in particular, are astonishingly lacking in women.

According to the 2009 report Corporate Women Directors International (CWDI), women accounted for only 17 of roughly 1,200 seats on the boards of Japan's 100 biggest companies—1.4 percent. Japan even lagged behind Arab countries, such as Oman, Jordan, and Kuwait, in the number of women directors its companies had. Some of the most truly international Japanese firms were the worst offenders. When the report was written, Toyota, Nissan, Honda, Panasonic, and Toshiba did not have a single woman director.

WOMEN HOLD A MINUSCULE 1.4 PERCENT OF THE BOARD SEATS IN JAPAN'S LEADING COMPANIES, LESS THAN IN OMAN, JORDAN, AND KUWAIT.

Japan's top universities turn out large numbers of exceptionally bright, talented women who then cannot find suitable employment in Japanese companies. In a phenomenon known as "gender arbitrage," Western firms are hiring these overachieving women, giving them responsible positions and good salaries. Japanese companies are missing out on this talent pool.

The biggest problem Japanese firms have in promoting women to directorships is that there are so few female managers to promote. Even companies whose customers are all women are generally run by men. In other words, a bias in hiring and a quite low glass ceiling after a woman enters a Japanese company create a self-perpetuating situation.

From any perspective, getting more women into work is the only economically rational choice for Japan. The population is both aging and shrinking; there is substantial resistance to increasing immigration; and the economy desperately needs ways to revitalize growth.

A recent study by Goldman Sachs examined this assertion and concluded that if the rate of female participation in the labor force rate could be raised to that of men (almost 80 percent), it would create more than 8 million jobs and add as much as 15 percent to the country's GDP. Because Japan is the only advanced industrialized nation with such a huge, skilled, untapped resource, the country has a golden opportunity to accelerate growth quickly and sustainably.

Conclusion

Changing Japan in these three areas—studying abroad, cultivating volunteerism, and promoting women—would be catalytic for society as a whole. One important area that could benefit is venture capital.

While it is true that Japanese corporations and financial institutions make microinvestments in venture companies, an American-style venture capital industry does not exist. The VC community in Japan is derided, perhaps harshly but not unfairly, as "very conservative" or even "very cowardly." There have been many attempts, especially at the Ministry of Economy, Trade and Industry (METI), to kick-start the entrepreneurial process. Several programs give loosely defined grants of between

$100,000 and $1 million to exceptional researchers and projects in universities or research labs. Unfortunately, many researchers use this money simply to fund more research, not to build businesses. In the past few years, these investments have returned less than 1 percent on average, compared with 3.9 percent for private venture capital, according to a 2009 Japan Venture Research report.

There are also government-backed VC companies that were created to invest both private and public money in entrepreneurial ventures. Unfortunately, these programs lack the kind of real-world experience that is essential to understanding the challenges facing venture companies. While the ideals underlying these and similar government programs are noble, they have become a moral hazard to Japanese entrepreneurs. Simply put, governments are not good at picking winners, nor should they be trying to do so.

In the United States, the principals of venture capital companies are usually former entrepreneurs themselves, so they understand the problems intimately. American VCs also expect to take an active role in their investees, not merely injecting cash but also offering hands-on management skills, personal contacts, and more. For every dollar in cash a venture capitalist invests, he also invests a dollar of know-how.

In Japan, venture capitalists typically take only observer seats, with no voting rights, on a company's board. These directors' ostensible purpose is to protect the VC firm from liability and criticism. The VC provides only small levels of capital and no management advice. This inactive, risk-phobic approach will never support a healthy venture economy.

To be successful, a venture capitalist must understand the needs of entrepreneurs and truly want to help them succeed, and must also understand the dynamics of the marketplace. Obviously, these qualities echo the three priorities I have identified for the Japanese economy.

Like the economy as a whole, the VC industry needs well-educated, insightful, analytical people—male or female. It needs creative problem solvers imbued with a broad, global perspective. And it needs people with the ability to understand multiple perspectives and a genuine desire to help other people become successful—an empathy that can be sparked through volunteerism at an early age.

I firmly believe that if Japan could harness only a fraction of the power in its disenfranchised female workers and foster a new generation with a broader global outlook and a willingness to help others, the country would not only revitalize its economy, but also become a model, once again, for other nations to emulate.

BUILDING STRENGTH THROUGH UNIQUENESS

JOHN CHAMBERS AND EDZARD J. C. OVERBEEK

THE BEAUTY OF JAPAN is renowned throughout the world; the country is celebrated for the refinement of its culture; its attention to detail; its operational excellence; its high standards and values.

Japanese society is, in part, defined by the great traditions of its rich history. These traditions are ingrained in its people and corporations. The country's greatest challenge is respecting these traditions, which in many ways define how Japanese companies work, while simultaneously instilling the flexibility and agility needed to thrive.

When we at Cisco meet our peers in Japan, we see that most companies understand global market dynamics. Implementing innovative approaches to benefit from those dynamics, however, is often difficult. Business practices and culture are never easy to change anywhere, of course, but Japan's particularly robust culture means challenging the status quo is more difficult still. However, once everyone in a Japanese company gets on the same, new page, the power of the culture allows its leaders to execute brilliantly.

Strategy and services

Japan is not a research and development center for Cisco. But the country's strengths in product quality, reliability, and attention to detail in process and technical refinement, are differentiating values. Japan is an important center for refining and perfecting new Cisco product categories and solutions created in our global centers of innovation. We coordinate closely with key customers in Japan.

John Chambers is chairman and CEO of Cisco. Edzard J. C. Overbeek is Cisco's president, Asia-Pacific and Japan.

Japan is also a key strategic market for us, particularly in the service-provider, enterprise, and small-business segments. Even during the past three trying economic years, Cisco's presence in Japan grew steadily.

The service-provider segment is particularly important. The standards used by Japanese service providers are world-class. New technologies, such as IPv6, LTE, and 4G, often are evaluated, tested, and implemented first in Japan. These "firsts" position Japan's telecommunications companies for leadership and provide the enterprises they serve with a golden opportunity to become the hub of a more global, "central nerve-system" for business. Japanese service providers are already exploring how new IT infrastructure concepts such as cloud computing can help them offer additional services. Such investments will further strengthen Japan's ability to increase productivity and create sustainable competitive advantage.

The Japanese government has recently begun to catalyze this type of innovation through investment and regulatory change; as a result, Japan has one of the world's most sophisticated broadband infrastructures. Japan needs to accelerate the adoption of these technologies to encourage the creation of new business models, solutions, and services.

For many years, Cisco has been working with Japanese stakeholders to discuss policy and regulatory frameworks for an innovative information and communications technology blueprint, including next-generation networks designed specifically for the Japanese market. In some cases, these networks are one to two years ahead of the rest of the world. They can host a range of data, voice, and video-enabled capabilities that could stimulate the development of online solutions and services, and thus create exciting new business opportunities.

Creating global buzz

To realize this potential, however, Japan will need to augment its outstanding credentials in quality, process, and technical excellence with a stronger entrepreneurial spirit. This spirit has historically been at odds with the traditional, and in many cases risk-averse, ways of thinking within the Japanese business culture.

According to the 2008 Global Entrepreneurship Monitor, only 26 percent of Japanese (compared with 69 percent of South Koreans and 63 percent of Americans) considered entrepreneurship a desirable career choice, by far the lowest figure of the 43 countries surveyed. In another measurement, Japan's total entrepreneurship activity (TEA) as a percent of GDP ranked last among 65 countries surveyed, at just 3.3 percent in 2009. The figure for the United States was 12.9 percent; even France, at 4.6 percent, had significantly higher TEA.

There are several things that Japan can do to change this attitude, starting with the broadband opportunities discussed earlier. A second initiative is to create an "Entrepreneurs Fund'" to funnel seed investment to students to start new ventures. Another idea is to design tax-beneficial schemes for companies to open centers of innovation or entrepreneurs' facilities, perhaps with special treatment for intellectual property.

Ultimately, the goal should be to create global buzz around "made-in-Japan."

Japan needs an innovation ecosystem like the one that sustains Silicon Valley, stimulating and maximizing returns from entrepreneurship. Of course, everyone would like to have the next Silicon Valley, and Japan has tried before. But it is important to keep trying. Entrepreneurship is at the core of innovation, and is a critical element for any country that wants to continue to create and evolve.

The evidence is that where Japan puts its will and its passion, it can be a world-class innovator. Japan is way ahead of the rest of the world in the use of robots and is a leader in the use of virtual technologies. Other industries in Japan, for example cars and consumer electronics, have hit a few bumps but are still world class.

Furthermore, we can see Japan taking on a far more active role in environmental technologies. Aggressive emissions-reduction targets may help make Japan a leader in the implementation of emerging "smart" grid technologies. The country is tops in the photovoltaic market, with a 45 percent market share.

Cultural evolutions

If Japan can figure out how to connect its leadership in communications and networking technologies to its unique culture, it could assure its place atop the global order for a long time to come. Doing so, however, will likely require another cultural shift.

Japan and its corporations prize the natural hierarchies of their society. Differences in status, whether based on academic achievement, position, or age, play a key role in day-to-day business. While the positive impact of such strong values cannot be underestimated, such norms naturally perpetuate hierarchical organizational structures in which only a small percentage of staff are expected or invited to contribute to innovation.

Japan has a tremendous opportunity to use its Internet leadership to evolve these structures in a way that fosters, rather than discourages, innovation. The Internet and social networking are redefining how corporations work. The next generation of dynamic networked organizations (DNO) is facilitating intelligent and dynamic interactions among knowledge workers. These workers use all kinds of social media (voicemail, instant messaging, microblogging, telepresence, and web conferencing) to make and implement decisions in real time.

You can liken this organizational change to an evolution from serial processing (doing one or few tasks at a time) to parallel processing (doing enormous numbers of tasks simultaneously and therefore finding faster, better, more detailed answers). We believe these knowledge-based organizations will be the foundation for 21st-century business. For a start, they can help to capture individual insights through collaborative social media. This activity, in turn, can become a major source of innovation.

Consider how this DNO concept could be applied to Japan, itself a social organism of extraordinary complexity and exclusivity. There are many unwritten social rules that only Japanese (and a handful of foreigners) know, and certain ways of doing things that everyone understands. If that social intelligence could be automated and connected into a collaborative platform, the result could be powerful.

For example, many Japanese do not like to present in public; therefore, their knowledge is not easily shared or distributed. At the same time, though, the Japanese are passionate adopters of digital social media. Encouraging more digital openness, then, could enable knowledge-sharing on an unprecedented scale. Unleashed via social media, Japan's unique social dynamics could become a real competitive advantage.

UNLEASHED VIA SOCIAL MEDIA, JAPAN'S UNIQUE SOCIAL DYNAMICS COULD BECOME A REAL COMPETITIVE ADVANTAGE.

If Japanese corporations look beyond their coastline, they will see that their global counterparts are already embracing these new ways of working. The best Japanese companies are already using social networking, too. For example, they are rotating their top talent in positions around the globe to expose these workers to experiences in different markets. When these executives return to Japan, they have a broader, deeper perspective on the world.

But these executives have to be careful not to be perceived as "Westernized Japanese," and thus in conflict with the way things are done in Japan. Still, these broadly based businesspeople know what is out there, and they know long term where to take the company, providing they can show respect to their culture, build trust, and create a collective notion of what change is needed. This effort can be time consuming and of course will not always happen, but the direction is clear.

Many Japanese companies understand what is happening. They recognize that to succeed globally, they need to be a *part* of globalization.

We believe Japan's corporate leaders see the choice before them very clearly. They can remain an economic powerhouse by adopting new, differentiated strategies that depend on a strong connection to the global economy. Or they can resist change and run the risk of become an introverted, isolated economy.

Theoretically, Japan could go either way. At Cisco, we don't see the country moving in the direction of introversion; at least in our business, we don't believe the "Galapagos Syndrome" is an issue.

Japan is, after all, one of the largest investors in China, where many skeptics were sure the two countries would never be able to work together. But work together they do, and it is this kind of pragmatic, innovative thinking that will form the basis for a reimagined Japan in the 21st century.

Japanese leaders know what is at stake and what it will take to keep Japan as an economic powerhouse. A strategy based on thinking globally and acting locally will deliver the best returns for Japan, now and in the future.

CAN JAPAN KEEP ITS CLEAN-TECH ADVANTAGE?

DAVID HENDERSON, PHILIPP RADTKE, AND SAKAE SUZUKI

MANY JAPANESE COMPANIES lead their sectors in the field of clean technology. It is tempting to conclude that in clean tech, as in the auto industry, the Japanese will remain formidable global competitors in decades to come, regardless of the uncertain outlook for the broader economy. In fact, however, Japan's lead in clean tech has become more precarious than is generally understood. Competitors from around the world are aggressively challenging the country's entrenched clean-tech leaders, threatening to filch billions of dollars of potential business in decades to come.

To stay ahead, Japanese companies must be faster on their feet and aggressively pursue scale and global reach. They have the capabilities needed to remain out front—world-class technology and quality management—but their responses over the next few years will determine whether they retain a global leadership role.

The clean-tech opportunity is huge, offers an economic lifeline to a country beset by declining domestic demand, and gives Japan an opportunity to play a role in crafting the solution to one of the largest global issues. McKinsey has found that more than 99 percent of the total investment required to address carbon dioxide abatement in 2020—69.6 trillion yen (about $840 billion)—will be made outside of Japan. In April 2009, Japan's Ministry of Economy, Trade, and Industry forecast that the global market for "green" goods and services could grow by 40 percent over the decade from 2005, reaching 49 trillion yen ($590 billion) and creating 2.6 million new jobs by 2015. That is roughly the same size as today's global automobile market and just under 1 percent of worldwide GDP.

David Henderson is a consultant; Philipp Radtke is a senior partner; and Sakae Suzuki is a consultant in McKinsey's Tokyo office.

Japan has a green-technology advantage, reflected in its relatively low figure of emissions per dollar of GDP: 0.25 kilograms per dollar, compared with 0.54 kilograms in the United States and 2.76 in China. Since 1990, sectors such as cement, chemicals, and steel have reduced their absolute level of emissions by more than 6 percent through higher energy efficiency and the deployment of new technology, even as they expanded. Japan boasts some of the world's most carbon-efficient industrial companies, which will have substantial business opportunities as green-tech markets emerge.

Japanese companies maintain a competitive advantage in many clean-tech fields, including electric and hybrid vehicles, solar, and carbon capture and storage. They lead in the secondary-materials and equipment industries and offer highly competitive technologies in gallium, glass, indium, and silicon—materials essential for producing solar panels. Japan is also a leader in industrial sectors like electrical power equipment. Both Toshiba and Hitachi stand out with their nuclear and carbon-capture-and-storage technologies.

METI ESTIMATES THAT THE GLOBAL MARKET FOR GREEN GOODS AND SERVICES COULD REACH $590 BILLION BY 2015.

Meanwhile, Japanese automakers enjoy an advantage in hybrid and electric vehicles. Toyota's well-known Prius, the first mass-produced hybrid, went on sale in Japan in 1997. Now marketed worldwide, the Prius has already achieved sales of more than two million units. Nissan's Leaf—a midsize, five-door hatchback electric with an average range of 160 kilometers—started shipping in December 2010 in Japan and the United States. It has already received preorders exceeding its 2011 sales targets, and Nissan expects to sell millions of units a year by 2015. Further up the value chain, Japanese players hold at least 80 percent of global market share in automotive batteries, motors, and other important components for electric vehicles.

That's the good news. But in reality, Japan's lead is narrowing in many industries. Chinese and South Korean companies have made big strides in cutting the cost of production, giving them a competitive edge as products commoditize. They also benefit from government financial support. Europeans have gained significantly in areas such as solar, biomass, and transportation. These companies too receive government aid to spur domestic demand for green goods. In the United States, vibrant new business models and technologies have emerged, bolstered by healthy funding from venture capital and the Obama administration's economic stimulus.

One clean-tech sector where the Japanese lead has clearly shrunk is solar panels. From 2001 to 2008, the global share of crystalline silicon solar-panel shipments from Japanese companies fell to 35 percent, from 41 percent, as new companies—such as Germany's Q-Cells—challenged their Japanese rivals. Over this same period, global production rose 18-fold, while Japanese production grew only eight times. In addition to facing a silicon shortage, Japanese companies mistimed their investments, leaving them with insufficient capacity to meet global demand. Meanwhile, competitors in China, Germany, Taiwan, and the United States quickly captured market share, thanks to timely investments and well-executed strategies capitalizing on new regulations to reduce greenhouse gas emissions.

Competitors are also eating into the Japanese lead in electric vehicles. One of the first sectors to face competition will be battery components like cathodes and anodes, which are on their way to becoming commodities. A low cost base will help Chinese companies, in particular, take a leading position in manufacturing and supplying these products.

What really threatens Japan's lead in clean tech is a frontal assault by entrepreneurs in Silicon Valley and other places around the globe. Worldwide venture capital investment in clean tech rose to $5.6 billion in 2009 as the number of deals in China, Europe, India, Israel, and North America exceeded 550. Solar energy was the leading category, with 21 percent of venture capital investment dollars in clean tech. During 2009, these investments outpaced those in software, biotechnology, and all other industry sectors. Moreover, 32 clean-tech IPOs around the world raised $4.7 billion in 2009.

© Illustration by Phil Couzens.

Although Asia accounted for fewer than 10 percent of global IPOs before 2009, in that year about 50 percent of clean-tech IPOs involved Chinese companies. In contrast, Japan's venture capital market makes roughly the same number of deals as the US market every year, but the size of an average deal is only one-quarter of the US average. Such small deals, in turn, are frequently insufficient to finance the basic research needed for commercializing many new technologies. Large Japanese companies, moreover, do not make up for this lack of funding; many are risk averse.

While the investment sums are eye opening, more impressive is the variety of innovations that receive funds. Here's a sampling: synthetic crude oil (crude, made from engineered algae, that can be refined into gasoline, diesel, or even jet fuel), thin-film photovoltaics (solar panels that use relatively inexpensive materials and manufacturing processes), syngas (synthetic gas made by gasifying solid waste), and high-altitude wind (turbine-bearing balloons that can intercept powerful, reliable breezes at altitudes of 300 to 5,000 meters).

THAT MOST OF THE INNOVATIONS WILL FAIL IS NOT AT ISSUE. WHAT MATTERS IS THAT A SELECT FEW WILL SUCCEED, AND THAT THESE MAY BECOME "CATEGORY KILLERS" THAT WIPE OUT COMPETING TECHNOLOGIES.

Most of the innovations will probably fail. What matters is that a select few will succeed and that these may become category killers, so disruptive that they wipe out competing technologies. Such innovations could be the greatest threat to Japanese companies. How can they maintain their lead in the face of intensifying overseas competition? Our review of global success cases identified several critical areas where Japanese executives should focus their attention.

- *Scale.* The market will grow to trillions of yen a year by mid-decade in many segments of clean tech. To take advantage of the opportunity, Japanese companies should prepare to finance and ramp up mass production. Surviving at small scale will be virtually impossible, since most clean-tech products are commodities; success will be measured, in large part, by cost performance, especially in cement, chemicals, lightweight materials, lithium-ion batteries, solar panels, and steel. The global market for such technologies will resemble the memory chip market much more than it will most high-tech or consumer electronics markets.

- *Speed.* In the past, green technologies, such as solar power and electric vehicles, took several decades to mature. Today's clean-tech market is evolving rapidly. This is no time for baby steps. Most US-based venture capital firms have horizons of no more than ten years, from first investment to exit. Among new clean-tech ventures, this mechanism will force rapid innovation, leading to a pace similar to that of the dot-com era or to the recent explosion of social networking. Japanese companies must adapt their product-development processes to achieve faster results, sometimes with less polished but usable technologies.

- *Globalization.* To maximize the clean-tech opportunity, it will be necessary to play on a global stage. Japanese companies must improve their ability to scan for opportunities around the world, to build relationships with business and government leaders in key markets, and to cultivate alliances with overseas business partners. Access to talent and technology is another reason to look abroad. Many Japanese companies share similar approaches, such as Sharp's and Sanyo's parallel bet on amorphous-silicon thin-film solar technology. Mixing with companies outside the country could spur new thinking and breakthrough ideas.

- *Mergers and acquisitions.* Overseas M&A could help Japan gain access to important markets more rapidly than might be possible through organic growth alone. By helping Japanese companies to promote their world-class technologies abroad, such purchases would boost their competitiveness and profitability, and the yen's current strength could facilitate deal making. In electrical vehicles, for instance, these companies might consider more aggressive investments in lithium-ion battery technologies, focusing on Chinese and South Korean players. Buying stakes in such overseas competitors would offer a low-cost base for Japanese OEMs, as well as provide upside growth potential for investors. Significant investments, coupled with technical alliances, would increase the likelihood of success.

Japanese companies must improve their M&A skills to make such investments worthwhile strategically, operationally, and financially. Among those skills: quicker decision making during negotiations, improved assessments and planning to capture value from synergies after acquisitions, and increased transparency to empower and provide incentives for managers at acquired businesses.

● ● ●

Japanese companies can remain global leaders in clean tech and help solve some of the most pressing environmental issues of our day. Their world-class technology should allow them to benefit from the growing demand for clean-tech products. Will they do enough to maintain their lead?

CHAPTER EIGHT: REFRESHING THE TALENT POOL

Photograph © Kazuhiro Nogi/AFP/Getty Images

TOWARD
A NEW MEIJI

TAKUMI SHIBATA

PEOPLE IN TODAY'S JAPAN seem content with what they have. They are very conservative, with a stagnant mentality, an isolationist drift. Their mindset is similar to the one that predominated in Japan during the latter half of the Tokugawa period (1603–1868), when the country's doors were closed to the rest of the world. Fortunately, that era was followed by the vigor and dynamism of the Meiji period (1868–1912), when Japan embraced the world. Unfortunately, I don't see another Meiji on the horizon, but we must try to rekindle that positive energy.

Japan's current public policies focus the country's priorities on pensions, healthcare, agriculture, and the like. Of course, it is very important to have an effective social safety net. But we also need to channel energy and resources toward building the future. We need to help young people, who are finding it increasingly difficult to find a proper job.

Unemployment in developed countries is one of the dark sides of globalization. Countries other than Japan have it much worse, of course. In France, the unemployment rate of those under age 25 has been above 20 percent for years. In Spain and Italy, the youth unemployment rate has sometimes gone above 40 percent. In Japan, however, full employment has been an important piece of the social contract; hence, a youth unemployment rate above 10 percent is clearly troubling in our society. In 2009, the employment rate of recent university graduates fell sharply, and because of the rigidity of Japanese employment practices, many of these people could end up as low wage earners forever. In addition, the number of young people working temporarily has risen. I think we, in Japan, need to pay greater attention to the young by training and valuing them differently.

Takumi Shibata is deputy president and COO of Nomura Holdings.

Post-Lehman, Nomura became a much bigger player on the Tokyo Stock Exchange.
© Toru Yamanaka/AFP/Getty Images

The only proper education students receive these days is at the best high schools and in corporate training programs. Otherwise, the Japanese education system simply misses the point. Looking back, I was a nonconformist student who didn't always follow the teacher's instructions; occasionally I was reprimanded for being a free thinker in exams or in class. Self-confident students can get away with that free-thinking attitude, but it should be encouraged in general.

The most important thing an education should deliver is the ability to think with an independent mind. The country's educational system needs a paradigm shift away from rote learning—unfortunately, still the focus of our education system— and toward the ability to think. Second, education should train people to reach a conclusion and to produce a solution. And third, the education system needs to provide a global perspective, away from Japan's "island mentality" and toward a "sailor's mentality." Our students need to get off the island and learn from the world.

In Japanese companies, it is very easy to find people who can follow instructions, which, unfortunately, is what most people in their 20s and early 30s are asked to do, even today. Because these workers have been neither schooled nor trained to think independently, they lack this critical skill when their employers start to demand it of them later in their careers. The country's education system creates a huge gap between the skills Japanese employees possess and the skills they need to succeed in today's world.

The reality is that the only thing certain in this world is uncertainty. To respond to uncertainty, one must exercise judgment. Instead, our social system essentially assumes that the world never changes. As a society, we place too much emphasis on succeeding in high school and on getting into the top Japanese universities, as if those who succeed at that stage will be winners forever. But the world does not work that way; it requires continuous learning and the ability to take initiative.

I saw this employee-skills deficit clearly in the aftermath of Nomura's 2008 acquisition of Lehman's Asian and European assets. Lehman was a good fit for us because over 20 years, we had not invested enough in globalizing our business and our organization. Nomura essentially exported and imported Japanese money and financial products—a shrinking, bilateral business in a growing, multi-polar world. The deal with Lehman gave us a chance to jump ahead and become a more global player. Before the Lehman acquisition, Nomura's market capital was the equivalent of about 6 percent of the total value of the Tokyo Stock Exchange; since the acquisition, our market capital is worth about 12 percent of the TSE.

What the acquisition of Lehman made apparent to me was the profiles of people who were successful: they were proactive and positive, and had no inclination to take their status for granted. As we began integrating the two companies, we appointed new senior managing directors from the ranks of both Japanese and non-Japanese. We wanted to find people who had the power to think for themselves, to challenge conventional beliefs, and to innovate. It was a process of discovery—a pleasant sort of discovery—to find the depth of talent that we had. The process confirmed that while good business leaders do exist, they are revealed through a kind of natural elimination. Not surprisingly, there was no correlation between employees' actual talent on the job and the scores they achieved in their high school years.

JAPAN'S EDUCATION SYSTEM MUST HELP YOUNG JAPANESE ABANDON THEIR CURRENT "ISLAND MENTALITY" AND DEVELOP A "SAILOR'S MENTALITY" INSTEAD.

Independence of mind is a key trait of leaders. While Japanese companies are good at *discovering or recognizing* leaders, I do not think enough of them are good at *producing* leaders—those people who can help their companies achieve big and bold progress. To create more leaders, among other things, companies need to change their incentive systems. Current practice encourages people not to take risks, not to make decisions, not to make enemies, and to stay in their organizations as long as possible.

With more leaders and a reformed education system, Japan could recapture some of the optimism of its Meiji era. I can imagine the future Japan as one of the richer countries in the world and one of the richer islands in a sea of prosperous Asian economies. Japan would take pride in its quality of education, its philosophy, and its ethics. It would be a peace-loving and environmentally friendly place.

Getting there will require a long process of large-scale change, not just one event. Japan is not on that track at the moment, unfortunately. But it might not be too late now to start.

UNLEASHING THE POWER OF YOUTH

MOTOYA OKADA

THERE ARE TWO THINGS I find most striking when I think about the Japan of recent years. The first is the population's aging, which is affecting society in general as well as private companies. We are aging at a rapid rate, and what worries me most is our young people. Japanese society has in many senses abandoned its youth, especially over the past 15 years. Companies are cutting back on hiring in order to protect older workers' jobs. The result has been an explosion of the younger and socially vulnerable forced into unstable irregular work—"freeters" (part-time freelancers) and temps.

Our "gray society" has led to this situation in which "the old" hold onto power in our private companies, the bureaucracy, and the political sphere. This power leads to organizations that are increasingly conservative, rigid, and noncompetitive. Looking at my own company, I find that I have been sitting in the president's chair for over 14 years and the top executives involved in our decision-making processes are getting on in years.

For an organization to remain competitive, it needs to have a younger generation that aggressively exerts leadership. Obviously, we should not ignore the experience and abilities of older workers, but it is important that we reassign them to other positions and not keep them on as leaders.

Sure, young people sometimes make mistakes. The point is that we need to create a society in which they are allowed to make mistakes as long as they keep trying to tackle ambitious challenges. Otherwise, Japanese competitiveness will continue to wane.

To take an example from my own company, one of the business issues we face is how to move into China and ASEAN. For people of my generation, China is viewed

---

Motoya Okada is president of AEON.

as a special country. We get caught up in wartime history and the image of a Communist state.

Young people do not have such prejudices. Jusco, one of AEON's largest subsidiaries, started off as a small distribution firm based in Kansai. We then shifted our headquarters to Tokyo and started opening outlets throughout Japan. We can take the same approach to entering the Chinese market. The power to enter this way comes from youth. Whether and how we cede this authority to young people is a major question for both our company and Japan as a whole.

At our company, we created something we call the Leadership Development Committee to bring the power of youth into our management in a substantive way. I direct this committee for middle management in their 30s and 40s. We identify younger people who have a reputation for excellence in the head office, subsidiaries, and stores, and interview various people to gather 360-degree feedback. We then use the results of these interviews to assign special missions and business opportunities. We want to give young employees a chance, and we want them to provide

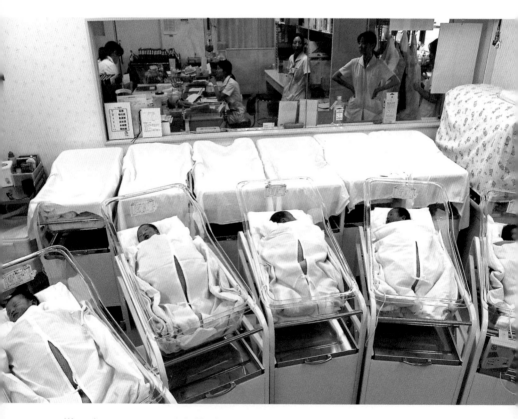

Wanted: a younger generation of leaders.
© Robert Gilhooly/epa/Corbis

new energy and vigor for the company as a whole. We have been focusing on young workers for over ten years and these efforts have produced a number of exciting ideas and innovations for us.

More than 10 years ago, our company abandoned the seniority-based wage system. We do not pay attention to employees' gender or education either; I do not even know from which institutions the other executives graduated. What is important to remember here is that these kinds of systems that seem obvious and commonplace today were in fact the results of decisions made about 15 years ago by people who came before us. We are the ones benefiting from the decisions of our predecessors.

We too must form an image of what Japanese society and companies will look like in another 10 or 20 years and make decisions accordingly—and there are a lot of decisions to make.

> JAPAN'S LARGE COMPANIES SHOULD DELEGATE MORE RESPONSIBILITY TO YOUNGER MANAGERS.

The decision about ceding authority to young people is among them. Another decision is to hire foreign workers and have them work alongside and on an equal footing with Japanese. But even before senior people begin to give young people authority, it is important that we proactively share our abundant experience, knowledge, and expertise with them. As managers, we tend to focus on protecting the current workforce, but we need to think about creating jobs for the next generation in the broader context of society as a whole and not think only about our own employees.

Japan is an aging country, and one of the duties of our generation is therefore to train the young people who will make our country and our companies strong and give them opportunities to work and advance.

The other pressing question I see is what Japan must do in order to become a true leader in Asia. I think two perspectives are of particular importance. The first is a decision to accept immigrants. Demographic trends clearly show that there will be a rapid decline in Japan's population. Japan is one of the most prosperous and free countries in Asia, and we need to accept people who want to move to Japan and achieve happiness as a result of their resourcefulness and hard work. Our willingness to accept immigrants is one of the responsibilities that Japan has to Asia, and it is also an effective policy for preventing population decline. What is important in this is that we Japanese have pride and confidence in our own country.

Large numbers of immigrants will mean exposure to many different ideas and customs. Some of these immigrants may find adapting to the customs and culture of Japanese society difficult, may not be able to adopt our customs, or may outright reject them. When that happens, many of today's Japanese are likely to view immigration as a mistake that needs correcting.

I think the constructive tension between Kyoto and its patrons provides a useful example of the kind of relationship that would be ideal between Japan and immigrants. Kyoto is a very "Kyoto-centric" place, in the best sense of the word. The *geisha* of Pontocho, the district known for Kyoto's finest *geisha* and tea houses, are certainly the most Kyoto-esque aspects of the city's culture, and they have traditionally been supported by the owners of the top companies of the day, not all of whom are Kyoto-born. If anything, most of these owners come from elsewhere to settle in Kyoto, where they start businesses and become successful. From Kyoto's perspective, they are immigrants.

Kyoto does not reject people who wish to become patrons of Kyoto culture. The city welcomes these people with open arms. However, Kyoto also takes pains to teach them "Pontocho etiquette"—that is, how to treat *geisha*. People who are unwilling to obey these unwritten rules are not allowed to become sponsors. Kyoto culture comes first. The city is unrelenting in this attitude, and thus rejoices when new sponsors master the protocols. The new sponsors are happy to spend money. Kyoto welcomes these sponsors as they emerge, and has no particular obsession with keeping hold of the old ones. Newly minted sponsors continue to enjoy the cultural delights of Kyoto as a symbol of their success. I think we could create the same kind of virtuous cycle in the relationship between Japan and immigrants.

Twenty years have passed since the Berlin Wall fell in Europe, but Asia has yet to tackle many of the issues left over from the post-World War II period: the relationship between China and Taiwan, the Korean Peninsula, US bases on Okinawa, the dispute between Japan and Russia over the Kuril Islands. China's response to territorial issues in late 2010 was vividly reminiscent of Cold War days.

These leftover issues are an extremely negative factor for Asian development, but are also an extraordinary opportunity for Japan. If Japan takes the lead in resolving these issues, our country will set the course for a new future in the most basic sense of the term. Certainly, these problems are difficult and deep-rooted, but they can be solved one by one with persistent, forthright negotiation, and doing so will be a significant opportunity for both our economic and national interests. I think the future of Japan depends on us doing so.

JAPAN'S NEXT BALANCING ACT

YOSHIE KOMURO

JAPAN HAS A LOW BIRTH RATE. The crude birth rate (CBR)—births per 1,000 people per year—is 7.41. This is the lowest in the world and still falling. According to *The World Factbook*, published annually by the Central Intelligence Agency, CBR levels for 2010 are 13.83 for America, 12.43 for France, 10.14 for Sweden, and 8.97 for Taiwan. The total fertility rate (TFR)—the average number of children born to a woman over her lifetime—is 2.1 for the United States, 1.9 for France, and 1.3 for Japan according to the World Health Organization's *World Health Statistics 2010*.

Over the last 40 years, having fewer children has become a global trend. But in some countries, the birthrate has leveled off or even gone up a little. This is thanks to more childcare facilities, parental leave for both men and women, regulations on working hours and other measures to create an environment where women can feel more comfortable about having children. In countries where both parents work, people are starting to think that it is okay to have more children in a stable, double-income household.

So why is it that Japan's birthrate just keeps falling?

There is an old notion in Japan that if the mother doesn't stay home for the first three years, the child will suffer. People believed there was a connection between low birthrates and women working—that if women work, they can't have children, and should therefore stay home and focus on the family. Ironically, this thinking led to the birthrate falling even further.

Men working and women supporting them at home has long been considered the norm in Japan. Men tend to expect women to be reserved and respect them rather than be assertive. By nature, women are sensitive to how they are seen by others, so

Yoshie Komuro is founder and CEO of the Work-Life Balance Company in Tokyo.

they become aware very early in life of what the world expects of them. Open-minded young girls realize they don't fit in when they're older if they're too outgoing.

I was ten years old when I figured out what was expected, and I quickly changed. I became very low key because I wanted the approval of teachers and boys. In high school and university, like most Japanese women, my dream was to become a housewife and support my husband. I was diligent and studied hard, but I didn't have any ambition.

Then in my third year at Japan Women's University, I met Kuniko Inoguchi. She was a professor at Sophia University for more than 20 years and then went into politics. She's known for her work on women's issues during the Koizumi administration (2001–06) and for serving as Minister of State

TO SOLVE THE ISSUE OF LOW BIRTH RATES, JAPAN HAS TO CHANGE, REALLY CHANGE.

for Gender Equality and Social Affairs. She gave a seminar at my university. I had to take the class, so I was not really motivated. But when she spoke, her words changed my life.

One thing she said was that, although Japanese women found it difficult to keep working after they had children, that situation would have to change—and the companies who leveraged women's knowledge would have a competitive edge in making products for working women. Professor Inoguchi also said that in Japan only about 10 percent of executives were women, while in some Western companies that figure was more like 40 percent. We could change the percentage of working women in Japan, she told us. She encouraged us to join Japanese companies.

This really struck me. Until then, I had believed that because women took maternity leave when they had children, Japanese companies were justified in not hiring us. I didn't think there was anything we could do about the situation. But Professor Inoguchi's words turned me around. She said that, to succeed, Japanese companies needed women even when they got married and had children. That message was an eye-opener for me.

Before her talk, I really envied men because I believed that if they studied diligently, companies would welcome them with open arms. Their hard work would be rewarded, so it was worth studying. But no matter how hard I studied, I would never have the same chance. Also, as a competitive person, I didn't feel like competing with people I would never be able to beat. That was one reason I wanted to become a housewife. The more I thought about Professor Inoguchi's predictions and expectations, the less I wanted to stay home. I felt like contributing to society in a different way.

After that lecture, I wanted to change my life. I decided to go to the United States for a fresh start. I didn't have much money, so I worked as a babysitter. That was another eye-opener. I worked at the home of a single mother who was returning to work after having a baby. During maternity leave, she had taken an e-learning course to get a certificate, and got promoted right after she returned to her job. That would not have happened in Japan, where you don't get any points for what you do during maternity leave. When I came back, I joined Shiseido and have continued to work ever since. I founded my own company in 2006.

Now, I lecture at a women's university. The students who sit in the front row and listen most intently are those who are under pressure from their parents to become lawyers or doctors. They work hard to get a job even if those career paths are not what the students themselves want. When I talk to them, as Professor Inoguchi talked to me, about being able to balance home and work and about Japanese companies needing women, those front-row girls are moved to tears. They realize that, even as women, they can have a career in the field they want. The students sitting in the back row have tears in their eyes, too. Like I did, these girls gave up on pursuing careers at a very early stage and simply see university as preparation to be a housewife. They come to realize that women are needed in the workplace.

It was 1996 when I attended Professor Inoguchi's seminar. As she predicted, there are more double-income households today than those in which wives remain at home. Yet surprisingly, society's idea of men in the workplace, women at home has hardly changed.

Money may be a reason why Japanese women don't have children—especially more than one. But perhaps a bigger factor is that often, after women have that first child, they become fed up. Their husbands are working until midnight, so the women have to take care of the child alone. If husbands keep working long hours and don't help with child care, I do not see that the birthrate will go up.

My husband worked at a government agency and would usually get home around 2 AM. I told him I would never have a second child because I had to take care of our son all by myself. We discussed this situation, and he changed his lifestyle. Now my husband contributes to child care; he picks up our son from nursery at least once a week. I am thinking about having a second child.

At first, trying to get off earlier caused my husband some hardship at work. As a work-life consultant, though, I was able to advise him. I told him to select the projects only he could do and delegate the rest to other people. He was surprised at how this motivated his staff. He shared more information so that they could take more responsibility. Even though he changed the way he worked, this hasn't affected his career path—he got promoted.

If only more men shouldered the burdens of raising a family.
© B.S.P.I./Encyclopedia/Corbis

And he receives huge support from the younger staff; he has become their role model for balancing family and work.

It is difficult for me to predict the future of Japan, but I know what I would like to see: a scenario in which each individual can balance responsibilities of home and work, where women can be fairly evaluated based on their productivity, and can get promoted. This scenario would be good not just for women, but also for Japan.

Right now, Japan is not leveraging its potential. In the United Nations' Human Development Index (HDI), which measures life expectancy, educational attainment, and income, Japan ranks eighth in the world. But in the Gender Empowerment Measurement (GEM), which shows how active women are in politics and economics, Japan is 59th. In other words, even though both men and women are well educated, half the population—the women—are excluded from government and business for reasons other than capability: gender discrimination. No other industrialized nation has such a gap between human development and gender empowerment. This is a sad fact, but you can give it a positive spin: Japan has a lot of talent ready and able to contribute to society.

A better work-life balance could help women be more active in society while raising children. More working mothers could help replace the working population that we will lose when a large number of baby boomers retire. And if we can stop men from working such long hours, many women may feel more inclined to have more than one child, putting a stop to the declining birthrate.

At least it would be a start.

PUTTING FAMILIES FIRST

KAORI SASAKI

OVER THE PAST 25 YEARS, Japan has become a much easier place for women to work—at least in legal terms. The Equal Employment Opportunity Law was enacted in 1986, and child-care and parental leave have also been established. Not long ago, women in some companies had to retire when they got married. Now many married women are working. More mothers work as well. By and large, companies have complied with the regulations to protect women's right to employment.

While the laws have changed, Japanese social institutions have remained more or less the same—and so have the attitudes of Japanese men. So, for example, while many companies now provide support for very young children (and Japan's nursery system is very good), as soon as the child enters elementary school, mothers get little help. So many women stop working then.

At my companies, UNICUL International and ewoman, we have a system in place to help parents care for children from the first year of elementary school to the start of university. When I work as an adviser to companies, I recommend support systems for women who have children up to age 18.

But that is only part of the answer. Japanese men need to change, too. It's all very well for men to say they support their wives working outside the home. But if women still have to do the same amount of work inside the home, they are not having much fun. Many women go along with their husband's attitude because having some work outside the home is better than having none. But I can't help but feel Japanese men don't value their families or private time as much as men in other

Kaori Sasaki is president of UNICUL International.

countries. Even if there was a better infrastructure to support families, I'm not sure Japanese men would use it, for example by leaving work early or taking leave.

Of course, some men do take leave; some men do stay home; and some men even cook for their families. I know they do because they get featured in the news—which shows just how unusual their situation is.

In a larger sense, I think we have lost something fundamental in our social system. For a long time, Japan focused on economic growth. People worked very hard. Even so, we were used to the idea that family members were close and it was important to keep good relations with neighbors. Somehow, without being aware of it, we've lost that ethos.

THE LAW CAN ONLY DO SO MUCH; THE VALUE SYSTEM NEEDS TO CHANGE.

When my elder child entered 10th grade, the coach for one of her extracurricular activities told her not to plan family trips so she could devote time to that activity during the summer vacation. One way of looking at this rule is that the school is teaching children not to spend time with their families so that when these young people start working for a corporation, they accept working long hours.

One thing that the government could do is to make the hiring of foreign help easier than it currently is. There are more than 100,000 foreign domestic helpers in Hong Kong—Filipinos, mostly. Tokyo has twice the population of Hong Kong, and nowhere near that many helpers. The government has made it unbelievably complicated for foreign domestic helpers to get a visa. I think the government's policy is deliberate. After all, many government officials are older men. Their wives worked at home, and they figure: why shouldn't today's women do the same?

Changing the law can only do so much; our value system needs to change, too. When we rebuilt Japan's economy after the war, our society forged a powerful "boy's network," with a common set of goals and values. That network functioned effectively and efficiently; one could argue that it was instrumental to Japan's rapid rate of economic growth. But the time has come for us to broaden that network to include new people and new values.

We must embrace diversity. I believe that when we learn to understand and accept multiple values, our companies and our country will be stronger, and we, as Japanese, will be happier.

Will she be able to crack the "boys' network"?
© Toshifumi Kitamura/AFP/Getty Images

MAYOR WITH A MISSION

FUMIKO HAYASHI

"WOULD YOU RUN for mayor of Yokohama?"

When this question was first put to me, I had absolutely no interest in politics or government. I was the president of a Nissan marketing company. In my 45-year professional life, all my experience had been in the private sector. I loved working in business.

But then someone told me something that changed my thinking: "There are far too few women leaders in local governments in Japan. This is a place where women should be active. Why don't you use your private-sector perspective to change how government works?" I had always felt that Japanese government lacked management sensibilities. It seemed to me that government moved too slowly, and there was little economic logic to its decisions.

The biggest issue facing Japan today is demography: birth rates are falling and everyone is living longer. Finding a solution to low birth rates will require a female perspective. We need to make greater use of women in the labor force, and our government services need to be better aligned with their lives—by providing them with assistance in childrearing, for instance. As I thought about these things, I made up my mind to run for mayor.

I have always tried to participate in and contribute to society through my work. I graduated from high school in 1965 and took a job at a major textiles manufacturer, but I had already been working for quite a while before that. From the time I was a fifth-grader, I had a part-time job making tea at a trading company. My family was poor, and I wanted to do what I could to help my parents. Even at that age, I had already begun to understand how enjoyable it is to work.

Fumiko Hayashi is mayor of Yokohama.

So I joined the company and finally got a real job, only to encounter restrictions and limitations on what women were allowed to do. It was a classic male-dominated society. Female employees could only serve as assistants to the men. We were really there only to take care of them.

Why wouldn't they let us work just like the men? Why couldn't women's abilities be put to use? In my case, adversity served as a springboard and gave me even greater motivation to work.

I was lucky because, at age 31, I landed a job in sales at an auto dealership, where there was little distinction between men and women; you were evaluated entirely on results. If you performed well and sold a lot of cars, your wages rose and your personnel evaluation improved. Eventually I became the company's first female branch manager, responsible not only for my own performance but also for that of my subordinates. At one point I was sent into a poorly performing dealership and tasked with rebuilding it. I guess my performance was noticed. Other companies began to scout me out and make offers. I moved from company to company, advancing my position as I went along.

Yokohama: a global port with world-class aspirations.

In 2005, I was hired to chair Daiei, a major distribution company that was in the process of being rebuilt by Marubeni and Advantage Partners. It goes without saying that 80 percent of the customers in a supermarket are women. About 80 percent of the people working at Daiei were women, too. So why were there no women managers? That appears to have been the idea behind hiring me. To be honest, no one was more surprised than I by the offer. Daiei was at one point a trillion-yen company. Bringing in a woman to lead it in the midst of an enormous rehabilitation project was a bold idea for Japan at this time.

My job at Daiei was demanding. In retail, a company can't expect sales to pick up simply because it has a new leader. Plus, when a company is rebuilding, it finds itself between the government (Industrial Revitalization Corporation of Japan) and multiple sponsors (shareholders) and must balance the often-conflicting interests of these different entities. What I felt most keenly was the need for trust, how much I was able to contribute in this position because I was a woman. Women are better able to accept other people's opinions. Women have the capacity to bring together multiple points of view. My ability to coordinate this project gave me a great deal of confidence. It also reaffirmed for me that, ultimately, human relationships bring a job to fruition. In the process, I like to think that I helped to expand the scope of what women can do in business.

MY IDEA WAS TO TURN YOKOHAMA INTO A MODEL OF THE JAPANESE CITIES OF THE FUTURE.

When I became mayor of Yokohama, I wanted to turn the city into a model of the future. Yokohama has a shortage of daycare centers, which are vital to women who want to continue working after they marry and have children. The unfortunate fact is that we are No. 1 in the country for numbers of children on daycare center waiting lists. But building daycare centers and training staff is costly—and not something a local government can do on its own. We decided to bring people together, pool their insights and wisdom, put emphasis on childcare assistance, and create a city that was able to make full use of its female workforce.

I think we can do more for retirees as well. We can create more opportunities than now exist for them to help out in the local community at after-school care centers, or to use their expertise and experience for the benefit of those around them.

Projections indicate that Yokohama's senior population will reach 1 million over the next ten years. We have devised an interim plan for our city that aims to support these individuals so they can contribute to their local communities. We want to create a society in which senior citizens can continue to be vital and active.

Joblessness among young people will be a factor that can lead to instability in the future. We have many recluses who find themselves unable to participate in society, and a considerable number of people who are unable to find regular jobs. To that end, we have created a Yokohama Youth Support Station to provide counseling and assistance for young people as they try to become independent. We also want to provide assistance in finding jobs to people who are recluses or who lack the confidence to be independent.

Yet another major issue Japan must confront is regional economic independence. Yokohama has a long history; its port opened to the world about 150 years ago. The city has been selected as a Strategic International Container Port under the national growth strategy and is now working to enhance the port's facilities. Unfortunately, the Port of Yokohama, in its current state, is inferior to other international hub ports in Asia like Hong Kong, Busan, and Singapore. The national government recognizes the danger and has decided to make concentrated investments in the Port of Keihin, which brings together Tokyo, Kawasaki, and Yokohama. We have responded to this initiative by privatizing our public company that manages the port so that at some point in the future our company can be integrated with the port management company in Tokyo to take advantage of economies of scale. We think that what will eventually be needed is a port authority to provide integrated management of the entire Tokyo Bay area, including Chiba and Yokosuka. We must think on this scale or we will never close the gap with Busan and the other ports.

We are also in the process of many other initiatives to improve the environment, stimulate small business, revitalize commercial districts, and promote tourism.

Up until this point, Yokohama has lived too long in Tokyo's shadow. We are directly connected to the major arteries of Japan; all *shinkansen* trains stop at Shin-Yokohama Station. Nearby Haneda Airport is also opening to international flights, and we can use this expansion to connect to the rest of the world.

We want to take advantage of these strengths to develop Yokohama-style solutions to the problems that will confront Japan. We want to be a model city. As a female mayor, I want to encourage sympathy and trust, never forgetting the perspectives of day-to-day life. I think that is how local communities can help to reenergize Japan. I am confident such a transformation can be made.

JAPAN IS NOT "LOST"

STEVE VAN ANDEL

OVER THE PAST 20 YEARS, in my roles as chairman of Amway and as former chairman of the United States Chamber of Commerce, I have been privileged to meet dignitaries, executives, and entrepreneurs from Japan. Each time I visit, I am amazed by the extraordinary kindness and dedication of the Japanese people. I believe these qualities bode well for Japan's future.

So, I am dismayed by the pessimistic tone of articles about Japan I read so often in the global press. It seems to me that many international business leaders and scholars are too quick to make negative judgments about Japan's prospects. They note that Japan is struggling, offer myriad reasons why, and lament that Japan will never change. While it's true that change often comes slowly in Japan, the country has proven its ability to adapt and influence the global economy in a positive way.

The way I see it, Japan is not "lost." Far from it. Japan is a wonderful place to do business. And when you work directly with Japanese entrepreneurs, as we do at Amway, you can see how strong Japan really is.

To understand what I mean, you don't need to look any further than one of our Amway plazas on a Monday morning. I have been to our Tokyo plaza many times on Mondays; it's quite a sight. The building is filled with people, most of them women, including a few who come pushing children in strollers. These people are our distributors. After a weekend with family and friends, they are back at work, building their businesses. The building is full of laughter and excited conversation, the sound of people helping other people succeed. There is a unique energy in the air.

All told, Amway counts more than 700,000 Amway distributors in Japan. About 80 percent of them are women pursuing their entrepreneurial dreams:

Steve Van Andel is chairman and co-CEO of Amway.

Amway cleans up, thanks to Japan's most underused resource.
© TWPhoto/Corbis

running their own businesses, seeking personal fulfillment, and earning extra money for their households. They are contributing to their family's stability in a way that fits cultural expectations.

When you think about Japan's changing demographics, it makes sense that women are playing an ever-increasing role in earning extra income for their families. Some experts say that, to counteract some of the challenges facing Japan, the country should consider aggressive fiscal policies and open-door immigration policies. I believe Japan already holds the keys to its future success in two groups: entrepreneurs and the nation's talented and capable women.

Japan has long been a country of ideas and innovation, but being an entrepreneur in Japan and bringing those ideas to market is sometimes very difficult. If you fail in Japan, more often than not you don't get much chance to to "try and try again." That is disheartening because failure is often a necessary prelude to success.

Amway's history shows that there is an entrepreneurial spirit in Japan, and that success is possible if society fosters and supports that spirit. In my experience, younger Japanese entrepreneurs have far fewer chances to benefit from coaching, mentorship, and professional development opportunities than their counterparts in many other developed economies. Japan's entrepreneurs would also benefit from greater access to funding through loans, venture capital, and grants.

To compete in the future, Japan's entrepreneurs will need to be developed, given the chance to fail a time or two, and granted greater access to funding and mentorship. These efforts will require greater partnership and collaboration between the public sector, academia, and Japan's business leaders.

Women are an even more underused resource than entrepreneurs. As a society, Japan has invested heavily in educating women. For the past 30 years, Amway has been offering an opportunity in Japan, to men and women alike. As a result, we have seen women who probably wouldn't have been given a chance in Japan's corporate culture flourish. These women have helped to make Amway the strong business that it is today in Japan.

I see significant, often untapped potential in this segment of Japan's workforce. According to Japan's statistics office, there are about 26.5 million women in the labor force today, which translates into a labor participation rate for women of just 48.7 percent, one of the lowest of any nation in the world. And more than half of the Japanese women who do work are part-timers. A recent government study found that women accounted for more than 90 percent of Japan's 8 million part-time workers; the study concluded that boosting women's role in the workforce could increase the labor pool by the equivalent of 4.5 million people. A gain of that magnitude would all but eliminate the need for Japan to permit mass immigration, an approach for which Japanese society so far has shown little enthusiasm.

Even a cursory consideration of such figures suggests Japan has a large pool of reserve workers who are educated and ready to work, and, if given the opportunity, could have a tremendous impact on Japan's GDP.

I believe that, in decades to come, Japan's women will silence critics of the nation's economy. But that can happen only if women are given the opportunity to excel in the Japanese business world, and given equal pay and motivation to remain a part of the workforce. Today, the United Nations Development Program ranks Japan eighth worldwide in human development, but much lower in gender development. Japan must aspire today to narrow that gap if it wants to secure its stability tomorrow.

I'm hopeful for Japan because I've seen Japan's innovative spirit. I also have seen how hard Japan's women—and men—can work. I have seen that when given a chance, entrepreneurs, both men and women, can achieve great things.

When I visit Japan and speak to our distributors, I spend a significant amount of time talking about opportunity, and what people can do if given a chance to prove themselves. We believe in providing an opportunity for everyone to own their own business. Anyone can join Amway. Anyone can work hard, learn, and maximize their potential. Anyone can succeed.

Overall, I see a bright future for Japan, a future in which Japan creates a more supportive environment for entrepreneurs, and an environment where women are given real opportunities to achieve their full potential. I have been impressed with Japan since my first trip 20 years ago, and I know I will continue to be impressed for the next 20 years and beyond.

A MATTER OF PRINCIPALS

KAZUHIRO FUJIWARA

JAPAN'S EDUCATION SYSTEM has become an impediment to growth of the economy and the development of society. If Japan's education system were a company, analysts would diagnose failures of investment and personnel.

To put it simply: society has changed, but Japan is educating children as it did 50 years ago. We still emphasize processing information: the ability to apply a formula and produce the right answer quickly. When you can answer "1492" to the question, "When did Columbus discover America?", you have processed. Japanese students process well, which is why they perform so well on international tests. But they are not skilled when editing information—that is, figuring out the best answer for a problem with multiple solutions by using knowledge, expertise, and experience. When you are able to edit information, you can address the larger question of how the world changed after Columbus.

There is an economic dimension to this weakness in students' abilities. Many employees can process information if they are given instructions, but are inept at defining problems or devising solutions. They fail not from lack of intelligence, but from a failure in the school curriculum.

Language lessons in Japan, for example, are unwaveringly focused on identifying a single, approved answer. When studying Shakespeare's King Lear, a typical question might be: "Why did the king act this way? Select the best answer from the four choices below." A better way to frame the question would be not to suggest answers but to leave the matter open. This approach, which would encourage

---

Kazuhiro Fujiwara is the first individual from the private sector to serve as a principal of a junior high school in Japan.

language skills through debate and develop creative thinking, is definitely missing in the curricula in Japan.

The cell phone lesson

In Osaka, I helped design a new type of high-school course called *Yononaka-ka*, which can be loosely translated as "How the World Works 101." During a visit to one of those classes, we tried an approach I found fascinating. The assignment asked students to work out where to open a hamburger store and how to operate it. To do the analysis, students brainstormed together. Then, using their cell phones, they e-mailed their ideas to a Web site set up by the teacher; these texts immediately appeared on a screen next to the blackboard at the front of the classroom. The teacher could point to any idea and ask students to elaborate. I liked this approach because it is a fact of school life that the same students tend to raise their hands and speak up. When everyone uses cell phones, though, everyone's idea gets some discussion.

I hope this type of lesson—active rather than passive—will be the norm in the classroom of the future, a classroom where students communicate with each other. Active learning increases the opportunities for students to edit information rather than merely process it.

How do we foster such qualities? I believe change needs to start at the top. Therefore, I'd like to see 3,000 new principals—one for every ten schools—recruited from outside the education sector. Let me explain what may seem to be an outrageous idea.

In Japan, principals have the right to change the curriculum; as long as their changes are legal and good for the children, these educators can do anything. But few do. Principals are so preoccupied with daily documentation—of reports ranging from bullying to nutrition to statistics on information technology—that they are up to their ears in detail.

Another problem is systemic. Because of the rigid, bureaucratic nature of Japan's education system, educators spend decades rising to the level of principal; by the time these educators are promoted, they are more concerned with protecting their position than making big changes.

As Peter Drucker might say, such a system is no way to create value.

Opening the system

Of Japan's 30,000 elementary and junior high school principals, fewer than 100 have been recruited from the private sector. Our schools are, in effect, a closed system, the enemy of creativity and innovation. Reforming education is a matter of management as well as education expertise; schools should be drawing from the best of Japanese society, not just from among education professionals.

From 2003 to 2008, I was principal of Wada Junior High School, which is in a middle-class residential area of Tokyo. When I started, the school had only 160 students, and was threatened with consolidation; it ranked 21st out of 23 schools in Suginami ward. Now the school has more than 400 students and is so well re-garded—it ranked first in the ward in 2010—that realtors single it out for praise.

I came to believe, particularly after living in Europe for a few years, that Japan needed structural change in education, health care and housing. I also believed that private education efforts would have only limited effect; to make economic sense, such efforts had to be in high-end private tutoring, which is already a well-estab-lished industry. I wanted to show that business know-how could help to transform public education—and that meant I had to work in a public school.

My journey to Wada Junior High School began in 1999, when Hiroshi Yamada was elected governor of Suginami ward. He named me to a "21st-century vision committee" to discuss the future of the area. Two years later, I became an adviser to the Suginami ward school board. We devised an action plan for principals, but it had little effect. I was convinced, however, that the plan had good ideas worth exploring. So I raised my hand at the Tokyo Metropolitan Board of Education and offered to be a principal. Two of the key decision makers on the board were familiar with Suginami ward, so they were receptive and eventually agreed to a five-year ap-pointment. Such an appointment was unprecedented; the board had never assigned a principal from the private sector.

Initially, the reaction at the school was not positive. I wanted to move fast, and the pace of change in Japanese schools is slow. The typical cycle goes like this: ob-serve the school for one year; suggest ideas in year two; consider ideas in year three; and implement them in year four. Using the principle of continuous improvement, or *kaizen*, I wanted to accelerate this process into weeks or months. That accelera-tion took some persuading.

So I made a point of developing good relationships with the teachers, in part by taking over duties they hated, such as dealing with student issues, and han-dling complaints from parents (including those who are so demanding that Japa-nese teachers sometimes refer to them as "monster parents"). They saw that I was committed to establishing policies that were good for children and based on clear criteria. And I took responsibility for my actions. Accountability is as important in education as it is in business.

My business background was with Re-cruit, which specializes in employment listings and career development. Recruit's slogan is "Create opportunity by my-self; transform myself by opportunity." I brought this mindset to Wada. Specifically, the Japanese education system tends to fa-vor equality of result and is almost suspi-cious of individual excellence. This attitude

But are they learning to think?
© Charles Gupton/Stone/Getty Images

is deeply imbedded in the attitude of the teachers' union. I put the emphasis on equality of opportunity.

Particularly in English, we achieved breakthrough results by creating ways to stretch our more talented students. At first, we got a lot of kneejerk criticism for this approach. People told us, "Supporting high-performing children goes against the spirit of equality and is harmful for struggling students."

TO PUT IT SIMPLY: SOCIETY HAS CHANGED, BUT JAPAN IS STILL EDUCATING CHILDREN AS IT DID 50 YEARS AGO.

Also, we could not find extra class time for existing teachers. So we brought in professional tutors and even university students—the kind of networking that was routine at Recruit.

What we found is that these efforts had a positive ripple effect. When people feel they are growing, they want to tell others about their progress, whether that progress is in baseball, *shogi* (a kind of Japanese chess), cooking, or schoolwork. So our better English-language students started teaching the middle- and lower-level children in the classroom, sometimes during recess, or on Saturdays. The children didn't learn just from their teachers; they learned from each other. Our test scores in English became the highest in Suginami ward and academic performance as a whole improved for five straight years.

It's important to note that just because we gave good English students more opportunities to learn, we did not neglect other subjects. For example, I wanted to find out at what points students fell behind. That is important to know because once students falter, they may find catching up very difficult. The business equivalent is to identify a weak division and fix it. At Wada, we identified one such weak point in math. To raise students' performance, we created a supplemental study course on Saturday, again led by private tutors and university students. Among other things, these tutors used Nintendo DS, a portable console with educational games that kids really enjoy. Finally, I applied modern time-management techniques. We changed the standard 50-minute lesson to 45 minutes, which increased the total number of classes by 10 percent, so that we could create extra periods for core subjects like English, Japanese, and math.

From criticism to action

Japan needs to figure out how to find more principals who are willing to take these kinds of chances. If these principals don't exist in academia, then we should turn to the private sector.

Japanese elementary and junior high schools now are like the night before the Meiji Restoration, when the country was closed but about to open up. If the country could attract 300 private-sector principals into the education system for each of the next ten years, I think we would create a hybrid curriculum that leverages the best of both worlds, something akin to the approach adopted by Oda Nobunaga, the military commander during Japan's Warring States period. Not all these principals would have to be recruited from the business sector, and in fact, there might not be that many businesspeople willing to take the pay cut that would probably be required. University professors, managers from private tutoring schools, education ministry officials, even leaders of shrines and temples—all could be part of the revamped system.

Principals hired from the private sector would have a different perspective on their community and draw in new ideas. They may, for example, be more skilled at building social networks, including among the 10 million baby boomers, who will retire in the next five years. And given these principals' networks of contacts and marketing skills, they also might be able to sell the idea of contributing assets—in the form of time, money or even buildings—to state schools.

I know these changes will not be easy. In many schools, particularly those where union or school factions dominate the school boards and personnel departments, there is no will to go in this direction. But if you begin from the position, as I do, that we need a second Meiji reform—an education one—then opening up the management of these schools has to be part of the process.

The one thing everyone recognizes is that we can't keep doing things in the same old way. Can we really bring about a revolution in Japanese education? Maybe, maybe not. But we made a revolution happen at Wada. That's a start.

A CHILD LEFT BEHIND

KUMIKO MAKIHARA

"WHAT ARE YOU GOING TO SAY if I don't make it?" my son asked me before he left for a long-distance ocean swim required by his school.

"I'll say, 'Can't you even do that? What a waste of tuition!'" We both laughed as I continued, "What did you want me to say? 'Nice try'? 'It's the effort that counts'?"

That such words of encouragement would be relegated to sarcasm reflects my son's experience of six years in a prestigious Japanese elementary school. All 122 of the sixth-graders, except for two who had been out sick or injured, swam one or two kilometers that summer. From the relief of the parents and children I saw after the event, it was clear that what mattered was not how hard the students tried but whether they actually went the distance.

My son soon graduates from one of the country's most elite, private elementary schools. I chose the school over our local public one because it offered better facilities, smaller classes, a broader curriculum, and an impressive list of alumni, including famous politicians, business leaders, and artists. In those six years, the school did a good job of imparting textbook knowledge and exposed him to a rich array of art, music, and sports. He will leave with an impressive body of facts at his fingertips and a solid foundation in math, reading, writing, science, and history.

My son's intellectual growth is another matter. Pervasive negative reinforcement from teachers and a competitive atmosphere that demoralized underachievers chipped away at his self-confidence and deflated any delightful childish dreams of winning a Nobel Prize or becoming a professional athlete. A constant and towering amount of work—from reciting ancient poetry to dissecting fish, sewing environmentally correct shopping bags, and memorizing historical events—pushed him to

Kumiko Makihara writes frequently about social and cultural trends in Japan.

view all school tasks as daunting. Mother-child relations spiraled downward as he came to view me as a despicable homework enforcer. I fear that instead of planting the seeds for a thirst for knowledge, the rigors of school may have discouraged the development of a probing mind.

That is an apprehension many experts have about the Japanese education system. "Are schools thinking enough about whether students can survive on their own after they graduate?" asks Masahiro Kozuki, director of the Policy Planning and Coordination Division of the Ministry of Science, Technology, and Education. Japanese students can recite facts, but they often lack the analytical skills and resourcefulness that are crucial in today's global economy. In the Organisation for Economic Co-operation and Development (OECD)-administered PISA tests, which rank 15-year-olds from dozens of countries, Japan still does well. Indeed, Japan advanced its standing in the most recent 2009 test. But it is troubling that in reading, for example, while Japan's students can identify what information is in a text, they have difficulty analyzing the content and relating that content to their own experiences. Since 2000, when the tests

PERVASIVE NEGATIVE REINFORCEMENT AND A COMPETITIVE ATMOSPHERE THAT DEMORALIZED UNDERACHIEVERS CHIPPED AWAY AT MY SON'S SELF-CONFIDENCE AND DEFLATED ANY DREAMS OF WINNING A NOBEL PRIZE OR BECOMING A PROFESSIONAL ATHLETE.

were first administered, Japan has dropped to ninth place (from first place) in math, and to fifth place (from second place) in science. In reading, Japan declined, then later regained its eighth place rank.

Did my son's school emphasize, along with getting the right answer, creativity, curiosity, flexibility, and communication skills? Sadly, I would say not enough. Our personal situation represents one extreme of Japanese primary education, since most children attend less-intense public schools. But the inability to groom outside-the-box thinking concerns all schools. That an institution with a legacy of producing leading members of society doesn't foster such characteristics is all the more distressing.

In 2005, my son began first grade on a verdant campus in suburban Tokyo. On the first day of school, his teacher played the guitar and sang a song to welcome the sparkling new pupils, many of whom had already studied for more than a year to pass the entrance exams, and their ambitious parents. The teacher circulated a small box and said, "There's a picture of the kind of child I like in there, so take a good look." I cherish the photo I have of my son peering into the box and smiling at his reflection in the tiny mirror pasted inside.

The first few years of school were ideal. The basics of reading, writing, and math were emphasized. Children were encouraged to play hard, and conflicts, even physical fighting, were not discouraged as long as they didn't cause injuries or weren't a result of bullying. As a parent of an only child, I appreciated the school's willingness to allow children to experiment with their own strengths and weaknesses. My son developed a love for his school and strong friendships during these years, and rushed out each morning to get in an extra few minutes of dodge ball or soccer on the playgrounds before class.

The dark side came in the latter half of elementary school as the academics became more advanced and the teachers emphasized results. To motivate students in a culture where people tend to define themselves by how they compare with others, student papers and projects were displayed on the walls or photocopied and distributed to parents. Test scores often noted the average mark and class rank, so that instead of receiving my son's report and saying, "Good job, 88 out of 100!" I would be prompted to lament, "Oh, just below the average of 91."

In an age when many educators encourage positive reinforcement, at my son's school, praise was doled out parsimoniously. In a certificate my son received for completing the two-kilometer swim, the words of congratulation from his instructor were followed by a list of "overall weak points that I want you to polish." During a conversation among the parents about the nautical feat, one mother felt obligated to say, "My daughter only swam one kilometer." *Only* one?

It is no wonder that, as the years went by, my son would say with increasing frequency, "I'm not good at that."

The amount of work was relentless. Homework for the sixth grade during the one-month-long summer vacation included math, science, and reading comprehension drill sheets, a book review, a hand-crafted invention, and a list of 234 Chinese characters to practice. Students also were told to keep diaries, read as many books as possible, and do independent projects. Throughout primary school, my son and I had almost daily arguments over homework. I would shudder when I read about the occasional murder of parents by children who later confessed they had been fed up with their parents' nagging them to study.

DID MY SON'S SCHOOL EMPHASIZE, ALONG WITH GETTING THE RIGHT ANSWER, CREATIVITY, CURIOSITY, FLEXIBILITY, AND COMMUNICATION SKILLS? SADLY, I WOULD SAY NOT ENOUGH.

Our most painful episode took place in the fifth-grade Japanese class. The teacher was a supremely confident man in his 60s, popular but intimidating for his entertaining and sharp tongue and revered by most parents for the advanced materials he taught. One day, he asked the pupils to raise their hands if the person sitting next to them had messy writing in their Chinese-character notebooks. The girl next to my son obediently put up her hand. Even though my son had tried, he had not been able to match the writing quality of his superachieving peers. The teacher circulated my son's notebook around the class as an example of sloppy penmanship. Instead of apologizing in shame, my son joked, "Handle with care! That's my treasure." When sending him to stand in the hallway still didn't elicit the expected remorse, the teacher took him to an empty classroom and slapped his face until blood streaked down the center of my son's shirt.

A resilient and optimistic boy with a hard shield that blocks out unpleasant thoughts, my son continued to attend that class happily. But I'm still harping on the disturbing values that I saw in the incident. The teacher met a lack of contrition

Smile! Learning is supposed to be fun!
© Paul Chesley/Stone/Getty Images

with violence. He also encouraged students to report on each other's weaknesses and intimated that poor schoolwork deserved to be hung out for humiliation. I wrote a letter with my thoughts to the teacher but received no reply. I didn't report the incident to outside authorities, because I didn't want to jeopardize my son's standing at the school. Besides, few other parents seemed to share my outrage, presumably feeling the teacher's strengths outweighed his severity and knowing their children would be obedient and were therefore not in danger.

Poor penmanship wasn't the only flaw stamped on my son's forehead. The children were required to pass a recorder test before they could audition to play other instruments at the school's annual concert. Who knows? My son might have had talent with the tambourine, but that path was closed because he never mastered the fingering for the treble recorder. His cooking skills were similarly discouraged after his group in a bread-baking class put too much water in the mix. The teacher complained bitterly that the children failed to follow instructions while he rekneaded the dough with more flour. Wouldn't a few weighty words on paying attention, plus a lesson on the tricks of rescuing gooey batter, have gone further to enhance these young cooks' efforts?

As graduation day approaches, I look back and wonder whether I would choose the same school if I could do it over again. Despite the disheartening aspects of the last few years, it's a tough call. I haven't come across a school in Japan that consistently tries to provide creative ways to spark the potential in every child, while also instilling a high level of knowledge. It's a sad commentary on the country's education that a top-level primary school won't take up that challenge.

When my son looks back on his elementary years, I hope he will remember that he mastered enough math to score an 88 and not that he scored below the 91 average; that he had the athletic prowess to swim two kilometers even though he didn't perfect his breaststroke; and that he had the dignity to accept, rather than resist, a teacher who beat his face. If my son can be happy with what he has achieved, and remain eager for more learning, I would deem his bumpy and bittersweet primary education by and large a success.

And I hope that when he leaves this school, he will still smile when he sees his reflection.

IN SEARCH OF PRIMARY GREATNESS

STEPHEN R. COVEY

I'VE VISITED JAPAN MANY TIMES over the years, and have met hundreds of senior executives at Japan's largest corporations. In those exchanges, I'm often asked to share my views about management and leadership. The two words are frequently used interchangeably. In my view, however, they are very different things—and the ability to distinguish one from the other is a prerequisite for doing either well.

Management is about systems, process, and methods; the focus is on execution, efficiency, and getting things done. Leadership is about people and ideals; the focus is on values, and what to do. Warren Bennis, a noted author and organizational consultant, put it this way: "Leaders are people who do the right thing; managers are people who do things right."

To me, one of the key distinctions between a manager and a leader is that the former seeks to control, while the latter seeks to empower. True leaders see their role as helping others identify and articulate a common purpose, then motivating them to work together in pursuit of that objective. My favorite definition of leadership is that it is the act of communicating to others their own worth and potential so clearly that they come to see it in themselves.

Both management and leadership are vital. You can't expect to achieve success as an organization—or as a country—by emphasizing one at the expense of the other. But my sense, affirmed in conversations with many top Japanese executives over the years, is that Japanese organizations, in both the public and private sectors, tend to be much better at management than at leadership.

Stephen R. Covey, the author of The 7 Habits of Highly Effective People *(1989), is cofounder and vice chairman of FranklinCovey.*

When it comes to systems and processes, Japan's largest manufacturers are second to none. And in visits to non-Japanese companies, too, I'm impressed at how Japanese ideas like *kaizen* ("continuous improvement") and just-in-time manufacturing have become standard practice around the world.

Japanese executives express less satisfaction with the efficiency of their organizations when it comes to administration, and many say they're concerned about the low productivity of the nation's service sector. But the larger struggle, Japanese executives tell me, is with broader issues: adjusting to external challenges, setting goals, formulating a strategy, articulating the mission, communicating with stakeholders.

I've heard many theories that seek to explain why leadership issues are more challenging than management ones in Japan. Clearly, one factor is that postwar Japan's economic and political institutions were geared for development, not mature growth. The postwar model mobilized resources brilliantly when "catching up" was the overwhelming goal. But Japan effectively caught up with—and in some key respects overtook—the West by the late 1980s. Since then, the postwar arrangements have served the nation poorly.

I've also heard that leadership suffers in Japan because the country's legal and economic institutions favor established firms rather than start-ups and entrepreneurs. For the handful of founding entrepreneurs whose companies have broken through—men like Konosuke Matsushita and Soichiro Honda, or, more recently, Masayoshi Son and Tadashi Yanai—visionary leadership comes naturally. The

Embracing the global Knowledge Age.
BLOOMimage/Getty Images

professional managers who succeed the founders, the theory goes, find it more difficult to take risks.

Wisdom of the ages

Regardless of the reasons, I see many Japanese organizations that remain rooted in outmoded economic paradigms. In the Industrial Age, the priority was to get predictable results: cars with zero defects, buttons that didn't fall off. To an Industrial-Age leader, people were akin to machines: they needed to be efficiently controlled and kept in compliance with orders from above. Then came the Information Age, in which individuals who could call up the most facts were the best placed to succeed.

But now we have reached the Knowledge Age. With the spread of the Internet, data is easy to find. Factual knowledge is therefore no longer a differentiator. The rigid mindset of the previous eras stifle the kind of initiative and resourcefulness organizations need to survive in a world of global interdependence and rapid technological change.

The Knowledge Age belongs to those who excel in creativity, and who also possess a strong analytical aptitude, a sense of foresight, and people skills. These are the inventors, the designers, the listeners, the big-picture thinkers, the meaning makers, and the pattern recognizers. They know how to optimize and creatively maneuver the facts, not just regurgitate them, and can do all this while working well with others.

For anyone seeking to direct a large Japanese organization, the implications of the shift to the Knowledge Age are profound. In the Industrial Age, workers could be motivated with carrots and sticks: a higher wage or the threat of dismissal. But in the Knowledge Age, if employees are to add value, they must be able to think and choose for themselves: to learn, to adapt, to innovate, and to capture opportunities entrepreneurially. Indeed, it is precisely those individuals most comfortable making independent choices who are likely to be the most valuable to an organization. These individuals cannot be managed (i.e., controlled), they can only be led (i.e., inspired and empowered).

In the Knowledge Age, therefore, successful leaders know to prize workers not for their ability to follow orders or to memorize facts, but for their unique contributions. Leaders must learn to let go, to value different (even disruptive) points of view, and to motivate people with zeal for their mission. This implies a far more fluid, freewheeling leadership style than is in place at most large Japanese companies.

The question Japan should be asking, then, is whether it is equipping its young people, both in school and on the job, for this new era.

Schools of greatness

I claim no particular expertise in Japanese politics or economics. So it's not for me to dissect the structural, institutional, or social factors underlying Japan's leadership deficit. But my company, FranklinCovey, has extensive operations in Japan; moreover, some 13,000 Japanese students are being taught "The 7 Habits of Highly Effective People" (the title of my 1989 book). My personal and professional experience leads me to believe that Japan could reduce and indeed eliminate its leadership deficit by rethinking its approach to education and training.

Education is the crucial element because developing better leaders is a goal that can't be imposed from above by policy directive or administrative guidance. True leaders must be grown. The habits and attitudes of leadership are best cultivated from an early age and, believe it or not, they can be learned at school.

I know this because for the past decade, I have been involved with educators who are teaching the leadership principles in *The 7 Habits of Highly Effective People* to elementary-school students. Those habits emphasize enhancing individual initiative; setting and achieving specific goals; focusing on what matters most; communicating and collaborating; and investing constantly in one's personal development. Critics of this approach have dismissed these habits as common sense, but it is surprising how uncommon it is for these skills to be exercised in daily life.

The goal of these programs is to teach young people how to succeed in the Knowledge Age by inculcating a heightened sense of what I call "primary greatness." Primary greatness has to do with who people are: their integrity, work ethic, creativity, treatment of others, motives, character, and discipline. It differs from secondary greatness, which has to do with positions or titles, wealth, fame, or rank.

The idea of primary greatness is inherent to Japanese students, as it is to young people in every culture. The mission of Japan's education system, then, must be to nurture and cultivate that sense of greatness, not merely to goad students into cramming for standardized entrance examinations. Japan will find its way forward by helping its young people to find the leader within.

• • •

My conviction that primary greatness is innate to Japan's people and its culture has been strengthened by the many acts of courage and sacrifice we've seen during the earthquake, tsunami, and radiation crisis. I have followed reports of the tragedy with great concern. I know that those who have lost loved ones in Tohoku are feeling the sort of pain that hurts deep in the soul. Japan is experiencing a time of mourning, healing, and rebuilding, a moment that will require strength and endurance, love and compassion. Many Japanese have risked danger to themselves to help others in need, and have reached out selflessly and with dignity, fortitude, and grace. I have heard of so many stories of people who didn't wait to be told what to do, but who quietly and independently took the initiative to pitch in and lighten the burdens of others. This spirit of community is the true spirit of Japan, and it is a spirit that inspires me.

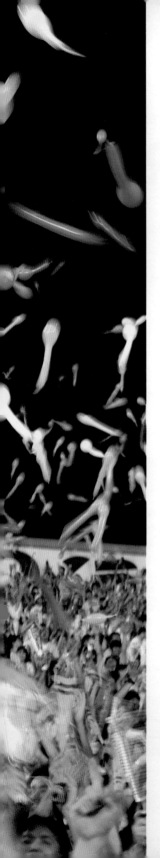

CHAPTER NINE: REINVIGORATING SOCIETY

Photograph © Robert Essel/Corbis

CULTURE OF CONNOISSEURSHIP

BERNARD ARNAULT

THESE ARE CHALLENGING times for Japan. Even before the terrible events of March 2011, its economy was struggling, and our luxury goods company, LVMH, and the sector more generally, have certainly felt the impact. Some people even take the view, admittedly extreme, that the luxury category in Japan is doomed. Allow me to state unequivocally that such beliefs are wrong. On the contrary, we remain very optimistic about the prospects for luxury goods in Japan.

Since the collapse of the "bubble economy" in the 1990s, Japan's economy has had its ups and downs. Yes, the attitudes of Japanese are changing, and their aspirations have shifted. But Japanese consumers' love for quality, excellence, and fashion has never faltered. Japan is still a country that launches trends, where the "new big thing," whether a store or a product, can attract huge crowds, and where the "Parisian look" remains a favored ideal. Why Japan is still important is not just that it is a large market, where per-capita incomes are high. It's important also because Japanese consumers are so extraordinarily discerning—the most demanding in the world. Their sophistication reflects high education levels and avid consumption of information.

Japanese consumers also have a remarkable awareness of luxury products and brands, and balance that awareness with a strong appetite for novelty. Appreciation of craftsmanship and heritage of luxury brands can be explained by an ethos of connoisseurship going back centuries and is, perhaps, intrinsic to Japanese culture. Japanese people appreciate and use, even on a daily basis, works of fine craftsmanship dating back centuries, whether in the form of ceramics, woodworks, or fabrics. Such craftsmanship is sometimes infused with contemporary flair through

---

Bernard Arnault is the chairman and CEO of LVMH Moët Hennessy Louis Vuitton.

the most advanced design or new technology to assist the creation. Japanese believe in not only keeping alive the heritage and craftsmanship, but also reworking and updating this heritage to match the modern lifestyle and aspirations. In Europe, we share these values, which are at the heart of our luxury brands, such as Louis Vuitton and Christian Dior.

One might argue that the global luxury industry has been structured on the basis of what succeeds or doesn't in Japan. Indeed, at LVMH, we think of Japan as our global reference market, a unique laboratory of creativity and innovation, especially in fashion, cosmetics, and architecture. The Japanese have made so many contributions in these areas; for example, LVMH has had wonderful collaborations with the noted architects Jun Aoki, Kengo Kuma, and Kazuyo Sejima, and the artist Takashi Murakami. Of course, Japan has been a longtime source of inspiration for Western designers, such as Hedi Slimane for Dior Homme, and others in the creative arts.

This world's luxury goods industry largely owes its development over the last 30 or 40 years to Japanese customers, whether they were shopping at home or abroad. In the early 1980s, for example, an important part of sales of LVMH brands such as Louis Vuitton came from the Japanese. Japanese tourists buying from luxury goods stores around the world led to the opening of Louis Vuitton stores in Hawaii and Southeast Asia, and helped to launch local luxury industries worldwide. Japan has been a crucial source of innovation for our brands: it was once a sacred cow at Louis Vuitton that all products should be under the same roof. But we moved away from that concept, and the first place we did so was in Japan, where we opened a separate men's store in Osaka and a separate watch and jewelry store in Tokyo's Ginza. Indeed, what we learn in Japan stretches our capabilities around the world.

The business model that we developed in Japan continues to inform our global strategy. That is one reason I regularly visit Japan. Customers from mainland China, as well as from Hong Kong, South Korea, and Taiwan, regularly visit Tokyo to shop for luxury products. They see Japan as the place in Asia where fashion is happening. As important, though, they are attracted by the quality of Japanese service and attention to detail and execution. We celebrate these attributes in a program called "The Art of Detail and Sophistication," which we run for our China management team. We bring Chinese managers to Japan for a week to observe at close quarters the country's culture of service. For starters, we might take our Chinese colleagues to a department-store opening at 10 AM to see the cordial manner in which the staff greets shoppers. These colleagues

Customers from around Asia come to Tokyo to shop for luxury products.
© Everett Kennedy Brown/epa/Corbis

ONE MIGHT ARGUE THAT THE GLOBAL LUXURY INDUSTRY HAS BEEN STRUCTURED ON THE BASIS OF WHAT SUCCEEDS OR DOESN'T IN JAPAN. might visit a school specializing in the art of preparing sushi, or experience a traditional tea ceremony, the intricacies of putting on a *kimono*, or the art of wrapping purchases. At bottom, the program is about bringing alive the sophisticated tastes and values of Japan and translating them into the kind of attention to detail and quality of service that is integral to the luxury experience.

The Japanese market is maturing, both demographically and in its attitude about luxury. The population is aging. More than 30 years have passed since Japanese women discovered and became passionate consumers of foreign luxury brands. Today, they have more choice in this category than ever. Also, fast-fashion mass brands have entered the Japanese market recently, and are giving shoppers an alternative to luxury brands in many buying situations. These developments suggest that Japan is becoming a market similar to the ones we observe in Europe and the United States. Consumers are becoming more demanding and sophisticated, requiring more for every yen they spend. They mix and match luxury goods with fast-fashion brands, trading up and down as they see fit. These consumers are less attached to brands and more inclined to shop around.

On top of that, these shoppers are trading physical goods for leisure. We see a shift from consumption emphasizing the acquisition of objects toward consumption that puts a premium on the quality of experience. Customers still appreciate fine products, but they want them to stand for something and be part of a larger context. In our luxury world, this preference translates into offering our Japanese customer unequaled craftsmanship, an enchanting in-store experience, and higher levels of care from our staff. For instance, we recently converted the top floor of our Omotesando house in Tokyo into a hall for art exhibitions and expert talks. Our obligation is to be ahead of these trends, as we have always been. We will continue to open boutiques in the most promising locations, as we did recently in Kobe, and upgrade or close those that do not meet our rising standards.

Japan remains an essential market for LVMH. We are committed to it and will continue to invest for the long term. Our Japanese customers are more demanding, aware, and sophisticated than ever. By meeting their high standards, we believe we will succeed not only in Japan, but also around the world.

THE POST-LUXURY ECONOMY

TYLER BRÛLÉ

THE WORLD'S LUXURY GOODS companies had the ride of a lifetime in Japan from the extravagant "bubble era" of the late 1980s until the early 2000s. But while the ensuing years have been hard on sales in Japan—particularly so immediately after the March 2011 Tohoku earthquake and tsunami—they've been kind to the peddlers of opinion, research, and talent: the industry's analysts, consultants, and headhunters.

As business began slowing in the early 2000s, some of the big European houses turned to analysts for elaborate data to explain why Japanese office ladies weren't buying as many deluxe handbags from Louis Vuitton as they did in the late 1990s. Others brought in consultants to figure out how retailers could rethink their stores and spark fresh spending, while headhunters made tidy bonuses bringing in bright-eyed directors to address sagging sales of low-heeled pumps and dainty evening bags.

What everyone has failed to identify, however, is that Japan has steadily transformed itself into the world's first post-luxury economy—and has become a more interesting place in the process.

All those trying to figure out how to sell more high-priced watches, woven leather tote bags, and butter-soft loafers to Japanese consumers have missed a simple fact: the banker in Marunouchi, the housewife in Kyoto, and the funky student in Fukuoka have quietly moved on, and they're unlikely to come back. This shift is not an aftereffect of the Tohoku disaster; it's been going on for the better part of a decade.

That is the unpalatable truth for those who've invested in building costly chains of luxury stores up and down the country and, for over two decades, have regarded Japan as their most important market.

Tyler Brûlé is the editor-in-chief of Monocle *magazine and a columnist for the* Financial Times.

Of course some luxury goods retailers—Hermès, for one—have been riding high, and for them, Japan is still a key market because the Japanese premium consumer values provenance and craftsmanship above all else. But other retailers pressed the panic button when they found they couldn't sell one more overpriced *meishi* (calling-card) holder or quilted handbag to Japanese consumers, and called in the consultants to figure out what went wrong.

Consumers are rediscovering the virtue of Japanese craftsmanship–like that of distinctive timber and leather furnishings made by Osaka-based Truck.
© Truck/Osaka

The less-creative advisers might have produced some dazzling charts explaining the impact of a souring economy on household spending power and then left their client to figure out the rest. More honest analysts might have looked a European CEO in the eye and told him that Japan's luxury goods market was saturated long ago.

And truly maverick consultants might have suggested their clients give up on the Japanese customer altogether, hire Mandarin-speaking staff, and re-merchandise their Ginza flagship stores to aim exclusively at the Chinese shoppers who have been flocking to the glitzy shopping district in recent years—at least, until fears of radioactive contamination from the damaged Fukushima nuclear power plant scared them away.

Indeed, many of the world's top luxury brands—including pioneers such as Ermenegildo Zegna, as well as LVMH, Cartier, and Coach—are at the very least funneling investment into their China operations. Others are leaving Japan altogether—just as Versace did in 2009—in part to focus on building their China presence. (Versace has since returned to Japan, albeit in a limited way, with its decision to market its wares through department store concessions in Tokyo and Osaka.) For many small Italian leathergoods and tailoring companies, the flight to China has cleared space on shop rails for more discreet and expensive garments. At the Milan menswear shows in early 2011, many midsize Italian companies reported double-digit growth in their Japan sales, as customers shunned more established labels in favor of smaller, emerging ones.

To get to grips with where the sharp (agenda-setting) end of the market is spending in Japan—and to understand where the rest might be heading—one only need peruse Japan's ever-popular newsstands and scan cover lines to get a flavor of the mood. The words "real," "authentic," "craft," "Nippon," "handmade," "rare," and "bespoke" pop up in everything from fashion to travel and food titles. The feature articles variously advise readers on how to order a unique canvas bag from a tiny atelier in Tokyo's Meguro district, how to make jam using a recipe from a small fruit stand in Kyoto, or even how to organize a tour of wooden-furniture makers in Hokkaido.

Many industry analysts would have the rest of the world believe that Japanese consumers are no longer spending on premium products and are simply staying at home to conserve their savings. The reality is that these former luxury goods consumers—the ones who transformed Japan in the early 1990s into the world's second-largest luxury goods market, behind only the United States—have merely relocated to a more exciting place. Essentially they're rediscovering the skills and traditions of Japan's best craftsmen and a new generation of homegrown designers, who are launching handmade brands that employ ancient manufacturing techniques and, in many cases, traditional materials. Rather than expire in the aftermath of the Tohoku disaster, this trend could well evolve into a cultural movement, as discerning and sympathetic consumers move to support the revitalization of small crafts workshops.

THE CONSUMERS WHO MADE JAPAN INTO THE WORLD'S SECOND-LARGEST LUXURY GOODS MARKET IN THE 1990S HAVE RELOCATED TO A MORE EXCITING PLACE.

Emerging brands like Kansai-based Bag'n'Noun, which uses duck canvas originally developed for Japan's imperial fleet to turn out a range of handmade bags, and Brooklyn, which produces in its Aoyama atelier high-quality leather products that can easily rival Hermès (at a better price point), have gained a loyal following in Japan as well as international attention. Then there is Tomorrowland, with its finely crafted clothing; Tabio, which has put a contemporary spin on Japan's traditional split-toed sock; Imabari Towel, with its superior towel products; and Truck, which began as a two-person business in Osaka and now has months-long waiting lists for its distinctive timber and leather furniture, lighting, and other furnishings.

On the food front, a new breed of innovative chefs has helped turn Japan into the world's most dynamic culinary economies. As a result, the Michelin stars showered on restaurants in Tokyo, Osaka, and Kyoto in the last few years have surpassed even France's huge constellation and put Japan on the world's culinary radar.

How did this shift come about? The simple explanation is that the Japanese post-luxury consumer wised up to the absurd margins charged by high-end European brands for a logo and a pattern applied to a bit of canvas, and became annoyed that most of these items were no longer made anywhere close to Paris or Milan, let alone France or Italy.

These consumers grew weary of seeing the same products show up in department store windows all over the country. And they also didn't like seeing those brands embraced by their neighbors to the west. In a more recent context, certain luxury goods seemed showier than ever in the months following the Tohoku quake.

The overall result has been a steady return to authenticity, a search for the lesser known and exclusive, and for tables at restaurants that require introductions from valued customers in order to secure a pair of seats.

This almost obsessive search for the lesser-known, hard-to-get, and limited edition has become a key narrative in Japanese spending patterns. Witness the hopeful customers lining up for a special edition backpack from a small manufacturer from Oregon, or micro batches of croissants from a French butter producer (Échiré's flagship butter store in Tokyo's central Marunouchi district has daily queues for its strictly limited production of baked goods).

It's easy to see not only why Japan's consumers and retailers lead in terms of personal style (they constantly remix) and innovation (never have department stores been reworked as much as those in Japan) but also why Tokyo sets the tone for the entire region. If boys and girls from Seoul and Shanghai are starting to look increasingly like they've walked off the streets of Tokyo's buzzing Harajuku district, it's because they have; Japan has become the benchmark for hairstyles, sharp cuts of denim, café culture, and new ways to fashion a scarf.

A NEW GENERATION OF HOMEGROWN DESIGNERS IS LAUNCHING HAND-MADE BRANDS THAT EMPLOY ANCIENT MANUFACTURING TECHNIQUES, AND IN MANY CASES, TRADITIONAL MATERIALS.

For "brand Japan," these developments are excellent news, as they have not only boosted domestic travel but also bolstered a whole new generation of entrepreneurs, designers, craftsmen, and chefs to keep the country's creative economy a step ahead of the pack.

While many European and US premium brands are only now waking up to the fact that moving all their production to China and Vietnam may not have been such a good idea, and that Japanese consumers are willing to pay for what might be called the "real thing," many companies are reaping the benefits of their "Japanese-ness."

Essentially, Japan has gone through a miniboom in small and midsize enterprises that has seen sacked bankers investing in vineyards and opening restaurants, even as the country has managed to boost the global reach of its soft power by introducing consumers, both at home and abroad, to new and indigenous labels, fabrics, tastes and textures.

The challenge for Japan now, as always, is to start marketing this movement in order to show other economies that there is, indeed, life after the gold-chain handbag and studded ballet slipper, and that taking the slower, more crafted approach might be the more rewarding and sustainable path.

In an increasingly crowded, globalized and impersonal world, is there anything wrong with taking the less populated, more unique and intimate path? Japan's shift to a post-luxury society that mixes its famed manufacturing might with a tradition of craft could well be the model for a new, more considered, thoughtful and prosperous nation state.

JAPAN'S CULINARY REVOLUTION

GWEN ROBINSON

EVERY DAY IN A SPRAWLING VILLA set amid the ancient temples and gardens of eastern Kyoto, elegantly coiffed and *kimono*-clad waitresses shuffle silently in their white *tabi* socks along polished wooden corridors. They bear trays laden with costly ceramic platters, each vessel a precious backdrop for intricate dishes described by one Western critic as "edible artwork."

The waitresses kneel to knock discreetly before sliding open the *washi* paper doors of each private dining room, bowing as they enter. Inside, the wood-paneled *tatami* room is adorned only with a scroll of flowing characters and a seasonal *ikebana* flower arrangement. Guests sit at a low table on silk cushions, gazing through a large window onto a classic Japanese garden and carp pond. The hushed atmosphere is broken only by the low, hypnotic tones of classical *koto*, or harp, music and the sound of running water from a nearby fountain.

Over several hours, a succession of 14 exquisitely presented dishes will showcase every key technique of Japanese cooking and a range of handcrafted tableware, in a seasonal feast intended as much to feed the eye and spirit as the stomach. The current theme is spring, dictating every aspect of the meal, from the pink-hued porcelain and pickled cherry-blossom garnishes to ingredients such as new bamboo shoots, lily bulbs, and *ayu* river fish.

This is *kaiseki ryori*, Japanese *haute cuisine*, at its finest. Those diners with an aversion to raw fish or unfamiliar textures might see it as a form of gastronomic torture. But in the annals of gourmet delights, a meal at one of Japan's top *kaiseki* restaurants is a prized, if costly, experience.

Gwen Robinson is a Tokyo-based journalist for the Financial Times.

Price is not necessarily a criterion for authenticity in *kaiseki*, and many restaurants in Japan offer elaborate "mini-*kaiseki*" courses for as little as 4,000 yen. In Kyoto, however, the ancient capital of *kaiseki* culture and still the center for Japan's top *ryotei*, or full-service *kaiseki* restaurants, a multicourse dinner can cost from 25,000 to 60,000 yen (about $300 to $730) per head—for food alone. With alcohol, *sake*, or, increasingly, Western wine, the bill can reach 70,000 yen or more.

For devotees, it is a price paid without hesitation. To them, *kaiseki* is not just about food. It is a gastronomic meditation on traditional aesthetics and, indeed, the very meaning of Japanese-ness.

In recent years, this insular world has drawn unprecedented international attention, particularly since the arrival in Japan of Michelin Guides—first with the controversial 2008 guide to Tokyo restaurants and hotels, and then with the fiercely debated Kyoto guide in 2009. Michelin has since bestowed more stars on Japan's two key gastronomic centers than any other city in the world.

IN THE GRAND OLD *RYOTEI* OF KYOTO, THERE IS MOUNTING CONCERN THAT ANCIENT TRADITIONS ARE BREAKING DOWN.

The international plaudits, however, have been somewhat tempered by food safety concerns following the March 11 earthquake, tsunami, and resulting nuclear crisis. Fears of radioactive contamination hit produce from the devastated northeast region, including vegetables, dairy, meat, and seaweed and seafood products. But Kyoto, in western Japan, with its own regional sources of fresh produce, seemed relatively insulated from such concerns. If anything, several chefs from western Japan told me, the food scares in the east have boosted demand for produce from the west, both domestically and abroad. In Tokyo and its surrounding regions, meanwhile, *kaiseki* and sushi restaurants were quick to modify their offerings, reducing their reliance on domestic seafood and diversifying their sources of supply.

Kaiseki culture has come under mounting pressure to reform its anachronistic model. In a sense, foreign scrutiny has ushered forces of "internationalization" into traditional Japanese cuisine, in much the same way they have been challenging timeworn practices in other fields of Japanese culture, sport, and business.

Increasingly, young Japanese chefs are venturing abroad for on-the-job training or to open their own restaurants, and in Japan, a Who's Who of international chefs has driven growth in high-end, Western dining. Meanwhile, the distinctive principles and techniques of *kaiseki* are influencing some of the world's top chefs, from Ferran Adria, of El Bulli fame, to France's Joel Robuchon, who operates four restaurants, three of them multistarred, in Japan. Robuchon opened his first Japanese restaurant, the one-star Yoshi, in Monaco in 2009.

Says Jean Luc Naret, the former director of Michelin Guides who led the group's push into Japan, "The world now recognizes that Japanese gastronomy has something totally unique, because of the high quality of its products and the way its superb culinary traditions are transmitted from one generation to the next, over centuries."

In 2005, when Michelin Guides decided to launch in Asia, the group's inspectors surveyed the region to determine which city should be the subject of the inaugural guide. "Japan—and more specifically, Tokyo—very quickly and very naturally became the *porte d'entrée*," says Naret. All the more ironic, then, that here, in the grand old *ryotei* of Kyoto—at the heart of a vast and highly acclaimed culinary culture—there is a growing sense that ancient traditions are breaking down.

Kaiseki cuisine is said to have originated from Zen Buddhist rituals and the 16th-century practice of serving small, refined dishes during protracted tea ceremonies. That practice evolved into a more elaborate affair, though always within rigid rules governing presentation, structure, and technique.

At its most exalted levels, there is still something of a religious quality to the *kaiseki* world, with its almost theatrical formality, severe rules, and reverence for ritual. Nearly all traditional establishments, for example, have an unwritten ban on accepting women trainees. Some top Kyoto *ryotei* still draw water from their own wells, as they have done for centuries. Many will not give itemized bills or accept credit cards.

Of course, for many diners, both Japanese and foreign, that is part of the appeal: the feeling of being transported, just for an evening, into a rapidly fading world. But this genteel nostalgia masks a darker side. In the austere backrooms of some of the biggest *ryotei*, some of Japan's most revered culinary traditions clearly rest on harsh labor practices and an increasingly unsustainable apprenticeship system.

Throughout the world, apprenticeship is an integral—and often brutal—part of restaurant training, as various chefs have revealed in tell-all memoirs. In Japan, however, on-the-job training can be particularly severe. In poorly ventilated old

Kaiseki: a gastronomic meditation on the meaning of Japanese-ness.
© Eric Rechsteiner

kitchens at several big *ryotei*, young *deshi*, or apprentices, typically work seven days a week, from 6 AM to 11 PM or later, with only a half-hour break and no more than three days off a month.

In two such establishments, each with more than 20 kitchen staff, monthly pay is fixed for a full five years at just 80,000 to 100,000 yen, equal to what a big customer might spend on a single meal, and well below the Japanese minimum wage. In this paternalistic, even feudal, system, most kitchen staff live on the premises in basic dorms for at least five years.

The unquestioned understanding—and indeed, the expectation—is that trainees will learn through the ancient system of *shugyo*, roughly translated as "severe training." In the big *ryotei*, which generally employ from eight to 30 kitchen staff, this training entails hard, menial tasks such as gutting fish, washing dishes, and even cleaning toilets. At some establishments, it takes

MANY OF JAPAN'S MOST REVERED CULINARY TRADITIONS DEPEND ON HARSH LABOR PRACTICES AND AN INCREASINGLY UNSUSTAINABLE APPRENTICESHIP SYSTEM.

years before a young chef is allowed to prepare food. Intimidation—verbal, if not physical—from senior chefs is common.

Even as a *deshi* slowly scales the hierarchy, the compartmentalized nature of traditional *kaiseki* means he is assigned for long stretches to a single task, perhaps cooking rice or grilling fish. It takes at least eight years to learn the key aspects of preparing a multicourse meal, and even then, only the top chefs hold the secrets of pulling it all together. Similarly, in smaller *kaiseki*—or less formal *kappo*—restaurants, with perhaps two to five

kitchen staff, trainees work punishing hours and handle the hardest tasks. They, too, can be subject to intimidation. Even so, a young chef in a small place inevitably gains knowledge and responsibility far more quickly.

For aspiring *kaiseki* chefs, who cannot afford the costs of a professional cooking school or who simply believe in traditional training, apprenticeship is the only way. Indeed, many who came up through the *shugyo* system vehemently defend it. *Kaiseki* trainees are expected to feel "lucky to get any money at all," a foreign chef who has worked at several top *ryotei* tells me. "The salary is considered a bonus because this is an education, seen as equal or superior to a culinary school or college education. The hard work and the long hours are tuition. It's said that in this world you don't truly master something without putting in 10,000 hours—that means eight to nine years. But it's not just about learning the techniques, it's about consistency and the spirit of practice."

Ichiro Kubota, a *kaiseki* chef whose family runs a two-star *kappo* restaurant in Kyoto, warns that Japan's new cult of culinary celebrity, hastened by the arrival of Michelin's star rankings, can "blind" chefs to the importance of traditional training, encouraging them to focus too much on "gastronomic hardware," or technique. The vital "software," he argues, is "something you can only learn from the masters." The purpose of apprenticeship is to learn not only *kaiseki* techniques and recipes, says Kubota, but also the spiritual rules. "Yes, it is hard, and it should be. To become a true chef, you must watch and learn from your seniors. They are living dictionaries."

Kaiseki cuisine is a crucial part of Japan's culinary future as well as its past, notes Michelin's Naret. But while many apprentices are reasonably treated, "some are treated very poorly, receiving from their 'master' the same harsh treatment he received from the generation before." Ultimately, says Naret, "this is a 'tradition' that has to stop. The *kaiseki* world is evolving, and this kind of training system will eventually break down."

Indeed, "evolution" could be a rallying cry for the emerging generation of Japanese chefs. Masaki Sugisaki, who has won acclaim for his "creative *kaiseki*" at Dinings, in London's Marylebone, quit his family's *kaiseki* restaurant near Tokyo to work in Europe. His hope was to develop a "modern version of *kaiseki* philosophy" and apply it internationally. Japan, he says, has a "remarkable and beautiful food culture, but it's just too old-fashioned. The way young chefs are treated seems almost to violate basic human rights."

Such sentiments highlight a shift away from *shugyo* training toward other means to professional qualifications. As a result, the big *ryotei* have been forced for the first time to compete to attract good staff, a development that has already led to small but significant reforms among the more enlightened *ryotei*. Several of Kyoto's three-star establishments, for example, have increased the days off for staff to as many as six per month from the standard two to three, while others have raised pay or improved their training regimes.

Even so, for ambitious would-be chefs, a *kaiseki* apprenticeship seems a bleak alternative to Japan's vibrant contemporary restaurant culture, with its ready rewards for creativity and entrepreneurship. Author and Japanese cuisine expert Kate Klippensteen says that a growing number of trainees are dropping out of the *kaiseki* system after just two or three years to start their own places, or "to just drop out." This development, she warns, is "transforming traditional *kaiseki* culture, and not in a favorable way."

The ensuing pressure on more rigid establishments is unlikely to recede. Younger chefs have grown up on a diet of television, the Internet, and affordable travel. "They know what's out there," says one Kyoto chef. "They've seen their contemporaries go overseas to work, or quit apprenticeships to open their own places, and they don't want to work like this anymore."

The big *ryotei* know that, without cheap labor, they could not survive, at least not in their current size and form. Indeed, a wave of Kyoto's *kaiseki* establishments faltered in Japan's postbubble years of the 1990s, and still more failed in the last five years.

For now, the apprenticeship system remains the backbone of the traditional *kaiseki* business model. Concern about the system's viability, however, has compelled some *ryotei* proprietors not only to reexamine old labor practices, but also to consider culinary innovations and other measures to attract new customers.

Despite the high prices paid by *kaiseki* diners, profits are surprisingly modest for most *ryotei*. Overheads are huge. Everything must be the best, including kitchen equipment and tableware. A single dinner plate by a contemporary potter can cost 40,000 yen (nearly $500), and a lacquer bowl, twice that. An antique platter might exceed 2 million yen ($24,000), while prices of kitchen utensils, such as handcrafted knives and forged metal pots, can make Western chefs wince. Then there are the daily deliveries from all over Japan of costly live seafood and the freshest ingredients.

In their bid to boost business, many of Kyoto's big *ryotei* have opened more casual, downtown branches serving cheaper set meals. Some are trying to increase sales of *sozai*, or packaged food, while others have experimented with special gift certificates, or cut-price corporate entertainment deals. Meanwhile, a growing crop of contemporary Japanese restaurants is becoming ever more competitive. As the big *ryotei* grapple with the decline in their loyal but aging customer base, they are seeing a fundamental change in the tastes of younger diners.

Rather than fork out for a formal *kaiseki* meal, many young Japanese would prefer to try a hot new restaurant they have read about in a magazine or on the country's myriad food blogs. Whether the fare is Western or Japanese, these diners are increasingly drawn to chefs in smaller or more stylish places, where the food is innovative, the atmosphere more relaxed, and the final bill much smaller.

When Michelin launched its first guide in Japan, many critics, including *kaiseki* chefs, derided the group's efforts to judge Japan's traditional restaurants. There were the "usual loud protests" over omissions and inclusions, shrugs Michelin's Naret. The important thing, he argues, is how quickly Japan's chefs discovered the boost that a star rating can give their business. Indeed, many in the industry now readily admit the guides have set a valuable global benchmark, for Japanese chefs to measure themselves not just against each other, but also against chefs worldwide.

Alain Verzeroli, executive chef for Robuchon's restaurants in Japan, sees a swing toward smaller, more exclusive restaurants that often combine traditional Japanese principles with contemporary European ideas. "Japan is really taking a different direction now," Verzeroli comments. "The chefs are young, but many are sophisticated enough to be able to create beautiful dishes. It's largely due to Michelin and the attention its guides can bring." The downside, he says, is the associated "ego-driven" race for star rankings and media attention. "So many young chefs now want to show off and compete...but something is missing. Many of these new restaurants lack soul."

Adding to pressures on the *ryotei* system is the rise of the professional cooking school in Japan and the exodus of young chefs to train abroad. One reason *shugyo* thrived for centuries was the absence of alternatives for aspiring chefs. Japan had no professional, Western-style cooking schools until the 20th century.

These days Japanese chefs can be found toiling in top restaurant kitchens overseas. Indeed, says Naret, "in many of the Michelin-starred restaurants of France, there is a Japanese employee. These employees are popular partly because of their traditions of perfectionism. They learn a lot, work hard, and practice a lot. When they go back to Japan to open a restaurant, many end up equal to or even surpassing their master."

At the same time, a growing number of young Japanese are prepared to pay the high fees to train at Tsuji Culinary Institute, the country's leading professional academy, or smaller rivals. Today, Tsuji boasts about 130,000 graduates, many working in Michelin-starred restaurants in Europe and Japan. At any one time, the academy has about 3,000 students, nearly 45 percent of them women, at 14 schools across eight campuses, including two chateaux schools in France. Notably, nearly half of all students elect to specialize at some stage in European cuisine, mainly French, or patisserie.

"APPRENTICESHIP IS HARD, AND IT SHOULD BE. TO BECOME A TRUE CHEF, YOU MUST WATCH AND LEARN FROM YOUR SENIORS. THEY ARE LIVING DICTIONARIES."

The price of a professional diploma—3.7 million yen for a full two-year course—is steep. A postgraduate year of French field training costs nearly that much again. But for ambitious chefs, the investment is well worth it. A Tsuji diploma virtually guarantees a job at a top restaurant or hotel, as the school's alumni records show. Nearly 90 percent of kitchen staff at Robuchon's restaurants and patisseries in Japan, for example, are Tsuji graduates.

Many of Japan's "new-breed" chefs—particularly those who quit the traditional *shugyo* system to open a restaurant or work elsewhere—see European cuisine as a refuge from the hidebound traditions of *kaiseki*. A growing number seek to combine elements of both culinary traditions, but remain wary of the *kaiseki* training regime. In European cuisine, even in Japan, changing jobs is an accepted method of moving up, and there is far more opportunity for women. In the *kaiseki* world, by contrast, moving employers means starting at the bottom; trainees who switch jobs are regarded with suspicion.

Increasingly, ambitious Japanese chefs see working abroad or gaining a professional diploma as a way to leapfrog the traditional system and earn the recognition required to open a successful restaurant. There are numerous examples to inspire them. Among them is Tateru Yoshino, one of the first Japanese chefs to train abroad. After working in France in the early 1980s, Yoshino eventually opened a restaurant in Paris, in 1997. He now holds a total of four Michelin stars across his three Tokyo restaurants, and shuttles between them and his Paris restaurant, Stella Maris, which won a star in 2006.

Yoshino began as a trainee in French restaurants in Japan. But, he notes, it was only when he first visited France, at the age of 39, that he realized the "huge difference in the sophistication level from Japan." It is vital for Japanese chefs to work overseas, he says. "We have to identify what is missing in Japan, by learning outside of Japan, to benchmark, instead of being satisfied with what we have."

Another trailblazing chef is Keisuke Matsushima, who went to France at the age of 20, after graduating from Tsuji. He opened his first restaurant in Nice at the age of 25, and a few years later gained his first Michelin star. Now barely 33, he opened his second venture, Restaurant-I, in Tokyo's Harajuku, in 2009, winning a Michelin star the following year. Then there is Shuzo Kishida of Quintessence, in Tokyo's Shirogane district, who learned on the job, mainly in multistarred restaurants in France. At the age of 33, a year after returning to open his restaurant in 2006, he made headlines by landing three stars in the inaugural Michelin 2008 Tokyo guide.

But perhaps the biggest inspiration is the story of Junichi Watanabe who, at 35, abandoned his career as salaryman at a construction company to retrain as a chef. Watanabe started as an unpaid dishwasher at a *kaiseki* restaurant before persuading another establishment to take him on as an apprentice. After five years of hard training, he opened Ichie, a small *kaiseki* restaurant in Tokyo's Hiroo neighborhood. A year later, in the week he turned 40, he won a Michelin star.

Such examples, of mavericks who find a fast track to success, only intensify the strains on the conformist world of traditional *kaiseki*. There are also other, more unlikely challenges—not least, the growing availability in Japan of a vast new range of ingredients. It is no longer enough for a *ryotei* to focus on time-honored seasonal dishes, explains Keiji Mori, a *kaiseki*-trained chef who runs Maru, a casual, Kyoto-style restaurant in Tokyo's Aoyama district. Not long ago, *kaiseki* restaurants "would all cook the same dishes," says Mori. "Now, many are trying to develop original recipes." That shift, he warns, threatens *kaiseki's* seasonal focus and could ultimately lead to the disappearance of "real, traditional Kyoto cuisine."

Under siege from within and without, proprietors of the grand *ryotei* know they must modernize their ancient model while maintaining valued traditions. They know, too, that reforming labor practices will require a rethink of the cost base and therefore the entire traditional structure. If this ossified world can make that transition, it could, perhaps, set an example for other fields. Along the way, however, many bigger establishments could falter or be forced to downsize, which would also hit suppliers, traditional craftsmen, and others who depend on their business.

Perhaps, in the future, there will be just a handful of grand, old *ryotei*, and a flourishing culture of small and midrange *kaiseki* restaurants. Already, the best of this new breed have proven they can innovate while preserving some key traditions. The purists—who defend long, hard *shugyo* training and reject culinary experimentation—may protest. Unfortunately, there are not enough of them to support the system as it stands.

There are already signs of change, not just in labor standards, but also in the growing dialogue between rival proprietors and chefs through Kyoto's industry associations. Slowly, owners and chefs are opening up to the world as they seek new ways to draw on the old. The *shugyo* system, meanwhile, may well go the way of the big *ryotei* that fail to meet the new challenges. For the survivors, however, there is a related term, *kugyo*: "to carry on while suffering."

How food fears are changing Japanese cuisine

Ask any *kaiseki* chef to name three vital ingredients of Japanese cuisine and he will most likely say *konbu*, or edible kelp; *katsuobushi*, dried bonito shavings; and water. These basic items, simmered in strict order, form *dashi* stock, the basis of Japanese cooking.

But after the March 11 disasters, the use of such essential fish and algae products, along with other traditional staples, triggered safety concerns—particularly in overseas markets. Many countries banned or restricted Japanese food imports after radiation leaks from the crippled Fukushima nuclear power plant northeast of Tokyo. The restrictions initially focused on produce, such as vegetables, dairy, and meat, from affected regions. But the news in April that moderately radioactive water had been released into the sea off Fukushima prompted some countries, including India, to ban all Japanese food imports—regardless of origin—for an initial three-month period.

Other countries, including Australia, China, and the United States, limited their restrictions to products from four or five prefectures near the nuclear plant, although some later widened the curbs to include 12 regions in eastern Japan. Still other countries introduced requirements for "radiation-free" certification of various food items.

Economically, the impact of such actions is small; food products account for barely 1 percent of Japan's total exports, according to the World Bank. But gastronomically, the effects could be significant. The increasing scarcity of key ingredients is forcing chefs of Japanese cuisine to seek alternative sources of supply—from China and Korea, for example—and to experiment with new ingredients and methods. If safety concerns undermine the popularity of Japanese produce abroad, and contribute to scarcities at home, traditional Japanese cuisine could change fundamentally.

At Zeniya, an acclaimed *kaiseki* restaurant in the western Japanese city of Kanazawa, foreign customers, who usually book far in advance, have cancelled reservations through the end of the year, according to proprietor Shin Takagi. A classically trained chef who travels the world to prepare *kaiseki* banquets, Takagi says that after the disasters, foreign clients asked him not to use Japan-sourced ingredients. By April, he was experimenting with substitutes—making *dashi* with chicken or duck bones, for example, or using salt instead of soy sauce. "There is no choice," Takagi shrugs. "We have to go back to zero and come up with new ways."

Masaki Sugisaki, of Dinings, a highly regarded Japanese restaurant in London, began developing a menu less reliant on Japan-sourced ingredients within days of the disaster. Even so, business fell sharply.

For chefs in Japan, the big worry has been supply shortages. Keiji Mori, owner-chef of Maru, a contemporary Japanese restaurant in Tokyo, warns that ultimately, Japanese chefs may have to use more imported products, including seafood, if key ingredients become more difficult to source within Japan. While that could promote innovation, Mori fears it could also hasten the decline of traditional *kaiseki* cuisine.

—Gwen Robinson

PEOPLE OF JAPAN, DISORGANIZE!

MASARU TAMAMOTO

IN JAPAN, THE LAND OF GROUP-THINK, even spontaneity is regulated. The first principle of action is to establish an alibi. Risk aversion is endemic. Acting on one's own initiative is tantamount to disrupting social harmony. Rule breaking is treated as a social disease.

The social order of modern Japan is conformist and consensual. Individuals achieve functionality by making themselves insignificant. The primary agents in this order are organizations, which often dictate to individuals their personal goals and the means to achieve them. Thus, individual Japanese are born into summoned lives and predetermined roles. Those roles are concrete and specific; playing them successfully demands acute awareness of social structure and context. In essence, today's Japanese have crafted for themselves a scripted world that tempers the onus—but also the privilege—of making individual choices.

This scripted world was designed to eliminate uncertainty. Social interactions, both public and private, were ordered by seniority. Decisions were prescribed—and constrained—by the premise of lifetime job security. The system was centralized and bureaucratic in the extreme, but it promised ever-increasing wealth, and safety and predictability for all. And for a time, the system delivered on that promise.

For two decades, however, the familiar script has failed to tell a coherent story. For Japanese under the age of 40, the quality of adult life is under constant threat from deflation, which exacts a tremendous psychological toll. Rising suicide rates across all age groups are a clear sign the old narrative has gone awry. There are many others: rising unemployment and underemployment, the spread of contract

---

Masaru Tamamoto is a research associate in the Faculty of Asian and Middle Eastern Studies at the University of Cambridge.

hiring over permanent employment, declining income levels, and an insolvent social security system. Feelings of pessimism, envy, and resentment now permeate all aspects of modern Japanese life. Japan's future is no longer certain—and to the extent that the future is knowable, it is bleak.

The old system consolidates organizational status and power in the hands of the old: aging leaders who recall the scripted world's halcyon comforts. But the minds of this graying generation are stuck in the past. They have squandered two decades in a futile effort to preserve the unpreservable, racking up vast public and private debt to bolster a spent order. Japan's entrenched, old guard has shown itself incapable of imagining an alternative script.

And in truth, the triumph of the old script was fleeting. The system of bureaucratic capitalism often referred to as the "capitalist development state," or more commonly "Japan Inc.," did not take solid form until the early 1970s and functioned effectively only until collapse of Japan's speculative financial bubble in 1991. The ensuing period of decay already has outlasted the system's moment of success.

> **AFTER TWO DECADES OF DYSFUNCTION, JAPAN HAS COME AT LAST TO AN HISTORIC TURNING POINT. THE OLD ORDER IS SPENT; IT IS PAINFULLY EVIDENT THAT THE NATION NEEDS A WHOLE NEW SOCIAL COMPACT.**

The very structures and habits that drove Japan Inc.'s success in the 1970s and 1980s now inhibit change. Organizations made Japan Inc., and Japan Inc. in turn wove organizations into the fabric of national life, making them the paramount social agents in an interdependent web. In Japan's tight corporatist world, no organization dared to challenge another, for to do so would risk inviting a counterattack. In this intricate arrangement of systemic mutual support and preservation of the status quo, dysfunctional organizations were allowed to limp along indefinitely, consuming capital and human resources that could have been more efficiently utilized elsewhere.

After two decades of dysfunction, Japan has come at last to an historic turning point. The old order is spent; it is painfully evident that the nation needs not just a handful of new policies or state-led initiatives, but also a whole new social compact. But where to find alternatives?

In times past, Japan has reinvented itself by borrowing eagerly, if eclectically, from the customs and institutions of other nations. In the push for modernization that began in the Meiji era (1868-1912), the Japanese took the German model of Prussian paternalism and—like the Germans themselves—ran it into the ground. In the postwar era, Japan embraced an American model first imposed by the US occupation; that, too, ultimately ran its course. The two models differed greatly, but in both cases Japan built its social and political models from imported parts. But today Japan has run out of models to emulate and seems to have lost its way. The nation's best hope is to look within, to reconstruct its own future without regard to outside examples.

There are three pillars of modernity, as defined by notions of progress and rationality that developed in Europe from the 17th century: the state as the highest level of social organization, capitalism as the wealth generator, and liberalism as the core ideology. Modern Japan has an understanding of the concept of the state, having experimented with authoritarian centralism, emperor-centered militarism, and democratic consumerism. So too with the key features of capitalism: open economy, imperial autarchy, and mercantilism. But the Japanese have never understood liberalism. This very lack of understanding leaves room for Japan to write a new script, to extricate itself from near-paralysis and certain decline.

PEDDLING LIBERALISM TO JAPAN ALL TOO OFTEN DRAWS THE RESPONSE: "ARE YOU SAYING WE SHOULD BECOME AMERICANS?"

Since Meiji, Japan's leaders have associated the idea of modernization with predictability; they sought to chart a course to a future already proven and "known." But a liberal future is, by definition, unknown and has no proven end. That very open-endedness is the essence of the Enlightenment idea of progress. Thus liberalism is fundamentally at odds with the old Japanese script.

Immanuel Kant could have been summing up Japan's problems when he defined the Enlightenment and its liberal project as "man's emergence from his self-imposed immaturity." Immaturity, he explained, "is the inability to use one's understanding without guidance from another. This immaturity is self-imposed when its cause lies not in lack of understanding, but in lack of resolve and courage to use it without guidance from another."

One key to Japan's conundrum lies in its nonlinear sense of time. Shuichi Kato, the late contemporary political philosopher, once observed how future and past are so often collapsed into the present—the "here and now"—in Japan. This sense of time is of course not particular to Japan, being premodern and experienced in other eras and places, including in the West. What is remarkable about Japan, however, is how the country achieved so much in the modern era without adopting the linear sense of time inherent in the idea of progress. Put simply, this achievement happened because modernity in the Japanese view could be had by "guidance from another." There was simply no need for Japan to construct a future of its own making until now.

In Western culture, Enlightenment became possible when society transcended the notion of Christian afterlife and embraced the idea of progress based on reason and the pursuit of peace, prosperity, and human happiness. It is time, now, for Japan to transcend "guidance from another" and emerge from its "self-imposed immaturity."

Yet, peddling liberalism to the Japanese all too often draws the response: "Are you saying we should become Americans?" The Japanese mind is so trained to deal with the concrete that a liberal society can only mean the United States, which many see as a land of unabashed individualism and attendant greed that wrought global financial mayhem. The Japanese find it difficult to conceive of liberalism in the abstract because doing so requires approximating a self-defined, desirable future.

Leaving aside the question of virtue, liberalism should serve Japan on practical grounds by enhancing innovation and economic productivity. In past eras, organizations served Japan's needs for industrial capitalism and a manufacturing economy. In organizations, each functionary was traditionally as necessary as—and equal to—every other, while discrepancies between individual capabilities were neutralized by the general effort. But today's era of late modernity and service capitalism puts the spotlight on the individual over the organization, and suggests it is high time to foster pluralism by making room for personal initiatives and expression of individual capabilities.

Talk of pluralism raises the vital and related challenge of immigration. While successive Japanese governments have been loath to deal squarely with this highly charged issue, it seems inevitable that Japan will eventually see a large influx of immigrants. A pluralistic society is naturally better suited to welcome people from the outside and resists the current impulse—reinforced by strict immigration and citizenship requirements—to reshape foreign arrivals, cookie-cutter style, into "acceptable" residents who easily fit into organizational Japan.

Japan's rapidly aging and dwindling population lies at the heart of the country's many problems. Already, 23 percent of Japanese are over 65, and there are 8.3 million over 80 in a country of 127 million people. With a steadily declining birthrate, present trends indicate there will be 30 percent fewer Japanese and an acutely geriatric society 50 years from now. On this front alone, liberalism is a perfect fit for a Japan in dire need of more labor and higher productivity to achieve sustainable economic growth.

Liberalism in its true sense requires embracing individual autonomy and liberty. Only morally autonomous individuals are capable of taking responsibility. But in modern Japan, where agency largely rests with the organization and not the individual, personal status is almost wholly defined by one's association with an organization and that organization's place in the long-established hierarchy. While the famous Japanese notion of "harmony" is understood as a central value, this harmony lacks a sense of time and movement. It is static, and underpins the ideology of a strictly stratified order to generate obedience.

Consider the issue of trust. Japan is widely hailed as a "high trust" society. And yet that belief cannot be the result of the fact that the Japanese are naturally trusting and trustworthy. Rather, trust in Japan today is the product of innumerable regulations governing the minutiae of everyday life, from formal law to social rituals and manners. These rules make behavior predictable. Normally, a society is more efficient when less effort is required to enforce cooperation. But it costs a great deal to establish regulations, and the Japanese regulatory system is costly because of its expansiveness and intrusiveness—not to mention the drag it places on initiative and creativity, which, by definition, are unpredictable.

Of course, all societies are established on rules. But authority in Japan assumes that Japan's citizens cannot be trusted to make wise decisions without precise rules to guide them. Members of a society so nurtured tend to retain the premodern mindset of peasants. Vulnerable to the whims of authority, peasants are fatalistic about forces beyond their control. Peasants' weaknesses make them devious; they must band together to gain strength in numbers, but they mistrust their fellows, for they know each other's weaknesses. In similar fashion, modern Japanese have demonstrated their distrust of authority and of one another. Japanese society has associated individualism with inequality, and a lack of trust and empathy. Yet it is possible to strive for a liberal Japanese future without socially disruptive inequality.

Liberal individualism is not about selfishness, as many Japanese tend to assume. Rather, the true goal of liberalism is to build a desirable community consistent with the ideals of liberty and individual autonomy. Similarly, the Japanese must shed their misconception that equality means "sameness"; equality of opportunity need not mean equality of outcome. Loneliness, bewilderment, and personal demoralization sometimes are cited as pitfalls of individualism. And yet, in what is perhaps the greatest irony of contemporary Japan, these are the very symptoms of the breakdown taking place in this organizational society. As things stand, in 20 years' time, one in four men in their 50s will be living alone; 29 percent of men and 23 percent of women will never marry.

In the name of "harmony," "stability," and "fairness," the old, organization-led Japan is creating a society of impoverished isolates, who live side by side in solitude and misery, straightjacketed by predefined social roles. That is a future Japan can and must avoid.

REVIVING A NOBLE BREED

MARTHA SHERRILL

ON MY FIRST VISIT TO JAPAN, 11 years ago, my baggage included the usual pre-conceptions. The Japanese were introverted and repressed, I gathered, except when they were drunk on the subway. The Japanese were guarded and noncommittal, unable to voice a strong opinion, and chronic foot-draggers. There were rigid codes of manners, which included elaborately wrapped gifts and other *Kabuki*-like transactions that were impossible to do correctly unless you had lived there forever.

Friends who had lived and worked in Japan warned that my husband and I would never make any Japanese friends, never be invited to dinner or even cross the threshold of a Japanese home. We weren't to expect any glimpses behind the *shoji*, in other words, because invisible barriers shielded outsiders from seeing anything real.

That is, if there was anything real to see. This was the subtext behind many remarks made about Japan. It was a nation of uniform drones.

It was nighttime when our train pulled into Kamakura, where we would be spending the winter. I drifted to sleep on a cozy futon with all those preconceptions floating in my head. The next morning, when I woke up, I began to see them all dismantled, one by one.

My husband and son and I made friends almost immediately. On walks to Kinokuniya market or climbing the stairs to the Hachiman shrine, strangers smiled. Bank tellers remembered us, monks joked and offered toys, and teenagers made shy attempts to communicate. We were invited to join a church playgroup so my son could meet other toddlers. We were invited to coffee and tea, then dinner, at our landlord's house, and several others. I was surprised by the clutter in these houses, the piles of shoes, stacks of books, little mountains of paper and mail.

Martha Sherrill is the author of Dog Man: An Uncommon Life on a Faraway Mountain *(2008).*

I was surprised, too, by the relaxed feeling, the playful atmosphere. Our hosts were funny and warm, gregarious and quick to laugh. Meals lasted a long time. Food was savored, small glasses and cups of beer and sake consumed, and the talk went on and on until it was interrupted by more laughter, sometimes loud, uproarious. Sitting around a dinner table or on the floor, I felt at home. My new friends reminded me of my mother's family of gregarious Italians.

Most of all, I was shocked by the depth of conversations, and their candor. The brutal honesty of the dialogue often startled me. It is rare to encounter people who can speak frankly about their lives and worldview. In the United States, where there is social pressure to appear successful and happy, people often describe their lives in an unrelentingly sunny light, using spin rather than reflection. Something very different seemed to be happening in Japan. Shrewd self-appraisals and poignant revelations seemed the norm. I wasn't fed lines, or told about job satisfaction or how marvelous a new son-in-law was. I was told the job was dull and the son-in-law. . . "Well, we think he's a bit odd."

Rather than characterless automatons, the Japanese I encountered seemed to be masters of the personal connection. And instead of groupthink and conformity, at every turn I saw individuals with quirks and differences. I met jazz nuts, vinyl freaks, rockers, steak lovers, and macrobiotic dieters. I met Zen students and Roman Catholics. I met a single-malt scotch obsessive, a monk who hung out at Starbucks, a secretary who taught yoga, and an elementary school teacher who surfed on weekends. I encountered self-reflection and thoughtfulness and such subtle consideration of the feelings of others that it was hard to fathom. And over and over, I was disarmed by the outspokenness of the Japanese.

Eventually I stayed long enough in Japan to witness some of the things that friends and colleagues had warned me about—the Japan of cliché—the guardedness, the foot-dragging, the drunken salarymen on the subway. I came to see how maddening it could be to do business in Japan, the endless negotiations, delays, indecision, and need for total consensus. Compared with the warmth and spontaneity I'd felt inside the homes of my Japanese friends, the practical realities of workaday Japan could be trying.

Why didn't the professional life of Japan contain more of the honesty and trust, the outspokenness and humor that I'd seen so often in private? What was gained by consensus? I understood its benefits, which included predictability. But what was lost—the vitality that comes from honesty, even confrontation—seemed to rob Japanese society of one thing it honored most: personal connection. And I began to suspect that the constraints of the workplace had sparked the need for passionate recreational pursuits, for the breathtaking individualism of the private hobbies and pastimes.

Wouldn't the fabric of all life in Japan improve enormously if private and public Japan were woven more closely together?

Many of these questions were alive in my mind when I returned to Japan, in 2005, to meet Sawataishi Morie, an engineer who had rescued the Akita dog breed from extinction during World War II. As I rode the bullet train into the vast valleys of the snow country, I wondered if my previous experiences in Japan had been an aberration. Maybe I wouldn't feel so comfortable in a rural area, or in the house of a man like Morie, who had not known many Westerners.

In guidebooks and various studies of Japan, much is made of the great divide between Tokyo, with its glittery sophistication and prosperity, and the bleak north. Even my Tokyo and Kamakura friends seemed surprised that I would want to go to such a backwater. Would my translator even be able to understand the thick northern accent?

My worries vanished within minutes of pulling up Morie's long driveway and arriving at the quiet house he and his wife had built on the secluded hillside of Mount Kurikoma. I received a hearty greeting at the door and inside, Morie, tall and barrel-chested at 89, presided over a dinner table where an atmosphere of warmth, informality, and humor prevailed.

Almost immediately, Morie and his wife, Kitako, disagreed whether their 1940 marriage was "arranged." They were opposites in many ways. He was a rugged country guy from Akita prefecture. She was raised in the fancy Azabu neighbor-

Japan's dog whisperer, Sawataishi Morie, shared the *kishou* spirit with the Akita breed he rescued.
© Mitsuo Aoyagi

hood of Tokyo. Had they been happy together? Morie was silent. "No," Kitako said. "There were many years I dreamt of leaving."

Again, the stunning candor. While the sizzling dishes of mountain cuisine kept coming, the Sawataishis and I talked for hours. After Morie went to bed, Kitako continued, until 3 AM. She vividly described the misery of her early years in the snow country—her loneliness, her sense of isolation. While walking for miles in the snow with a baby on her back, she thought of her city life and dreamed of going back there.

RATHER THAN LOOKING FOR CONSENSUS AND APPROVAL, MORIE LOOKED WITHIN HIMSELF. HE GUIDED HIS LIFE BY INSTINCT.

Morie had arrived at rural life by a circuitous route. He had gone to the prestigious Yokosuka Naval Academy, then fought in China in the late 1930s. He was serving on a minesweeper in the Yangtze River when an explosion, which killed many others, blew him overboard.

Here is where Morie's story begins to swerve radically from the norm. Rather than accepting the job offered him in Tokyo, which his friends and family expected him to do, he moved with Kitako to one of Japan's remotest areas, where homes were lit by oil lamps at night, dinner was cooked over a smoky wood stove, and isolated villages were buried under snow five months a year. He explained to Kitako that city life bored him. "Let's have an adventure instead."

He built and ran many of the Mitsubishi power plants in the north, a job he loved, but his real passion was dogs. In 1944, when he learned that only 12 Akita dogs were left in Japan—the dogs had been slaughtered and their pelts sold to the military—Morie spent six months' salary on a puppy with a prized pedigree, and hid it in a shed behind his house. He not only kept the dog alive and fed throughout the war, when food was scarce, but also kept it a secret from his in-laws, who had taken refuge under his roof after bombs had destroyed their Tokyo homes.

As soon as the war ended, Morie's passion went public. He held the first unofficial Akita Inu show in his backyard and over the next 60 years, he played a major role in the restoration of the breed. To Morie, the rugged Akitas embodied the quintessential qualities of old Japan. While over the years he and Kitako made many sacrifices for the dogs, and endured sporadic poverty because of them, Morie refused to sell a puppy for money. His efforts with the dogs, he said, had already been amply rewarded.

What he admired most about his dogs, he said, was their *kishou*. As he defined it for me, the word means "energy, vitality, assertiveness, spirit." These were qualities that Morie hoped to nurture in himself and worried were becoming lost in the modernization of Japan. "Having *kishou* means having a fighting spirit," he told me. "And I think it's a fighting spirit that has allowed the Akita to survive for centuries."

On one level, the tale of Morie and the Akita is a rescue story, a tale of courage and heroism, in which one man almost singlehandedly saves a breed from extinction, at great cost to himself and his family. On another level, it is a story of a marriage, and how opposites can find not just accommodations but a shared vibrancy.

It is also the story of Japan in the last century, its quick march to the computer age and more Western values, and of how the snowy isolated towns of Akita and Miyagi prefectures were left behind.

But on the deepest level, Morie's life is about *kishou*. He is the rare person who dreams of the life he wants and skillfully steers himself there, unfazed by the obstacles thrown in his way. Rather than looking for consensus and approval, he looked within himself. He guided his life by instinct.

When Morie retired in 1975, he went deeper into the wild. His dogs needed the mountains—and daily challenges—to stay vigorous and strong. And so did he. Morie built a house in the middle of nowhere, started hunting bear, and befriended a traditional *matagi* hunter who roamed the forests of the north with a knife and shotgun.

By the 1990s, his dogs were an anomaly in the Akita world, when Morie's last rugged champion, Shiro, won his national prize. All the other dogs in the ring were sweet and more docile, and without signs of *kishou*. "It used to be that a leader was a dog that knew how to hunt," Morie told me. "Now the dog that succeeds is a pet that simply exists to please its owner and receive affection."

In the United States, a man who leaves society behind, moves to the mountains, and rescues a breed of dog could easily wind up the hero of a Disney movie. Americans admire individualism and crave reminders of its rewards. It isn't easy to plow your own path and live on your own terms, no matter where you live. In Japan, there may be less admiration for an individual like Morie, a man who is driven by passion and not fear. But the qualities that he tried to instill in himself and embody, both privately and professionally—boldness, resourcefulness, vitality, and drive—are things that keep a society flourishing and strong.

Before Morie died in 2008, he regretted not being able to do more for the Akita dog. He'd saved the breed, he told me, but not what really mattered—its *kishou*. But maybe the most important thing is that he saved *kishou* in himself.

THE MORE THINGS CHANGE

PICO IYER

ONE JAPANESE INDIVIDUAL commits suicide every 15 minutes. More than a million Japanese people are *hikikomori*, meaning that they almost never leave their houses. Even as the country is suffering through one recession after another—shuttered stores seem to be as common as departing prime ministers—the social fabric of my adopted home, sustained and refined over centuries, is beginning to crack. Some older couples are hiring young actresses to visit them on Sundays, to say, "Hi, Mom! Hi, Pop!" because their own daughters no longer do.

Yet even as all the external registers suggest a society in decline, and even as the horrifying earthquake and tsunami of March 2011 literally reduced parts of the country to rubble, the Japan I see around me seems much stronger and more durable than statistics suggest. It remains—becomes ever more, I sometimes feel—the pop cultural model that countries from Taiwan to Singapore are keen to follow, in its street fashions, its gizmos, its convenience stores. Japan is still a byword for quality and efficiency. Its people, in moments of stress (as after the tsunami) summon a fortitude, a resolve, and a community spirit at which the rest of the world rightly marvels. And when Richard Florida at the Rotman School of Management in Toronto conducted a survey of 45 countries a few years ago, Japan ranked first in the "values index"—a register of how much the country holds to the traditional. For Florida, this ranking was not an advantage, but for those who worry that Japan has left its past behind without ever quite arriving at an international future, the result could be both a surprise and a consolation.

I look around me in the Western-style suburb near Nara where I've lived for 18 years, and the external changes are startling. When first I arrived in Japan, in 1987,

Pico Iyer is a Japan-based author and essayist.

my neighbors in California were being told that their towns were about to become suburbs of Shinjuku. Columbia Pictures was suddenly Japanese, Rockefeller Center was mostly Japanese—and magazines were reporting that the Imperial Palace alone was worth as much as the state of California.

In the decades since, the country's economy has failed to consolidate that rise—or to take over the planet. And socially, on the surface, the place is ever more mongrel and untraditional. The teenage girls who looked so demure when I arrived, so different from their counterparts abroad in their ritualized innocence and lack of make-up, now look like tigerish creatures who could be modeling for Armani. Their boyfriends wear oversized Lakers T-shirts and baggy shorts, as if they're auditioning for an LA street gang. Every few months, some new outrage—schoolgirl prostitution or a horrific act of violence—makes my Japanese wife

JAPAN'S STRENGTH MAY NOT LIE IN ITS FUTURE BUT IN ITS PAST, OR AT LEAST IN ITS TRADITIONAL SENSE THAT TIME MOVES ROUND RATHER THAN ALWAYS PRESSING FORWARD.

and neighbors talk about the Land of *Wa* (or Harmony) as if it were a distant suburb of Detroit. Last year, on a train platform in Nara, a schoolboy, in the midst of morning commuter crowds, buried a kitchen knife, with a 17-centimeter blade, fatally, into a classmate. Why? "His attitude at school always made me sick."

When I look around me, though—at the way people here speak, don't speak, bow to their cell phones, or instantly open their doors and share scarce water and food after a natural disaster—I wonder how far they have really moved from the traditional Japanese model. Reports of imminent changes in Japan are, after all, as regular as the harvest moon. People are always expecting this ancient archipelago to lose its distinctive character tomorrow. Every autumn, so it seems, the old in Japan express the fear that their country is going to lose its soul—and the young express their fear that it's not.

Nara itself could serve as a diagram of the increasing tensions—the competing tenses—in Japan. At the heart of this city of 400,000 stands a deer park, in which 1,200 four-legged creatures wander freely among rolling hills, pagoda spires, a giant Buddha in what is said to be the world's largest wooden building, and pavilions sitting picturesquely on ponds. Nara became the first permanent Buddhist capital of Japan, in 710, but it lost the court in 784. As a result, it has spent more than 1,200 years as a kind of forgotten place of ghosts, whose road signs point to "Primeval Forests" and whose maps direct you to "burial grounds."

The most sacred Shinto shrine in the land (outside of Ise) is here, as is a treasure hall remembering the city's status as the eastern terminus of the Silk Road. White-gravel pathways lead through groves of trees and past 2,000 stone lanterns. Turn one way, and you come to an old wooden building, in a grove of wild plum trees, that used to house Buddhist sutras; turn another, and you end up at the Nara Hotel, 100 years old in 2009 and adorned with photographs of the emperors who have offered sepulchral waves here.

Immediately outside the park, however, is all the clatter and cacophony of any postwar Japanese metropolis. Beeping machines, automated voices, flashing lights, and pachinko clangor ricochet around a labyrinth of covered shopping arcades. Falafel joints, Vietnamese restaurants, McDonald's outlets, and Indian cafes make you feel as if you're walking through a World's Fair as giddy as it is globally generic. And as you move out into the suburbs, you come to areas such as mine, with Western-style homes laid out on straight, carless streets, and huge buildings called Life and Aeon (the local versions of Costco and Wal-Mart) standing guard above the commuter stations. The neighborhood where I sleep is called Shikanodai—or Deer's Slope—and it includes no temples, no shrines, not even any jagged streets or alleyways. Late-model Mercedes doze outside hair salons on School Dori, and almost nothing is older than my 30-year-old son.

Farther out, when I walk just beyond the boundaries of my ten-square block neighborhood, are valleys and large rural spaces filled with fantastical structures that look as if they had been airlifted from some science fiction writer's imagination. One building has a nine-story front window that reflects a giant image of Albert Einstein sticking out his tongue. Across from it is a research lab built in the shape of a seven-story retina. There are great telecommunications centers set along these broad and largely silent boulevards; buildings with rainbowed surfaces bring home the face of the 23rd century. Established during the excitement of the bubble years to serve as a Science Town of the future, the structures look now like beached whales, monuments to outsized dreams, their parking lots empty and cobwebs clogging their state-of-the-art doors.

Nara, where the past lights the future.
© Jiji Press/AFP/Getty Images

I've never been in a position to offer the expert, Tokyo-driven diagnoses of the many professional Japan-watchers who fill this volume. My interest has always been the private Japan. As I look around the city I've made my home—at the deer grazing just outside the glass-and-concrete City Hall—it's hard not to wonder if the country's strength lies not in its future but in its past, or at least in its traditional sense that time moves round rather than always pressing forward. Fashions change in Japan, famously, more furiously than anywhere else, and there are few places more full of surging crowds, flashing images, and all the apparatus of tomorrow. But the ideas underlying all these spinning surfaces often suggest that progress is cyclical, not linear; that moments keep returning as the seasons do; and that change itself can be a constant, much as autumn's rites of passage are. Every year, the details shift—but the pattern looks very much the same.

When friends from California visit, they point out how much the old Buddhist capital of Nara looks like a version of Los Angeles's San Fernando Valley. Mothers in Japan now aspire to look younger than their daughters (as in the Golden State of eternal summer) as fast as their daughters contrive to look older than their mothers. Those not possessed of surfer or hip-hop styles seem to be taking their cue from old punk records or the *Full House* sitcom that was shown for years on Japan's educational channel. There are many more 7-Elevens in Japan than in the United States. But in a sense, this is a San Fernando Valley violently lost in translation. As soon as my friends start talking to Japanese people, they find much less faith in the future tense than there is in the Far West—and a much keener sense of the past.

I remember the first time I spoke to Toshi Okazaki Satow, the elegant manager of Tawaraya, the 18-room inn, at the center of Kyoto, that is often called the best hotel in the world. Tawaraya has opened its doors to European kings and the first prime minister of Japan, to Marlon Brando, Willem de Kooning, and J. Robert Oppenheimer. "The spirit of Tawaraya has not changed in 300 years," said Mrs. Satow, the 11th-generation owner of the inn, as she served me tea in the compact library and lanterns came on in the narrow lane outside. "But the style has to change to keep that spirit alive." True to that creed, she brought in design elements from China and Indonesia and Egypt—then wove them together into a distinctly Japanese whole. She installed televisions and telephones in every room but covered them in elegant fabrics, so that visitors could imagine themselves in classic *tatami* quiet. What she was saying, I think, is that Japan remains Japanese by constantly bringing in new elements to sustain its traditional ways, the way the shrine at Ise is carefully rebuilt every 20 years to remain in the same state of weatheredness.

JAPAN REMAINS JAPANESE BY CONSTANTLY BRINGING IN NEW ELEMENTS TO SUSTAIN ITS TRADITIONAL WAYS.

Issey Miyake draws on a classically Japanese sense of design to make Western-style clothes for the global market. Hayao Miyazaki brings together the Prussian-blue skies of Hiroshige and a Shinto sense of spirits alive in every river, tree, and even desk to make Academy Award-winning animated films so popular that Disney buys them. In Kyoto, tradition is so much in fashion—thanks in part, perhaps, to interest from the West—that design studios are now setting up offices in *machiya*, or traditional wooden houses; temples are opening their gates after nightfall (to show off the autumn colors—and to put more money in their coffers); and platinum blond–haired local girls are paying $150 to dress up for a day in *geisha* clothing.

Of course it's much easier to adapt foreign images to a Japanese model when it comes to fashions, films, and food than to global diplomacy or international trade, both of which hold to worldwide standards. And no one would suggest that a place as exclusive or as exquisite as Tawaraya could serve as a useful model for democracy. But what I heard Mrs. Satow imply—and implication, inevitably, was part of the point—was that Japan was still much better at being itself than at being a mock-California or proto-Shanghai. It does not take a visitor more than a few days in Tokyo to see that (as is not the case in Beijing or Bangkok) the same women who look so natural and at ease in traditional dress often seem strikingly ungainly in Western fashions, as if they do not know how to match content to context. The only part of Nara that does not seem confused to me is its 1,300-year-old center, which has very much stayed in place.

The recent power and popularity of Japan, such as it is, has come not from its trying to diminish its distance from the world so much as from trying to turn that distance to advantage. The brilliant miniaturism of its TVs and smartphones arises from a land that has long liked to work in small spaces—think *haiku* and *bonsai*. The *manga* and *anime* that have swept the pop-cultural globe come from a culture that has long thought in images more readily than in words. The planetary phenomenon that Yorkshiremen call "carry-oke" derives from a country whose people are at once publicly shy and yet strikingly confident when it comes to playing a part.

Japan has long been less like anywhere else than anywhere else I know, and when the country sees that as a strength, it finds its place on the international stage. Who would have thought, for example, that people from Bombay to Rio would be devouring raw fish? In an era of globalization, the local has a new and particular force.

Posters everywhere, as autumn approaches again this year, are drawing me to the autumn carnival in department stores. McDonald's is serving up *tsukimi*, or moon-viewing burgers (with fried eggs between the buns), on the occasion of the harvest moon. Plastic maple leaves are soon to appear around the sets of TV shows, and pumpkin churritos and Halloween masks are showing up in Universal Studios in Osaka. This can all seem rather hokey to a visitor—ancient Chinese customs adapted to a deracinated Westernized world.

And yet, the reverence for autumn remains, deep down, as Japanese as it's ever been. I watch as my neighbors stream into the parks again—to admire the same trees in the same light as last year, and every year before—and then to pose for the same photos and murmur the same phrases among the deer, around the shopping arcades, in my artificial suburb, and along the rusting streets of Science Town. It's hard not to feel that people here are sustaining themselves—not desperately or nostalgically, but instinctively—by noticing what doesn't change even as their own lives move naturally toward the cold and dark of winter.

Their economy is stalled, their political system looks bankrupt, their land was hit by an apocalyptic series of traumas, and their kids are acting out. But when Japan looks toward the future—and this was not the case in the England I grew up in or in California when I lived there—it sees something that looks as familiar as the falling leaves and brilliant skies of November. The things that don't change give a meaning and a perspective to the many things that do. Autumn turns to winter, and then to spring again.

JAPAN AFTER PEOPLE

ALEX KERR

Dateline 2020

Tokyo

JAPAN HAS LARGELY RECOVERED from the 2011 earthquake and tsunami, in
which tens of thousands died.

But since those disasters, a different kind of wave quietly has been sweeping
people from the Japanese archipelago. Japan's low birth rate has reduced the nation's population year by year. Census results show that millions of people have, in
effect, vanished from Japan over the past decade.

In Tokyo few have noticed. A decade of massive reconstruction has infused the
economy with cash, and the capital is thriving as never before, having grown a full
10 percent larger in population than it had been in 2010.

The nation has a new prime minister, and now that the post-tsunami rebuilding
is coming to an end, the government has proposed a new huge stimulus plan. But
we have seen many prime ministers and countless stimulus budgets since the late
20th century. Regardless of the politicians' comings and goings, the big ministries
such as the Ministry of Economy, Trade and Industry (METI) continue to manage
the country with their usual finesse.

Despite China's rise and the slow collapse of many Japanese industries, Japan
as a whole has shown resilience. The economy isn't growing much, but by relying
on homegrown multinationals, such as Toyota, and specialist technologies, it hasn't
declined either. Tokyo looks more or less as it always did. But areas beyond the
lights of the big cities tell a different story.

Alex Kerr is an author and expert on the arts and environment of East Asia.

Nanjo[1]

The pattern of demographic decrease in Japan's early 21st century has been uneven. The nation's giant metropolitan centers actually continue to expand; midsize cities are contracting slowly; smaller cities are shrinking quickly.

From the 1960s onward, foreign observers of Japan, impressed by the crowds of well-dressed people thronging Shibuya, Ginza, and Harajuku, had largely failed to notice that *shatta-gai* ("shuttered streets") began spreading through small towns in the mid-1990s. Long before 2006, when the population of Japan as a whole began to fall, the nation's small towns already were in decline.

JAPAN 2060: THE GOVERNMENT HAS AGAIN BUDGETED A HUGE ECONOMIC STIMULUS, AND A NEW PRIME MINISTER HAS JUST TAKEN OFFICE. THE MINISTRIES OF COURSE STILL HAVE EVERYTHING UNDER CONTROL.

The town of Nanjo (pop. 70,000), on the western island of Kyushu, has lost more than 20 percent of its residents since the 1980s. Faced with a rapidly aging population, the local government is commissioning a study on how to save the town through tourism.

By 2000, tourism was the world's largest earner of foreign exchange, exceeding computers, cars, and even oil. Japan, preoccupied with manufacturing, failed to recognize tourism's potential, but is now determined to make up for that oversight.

In 2008, Japan established a Tourism Agency, opened the floodgates to Chinese tourists, and created a subsidy scheme for local governments to conduct studies on how to develop tourism in their communities. Suddenly, towns throughout Japan began to look upon their crumbling old city centers and quaint farmhouses as potential lifelines.

Kyoto, however, is going in another direction. The local authorities know visitors will always come to this cultural center, no matter what the town looks like, as long as it still boasts famous temples such as Kiyomizu and Kinkakuji. But are temples enough? The city government has built a huge aquarium on a site near the station to prove to the world that Kyoto is thoroughly modern.

One effect of the 2011 earthquake and tsunami was to imprint firmly on people's minds the belief that Japan must be protected from further natural disasters by heavily concreting the shore and the land. Although civil engineering works were declining in the early 21st century, they revived in force after the tsunami. Compared with the kind of work done in the 1980s and 1990s, however, Japan's public works programs have metastasized; beyond the megaprojects like the massive new Tohoku seawalls, government construction projects take the form of tens of thousands of miniprojects: a waterfall here, a creek there.

Kariyo

The smaller the town, the more drastic the problems. The little island of Kariyo, off the west coast of Nagasaki, proves that rule. With most of its 2,700 inhabitants now

---

1 "Nanjo" and "Kariyo" are pseudonyms.

over the age of 60, the town can claim fewer than half the residents it had in 1980, and barely a third of its population in the 1950s.

Ten years ago, Kariyo made a gamble. It shortened the study process and instead spent its share of subsidy money on restoring old houses in its quaint harbor, converting the area into a resort destination. It also hired an international sales firm. The bet paid off, bringing streams of affluent tourists.

But elsewhere in Japan, the situation is grim. The phenomenon of empty hamlets known as *genkai shuraku* ("terminal villages") had become apparent as early as in the 1980s. Today, large numbers of these hamlets stand totally abandoned.

As people evaporate from the towns and villages, Japan's once varied trees and forests are also undergoing a transformation. In the mountains, plantation of *sugi* (cryptomeria cedar) monoculture continues as one of the government's priority projects. At the time of this report, *sugi* account for about 70 percent of Japan's forests. In the cities, trees are not popular because people see falling leaves as "untidy." In most towns it is common practice to cut tree branches and trim down the trunks—or to remove the trees altogether.

International Relations

Japan is still a close partner of its oldest ally, America, despite the occasional spat over trade or protest over the US military presence in Okinawa. It's obvious that America's burgeoning debt, chaotic politics, and military exposure are sapping its international leadership role, but nobody knows how Japan could become more independent of its longtime ally. Perhaps the incoming prime minister will have a better idea.

Dateline 2060

Tokyo

The government has again budgeted a huge economic stimulus, and a new prime minister has just taken office. The ministries, of course, still have everything under control.

Osaka's population has fallen by 35 percent and Tokyo itself is beginning to shrink, finally following the rest of the country. The decline in Tokyo's population came slowly at first, but is gathering speed as the population ages.

The 20 percent decline in Tokyo's population, while far less than that of other cities, has affected the outer neighborhoods, which are gradually decaying into rust belts. However, the urban core within the JR Yamanote railway commuter ring has lost none of its vibrancy, and Japan's economy remains stable. Ironically, this picture translates into a higher GNP per capita, so despite the rapid increase in unproductive retirees, in Tokyo at least, life is comfortable.

Charles Darwin once marveled at the strange forms of life that evolved in isolated environments such as the Galapagos Islands. A similar phenomenon has affected Japan's goods and internal systems. ATM cards, hotel reservation policies, toilet technology—all these things have taken on fascinating new forms that bear little resemblance to their equivalents in other nations. Japanese cell phones are admired everywhere as marvels of unexpected design; they cannot, however, communicate with non-Japanese phones. Beyond technology, key to Japan's mid-21st century evolution has been a growing emphasis on "germ-free" cleanliness. In 2050, Japan announced a plan to rid the country of all germs within the next 50 years.

After a slow start at the beginning of the century, Japan is putting serious efforts into robotics. It is hoped that robots will save Japanese industry and society, even though the results may not be seen for decades.

Nanjo

The tourism study commissioned by Nanjo in 2020 recommended a second study which, naturally, led to a third. The city government put money into restoring a few historic houses and an old town hall. But unlike Kariyo, Nanjo lacked a strategy to attract foreign visitors. Despite this brushup of the old town, tourists stayed away. The population has plummeted to less than half its peak. The town is applying to the government for a grant to support another study.

By now, 90 percent of Japan's forests consist of *sugi*. Most native wildlife (such as deer, boar, monkeys, and pheasants), which can't survive in the "*sugi* deserts," have disappeared.

IN 2050, JAPAN ANNOUNCED A PLAN TO RID THE COUNTRY OF ALL GERMS WITHIN THE NEXT 50 YEARS.

Civil engineering works meanwhile have shifted focus to the repair and enlargement of earlier projects. Old roads must be widened. Most of the big dams have silted up, so even larger ones must be built upstream. Unfortunately, the civil engineering works, conducted in the name of economic growth, undermine the appeal of rural areas for tourists, the country's best hope for salvation. Meanwhile, agriculture, forestry, and fishing are all in terminal depression.

Not only is Nanjo in trouble, but demographic decline is now striking cities as large as one or two million in population. Kumamoto, Okayama, Himeji, Niigata, and Aomori are among the cities that have condemned and demolished large stretches of empty *shatta-gai* and abandoned houses. Poorer cities simply let their old centers decay.

Small towns, having destroyed their original historic appeal, while the surrounding countryside has been covered with *sugi* plantations and concrete, have little left to draw travelers or new businesses. These towns' dependence on government-funded concreting is near total, but the shrinkage of the national tax base means that with each passing year, less money is available for the concrete that is their lifeblood.

Kariyo

Kariyo achieved international fame through astute marketing and investment from spa operators. Aman Resorts took over the northern part of the island; developers built villas and summer homes. The population has stabilized at about

2,000, consisting largely of young people employed by the rental homes and luxury villas.

In general, tourism has become a success for Japan, with inbound numbers rising to 25 million per year, six times the level of the early 2000s. As 20 million of the total visitor numbers are Chinese tourists, their tastes dominate; that is to say, Japan is building more amusement parks, skiing facilities, and shopping malls. The Chinese even overtook the Australians in Hokkaido, bringing in vast sums of money to develop Niseko and other ski resorts in the northern island.

Kyoto, meanwhile, correctly foresaw its future. It is not the city's venerated cultural attributes that draw tourists, but the aquarium, now joined by a planetarium, indoor wave-maker and surfing tank, and a massive shopping mall where Nijo Castle once stood. Nijo has been moved to Meiji Mura, the historic architectural theme park, near Nagoya.

Among the tourists there is a small but steady minority who are drawn to traditional culture and the natural environment. These individuals flock to places such as Kariyo. However, only a few dozen towns were able to rein in the public works and consultancy studies in time. For most of the others, it's now too late to change course.

Rural Japan: going to seed?
© Yukihiro Fukuda/AmanaimagesRF/Getty Images

Thus, despite the impressive headline numbers, tourism has rescued only a few places. Most villages fall into the *genkai shuraku* category. Of the towns and villages that in 2010 had a population of 10,000 or less, currently more than 60 percent have lost all their inhabitants and stand deserted.

International Relations

Japan is not the only country struggling with depopulation. The problem (evident in Italy and Austria from the early 2000s) has hit Europe as well. China, too, is facing similar pressures. Only the United States resists the trend. More religious than ever, Americans keep having children, and the country remains a magnet for immigrants.

In the 2030s, first America and then China established colonies on Mars and the Moon. Japan moved forward under the US umbrella, and Japanese companies soon grabbed a large percentage of America's space business, designing and constructing facilities on other planets.

The Japanese economy is resurging on tourism and the space business. Fewer youth can be found in Tokyo, but the inner city is still full of shops, restaurants, and well-dressed people thronging Shibuya, Ginza, and Harajuku.

Dateline 2110

Tokyo

The new government has budgeted a huge economic stimulus program.

Even in Tokyo, population decline has wrought radical change. From its peak of 130 million in 2000, Japan's total population has contracted to 45 million. Japan in 2110 has the same number of inhabitants as it did in 1900. Tokyo has also contracted in geographic terms, and is now 50 percent smaller than in the preceding century. Large stretches of land outside the Yamanote line have been abandoned, much of them converted into public plazas.

The economy in Tokyo has not suffered as badly as many prognosticators had feared. Most of the shoddily built stock of 20th century apartments and offices needed to be torn down, resulting in decades of profitable work for construction companies. Tokyoites have benefited, as available living space doubled as a result.

In terms of industries, only tourism, space, and *anime* survived the economic onslaught from China. But these sectors are proving strong enough to support Japan's economy, which has remained stable for a century—proof, at least, that the bureaucrats are doing their job.

Meanwhile, tourism has remade the country. The redesigning of towns in the name of tourism that began with Nanjo and Kariyo nearly a century ago is now also boosting Tokyo. It was increasingly apparent that the national Diet, or parliament, building was underutilized, so last year, the politicians were moved to a warehouse in Koto-ku, on the outskirts of the city, and the building was transformed into a Museum of Parliamentarianism. An exclusive Aman Resort occupies the upper floors.

Nanjo

Unfortunately, Nanjo has disappeared completely, except for a handful of old buildings, which a curator from nearby Fukuoka looks after on the weekends. But the government is still commissioning studies, as the town has been a boon to generations of consultants. The studies come to thousands of pages, ensuring that Nanjo will go down in history, even if nobody lives there.

Kariyo

The town still exists, even thrives, with a steady population of 2,000, mostly villa and hotel staff who have moved in and replaced the locals. Compared with towns like Nanjo and countless others that simply disappeared, Kariyo is a success—a "recycled countryside."

Meanwhile, as part of the "germ-free" policy, in 2080 the government banned deciduous trees once and for all, exempting those growing in a few tourist areas such as the leafy *keyaki* (zelkova elm) in Tokyo's Omotesando boulevard, and colorful maples in Kyoto's gardens.

The *sugi* plantations in the countryside are now old growth, boasting massive trunks like those in the ancient town of Nikko, north of Tokyo. There is little need for the lumber since, within Japan, all housing is mandated to be 100 percent plastic and aluminum as part of the "germ-free" policy. Nevertheless, the *sugi* budgets, established 150 years earlier, still exist, so trees are periodically cut down anyway, to make room for ongoing reforestation projects.

International Affairs

America's population, bucking a trend among the world's richer nations, continues to grow. The combination of Japan's population shrinkage and America's increase means that the United States, which had been 2.5 times more populous than Japan in 2010, now has more than 10 times as many people. Thus America is still very much a power to be reckoned with.

Japan's economy was saved by the space industry. In "germ-free" Japan, outer space has a particular appeal, since the Japanese countryside is devoid of most natural life other than industrial-use cedar, the mountainsides and rivers are covered with cement, and towns are empty of people and foliage. Japan's modern inhabitants feel little nostalgia for Earth. They're happy working in space stations and rarely need to be repatriated to their hometowns.

Overall

Inside the *sugi* forests devoid of animals and birds, peace and quiet reigns. Towns and suburbs lie still as elderly hangers-on pass away, leaving jumbled vistas of mouldering plastic and aluminum stretching for tens of kilometers, where people once lived. Even the sparkling new towns built in Tohoku after the tsunami stand mostly empty, as these areas were already suffering from depopulation before the wave hit, and after the disaster, no amount of money could induce new residents to move in. Expressways and high-speed trains whisk tourists past the *sugi* and the ghost towns toward bustling Chinese amusement parks dotting the coasts.

Agriculture has disappeared from the countryside except for some showpiece rice paddies in the northern region of Akita, maintained by the Agency for Cultural Affairs. The Akita farmers, who know how to plant and harvest rice, have been declared Intangible Cultural Assets, and are much in demand at tourist events.

In the late 20th century, Japan's staple food began to switch from rice to mayonnaise, and by now the transformation is complete. Luckily mayonnaise can be manufactured from petroleum by-products, or even from used tires. The few people who still seek rice can purchase it over the Internet from the Akita Foundation.

Agriculture does exist, but in a new form: plants grown in nonsoil nutrient docks housed in large buildings. This industry is, of course, germ-free and can be managed by robots. Fishing also has moved indoors, with companies farming fish in tanks located within reengineered schools and universities. Smaller fish thrive in classrooms, while larger fish such as tuna adapt well to auditoriums and stadiums. Aquaculture, too, can be mostly tended by robots, so fresh sushi continues to be available.

Midsize cities shrank to roughly a fifth of their population by the end of the 21st century, leaving behind tens of thousands of untenanted office blocks and empty apartment buildings. This shrinkage spurred the growth of a new industry, "urban mining," which extracts iron, copper, and rare earths from buildings in the slums and outer suburbs as they are demolished.

Tokyo and the Kansai complex (Kyoto, Osaka, Kobe) have managed fairly well. The population loss has not been such a bad thing, as it lowered cripplingly high real estate values and encouraged fresh investment in a new generation of high-quality structures in the surviving urban cores. Living space per capita continues to improve.

Robots take care of most needs, including many formerly human interactions. Town centers are largely tree-free, and germ-free, making them the safest places to live on earth. And foreign experts continue to observe to their satisfaction that life is comfortable in Tokyo, with lots of well-dressed people thronging Shibuya, Ginza, and Harajuku.

Dateline 2210

Tokyo, Nanjo, Kariyo
No change.

COOL IS NOT ENOUGH

CHRISTOPHER GRAVES

If you aren't remembered, then you never existed.
~from the Japanese *anime* series, *Serial Experiments Lain*

Do your work with mastery.
~The Buddha

IN 1856, FELIX BRACQUEMOND, a Parisian engraver, printmaker, and ceramicist, received a package of ceramics from Japan. Bracquemond was immediately stirred, legend has it, by the flat, bold style of the images on the paper used to protect the ceramics. He showed these woodblock prints to his artist friends, including Manet, Degas, and Whistler, who swiftly began incorporating Japanese motifs in their work. The Western love affair with Japan had begun.

A century and a half later, young Americans are flocking to Japanese-sounding conventions like Ohayocon in Columbus, Ohio, or Sogencon in Sioux Falls, South Dakota. They handcraft costumes of the characters they adore from Japanese *anime* (animated cartoon films). This dressing-up and role-playing is called "cosplay," short for "costume play," and has launched a global subculture. There are zillions of Facebook groups and Web sites. There is a *Cosplay in America* coffee table book. There are pilgrimages to famous *anime* sites. It all feels a bit like a mania.

This wave of fantasy appears to be out of sync with the country. Even before the March 2011 earthquake and all that followed, Japan was struggling—not only with aging but with the emergence of a significant number of young people who are un-

Christopher Graves is global CEO of Ogilvy Public Relations Worldwide.

motivated and unemployed (known as "freetas," or freelance part-time workers) or disenfranchised ("NEETs," not in education, employment, or training).

The heated debate over cool

Amid this angst and ennui, the government of Japan has launched an initiative called "Cool Japan."

The last time a nation associated itself with "cool" was the United Kingdom. Shortly after Tony Blair's Labor government took power in 1997, it linked itself to the term, to widespread derision. It's important to remember, though, that foreigners introduced the notion of "Cool Britannia" to describe the Britpop cultural wave—not the Brits themselves and certainly not the government. The US ice cream brand Ben & Jerry's, known for its laid-back, funny, and pop-culture-meets-parody names for its flavors, launched a contest in 1996 to name a new flavor that would embody the trendy hipness of British fashion, art, and pop music at that moment. "Cool Britannia" won. *Newsweek* followed with a cover story ("London Rules... Inside the world's coolest city") and then *Vanity Fair* ("London Swings Again!"). Britain was, indeed, downright cool. So when the Blair government tried to co-opt the idea, it was surfing a spontaneous wave. In the end, though, cool is evanescent, and Britain lost it. Cool Britannia became a joke.

WHILE THE *OTAKU* SUBCULTURE MIGHT CATCH FIRE, THAT DOES NOT NECESSARILY TRANSLATE INTO AN EFFECTIVE INDUSTRIAL POLICY.

The story is a classic example of how governments and tourism boards struggle to present their countries to the world—how, in effect, to "brand" them. Cool Britannia is worth remembering in particular because now Japan is betting on cool: the government is touting "Cool Japan" as a strategy of economic rebirth. The Ministry of Economy, Trade and Industry (METI) has even set up a special division, called Cool Japan, to boost the country's pop-culture power. METI wants nearly to quadruple global pop-culture sales, to $200 billion, by the year 2020. That's a lot of cool.

But as any teenager will tell you, one cannot pronounce oneself "cool." A government agency like METI laying claim to the title risks all the awkwardness of a middle-aged father trying too hard to win the acceptance of his teenage daughter's friends by mangling their slang.

Then there is the issue of just what cool means. The Japan television show *Cool Japan* asked foreigners new to Japan what they found coolest. Their top answer: high-tech toilets. That's probably not what METI had in mind.

Japan's efforts to claim "coolness" beg two key questions: first, can Japan build an entire industrial policy based on cool? And second, can the country revive its dynamism through creative content and ideas, especially content around fantasy and virtual worlds? Roland Kelts, author and Japan pop-culture commentator, puts it this way in his book, *Japanamerica: How Japanese Pop Culture Has Invaded the US*: "*Anime* is seeking to answer to what may be the most critical question for Japan in the new century: can its ideas be exported without the gadgetry to go with them? Is Japanese thought exportable on its own?"

Countries have long tried to exercise "soft power" by linking their brand image and influence to pop culture exports. Korea has had its *Hallyu* and K-wave of TV soap operas and pop singers. Japan has a whole host of J words, including J-Pop, J-Rock, and J-Cool. It all adds up to J-Cult (short for Japan culture).

For nation-branding to be effective, the pop culture needs to do more than enlist foreigners into songs or fashion or even cosplay. It needs to make people think of, understand, seek out, and love the country of origin. The problem with the export of *anime* and *manga* (Japan's distinctive book-length comics) is that they may be loved simply for what they are, rather **AS ANY TEENAGER** than for enlightening anyone about Japan. Indeed, many **WILL SAY,** countries now have their own versions of *manga*. **ONE CANNOT**

There may be some indistinct sense on the part of *anime* **PRONOUNCE** or *manga* fans that the art form comes from Japan, but they **ONESELF COOL.** seem to like the style regardless of who creates it. The Japan connection has been lost. In an August 2010 report, "100 Actions to Launch Japan's New Growth Strategy," Japanese government officials acknowledged the complexity of converting "cool" to cash.

Japan's *anime*, fashion, and safe foods are so popular in overseas markets that these industries have the potential of expanding their business globally; however, the popularity of Japanese culture overseas has not necessarily led to business.

While the subculture of *otaku*—serious, even obsessive fans of *anime, manga*, and video games—may catch fire, that does not necessarily translate into an effective industrial policy. There is, for example, the matter of timing. The government is pushing the idea of an *otaku* export economy as sales of *anime* and *manga*, both in Japan and globally, have been declining for years (in part, admittedly, due to piracy).

Sure, cosplay conventions draw the believers, just as Star Trek conventions do. But Star Trek was never the core of American nation-branding. So while *anime* gatherings nearly always have some tie-in to Japan, the connection is tenuous.

This lack of a strong tie between the export and the country is what Waseda University professor Koichi Iwabuchi labels "culturally odorless," meaning that the export erases its telltale country-of-origin smell. He wonders if Western fans of Japanese pop culture admire an "animated, raceless, and culture-less, virtual version of 'Japan.'"

The American fans swarming into *anime* cons are imagining a Japan of their own, rather than one whose present is grounded in thousands of years of tradition. If anything, for these fans, Japan stands for escapism and fantasy. It is a land where men pay to have a virtual girlfriend on their phone (Love Plus dating simulation) and can even check into a hotel catering to virtual relationships.

If Japan truly exports its wide array of *anime* and *manga*, foreign fans will discover that the content ranges from *kawaii* (super cute) to *hentai* (sexual perversion) interlaced with violence and dark apocalyptic visions. Real *manga* is not all childlike and could cause an uproar in countries like the United States, whose people are likely to be outraged by scenes of rape or sex with an octopus. Indeed, in 2010 such *manga* caused a huge controversy in Tokyo, where the mayor has shepherded in new anti-obscenity laws. That's hardly a solid footing for a national brand.

One alternative to an *otaku*-centered brand strategy is to link Japan's age-old traditions—the Zen rock gardens, *bonsai*, the tea ceremony, and so on—to a more contemporary image of the nation. But the dialectic of modern and traditional has become a cliché in nation-branding: is there any place that is not a "land of contrasts"? Think of travel and tourism photos of a Kyodo *geisha* trainee with a cell phone, for example. The Japan pavilion at the 2010 Shanghai Expo tried to pull off the pairing of tradition and high tech, but it came across as muddled. The official positioning statement of the National Tourism Organization is "Japan: endless discovery," but it is a traditional sense of discovery that appears to be on offer. As wealthy tourists age, they crave a new form of self-mastery that implies a sort of inner discovery as well.

THE FANS SWARMING INTO *ANIME* CONVENTIONS ARE IMAGINING A JAPAN OF THEIR OWN, RATHER THAN ONE GROUNDED IN REALITY.

Mastering a new brand

Is there a unifying idea that could pull together these widely diverging—and entirely authentic—aspects of Japaneseness? Or must Japan brand itself completely differently when talking to different audiences? Is there, in short, a brand strategy that can successfully appeal to great-granddad and today's teenagers? I think there is.

Consider this insight from Fukukawa Shinji, the chair of the Japonesque Modern Committee, a public–private initiative launched in 2006 to promote the Japan brand. Explaining the committee in 2008, Fukuwaka said, "Much more than a new Japanese brand of 'cool,' Japonesque Modern unites Japanese culture, design, and aesthetics with advanced technology, bringing traditional values to enrichment of contemporary living."

Backed by METI, Japonesque curated a collection of 116 objects it felt embodied this spirit, ranging from the Lexus hybrid and artificial blood vessels to the Kadokeshi eraser and the Saika *bonsai*. Deep in the DNA of each of these disparate objects, Fukuwaka said, was a "devotion to mastery." He defined the term as "Japan's cultivation of superior technical skills by learning traditions, techniques, and ideas from others that have been passed down in society."

This idea is beginning to resonate. A new tourism niche, called "creative tourism," is emerging to serve people who long to master a new skill, such as woodworking, cooking, or art. The concept seems to fit the needs of many global baby boomers, the first of whom have reached 65 this year and will start to unleash some of their $2 trillion in accumulated wealth. These baby boomers tell marketers that they want to travel and learn a new skill or hobby. Creative tourism hits the mark.

Anime in Anaheim: American cosplayers at an expo in California.
© Damian Dovarganes/AP Photo

Meanwhile, behavioral research indicates self-improvement and the urge to master a craft or skill is a basic human desire ("mastery motivation" theory). People build satisfaction and reward through becoming more expert at something and then, in turn, are acknowledged for that expertise. According to Daniel Pink, author of *Drive: The Surprising Truth about What Motivates Us*, people are only truly moved by three intrinsic elements: autonomy, purpose, and mastery, the latter defined as getting better and better at something that matters.

Japan's history, culture, and DNA are built on this "devotion to mastery" in all things, from crafts to theater to food to factories. Slapdash just doesn't cut it in Japan; even a humble bowl of noodles can be a masterpiece of detail. And this is, of course, true of industry as well. Canon, for example, anoints skilled printer assembly workers as "meisters" and those who learn all 600 processes are "super meisters."

Devotion to mastery, I believe, could become the unifying thread that weaves pop culture and tradition into a distinctive national brand that Japan can market under the umbrella of creative tourism. Some private-sector companies already excel at approaching consumers through their passions. For example, the Genius Bars in Apple stores feature software and hardware *sensei* who, for no charge, improve your computing experience while making you more of an expert. Nike and Adidas have created services built upon processing biodata for runners: creating a mash-up of songs, data, training advice, and community support. When Ford wanted to enter conversations in social media, it moved beyond the direct and literal (for example, car buyer forums) to communities centered on other interests such as the environment, design, parenting, and personal finance. In a similar fashion, Unilever (owner of health and beauty brands such as Lux, Ponds, and Dove) enters gently into online conversations about travel, fitness, wellness, cooking, and parenting, and doesn't limit itself to beauty product sites.

The analogy to Japan is that these companies are building a reputation and a strategy for more than their products; they are creating value on the basis of processes, expertise, and community. In the same way, Japan must do more than pique people's curiosity; it must connect them to the craft they wish to master. Creative tourism requires creating real avenues of learning.

To do so, Japan needs to leverage social media and community-building. Wherever online communities long to learn, want to improve themselves through mastery, Japan needs to enter the conversation. In addition to traditional demographic targeting or segmentation, this goal requires entering online communities—these tribes of the mind—through their own passions.

Thus, Japan could try to enter the community of hobbyist and serious woodworkers, linking them to traditional Japanese woodworking design. For gardeners: *ikebana* and *bonsai*. For foodies: the art of *ramen*, sushi, and preparation. For *anime* and *manga* lovers: film and drawing workshops and programs. Japan can bring an inner satisfaction for those yearning to begin to master something they love and longing to become better versions of themselves.

In approaching such communities, style, sincerity, and tone will make all the difference. Entering others' turf online is not the same as running your own Web site. Japan already manages Web sites such as the comprehensive Japan National Tourism Organization, and Visit Japan 2011. But leveraging social media effectively means enabling online communities and creating content seen as clever enough, useful enough, and, yes, cool enough to be passed along. It is this grass-roots passion that builds momentum. Even when companies create their own sites (see a good example at www.thefordstory.com), they need to stimulate fans into telling their own stories and creating their own content.

Strong bonds connect communities of passionate devotees, whether *bonsai* amateurs or *manga otaku*. Social media lend themselves to the creation and nurturing of these communities as the students of the craft find and begin to talk to each other within its tightly framed subculture and argot.

The goal, then, should be to combine two powerful ideas: (1) Japan as devoted to mastery, tapping into the intrinsic desire for self-improvement, and (2) linking back to Japan private passions and communities of interest within social media.

In a sense, then, Japan can create a new—and profitable—global brand for itself by tapping into that most enduring human desire: the drive for individual self-discovery. And in that sense, it is truly an "Endless Discovery."

CULTIVATING THE VERTICAL GARDEN

MINORU MORI

RAPID ADVANCES IN GLOBALIZATION and information technology have increased the flow of people, products, money, knowledge and information to cities around the world, particularly those that have the greatest appeal and largest number of business opportunities. For Japan, with its shrinking population, it is essential to create cities that can draw in people from around the world. The recovery of the Japanese economy is, therefore, intrinsically linked to urban design.

Tokyo is one of the world's largest cities, with a population of 13 million (35 million if the greater metropolitan area is included). Tokyo was ranked first in a 2008 "Global City GDP Ranking" (a survey conducted by PricewaterhouseCoopers LLP). Similarly, in the "Global Power City Index 2010" a scorecard devised by the Mori Memorial Foundation, Tokyo ranked fourth, after New York, Paris, and London. However, in the World Competitiveness Yearbook Results for 2010, prepared by the Swiss-based International Institute for Management Development, (IMD), Japan's position fell significantly, to 27th place, compared to 17th in 2009. And the rest of the world is not standing still. At a time when the developing cities of Asia are driving hard to catch up, Japan is digging out from the devastation of the earthquake in March.

What kind of cities would be most effective in helping Japan to recover? Taking Tokyo as an example, I would like to present an urban redevelopment concept that will contribute to reawakening Japan's vitality and appeal.

As I see it, Tokyo and, by extension, Japan have to deal with five critical issues.

1. *Coming to grips with globalization*

Although global players recognize the appeal of the massive market of the greater Tokyo metropolitan area, there is also a pervading image of Japan as a

Minoru Mori is chairman of Mori Building.

"far-off country," because of such factors as numerous regulations, an inconveniently located airport, and language difficulties. The recent reopening of Haneda Airport to international flights is welcome news, but to attract top-class people to Tokyo, it is equally important to proceed with legislative reforms that will bring the entire transportation infrastructure into line with accepted international standards.

THE CENTER OF TOKYO IS NOT EFFICIENTLY UTILIZED, RESULTING IN A SPRAWL OF JAM-PACKED BUILDINGS STRETCHING OUT TO THE SUBURBS.

To maintain national vitality with a shrinking population, it is important to encourage large influxes of tourists and to attract excellent human resources from around the world and keep them here for as long as possible. For these influxes to happen, it is absolutely essential to bring living and business environments up to safe, global standards; provide more attractive tourist resources and events; and expand opportunities for exchange and collaboration. In particular, given that the wealthy and middle-income sectors of Asian society will rapidly expand, it is vital that we create open-minded systems and urban design that will make these people want to visit Japan repeatedly.

2. *Transforming Japan into a knowledge- and information-based society*

Japan is still overly dependent on its successes from the industrial age and is lagging behind in the transformation to a knowledge- and information-based society. Despite the fact that tertiary industries already account for approximately 70 percent of GDP and employment, government policies and urban structure have not broken away from the frameworks that were developed for an industrial society.

The driver of Japan's future growth will undoubtedly be "soft power," such as planning and development, design, and strategy based on knowledge and sensitive discernment. Secondary industries are already relocating to overseas production hubs, and the major departments left at home are those dedicated to soft power. Moreover, Japanese *anime*, games, fashion and food culture, which have always been given scant regard as economic sectors, have gained global acclaim.

Knowledge-creation flourishes when there are seamless links between work and daily living. Similarly, to achieve a better work-life balance, it is essential to move away from the urban structure of an industrial society, where work and daily life were rigidly segmented. Instead, we should move toward a concept that offers a multipurpose urban infrastructure. In this way, we can enable more people to enjoy a life where work and home are close to each other and commuting time can be minimized.

3. *Addressing environmental concerns, including global warming*

Land in the center of Tokyo is not efficiently utilized, particularly in the vertical direction. There are relatively few high-rise buildings juxtaposed into a sprawl of jam-packed buildings stretching out to the suburbs. An urban structure that relies on dense development in the horizontal plane results in high levels of energy use for transportation and a consequent degradation of the natural environment. The life span of residences is short; Japan's culture of scrap and build wastes resources.

Japan has outstanding building and environmental technologies that can address the land-use issue. I would like to see these technologies brought together; Japan could lead the world in redeveloping highly energy-efficient, ultrahigh-rise cities that are in harmony with nature. If this vision could be realized, we would create a city that could showcase Japan's technological excellence and open up major business opportunities.

4. *Managing earthquake risk*

In Tokyo, the Great Eastern Japan Earthquake registered a strong 5 on the Japanese scale of 7, but few buildings in the capital were damaged and social order was maintained. While the world lauded Japan's construction technology and the calmness of its people, many Japanese feared an economic slowdown caused by recovery efforts and power-supply problems. They also worried about the risk of a stronger earthquake hitting the capital.

As soon as possible, we need to launch a project to revive Tokyo, creating buildings and communities where people will seek refuge, not flee, even in the event of a number 7 earthquake. This effort will involve integrating areas with narrow, winding streets, and redeveloping them into high-rise vertical communities that are highly quake-resistant. By increasing the number of high-rise communities that are equipped with disaster-prevention facilities, including stocks of emergency supplies, we would enhance the overall disaster-preparedness of our cities.

Japan has the technology. Tax revenues should go to rebuilding the stricken areas; moreover, deregulation should be used to help maximize the expertise and capital from the private sector and overseas to redevelop Tokyo.

5. *Addressing the demographic challenge*

The increasing financial burden of Japan's shrinking working population and aging society is expected to hinder the country's economic performance. If Japan implemented policies such as accepting more overseas residents, boosting the employment rate of seniors, and creating an environment conducive to raising children, it would be possible to stop the decline in the working population.

From an urban perspective, the acceptance of overseas residents overlaps with the challenge of coming to grips with globalization. Although there may be resistance to such a policy, this hurdle needs to be overcome in order to create a global city.

For the other two points—creating a knowledge-based society and addressing environmental concerns—the key will be a transformation to an urban structure where workplaces and homes are in closer proximity. Employment opportunities are concentrated in the city center; if it were possible for people to both live and work there, seniors and women with children would find participating in the workforce easier.

An aging population in a knowledge- and information-based society is by no means a disadvantage. Older people can contribute by drawing on their experience and knowledge, communication skills, networks, and maturity.

"Vertical Garden Cities" for Japan

To address these five issues, I have proposed the "Vertical Garden City." Mori Building's Roppongi Hills development is based on this concept, which has become all the more significant since the earthquake.

A Vertical Garden City is an urban development that maximizes the utilization of space above- and belowground to greatly expand total urban space, opening up aboveground surfaces and man-made foundations for greenery and people. While a Vertical Garden City contains ultrahigh-rise buildings, it aims to be full of greenery. If earthquake resistance and disaster prevention are enhanced, and independent power generation incorporated, these buildings could also become refuges during times of disaster.

Looking at the big picture, the Vertical Garden City proposes the creation of advanced urban models around the world where, by concentrating human activities, it will be possible to use remaining land to revive nature and ecosystems. Moreover, by bringing these microcosms of nature to the city and improving energy efficiency, it will be possible to curb the emissions of greenhouse gases that cause global warming.

Eight foundations for implementing the Vertical Garden City

Based on our experience, the principal requirements for implementing this concept include the following.

1. *Integrate small parcels of land into developments of between 2 and 10 hectares*
   Expanding an urban area and, at the same time, completely redeveloping roads and other lifeline infrastructure, boost the degree of freedom in urban planning. This kind of expansion enables the creation of attractive city plans and is also useful for the realization of a community that is well prepared against disasters.

2. *Raise the floor–space ratio while keeping the building footprint-to-land ratio low*
   By building upward instead of outward, the space between buildings can be increased, making it possible to create wide-open vistas. These green spaces provide a place for people to relax or enjoy sports. In times of disaster, they also create firebreaks and ensure that residents have a place where they can evacuate safely. Green vistas can also be effective in reducing the heat island phenomenon.

3. *Maximize use of space below ground*
   Creating enormous spaces underground provides further freedom for building design and placement of appropriate facilities aboveground. Structures that should be aboveground are those that require sunlight, including

offices, residences, hotels, social areas, and cultural facilities. Belowground facilities should be those that do not need sunlight, such as concert halls, shops, movie theaters, parking lots, energy plants, roads and railroads, and other lifeline infrastructure.

Although still in the research phase, if we could dig into the firm bedrock 20 to 40 meters below the ground and construct an enormous underground space in conjunction with the construction of foundations for aboveground buildings, we could devise a whole range of new possibilities for strongly earthquake-resistant, temperature-stable underground spaces.

4. *Use underground spaces to separate the means of transportation and movements of people*

By positioning roads and railways underground or under man-made foundations, it is possible for people, including those in wheelchairs and strollers, to move around safely. The aboveground spaces can be used for green zones, parks, jogging courses, and other purposes. By separating the means of transportation in a vertical manner, for short distances, people can move around on foot or on bicycles. For medium distances, they can ride electric-powered buses or trams, and for long distances, they can move around on railways and expressways. This structure makes it possible to reduce traffic congestion and accidents.

5. *Create a compact, vertically integrated city where everything is accessible on foot*

In contrast to existing urban structures where workplaces and residences may be separated by considerable distances, the Vertical Garden City makes possible a dramatic reduction in transportation time and energy. This kind of construction increases the free time that residents have to spend with their families or on their own pursuits. This way of living is well suited to a knowledge- and information-based society, because work and daily living are linked seamlessly.

6. *Make sure every corner of the city is stimulating and healing*

At Roppongi Hills, we have established a modern art gallery on the top floor of the central tower, as well as a private members' club, a library, and a school targeting professional working people. With these facilities, we have created a wealth of opportunities for people to come into contact with outstanding individuals and artworks, thus providing additional avenues for intellectual stimulation and self-development. On the ground level, there is a Japanese garden as well as various public artworks, street furniture, open-air cafes, and a vari-

Roppongi Hills: One man's vision of Japan's urban future.
© Shizuo Kambayashi/AP Photo

ety of restaurants. These facilities are vital for people to be able to sit back and relax, recover from fatigue, and enjoy some downtime.

Roppongi Hills is a city where there is always some sort of unique event taking place that is reported to the rest of Japan and the world. Gathering together people is the key to maintaining the freshness and cutting edge of a city. We aim to create cities where people are connected with the rest of the world 24 hours a day, where English is readily understood, and where offices and residences meet global standards.

7. *Ensure energy self-sufficiency*

The Vertical Garden City that is home to a range of diverse functions is able to achieve an equalization of electrical power load, using waste heat efficiently for power generation. Although the total energy consumption is large, efficiency is high and it is possible to significantly reduce power transmission energy loss. Even if lifelines are disrupted in a disaster, the Vertical Garden City does not lose power, so businesses and homes are able to continue with their activities.

8. *Practice "town management"*

Town management is a concept that we have introduced at Roppongi Hills, and it has been extremely effective for maintaining the complex's freshness and vitality. We coordinate and control the diverse facilities, listen to the opinions of our tenants, and consider their interests as we plan the events and promotions that further raise the appeal of the city. In this way, the Vertical Garden City functions as a media source in its own right, serving to send out information and messages to Japan and the wider world.

Japan's future hinges on the speed of urban redevelopment

The urban concept I have described is not fully appreciated in Japan. However, with the birth of Roppongi Hills eight years ago, many people have been able to experience this kind of living firsthand and the concept is now better understood. Since the March 11 earthquake, which focused attention on safety and self-sufficiency, the Vertical Garden City idea has received much support.

Although I have focused on Tokyo here, my thinking also applies to revitalizing regional cities and rebuilding stricken areas. A compact urban design with concentrated functions may help balance the needs of an aging society with the availability of welfare services.

Speed is critical. I was involved with the Shanghai World Financial Center in China, which opened for business in 2008, and experienced for myself the amazing pace of its development. We may have only a limited time before Shanghai catches up with Tokyo.

What position Tokyo (or Japan) will hold in the world 20 or 30 years from now depends largely on the effective implementation of urban policies and the speed of administrative action. Recovery from the Tohoku disaster and urban redevelopment are investments for the future.

GO BACK TO GO FORWARD

EDWARD SUZUKI

IN THE OLD DAYS, the Japanese wisely employed the concept of *shakkei*, meaning "borrowed scenery" to enlarge and enrich their invariably small pieces of property by utilizing neighboring vistas in the design of their own living spaces.

Sadly this practice—like so many other aspects of traditional *nihon kenchiku*, or Japanese architecture—is fast disappearing in the rapid growth of Japan's densely populated urban centers. Indeed, in stark contrast to past eras, the crowded cities have become places inhabitants want to escape from or shut out, rather than be a part of.

As a result, contemporary Japanese architects often find themselves having to design "defensively," to block out unsightly or overbearing neighboring aspects. Over time, I developed a design feature I came to call the "interface." Quite simply, this feature is a distinct yet unobtrusive demarcation of a property's boundaries via a fence or a screen of sorts. Typically, the screen would be covered by bamboo or some other greenery, producing what could be called a soft interface between interior and exterior.

At one point I realized, however, that what I thought I had developed was not truly original but had deep roots in traditional Japanese architecture.

Similarly, the *engawa*, a long and usually elegant corridor surrounding the periphery of many traditional Japanese houses, is neither outside nor inside, but is simply yet another interface between the two worlds. As I delved more deeply into ancient design concepts, I realized there was a wealth of vocabulary and principles that Japan's contemporary designers could learn from and apply to their daily work.

Edward Suzuki is a Tokyo-based architect and founder of Edward Suzuki Associates.

Japan's age-old design traditions, such as the *engawa*—a peripheral corridor that connects inside and out—can be used in ways both traditional (left) and modern.
© Courtesy of Edward Suzuki Associates

In some circles of Japanese architecture today, there is a revival of interest in these time-honored design traditions. If Japan could effectively revive the wisdom and know-how of traditional daily living and apply it to contemporary lifestyles, so much could be accomplished by combining these old ideas with the exciting new materials, technology, and design concepts now emerging.

There are numerous areas in which these ideas, old and new, can converge. In the Edo period there was great emphasis on conservation and recycling, for example, through simple but ingenious systems to catch rainwater for household use. Houses were carefully designed in a sparse, yet elegant, minimalist style, with cleverly placed vents to allow maximum air circulation in summer, and shutters and simple valves on vents to help seal off drafts in the colder months.

In the *engawa* all the storm windows and the *shoji* (rice paper screens) would be taken out to allow cross-ventilation in the hot summer months. In the winter, the windows and the screens would be put back to increase thermal insulation and to minimize heat loss.

Traditional building materials were, of course, all natural, and great emphasis was placed on nature as a means of ventilating, cooling, and heating through the channeling of sunlight, wind, and water, and the use of greenery and earth.

Alas, such ideas were steadily abandoned, especially after World War II, in Japan's eager rush to embrace the "Modernism," or the "International Style," that was prevalent in the West. As a result, the ingenuity inherent in the old ways of Japanese building techniques and lifestyles was lost in the name of modernity.

Now, some Japanese architects are trying to relearn and reapply the principles that at one time made the country's architecture a much-admired model of simplicity, style, and utility.

This return to simplicity should above all remind us that, even as Japan races headlong into expanding its urban sprawl and revels in its futuristic high-tech innovations and popular sci-fi animations and *manga* of "Cool Japan," the country should be mindful of its past wisdom, whether in design principles or more fundamental values.

AFTER THE WAR, THE INGENUITY INHERENT IN THE OLD WAYS OF JAPANESE BUILDING WAS LOST IN THE NAME OF MODERNITY.

The swing back to traditional principles of Japanese architecture also points to a broader revival of interest in the homegrown approach to synthesizing and developing styles and ideas, particularly in the culinary, fashion, and arts and crafts fields. In such areas lie a wealth of unique design ideas that are yet to be fully tapped, and which, I believe, in time will be shared around the world.

Perhaps because Japan is an island country that lacks natural resources, the Japanese cultivated a knack for emulating and improving on whatever they imported. In many cases, they developed products that not only surpassed the originals but also gave them a uniquely Japanese twist.

Take, for example, culinary culture. The immense wealth of delicacies in Japan spans "original" Japanese foods, such as sushi, *tempura*, and *sukiyaki*; more hearty, earthy dishes that borrowed from other cultures, such as *tonkatsu* (deep-fried pork cutlet), curry rice, and *ramen* noodles; and wholly imported cuisines from France, Italy, Spain, and elsewhere. As evidenced by international accolades, including the awarding by Michelin Guides of more stars to restaurants in Japan than to those in any other country, the quality of "foreign" cuisines in many of Japan's best restaurants now exceeds that of food served in the original countries.

Similarly, the Japanese have developed Zen Buddhism, based on concepts borrowed from India by way of China and Korea. The Japanese *kanji* characters, too, were imported from China. So many aspects of Japanese society, in fact, did not originate in Japan. Nonetheless, the Japanese have made these ideas into something uniquely Japanese, and often sought after by the rest of the world.

This, I believe, is a source of wealth and strength that, unfortunately, most Japanese are not even aware of. If and when they do become aware, my guess is that, for good or for bad, foreign influence will again have triggered it.

Similarly, in the revival of traditional architectural concepts, one can see the synthesis of the old and homegrown, and the new and borrowed ideas. Perhaps more importantly, this trend is one of the most potent reminders for Japanese society: sometimes to go forward, it is essential to look back.

Fushimi Inari shrine, Kyoto, Japan
© Fototrav

CONCLUSION

A 20-YEAR ROAD MAP FOR THE FUTURE

HEANG CHHOR

WHEN THE MOST POWERFUL EARTHQUAKE in Japan's history devastated northern Honshu in March, it rocked buildings in Tokyo, and the tsunami that came after touched the shores of Oregon and Chile. Countries from South America to Canada went on the alert.

The event was, first and foremost, a national tragedy of historic scale; Prime Minister Naoto Kan was right to call it Japan's most difficult crisis since World War II. But the reckoning will be global. In the most terrible way, the earthquake was a reminder of just how much Japan matters.

For a start, dealing with the wreckage will place terrific strains on the country's finances, already burdened by the rich world's highest level of debt. A generous donor, Japan may cut back on its assistance to poorer countries. Supply chains in a variety of industries were disrupted. Shipments of goods stalled. Commodity prices for everything from oil to rare earths were affected. The long-term effect on the nuclear industry is sure to be profound, with consequences for the Japanese and the global energy supply as well as for continuing efforts on climate change.

But let us remember, too, what the earthquake revealed about the strengths of Japan. The country's strict and rigidly enforced construction codes meant that the death toll, albeit awful, was orders of magnitude less than it would have been almost anywhere else. The government responded with greater speed, precision, and effectiveness than it did after the 1995 Kobe earthquake; the country's massive investments in prevention and preparedness clearly paid off. And the citizens of Japan, even in their grief, were models of civility and calm.

Heang Chhor is a senior partner at McKinsey & Company, and the head of McKinsey Japan.

• • •

Although we began work on *Reimagining Japan* long before the earthquake hit, the issues the book addresses are no less relevant in its aftermath. When it comes to the forces of nature, all any country can do is try to anticipate and then to react intelligently. The same is true of man-made forces, and it is these that are at the heart of this volume. Among them: the rise of China; Japan's aging, shrinking population; a stagnating economy; an increasingly inward-looking orientation; and a turbulent, ineffectual political order. These are among the factors that have led many observers to predict an era of inevitable decline and second-tier status for Japan.

Japan's long-term decline is a sobering thought—and one that would not have occurred to anyone only a generation ago. Yet this destiny is not the only one available to Japan. The country's business, government, and social leaders can take practical steps that would allow Japan to forge a very different future. That will be a daunting task, as the essays in this volume make clear. Still, it is far from an impossible one.

In this essay, I offer a 20-year road map that suggests the direction the country should take. Why 20 years? Because Japan must make fundamental changes. The nation will need time to assess the implications of these proposals, to win acceptance for them, and to implement them on a large scale. Reimagining Japan cannot be done otherwise.

Among the priorities: restructuring and globalizing Japanese companies, changing the educational system, adapting to troubling demographic trends, attracting foreigners, and building closer ties with Asia. One consistent element running through this list—and indeed throughout *Reimagining Japan*—is the need for more openness and collaboration with the rest of the world.

To move in this direction, Japan's leaders will have to take a number of difficult, unpopular actions—and that's a problem. I cannot count the number of times I have heard from Japanese leaders, "I agree that we need radical changes but I would never say that." Such fear of change and, in a larger sense, fearfulness about the future, are forms of anxiety the country can no longer afford. To stay in the global game, Japan needs leaders who will speak frankly, set goals, and inspire their fellow citizens to revitalize the country.

A divided society?

To begin with the problems: Japan's public debt could reach 300 percent of GDP before long, and the deficits of the pension and health systems are also growing. The population, already the world's oldest, is beginning to shrink—meaning that there are fewer citizens to buy government bonds or produce the wealth that can finance the country's debts. The economy is in a third "lost decade" with declining consumption and weakening competitiveness in major industries. Not surprisingly, Japan's influence on the world is likewise fading.

These facts alone justify full mobilization. But the most urgent reason to act is for the sake of the young. Persistently slow economic growth has produced millions of young Japanese who feel left out or unwanted. Although unemployment is not as high in Japan as in many other places—10 percent among 15- to 24-year-olds and 6 percent among those 25 to 34—the reality is still troubling. The unemployment figure fails to take into account the many women dropping out of the workforce or the huge number of temporary employees, who tend to have lower, less stable incomes. In 2009, they accounted for 34 percent of the labor force, up from 20 percent in 1990.

What happens if these millions of un- and underemployed workers fail to find their footing? Lacking confidence in their ability to contribute, they may hesitate to marry, with social and demographic consequences that cannot be benign. Then consider the increase in rural poverty, the rising number of lonely and struggling elderly, and the uncountable number of alienated people.

Add this all together, and Japan begins to look like something new to itself: a society of "haves" and "have-nots." For a society that has long prided itself on its cohesive and egalitarian values, the prospect of such a divided society is horrifying.

A 20-year road map for change

Transforming Japanese companies
No country can prosper without a dynamic private sector. Japanese executives, working with the government, should focus on the following issues.

- *Reducing overcapacity.* In industries such as consumer electronics, retailing, banking, and beverages, companies must restructure their domestic operations by selling or swapping underperforming businesses. Japanese companies are often so busy fighting and investing resources in a shrinking domestic market that they overlook other opportunities—for both innovation or internationalization.

   Take Japan's mobile-phone industry. The companies in this sector compete fiercely on price within the domestic market, but none managed to launch a compelling smartphone. That left the field wide open for Apple's wildly popular iPhone. In other words, Japanese companies have chosen to fight local competitors and preserve overcapacity rather than adapt to fast-changing consumer needs.

   Japanese managers avoid reducing capacity in part because doing so might imply a defeat or an acknowledgement that a predecessor made a poor choice and in part because closing or selling businesses and factories costs jobs. These reasons speak to Japan's enduring social values. In an ever more competitive world, though, these values must evolve. The government could help force the pace by doing more to retrain those who lose their jobs, helping them relocate, and offering additional unemployment benefits. Such measures are costly but essential; several European countries have models worth looking at.

- *Creating global champions.* Global champions are profitable, powerful job creators and innovators boasting leadership positions and the ability to attract the most talented employees. Canon, Komatsu, and Toyota are members of this club; Shiseido and Uniqlo might join it one day. Japan needs many more, particularly in consumer electronics, to compete against Apple, HP, Nokia, and Samsung; in retailing against Wal-Mart, Tesco, and Carrefour; and in banking against Citibank and HSBC.

Mergers and acquisitions could speed up the pace. In recent years, Japanese companies have made a number of bold deals, including Takeda's acquisition of Millennium, a US pharma; Canon's purchase of Oce and Suntory's acquisition of Orangina-Schweppes, both European targets; and Nomura's absorption of Lehman Brothers Holdings in Europe and Asia. Still, Japan's record remains relatively modest compared with the scale of M&A among major Chinese, Indian, and Western enterprises. One result: Japanese companies lack top-level foreign talent and global experience in their executive ranks.

- *Refining the performance culture.* In the 1980s and '90s, Japan's distinctive corporate structure was widely lauded as a permanent competitive advantage. Now, however, parts of it have clearly become an impediment.

Performance management, for example, has a bad name in Japan, where it is often associated with a narrow, Western, bottom-line mentality. Instead, many companies would rather just *gambaru*—essentially, "hang in there and try your best." Too often, Japanese executives measure employees on the basis of input and effort rather than output and effectiveness.

The world's most successful companies go beyond either of these approaches. They see performance in broader terms, taking into account innovation, quality, talent, and growth. These factors can be difficult to fit into the Japanese context. Pursuing innovation, for example, invites failure. But Japanese executives typically have detailed action plans to guarantee a 100-percent success rate. Unfortunately, the world doesn't work that way.

Another barrier to innovation and growth is the "we are unique" mentality. Too many Japanese executives resist the idea that they can learn from other companies' experiences. Many Japanese firms have an "inside-out" orientation: a company creates a product, then presents it to the world. But there should also be a place for "outside-in" thinking: adopting global best practices regardless of their country of origin. Beginning in the 1980s, remember, that is what many US and European car companies did, imitating Japanese practices in detail and improving the quality of their products significantly.

The opportunities of an outside-in approach are almost limitless, particularly given fast growth in emerging markets. General Electric, for example, is developing more than 25 percent of its new health care products in India, with explicit plans to sell them in developed countries as well. Japanese companies should open themselves to such innovative models.

Finally, maximizing performance requires having the right people, with the right incentives, in the right jobs and locations. Japan's tradition of lifetime employment for managers, for all its virtues, has become a handicap because it prevents, or at least slows, the renewal of talent and fresh thinking. More flexible policies are necessary. Along those lines, Japanese companies must develop more effective career paths, internal training, and personnel systems. In many large corporations, younger employees can spend their first five to ten years in roles that barely tap their potential. They need more stimulating assignments, to learn by doing, to take risks, and to interact with foreign cultures. Recruiting mid- to senior-level managers from other Japanese and foreign companies must also become more routine.

- *Unleashing entrepreneurship.* After World War II, an exceptional group of entrepreneurs, including the founders of Toyota, Honda, Sony, and Matsushita, led the country's march to prosperity. As Japan became more successful, however, later generations became less interested in taking risks. Instead, Japan's best and brightest opted for the security of lifetime employment in big companies or for the prestige of government ministries.

That career model is limiting; Japan should actively encourage young people to dare to be entrepreneurs. Creating a vibrant culture of entrepreneurship requires a big change in educational philosophy (see below) and concerted efforts to take advantage of the country's excellent engineering and technology resources. Government and the private sector could, for example, start a venture capital fund aimed at promoting next-generation businesses through open innovation. Encouraged widely, the spirit of entrepreneurship might in turn fuel risk and initiative taking inside bigger organizations. The country's leaders should encourage a Silicon Valley mentality so that more young people follow the path of the high-energy Japanese entrepreneurs who have created success stories like DeNA, Nitori, Rakuten, and SoftBank.

The case for radical educational reform

Japan's future prosperity depends in large part on transforming education. The system produces too many graduates who are not especially useful to Japanese companies struggling to compete globally. The scale of the challenge requires mobilizing the country's political and business leaders. Incremental efforts—or, worse, inertia—will stunt Japan's long-term competitiveness.

- *Developing more independent-minded students.* A reformed education system should seek to develop graduates who are mature, independent thinkers willing to lead. Japan should reduce the emphasis on rote learning in favor of a curriculum that encourages students to think critically, express their views, challenge conventional beliefs, and talk openly.
- *Creating global citizens.* Comparatively few Japanese study abroad—and the number is falling. Meanwhile, there are more overseas students than ever from China, India, and South Korea. Japan should seek to reverse this troubling trend by, for example, making it compulsory for university students to spend a year outside Japan. Educators should also encourage more ex-

changes between Japanese high-school students and their counterparts in other countries.

Here is a specific idea: Japan should create a national program to send 100,000 students or employees overseas each year, for at least one year, with, say, a $25,000 to $50,000 government subsidy. One could also envision giving 100,000 young foreigners the same subsidy to encourage them to study in Japan for a year or two. These two programs would cost $5 billion to $10 billion a year, a trifling addition to the country's trillion-dollar annual budget. And think of the payoff: in ten years, Japan could have a pool of one million workers with international experience and one million foreigners familiar with Japan.

Another bold but challenging move would be to make English a second national language, with schools teaching it from a young age. Taking drastic action to promote a wider role for English could be transforming. If Japan were to do so, by 2030 millions of young Japanese would have the language skills to work abroad. Japanese companies would be better equipped to sustain their global presence. And more tourists might be attracted to Japan if they could communicate more readily.

● *Reconnecting with business.* Japan must produce more students with skills that match the needs of its companies. University students should have more work experience before graduating; for example, internships should be a compulsory part of the curriculum. (One-year corporate internships have become the norm in the leading graduate schools in countries such as France and Germany.) Getting more business leaders to sit on the boards of Japanese universities would also help; executives could help to make academic programs more business friendly.

● *Making leading Japanese universities regional academic centers.* Universities could merge their best research assets, human and physical, to turn themselves into regional research centers that attract the best students and teachers from around Asia and the world. English should be the language of instruction. This approach could inject into Japan an element of diversity and creativity that it needs. The country should build on the disciplines in which it excels or would like to excel—clean technology and health care, for example—making it more attractive for top talent in those disciplines to relocate.

Turning demographic change into opportunity

Japan's population is getting older and smaller. By 2030, people over 65 years of age could account for one-third of the population, compared with 20 percent in 2005. This dramatic demographic change contains the seeds of opportunity.

● *Developing businesses related to seniors.* Savers 55 years old and above hold 70 percent of Japan's $16 trillion in financial assets. In the cosmetics sector, some companies are producing brands specifically for women aged 50 and older. Retailers could invest in home delivery for consumers who can't or don't want to go to a store. Older consumers may need electronic devices with simple touch screens that make ordering straightforward. Travel and entertainment companies, which currently focus on younger consumers, could greatly expand offerings for older people. These models, fine-tuned at home, could help Japanese companies in their globalization efforts as the population ages in many parts of the world.

- *Becoming a world center of excellence on aging.* Other countries will eventually face similar demographic challenges, including how to deal with a large elderly population and what to do about the depopulation of rural areas. Japan, however, will be dealing with all of this first. It should seek to become the place others look to for expert advice on caring for seniors, providing them with health care, managing pensions, and related issues.

- *Taking advantage of a highly educated female workforce.* Japan is wasting the talent of its women. The country no longer has the luxury of holding back so many of its highly educated and most productive citizens. Cultural issues notwithstanding, as Japan's population shrinks, there's no getting around the need to make women a more important part of the formal workforce. Just 70 percent of women remain in it following marriage; that percentage drops to about 50 percent after the birth of the first (and often only) child.

In Japan, retaining women in the workforce after they start families will require improving the country's child care infrastructure. While about 50,000 children are on the official waiting list for nurseries, the true figure is more like several hundred thousand. Companies must speak out forcefully—their long-term interests will be served by maximizing the number of qualified workers.

Demographic trends also suggest that Japan should provide incentives for young couples to have more children. It could learn from countries that have reconciled a higher fertility rate—the average number of children born to a woman in her lifetime—with a higher workforce participation rate for women. Sweden, for example, has increased its fertility rate from 1.5 in the early 1990s to 1.9, and 80 percent of Swedish women 25 to 49 years old are employed. Both figures are substantially higher than those in Japan.

- *Seeing immigration as a source of possibility.* The Japanese government obviously has the right to decide whether to open the country's doors wider and, if so, how. Less than 2 percent of Japan's population is of foreign origin—the lowest percentage in the Organisation for Economic Co-operation and Development (OECD). Immigration is a controversial issue in Japan, as it is in many countries. But there's a difference between mass and selective immigration. The government and business must develop a plan to attract the right talent.

One could imagine at least three entrant profiles: students, service workers, and corporate managers. As mentioned, foreign students would arrive in the context of a Japanese program offering education and experience in regional research centers. They might later stay on to work for Japanese organizations.

As the population ages and more women enter and remain in the workforce, demand for nurses, babysitters, retail clerks, and construction workers will rise. For this population, the biggest obstacle is the Japanese language; there is no easy solution here. Intensive courses in Japanese will be necessary but so will increasing the number of English-speaking Japanese supervisors and co-workers.

Companies desperately need the outside perspective that foreign managers could bring, and thousands of young US and European managers are looking for opportunities in Asia. Japan should try to capture its share of these talented workers and not let most of them go to China, where jobs are easier to find.

Ingesting such an influx, even if it is well regulated, will not be easy. But it is important to consider the possibility that a virtuous cycle could begin to form. That is, as Japan becomes more diverse and more global—accepting more foreign-born workers and becoming more comfortable with the outside world—the idea of immigration could be less daunting and perhaps even routine.

Looking to an Asian future

The United States and Europe will remain important markets and partners. But Asia will be an even more formidable source of opportunities: the region's markets are growing faster than those of the United States and Europe; they are also an increasing source of demand for Japanese companies. Japan needs the growth that comes from exports to Asia. (China is already Japan's leading trading partner.) In fact, Japan can leverage its technologies to foster integration with Asia and benefit from its vitality.

As the region's most advanced and second-biggest economy, Japan can capture significant business opportunities in sectors from telecommunications to health care. It can also use its technology and know-how to help Asia grow. India, for example, could benefit from Japan's expertise in infrastructure and China from its experience in combating pollution. Japan's government says it wants to increase infrastructure exports such as high-speed rail and water-related projects. South East Asia is fertile ground for Japanese investment, and Japan is determined to help Association of South East Asian Nations (ASEAN) in its connectivity infrastructure initiative.

The country must also continue to pursue free-trade agreements. In October 2010, Japan and India concluded such a deal; there's huge potential in the relationship. In 2009, bilateral trade between India and Japan came to only $10 billion, compared with more than $250 billion between China and Japan. In general, Japanese farmers oppose free-trade pacts, fearing competition from lower-cost producers. But the rest of Japanese business—not to mention consumers—stands to gain considerably from reduced tariffs.

Japan could benefit from allowing more Asians to study, work, and settle in the country. In return, Japan could use its retired and older unemployed managers to train workers, teach, run factories, and build schools and hospitals in the region. Such projects would help redundant Japanese workers contribute to society and promote closer relationships with Asia. When those economies grow, they become bigger markets for Japanese products.

Leadership for a new era

How can Japan carry out these challenging reforms? The answer is clear: leadership. This was true before the natural disasters of March 11; it is even more true in their wake. Japanese leaders will have to restore confidence and act boldly to get Japan back on track. In the 1970s and 1980s, US and European companies were caught resting on their laurels, and Japanese executives took advantage of the West's sluggish innovation, poor product quality, and ineffective manufacturing practices to build market share around the world. Japanese managers then exhibited exactly the right leadership qualities: high aspirations, creativity, risk taking, open-mindedness, and the ability to change. These were coupled with detailed planning for large-scale execution, discipline in implementation, and a standardized approach to internationalization.

Japan's success woke up the competition, which worked hard during the 1980s and 1990s to improve efficiency and quality. As a result, many companies in China, India, South Korea, and the West have learned to execute as well as the Japanese did—and sometimes faster. Execution in Japan has become a source of weakness. Decision making is much too slow at a time when anticipation, rapid adaptation, and the ability to make radical changes are the keys to success.

Moreover, the leadership skills that made Japanese companies so successful in the 1970s and 1980s have not been transmitted to the present generation of managers. There is a lack of independent thinking for bold strategies—especially internationally driven ones—and for radical change. Risk aversion is the rule. In sum, Japan and its companies do not have enough leaders to address all the challenges.

Making leadership and performance a priority

Japanese companies are led by well-meaning and committed people who want to do the right thing. The problem is that they don't always know how. They are brilliant at running the trains on time but much less so at 21st-century skills such as evaluating risks, appointing the right people, and developing a long-term vision. Executives urgently require coaching and incentives to become more performance oriented. The emphasis should be on taking initiative, focusing on results, and confronting difficulties—not on how hard executives try or how adept they are at building consensus. Risk taking should be encouraged, and failure should not cost executives their chances for promotion. Companies such as Recruit, SoftBank, and Takeda exemplify such an approach, but they are outliers.

Today, a typical Japanese company brings managers along very deliberately. In their first years on the job, their skills develop at an achingly slow pace and they have limited responsibilities. This model is out of step with modern corporate challenges. The leadership qualities required of today's executives must be taught and allowed to flourish among people at younger ages—in universities, when students join companies, and when they become managers.

Globalizing corporate management

Hundreds of capable foreign executives could fill jobs in Japanese companies, injecting new ideas and energy. The counterargument, too often heard, is that Japan's unique management style must be preserved because it is embedded in the country's unique culture. This notion is an excuse for stasis; moreover, it is no longer persuasive, given the glaring competitiveness issues in too many Japanese industries.

Of course Japan is unique. So is Germany, for that matter, or Canada; the difference is that in these countries, corporate management is also much more internationalized. Japan's corporate leaders need to think through and courageously implement the operational changes, ranging from language to work practices to incentives, required to attract more foreign talent. The evidence is clear that even in Japan, a more global leadership can expand a company's options and help to make it stronger. In a number of cases, for example, foreigners have helped to lead turnaround efforts; these are often more difficult for Japanese to manage because they feel more culturally constrained when it comes to painful restructuring.

The idea of bringing in more foreigners is not to make Japan more like someplace else; it is to make it easier to bring the best of global thinking and best practices (including, of course, those from Japan) to the nation's companies. And this should not be a one-way ticket. Enterprises could also send young Japanese managers to work and train abroad and then return to take leadership positions. Companies like Komatsu, Sony, and Toshiba have moved in this direction. Government could facilitate the process by granting tax breaks for the cost of sending young managers to foreign countries.

Promote leadership development

Japan should make leadership development a priority—like the successful national efforts on energy efficiency or product quality. In the last few years, some nonprofit organizations have developed programs to teach leadership skills to young people. Japanese executives and government leaders should support these efforts, whose popularity suggests that there's growing public interest in the topic.

● ● ●

Japan is a rich society where most people live comfortable lives. At the same time, long-term economic factors have undermined the country's confidence and called into question the system that fostered these benefits. Over the last 20 years, Japan has suffered from slow growth, deflation, political scandals, a revolving door in the prime minister's office, and intense competition with Asian rivals. Confidence is so damaged that it appears to be difficult for Japan's business and political leaders to make game-changing moves.

Still, Japan has many unexploited assets, including the world's support of and affinity for Japan. A 2010 poll by the BBC World Service found that the global general public put Japan number two, after Germany, as a country with a mainly positive image. Japan must have been heartened by the overwhelming support and sympathy from the rest of the world in the aftermath of the Tohoku disasters.

But something has to give. Many Japanese recognize that the changes described above—and these are by no means comprehensive—are necessary. Corporate Japan must demonstrate exceptional daring to change the tenets of business as usual. Government must support these tough decisions and invest in an educational system that suits future needs. And the public and private sectors must collaborate closely to support the nation's long-term interests, not to protect vested ones. Japan's leaders must, in short, reimagine their country. The destiny of future generations is at stake. The tragedies of March 2011 make the case for faster, more radical action with even greater urgency.

This 20-year road map is not intended to imply that Japan has only one way to get where it wants to go, any more than a map sets out only one route to reach a destination. Change will come in many ways—from the micro choices of individual men and women to the macroeconomic policies decided by the nation's famed bureaucrats to the day-to-day actions of line managers in thousands of companies.

A map, after all, is only a map. It is the driver—Japan and its people—who will make the journey.

CONTRIBUTORS

BERNARD ARNAULT is the chairman and CEO of LVMH Moët Hennessy Louis Vuitton, the world-leading luxury goods group. LVMH has a portfolio of more than 60 prestigious brands, including Louis Vuitton, Fendi, Christian Dior, Guerlain, Moët & Chandon, Dom Pérignon, Hennessy, TAG Heuer, Chaumet, Sephora, and others.

GERARD J. ARPEY is chairman and CEO of AMR Corp. and American Airlines.

GOVINDA AVASARALA is a research assistant with the Energy Security Initiative at the Brookings Institution.

DOMINIC BARTON is the global managing director of McKinsey & Company. Prior to his current role, he was based in Shanghai as McKinsey's Asia chairman from 2004-09, and he led McKinsey's office in Korea from 2000–04. He is co-author of *Dangerous Markets: Managing in Financial Crises* (2002, with Roberto Newell and Greg Wilson) and of *China Vignettes: An Inside Look at China* (2007, with Mei Ye). Barton is a trustee of the Brookings Institution and is the chairman of the International Advisory Committee to the President of South Korea. In 2009, the Shanghai government awarded him the Magnolia Gold Prize for his contributions to the city's development.

HANNAH BEECH, Beijing bureau chief of *Time* magazine, has lived in Asia for almost 15 years and reported extensively throughout the region.

PAUL BLUSTEIN is a non-resident fellow in the global economy and development program at the Brookings Institution, and senior visiting fellow at the Centre for International Governance Innovation. A resident of Kamakura, he spent much of his career as a reporter for *The Washington Post*, including five years as a correspondent in Tokyo. He is the author of three books about international economic institutions, including the IMF and WTO, and is working on another book about the global financial crisis.

TYLER BRÛLÉ is founder and editor-in-chief of *Monocle* magazine, whose operations include retail shops in London, Los Angeles, Hong Kong, Tokyo and New York, as well as an e-commerce site. Brûlé is the Fast Lane columnist for the *Financial Times* and was the founding editor of *Wallpaper**.

IAN BURUMA is a professor of human rights at Bard College. He studied film at Japan's Nihon University in the 1970s and has written several acclaimed books about modern Japan, including *The Wages of Guilt: Memories of War in Japan and Germany; The Missionary and the Libertine: Love and War in East and West;* and *Inventing Japan: 1853–1964*.

CLAY CHANDLER is Asia Editor for McKinsey & Company. Prior to joining McKinsey, he was Asia Editor of *Fortune* (2001–2008); Hong Kong bureau chief (1999–2001) and Washington, DC-based chief economic correspondent (1992–1999) for *The Washington Post*; and Tokyo correspondent for *The Wall Street Journal* (1989–1992).

JOHN CHAMBERS is chairman and CEO of Cisco.

HEANG CHHOR is a senior partner at McKinsey & Company and the head of McKinsey Japan. He is a long-time observer of Asian and Japanese economies and societies.

MARK CLIFFORD is executive director of the Asia Business Council, an independent organization of top executives that conducts research and holds forums on topics ranging from intellectual property to education to energy efficiency. Prior to joining the Council in May 2007, Clifford was editor-in-chief of both of Hong Kong's major English-language newspapers, *The Standard* and *The South China Morning Post*. He is the co-author of *China and the WTO: Changing China, Changing World Trade* (2002) and the author of *Troubled Tiger: Businessmen, Bureaucrats and Generals in South Korea* (1997).

STEPHEN R. COVEY is an expert on organizations and leadership. A prolific author, he has sold more than 20 million books, including *The 7 Habits of Highly Effective People* (1989), *Principle-Centered Leadership* (1991) and *The Eighth Habit*

(2005). He is cofounder and vice chairman of FranklinCovey, a global professional services firm with offices in 123 countries.

GERALD L. CURTIS is the Burgess professor of political science at Columbia University; concurrently, he is a visiting professor at Waseda University and senior research fellow at the International Institute for Economic Studies and the Tokyo Foundation. Curtis is the author of *The Logic of Japanese Politics* (2000) and numerous other books and articles. His most recent book, written in Japanese, is *Politics and Sanma: 45 Years Living with Japan* (2008). In 2004, Curtis was awarded the Order of the Rising Sun, Gold and Silver Star, by the Emperor of Japan.

JOHN W. DOWER is a professor emeritus of history at the Massachusetts Institute of Technology and the author of many books about Japan, including *Embracing Defeat: Japan in the Wake of World War II* (1999), which won the Pulitzer Prize for general non-fiction, the National Book Award, and the Bancroft Prize. His most recent book is *Cultures of War: Pearl Harbor/Hiroshima/9-11/Iraq* (2010).

NICHOLAS EBERSTADT is the Henry Wendt Scholar in Political Economy at the American Enterprise Institute in Washington. A political economist and demographer, he is a senior adviser to the National Board of Asian Research, a member of the visiting committee at the Harvard School of Public Health, and a member of the Global Agenda Council at the World Economic Forum.

CHARLES K. EBINGER is director of the Energy Security Initiative at the Brookings Institution. Ebinger has served as an energy policy adviser to more than 50 governments, working with them on restructuring, privatization and the creation of regulatory regimes. He is also an adjunct professor of electricity economics at the Paul H. Nitze School of Advanced International Studies at Johns Hopkins University.

MOHAMED A. EL-ERIAN is CEO and co-CIO of PIMCO, a California-based global investment firm that has more than $1.2 trillion in assets under management. He is the author of *When Markets Collide: Investment Strategies for the Age of Global Economic Change* (2008).

BILL EMMOTT is an independent writer and consultant on international affairs. From 1993 to 2006, he was editor-in-chief of *The Economist*. His latest books are *Rivals—How the Power Struggle between China, India and Japan Will Shape our Next Decade* (2008) and *Forza, Italia: Come Ripartire Dopo Berlusconi* (2010).

KAZUHIRO FUJIWARA was a longtime executive with Recruit in both Tokyo and Europe. In 2002, he joined the Suginami Ward Education Committee. From

April 2003 to March 2008, he was principal of the Suginami Ward Wada Junior High School—the first individual from the private sector to serve as a principal of a junior high school in Japan.

GLEN S. FUKUSHIMA is chairman of Airbus. After practicing law, he was a senior official at the Office of the US Trade Representative, 1985–90. Since then, he has been a senior executive at AT&T, Arthur D. Little, Cadence Design Systems, and NCR. He also served as vice president and president of the American Chamber of Commerce in Japan (1993–99) and on the boards of companies and nonprofit organizations in the US, Japan, and Europe. A graduate of Deep Spring, Stanford and Harvard, he was a Fulbright Fellow at the University of Tokyo, 1982-83.

YOICHI FUNABASHI is a former editor in chief of the *Asahi Shimbun*, one of Japan's largest daily newpapers. During his journalism career, he was posted to both Beijing and Washington, and was chief of the *Asahi Shimbun* American General Bureau from 1993–97. He won the Japan Press Award in 1994 for his columns on foreign policy. Funabashi has written several books, including *The Peninsula Question: A Chronicle of the Second Korean Nuclear Crisis* (2007) and *Alliance Adrift* (1998) and served as a visiting professor at universities in both Japan and Korea. He was a member of the Prime Minister's commission on the future of Japan (1999–2000).

VICTOR K. FUNG is chairman of the Li & Fung group of companies, chairman of the Hong Kong-Japan Business Cooperation Committee, chairman of the Greater Pearl River Delta Business Council, and honorary chairman of the International Chamber of Commerce. He is also a member of Chinese People's Political Consultative Conference.

YUJI GENDA is a professor of labor economics at the University of Tokyo Institute of Social Science. He has written and spoken extensively on youth, labor markets, economic insecurity and other social trends.

CARLOS GHOSN is chairman and CEO, Renault-Nissan Alliance.

BRAD GLOSSERMAN is executive director of Pacific Forum CSIS, a nonprofit, foreign policy research institute affiliated with the Center for Strategic and International Studies in Washington, D.C. He is co-editor of *Comparative Connections*, the Pacific Forum's quarterly electronic journal, and co-authors the regional review. A member of *The Japan Times* editorial board, he has written dozens of monographs on US foreign policy and Asian security relations, including *The Guillotine: Japan's Demographic Transition and its Security Implications* (with Tomoko Tsunoda, 2009).

SENAPATHY GOPALAKRISHNAN is CEO and managing director of Infosys Technologies, which he helped to found in 1981.

CHRISTOPHER GRAVES is global CEO of Ogilvy Public Relations Worldwide; he also serves on the Ogilvy & Mather Group board of directors. Before joining Ogilvy, he worked in news for 23 years, including serving as head of television news for *The Wall Street Journal* and Dow Jones, and head of network news for CNBC in Europe and Asia. He was elected a life member of the Council on Foreign Relations in 2010.

MICHAEL J. GREEN is senior adviser and Japan chair at the Center for Strategic and International Studies in Washington, D.C., as well as associate professor of international relations at Georgetown University. He served on the National Security Council staff from 2001 through 2005, including as special assistant to President Bush, and senior director for Asian Affairs.

YASUCHIKA HASEGAWA is president and CEO of Takeda Pharmaceutical Company.

FUMIKO HAYASHI was elected mayor of Yokohama in 2009, the first woman to hold that post. She is also the former president of BMW Tokyo, CEO of Daiei, and president of Tokyo Nissan Auto Sales.

DAVID HENDERSON is a consultant in McKinsey's Tokyo office.

KENSHI HIROKANE is an award-winning *manga* artist whose work often addresses social issues. His long-running *manga* series featuring a fictional businessman, Kōsaku Shima, follows his career from section chief to president of a consumer electronics company. Hugely popular in Japan, the series is considered a tellingly accurate portrayal of corporate life.

KEIJI INAFUNE is founder and CEO of Comcept, which designs and develops video games. He is the former head of global R&D and production at Capcom, an Osaka-based video developer and publisher. Inafune worked on the graphic design for the *Street Fighter* and *Rock Man* game series before producing the action-adventure game, *Onimusha*, and the horror title, *Dead Rising*.

PAUL J. INGRASSIA has written about automobiles and the auto industry for 25 years. As *The Wall Street Journal's* Detroit bureau chief from 1985 to 1994, Ingrassia won a Pulitzer Prize—along with his deputy, Joseph B. White—in 1993 for coverage of General Motors. His latest book, *Crash Course: The American Automobile Industry's Road from Glory to Disaster* (2010), is a behind-the-scenes account of the bailouts and bankruptcies of GM and Chrysler.

NATSUMI IWASAKI is the author of *What If the Female Manager of a High-School Baseball Team Read Drucker's* Management? The fictional book was Japan's top seller in 2010.

NAOYUKI IWATANI is a partner in McKinsey's Tokyo office.

PICO IYER is the author of two novels and seven works of non-fiction, among them *Video Night in Kathmandu* (1988) *The Lady and the Monk* (1991), *The Global Soul* (2001) and, most recently, *The Open Road* (2008). An essayist for *Time* magazine since 1986, he writes regularly for *The New York Review of Books*, *The New York Times*, *Financial Times* and many other publications. Iyer has been based in Japan since 1992.

LUDWIG KANZLER is a partner in McKinsey's Tokyo office.

RICHARD KATZ is the editor of *The Oriental Economist Report*, a monthly newsletter on Japan, and of TOE Alert, a semi-weekly briefing service on Japan. He is the author of *The System That Soured: The Rise and Fall of the Japanese Economic Miracle.*

PETER KENEVAN is a partner in McKinsey's Tokyo office.

ALEX KERR, a longtime resident of Japan and Thailand, is an expert in the traditional arts and environment of East Asia. Kerr has written several books, including *Bangkok Found: Reflections on the City* (2010); *Lost Japan* (Japanese, 1993; English, 1996) and *Dogs and Demons: Tales from the Dark Side of Japan* (2001), about the country's post-1990 malaise.

JESPER KOLL, a resident of Japan since 1986, is managing director and head of Japanese equity research at JP Morgan Securities Japan. He has written two books in Japanese, *Towards a New Japanese Golden Age* and *The End of Heisei Deflation.* He is also one of the few non-Japanese members of the *Keizai Doyukai* (the Japan Association of Corporate Executives).

YOSHIE KOMURO is founder and CEO of the Work-Life Balance Company in Tokyo.

KENNETH LIEBERTHAL is director of the John L. Thornton China Center and senior fellow in Foreign Policy and Global Economy and Development at the Brookings Institution. He has authored 17 books and monographs and more than 70 articles, mostly dealing with China. He also served as special assistant to the president for national security affairs and senior director for Asia on the National Security Council from August 1998 to October 2000.

PETER LÖSCHER is president and CEO of Siemens AG.

SHINZO MAEDA is chairman of Shiseido, and was president and CEO from 2005 to early 2011.

KUMIKO MAKIHARA is a freelance writer and translator who often writes about social and cultural trends in Japan. Previously, she was the features editor of the *Moscow Times*, a correspondent for *Time* magazine in Tokyo and a reporter for the Associated Press.

KEVIN MASSY is assistant director of the Energy Security Initiative at the Brookings Institution. He was previously a contributing writer to *The Economist* on energy and technology; and an associate editor for CBS, where he covered transportation and alternative energy.

BOB MCDONALD is chairman, president and CEO of Procter & Gamble.

ALLEN MINER is the founder/chairman and CEO of SunBridge Corporation, founder/director of Japan Venture Research, and cofounder of the Japan Venture Capital Association. He was Oracle's first on-the ground employee in Japan in the 1980s and helped to found Oracle Japan. SunBridge is a Tokyo-based venture capital, IT and professional-services firm that has worked with more than 45 Japanese technology startups. The market cap of companies backed by SunBridge is more than $21 billion.

MINORU MORI is chairman of Mori Building, a privately held and nonlisted firm that is one of Japan's leading property developers. Among its major projects are the 101-story Shanghai World Financial Center and the Roppongi Hills development in Tokyo.

ULRICH NAEHER is a senior partner in McKinsey's Tokyo office.

TOMOKO NAMBA, a former McKinsey partner, is the founder and CEO of DeNA, one of the largest mobile game companies in Japan.

MOTOYA OKADA is president of AEON, one of the largest retail groups in Japan.

TAKESHI OKADA was coach of Japan's national soccer team from December 2007 to August 2010. He led Japan to a ninth-place finish at the 2010 World Cup, its best performance ever.

GORDON ORR is a senior partner in McKinsey's Shanghai office and the chairman of McKinsey Asia.

EDZARD J. C. OVERBEEK is president of Cisco Asia-Pacific and Japan.

ADAM S. POSEN is an external member of the Monetary Policy Committee of the Bank of England, by appointment of the Chancellor of the Exchequer, and a senior fellow at the Peterson Institute for International Economics, a private, nonprofit, nonpartisan research institute. An expert on macroeconomic policy, Posen is author of *Restoring Japan's Economic Growth* (1998) and co-author (with Ben Bernanke, et al.) of *Inflation Targeting: Lessons from the International Experience* (1999), and *The Japanese Financial Crisis and its Parallels with US Experience* (2000, with Ryoichi Mikitani).

PHILIPP RADTKE is a senior partner in McKinsey's Tokyo office.

T.R. REID, a former bureau chief for *The Washington Post* in Tokyo and London, is the author of several books, in both English and Japanese, including *Confucius Lives Next Door: What Living in the East Teaches Us About Living in the West* (1999). He is a regular commentator on National Public Radio's "Morning Edition" and has made documentary films for National Geographic TV, PBS, and the A&E network.

STEPHEN S. ROACH is a senior fellow in the Jackson Institute for Global Affairs at Yale University and non-executive chairman of Morgan Stanley Asia.

GWEN ROBINSON has worked for the *Financial Times* since 1995 as a reporter in Asia and the US, and as the paper's online news editor and comment editor. She has been based in Tokyo since 2007, covering global finance and business and, on occasion, food, lifestyle and the arts.

WILLIAM H. SAITO is a US-born authority in the fields of encryption, authentication and biometric technology. In 1991, he founded I/O Software, Inc., which became a global leader in security software development; he was named Entrepreneur of the Year in 1998 by Ernst & Young, NASDAQ and USA Today. After he sold the company in 2004, Saito moved to Japan and founded Intecur KK, a consultancy that helps companies identify and develop innovative technologies. He also serves as an adviser on innovation and entrepreneurship to government agencies in the US and Japan.

MASAHIRO SAKANE is chairman of Komatsu, Ltd. He served as president and CEO from June 2003 to June 2007.

BRIAN SALSBERG is a partner in McKinsey's Tokyo office.

DAVID E. SANGER served as the Tokyo correspondent and bureau chief for *The New York Times* from 1988–94. He is now chief Washington correspondent for the *Times* and an adjunct professor of public policy at Harvard University's Kennedy School of Government. He is also the author of the best-seller, *The Inheritance: The World Obama Confronts and the Challenges to American Power* (2009).

KAORI SASAKI is president of UNICUL International, a Tokyo-based international communications consulting company, and president and CEO of ewoman.

HOWARD SCHULTZ is chairman, president and CEO of Starbucks.

KLAUS SCHWAB is the founder and executive director of the World Economic Forum, a non-profit foundation whose annual meeting in Davos, Switzerland, is a magnet for global leaders. He is also co-founder, with his wife Hilde, of the Schwab Foundation for Social Entrepreneurship. Since 1979, Schwab has published the *Global Competitiveness Report*.

WAICHI SEKIGUCHI is an editorial writer specializing in information technology for the *Nihon Keizai Shimbun* newspaper, the largest economic daily in Asia, and a news commentator on the *Nikkei Japan Report*, a program of NHK World TV. Sekiguchi is a visiting professor at Hosei University Business School and International University of Japan. A former Fulbright fellow at Harvard University and Washington correspondent for *Nihon Keizai Shimbun*, he is a member of the government's ICT Taskforce Team and a member of the School Informatization Council of the Ministry of Education.

MARTHA SHERRILL is an author and writer who explores the tension between the individual and society. From 1985-2000, she was an award-winning writer for *The Washington Post*. Her first book, *The Buddha from Brooklyn* (2000), was about the lives of the monks and nuns of the largest Tibetan Buddhist monastery in the West. *Dog Man: An Uncommon Life on a Faraway Mountain* (2008) tells the story of Morie Sawataishi, the rescuer of the Akita dog breed.

TAKUMI SHIBATA is deputy president and COO of Nomura Holdings.

MASAYOSHI SON, chairman and CEO, founded SoftBank in 1981 at the age of 24, after graduating from the University of California/Berkeley. A leader in Japan's digital economy, SoftBank was an early partner of Microsoft and brought Yahoo to Japan. SoftBank is also a major player in the mobile phone business; it bought Japan Telecom and Vodafone Japan. SoftBank is the official carrier in Japan for Apple's iPhone.

DEVIN STEWART is senior director of corporate, policy and lecture programs at the Japan Society in New York City. He is a Carnegie Council Senior Fellow, Truman Security Fellow, and Next Generation Fellow. He also teaches a course on Asia at New York University.

AKIRA SUGAHARA is a senior partner in McKinsey's Tokyo office.

EDWARD SUZUKI, founder of Tokyo-based Edward Suzuki Associates, is an award-winning architect who has worked with Buckminster Fuller and Isamu Noguchi.

SAKAE SUZUKI is a consultant in McKinsey's Tokyo office.

MASARU TAMAMOTO is a research associate in the Faculty of Asian and Middle Eastern Studies at the University of Cambridge and a senior fellow of the World Policy Institute in New York.

HITOSHI TANAKA is chairman of the Institute for International Strategy at the Japan Research Institute; visiting professor at the Graduate School of Public Policy at the University of Tokyo; and senior fellow at the Japan Center for International Exchange. He was Deputy Minister for Foreign Affairs from 2002–05, the ministry's second-highest civil service post. His recent publications include *Purofeshonaru no Kosho-ryoku* (*The Logic of Strategic Negotiation*, 2009) and *Gaiko no Chikara* (*The Power of Diplomacy*, 2009).

PETER TASKER is a founding partner of Arcus Investments, an investment management firm that specializes in Japanese securities. He has written several books on Japanese economics and society, including *Japan 2020* (1997) and *The End of the Japanese Golden Era* (1992). He is the author of several novels and works of non-fiction in both English and Japanese, and has written for *Newsweek*, *Financial Times*, *The Economist* and other publications.

HENRY TRICKS is the Tokyo bureau chief for *The Economist*. He joined *The Economist* as capital markets editor in January 2006, and then became finance editor. He previously wrote for the *Financial Times* in London, was *FT* bureau chief in Mexico, and worked for Reuters in the US, Mexico, and Central America.

BOBBY VALENTINE is a baseball analyst with ESPN. A former major-league player, he has managed in both the Japan and US major leagues.

STEVE VAN ANDEL is chairman and co-CEO of Amway.

EZRA F. VOGEL is a former Harvard professor and director of its East Asian Research Center. He has written many books on China and Japan, including *Japan as Number One: Lessons for America* (1979), which is the all-time nonfiction bestseller in Japan by a Western author. Vogel officially retired in 2000 but remains active in research and East Asia-related activities.

INGO BEYER VON MORGENSTERN is a senior partner in McKinsey's Shanghai office.

ROBERT WHITING is an author and journalist who has written several acclaimed books on contemporary Japanese culture. *You Gotta Have Wa* (1989) was a Pulitzer Prize finalist; *Tokyo Underworld* (1999), an account of the corrupt side of US-Japan relations, was a bestseller in Japan. Whiting's other works include *The Chrysanthemum and the Bat* (1977), chosen as the best sports book of the year by *Time* magazine; *Slugging It Out In Japan* (1992); and *The Meaning of Ichiro* (2004). A graduate of Tokyo's Sophia University, Whiting has spent 33 of the past 48 years in Japan.

MASAHIRO YAMADA, a sociologist at Chuo University, is credited with creating such terms as "parasite singles" and "gap-widening society."

SHLOMO YANAI is president and CEO of Teva Pharmaceutical Industries.

TADASHI YANAI is chairman, president and CEO of Fast Retailing, whose major subsidiary is Uniqlo.

ACKNOWLEDGEMENTS

IT TAKES ALMOST A VILLAGE to put together a book like this one.
Reimagining Japan would not have been possible without extraordinary support from our partners at Shogakukan. We are especially grateful for the dedication and hard work of Takeharu Chris Kusuda, multilingual publishing editor from the Office of the President of Shogakukan Incorporated; Shin Komatsu, marketing; and Naoyuki Goto, of the Management Printing and Bookbinding Division.

We benefited enormously from the judgment, Japan savvy, and sheer stamina of our two external editorial consultants, Paul Blustein and Gwen Robinson, as well as from swift and sure copy editing by Susan Schwartz. For help with this book's design, we enlisted the genius of graphic consultants Robert Newman and Linda Rubes.

Others outside McKinsey & Company helped us contact and communicate with authors. They included Katharina Ahrens, Doug Beck, Orlando Camargo, Greg Clark, Pär Edin, Ken Ehrhart, Carsten Fischer, Barbara LeMarrec, Pamela Mar, Cécile Maisonneuve, Pascal Martin, Coco Masters, David McCulloch, Kyoko Morisawa, Suzana Nahum-Zilberberg, Kiho Ohga, John Parker, Emmanuel Prat, Phillip Raskin, Ravit Shem-Tov, V. Sriram, Akira Tsuchiya, Herman Uscategui, Jean-Baptiste Voisin, Peter Witts, as well as the Office of the President of the African Development Bank. Thank you all!

At McKinsey, people from many different departments and many different countries contributed their time and talent.

From McKinsey Global Publishing, Allan Gold in Washington, DC, and Cait Murphy in New York played key roles in editing essays and managing the copy flow. In Chicago, editors Nicole Adams and Roger Draper oversaw the copyediting process. We also benefited from the editorial assistance of Liza Cornelius, Drew Holzfeind, and Mary Kuntz.

Therese Khoury and Val Titov, in Sydney, handled production and layout, with support from designers Veronica Belsuzarri and Delilah Zak, in Chicago. Katharine Bowerman, Sandrine Devillard, Allen Fung, Acha Leke, and Jean-Christophe Mieszala opened their files to introduce us to possible authors. David Sandgrund and Antony Wyatt provided legal advice. Paul McInerney, Peter Schoppert, and Shizuko Yamasaki assisted with marketing and promotion.

In Tokyo, Maiko Hirata, Helen Iwata, Junko Nakamura, Andrew Nichols, Yumi Sato, and Tami Tsukahara provided a wide range of editorial services, in both Japanese and English. Shinichi Yokohama offered advice on Japanese editing. Tomoko Hibino-Niitani, Fumiko Okada, and Shiomi Sato helped with research and fact checking. In Seoul, Alex Kim also aided with research.

Tomoko Kamitani, Satoshi Erdos Kato, Hiroki Kitajima, Chloe Lau, Kumiko Nagashima, Bumpei Noda, Chigusa Sato, Arei Shirai, Junko Tashiro, Hiroyuki Tokunaga, and Miori Tomisaka fielded a dizzying array of duties—including communicating with authors, keeping track of editorial drafts, and assisting the translation—with great aplomb. We also were supported by Tokyo office interns Laurent Lahmy and Yalinna Ya.

Throughout the project, Rik Kirkland, head of McKinsey Global Publishing, provided support, editorial direction, encouragement, and inspiration.

Finally, we wish to express our gratitude to all members of McKinsey's Tokyo office, this year celebrating the firm's 40th anniversary in Japan, for supporting *Reimagining Japan* from its inception in a variety of ways, both large and small.